PUNISHING THE MENTALLY ILL

SUNY series in New Directions in Crime and Justice Studies
Austin T. Turk, editor

Punishing the Mentally Ill

A Critical Analysis of Law and Psychiatry

Bruce A. Arrigo

STATE UNIVERSITY OF NEW YORK PRESS

Published by
State University of New York Press, Albany

Printed in the United States of America

For information, address State University of New York Press,
90 State Street, Suite 700, Albany, NY 12207

Production by Cathleen Collins
Marketing by Patrick Durocher

Library of Congress Cataloging-in-Publication Data

Arrigo, Bruce A.
Punishing the mentally ill : a critical analysis of law and psychiatry / Bruce A. Arrigo.
p. cm. — (SUNY series in new directions in crime and justice studies)
Includes bibliographical references and index.
ISBN 0-7914-5403-7 (alk. paper) — ISBN 0-7914-5404-5 (pbk. : alk. paper)
1. Insane—Commitment and detention—United States. 2.
Insanity—Jurisprudence—United States. 3. Punishment—United States. I. Title. II. Series.

KF480 .A973 2002
346.7301'38—dc21

2001049407

10 9 8 7 6 5 4 3 2 1

For Chris:

Whether as student, teacher, friend, or mentor,
thank you for reminding me
that we are all philosophers.

Contents

Foreword

Mental illness has been present since the beginnings of humankind, and throughout the centuries the mentally ill—"the different"—have been dealt with in various ways. They have been seen as repulsive and frightening, and they have been ostracized, rejected, and abandoned, or confined to the back rooms of family homes, rudimentary prisons, "insane" asylums, and hospices. At one time, they were even collectively gathered on the so-called Ship of Fools, a boat that went up and down the Rhine, obviously excluding them from contact with the mainland and its inhabitants. Throughout history their victimization appears to have been a cyclical Vichian presence.

The mentally ill may face people with the most devastating infirmity, the "loss" of one's mind, the most cherished part of one's self. This is a frightening realization, a traumatic event the thought of which cannot be sustained by the so-called sane majority, and it may contribute to a strong reaction formation leading to the exclusion of the mentally ill from mainstream society and at times even to their annihilation. Indeed, from the time of ancient Sparta to the middle of the twentieth century they have been eliminated, at times with drastic measures, because they were thought not only to be different but to be a burden, even being seen as evil.

The old psychiatric hospitals, often more "snake pits" than hospitals, saw the mentally ill languish to the point of inanition. Great scholars and benefactors such as Vincenzo Chiarugi, Philippe Pinel, and Dorothea Dix attempted to rescue the mentally ill from their humiliating conditions and partially succeeded in returning them to a humane state, even though they were still confined and later subjected to moral therapy. The third psychiatric revolution, subsequent to the development of psychotropic medications, that of the sixties, brought about mass deinstitutionalization of the mentally ill. The subsequent confusion created the emargination of many of these people and the unconscionable criminalization of a great number of them.

Bruce Arrigo presents a critique of the present-day psychiatric and legal approaches to the mentally ill in court proceedings, whether for civil or criminal commitment. He believes that this way of dealing with the mentally ill is an injustice. He is of the opinion that at the basis of the policing of the mentally ill is, in fact, their being seen as "different" from others. His disquisition is not only theoretical and philosophical, but practical, aimed at demonstrating the unfairness of the civil and criminal laws regarding the mentally ill enacted by the justice system. His basic tenet is that "being different" is a category in itself and it is assessed by symbolic language that sustains and legitimizes inequalities before the law. In his criticism of the psychiatric-legal manner of dealing with the mentally ill he uses Lacanian psychoanalytic theories. He moves through Lacanian semiotics, through the Three Orders of the psychic configuration of the unconscious: the symbolic, the imaginary, and the real with the easiness of the expert he has proved himself to be. He explains the frequent presence of metaphors and metonymical expressions in the conventional thought of psychiatric-legal debates concerning the mentally ill relative to the discourse of Foucault's involuntary confinement. Psychiatric-legal justice, he says, and the enactors of clinical-legal discourse (the players in a court of law) attempt to affirm values consistent with logic that upholds unity, homogeneity, stability, and order. This is in essence the symbolic language of Lacan, a spoken language that cleanses, sanitizes, and corrects difference. In so doing, the real self of the mentally ill is not taken into consideration, its uniqueness is not given proper appreciation. This reminds me that our expertise in courtrooms is too often only a behavioral assessment and not a thorough inquiry into the deeper conflicts and motivations for the behavior of the mentally ill, and, obviously, does not elicit and put forward the still untouched-by-illness positive self of these individuals. Courts limit themselves to facts, and the clinical psychiatric-legal language, the symbolic communication of the players, follows suit.

This book says much more than the above in its well-written, well-thought out pages. Significantly, in Arrigo's concluding thoughts he introduces three perspectives on how the mentally ill are assessed, or should be assessed, in the courts: The Medical Model Perspective upholds the use of present-day clinical legal language, the symbolic language; the Mainstream Legal Perspective, which, even though subscribing to the same approach, admits that at times this approach may erode the rights of mentally ill citizens and should be amended if harmful to these persons; and the Critical Perspective, which, instead, proposes that violence is done to the mentally ill through the various symbolic activities and qualifying statements, such as "disease, sick, incompetent or diminished," at times used by court players, unconsciously and without recognizing the consequences of such labeling. This book is, indeed, a critical analysis of the present-day labeling of mental illness, its logic sponsored by mental health and legal professionals, and accepted by the justice system at large. Arrigo, who favors the last view—the Critical Perspective—believes that the process of justice for the mentally ill is irreparably flawed and suggests the elimination of civil and criminal confinement for this category of people, or, at least, a reassessment of the "theoretical premises and epistemological assumptions underscoring all legal and psychiatric decision making." He demonstrates not only a great deal of empathy for what has become the legal plight of the mentally ill, but a deep sense of humane concern. He feels at one with the "different" and he firmly believes, in his objective rigorous analysis, that they are being wrongly punished by the system. I agree with his view, and I also believe that, while obviously needing understanding and treatment, even when they perpetrate violent crimes, the mentally ill in general do not belong in the justice arena.

However, if they do not belong to the justice arena, where do they belong? Even though this book does not answer the question, it certainly gives strong indications for reflection. Arrigo has lifted the lid of a Pandora's box. His voice should be listened to, and his concerns properly assessed. This book presents an intellectual challenge to the reader, and, at the same time, it sends an important message to policy makers. Society can only benefit from a critical analysis of its shortcomings, especially when they involve some of its weakest members: To be different is not a crime.

George B. Palermo, M.D.
President, Center for Forensic Psychiatry and Risk Assessment
Clinical Professor of Psychiatry and Neurology,
Medical College of Wisconsin
Adjunct Professor of Criminology and Law Studies,
Department of Cultural and Social Sciences,
Marquette University, Milwaukee, Wisconsin

Preface

One of the few memories from my introductory philosophy course in college—over 35 years ago—is the parable of the blind men and the elephant.

> Four blind men come across an elephant. They decide to feel the elephant to determine what sort of creature it is. One blind man feels the back leg of the elephant. He says, "An elephant is like a tree." The second blind man feels the trunk. He says, "An elephant is like a snake." The third blind man feels the tail. He says, "An elephant is like a rope." The fourth blind man is afraid. He doesn't feel the elephant at all.
>
> The three blind men argue a long time about what an elephant is and based on their own personal experience each is right.[1]

This affected me greatly, when I first heard it at age 18, and it has stayed with me to this day. It seems to explain so much of our social, intrapsychic, political, and cultural behavior, especially the "disconnects" we all frequently experience in everyday work and professional life. When I started writing about the meretricious allure of "ordinary common sense" in legal theory,[2] I realized that that parable helped explain our distorted thinking processes that have led to such incoherence in, for example, our insanity defense policies.[3]

When I read the manuscript of Bruce Arrigo's brilliant new book, *Punishing the Mentally Ill: A Critical Analysis of Law and Psychiatry*, the parable came back to me in a very different way. For what Professor Arrigo has done is to expose the failures and shortcomings of those methodologies that insist on looking at the "mental health system" through one perspective only—be that the clinical, the legal, the behavioral, the empirical, the political, or the theoretical. Professor Arrigo—who demonstrates in this book a prodigious knowledge of *all* of these approaches—aims to do more, and he sets out that aim clearly.

In the first pages of his Introduction he says this:

> I am interested in exploring the depths of punishment enacted first unconsciously in symbolic form and subsequently legitimized, knowingly or not, in social effect. In other words, this project seeks to link clinicolgeal practices (e.g., predicting dangerousness, executing the mentally ill) with unspoken desires (e.g., the metaphysics of presence, the social control thesis), revealing how ideology and circumscribed knowledge inform the behavior of law and psychiatry.[4]

His thesis is that we cannot possibly understand the mental health system without confronting ideology, desires, and unconscious imagery. He also argues that this perception controls whether we are looking at civil or criminal mental disability law, at institutional or community mental disability law policy, or questions of mental health advocacy. And I agree. By framing his arguments as he does, he recognizes that what is really going on in mental disability policy decision-making is complex, and is informed by a discourse that is highly dependent on our understanding of the depths of our punitive urges, and the roots of our need to control those perceived to be deviant.[5]

Professor Arrigo shows how these attitudes inform our clinical policies and out legal policies, whether we are looking at involuntary civil commitment, the provision of community treatment, the right to refuse treatment, an insanity defense trial, or the decision making involved in determining whether a person with mental disability can be executed. By doing this, he forces us to leave the comfortably narrow cocoons of our own substantive specialties (and professional calling), and makes us understand how a set of unconsciously integrated attitudes explains why we do what we do—especially in the name of the state—in the way we deal with persons with mental disability.

I am interested in all of the topics that Professor Arrigo has brought to the scholarly table, and have written about many of them.[6] I was most interested, however, in his chapter on "the ethics of advocacy for the mentally ill." This is a topic that has been severely underconsidered over the years,[7] and about which there has truly been little that is original or controversial. Professor Arrigo's thesis here is clear: "Each time the mentally ill (or their representatives) engage the law, they strengthen and bolster their dependence on it, and, further, *become somewhat disempowered because of it.*"[8] This, he concludes, establishes the "profound paradox" faced by persons with mental disability: "to endure without rights (as the law has taken them away), or seek rights from the law, which, in turn, fortifies the power of the law."[9] And this leads him to his ultimate question on this topic:

> If advocacy in mental health law is anchored by clinicolegal interpretations of rights, illness, competency, and the like, and if

> confinement decisions hinge, fundamentally, on an appeal to established structures of civil and criminal institutional authority, what room, if any, is legitimately left for the disparate voices of the psychiatrically disordered? Indeed, given these constructed realities, on whose behalf is the advocacy truly initiated?[10]

This is, of course, very unsettling, perhaps more so to someone like me who spent 11 years representing persons with mental disabilities (3 as a Public Defender, specializing in cases involving incompetency status determinations and insanity trials, and 8 as director of the NJ Division of Mental Health Advocacy, a state-funded, subcabinet office vested with the power to provide legal representation in both individual and class action matters for persons with mental disability), who, for the past 17 years, has taught students, in both classroom and clinical settings, to do the same,[11] and who employs different modes of legal analysis as a means of expanding the rights of persons with mental disabilities through mental health advocacy.[12] Professor Arrigo's arguments here "push the envelope" in directions new to interdisciplinary scholarship, and will, I hope, inaugurate a new and important dialogue in the mental health "rights community."

For the past decade or so, I have focused my own writing on what I term *sanism* as well as what I term *pretextuality*. Simply put, sanism is an irrational prejudice of the same quality and character of other irrational prejudices that cause (and are reflected in) prevailing social attitudes of racism, sexism, homophobia, and ethnic bigotry. It infects both our jurisprudence and our lawyering practices. Sanism is largely invisible and largely socially acceptable. It is based predominantly on stereotype, myth, superstition, and deindividualization, and is sustained and perpetuated by our use of alleged "ordinary common sense" (OCS) and heuristic reasoning in an unconscious response to events both in everyday life and in the legal process.

And, "pretextuality" means that courts accept (either implicitly or explicitly) testimonial dishonesty and engage similarly in dishonest (frequently meretricious) decision-making, specifically where witnesses, especially *expert* witnesses, show a "high propensity to purposely distort their testimony in order to achieve desired ends." This pretextuality is poisonous; it infects all participants in the judicial system, breeds cynicism and disrespect for the law, demeans participants, and reinforces shoddy lawyering, blasé judging, and, at times, perjurious and/or corrupt testifying.[13]

I turned to these concepts as a way of explaining why and how mental disability law has developed as it has. And I believe that the perniciousness and malignance of these concepts *do* so explain that law, whether we are looking at assisted outpatient commitment law, sexually violent predator laws, assessing defendants' competence to plead guilty, the right of institutionalized patients to sexual interaction, or any of the other "standard" topics of mental disability law about which courts decide cases and scholars write articles.

I have sought—especially in my earlier writings of the topic—to explain the historical, religious, and political sources of sanism, and how, to a great extent, these sources still animate current attitudes and behaviors.[14] But, having said that, I always have wondered if there were still "something else" to be added to help solve this most difficult of social policy puzzles. Professor Arrigo provides that "something else" in this book, and he does so clearly, provocatively, and persuasively. It is one that we will be thinking about for a long, long time.

Michael L. Perlin
Professor, New York Law School

Acknowledgments

This book is the product of many people whose expertise, generosity, and thoughtfulness made the work possible. I especially want to thank the folks at the State University of New York Press. In particular, my editor, Nancy Ellegate, encouraged me throughout the process, offering concernful guidance, constructive criticism, and skilled attention to detail. In addition, I have always been fortunate to benefit from the assistance of many fine doctoral students. I am indebted to Rachel Latter, Petra Smith, Natalie Claussen, Jennifer Krantz, and Elizabeth Gibbons. Their exhaustive contributions to the manuscript, including assistance with citations, references, and the index, helped produce a level of completeness and accuracy that, I believe, would otherwise be missing from the finished document. I am also grateful to many colleagues who read previous drafts of this work in total or portions of it, or who were kind enough to discuss and comment on the ideas entertained throughout the manuscript. A full list of these individuals is simply not possible; however, many of them are members of the Critical Criminology Division of the American Society of Criminology, or are affiliated with the American Psychology-Law Society of the American Psychological Association. Thus, I draw attention to these organizations and to those associated with them whose observations inspired me to make the book better. Finally, I thank my wife, Beth, and our two children, Rebecca and Anthony. I remain devoted to them and, fortunately for me, they supported the time I needed, away from them, to complete this project. They are the source of my enduring love.

Portions of chapter 5 were previously reprinted in "Transcarceration: A Constitutive Ethnography of Mentally Ill Offenders," *The Prison Journal, 81* (2): 162–186, copyright 2001 by Sage Publications, reproduced by permission of Sage Publications. Portions of chapter 3 were previously reprinted in "The Logic of Identity and the Politics of Justice: Establishing a Right to Community Based Treatment for the Institutionalized Mentally Disabled," *The New England Journal on Criminal and Civil Confinement, 18* (1): 1–31, copyright 1992. Portions of chapter 7 were previously reprinted in "Law, Ideology, and Critical Inquiry: The Case of Treatment Refusal for Incompetent Prisoners Awaiting Execution," *The New England Journal on Criminal and Civil Confinement*, 25 (2): 367–412, copyright 1999. Portions of chapter 4 were previously reprinted in "Chaos Theory and the Social Control Thesis: A Post-Foucauldian Analysis of Mental Illness and Involuntary Civil Commitment," *Social Justice*, 26 (1): 177–207, copyright 1999.

Introduction

Historically, society's response to mental illness has been marked by grand reformist efforts producing disappointing, if not disastrous, results (Grob, 1994). Typically, these results have led to civil incarceration, criminal confinement or other forms of liberty deprivation (Perlin, 1999). Along the way, both law and psychiatry have exercised considerable decision making and discretionary authority. According to some observers, their ongoing involvement has fostered a system of care that has led to the abandonment of the mentally disordered (Isaac & Armat, 1990; Torrey, 1997). In the extreme, I have questioned this abandonment suggesting, instead, that psychiatric citizens are punished for being different (Arrigo, 1996b). This book specifically considers why efforts at reform, particularly during the past 25 years, have failed, mindful of how punishment underscores decisions made at the crossroads of law and psychiatry.

Other investigators have examined the disciplining of mental illness in varying degrees. Indeed, philosophical (Foucault, 1965, 1977), historical (Scull, 1989; Rothman, 1971, 1980), psychiatric (Szasz, 1963, 1987), legal (Perlin, 1999, 2000), and sociological (Warren, 1982; Holstein, 1993; Scheff, 2000) explanations abound. However, unlike these works, I am interested in exploring the depth of punishment enacted first unconsciously in symbolic form and subsequently legitimized, knowingly or not, in social effect. In other words, this project seeks to link clinicolegal practices (e.g., predicting dangerousness, executing the mentally ill) with unspoken desires (e.g., the metaphysics of presence, the social control thesis), revealing how ideology and circumscribed knowledge inform the behavior of law and psychiatry (Arrigo, 1996a).

The significance of this research should not be underestimated. Indeed, if symbolic violence, activated deep within the inner network of psycholegal thought, shapes mental health law and policy decisions, then the legitimacy of any forensic trial, administrative hearing, medical intervention, or liberty protection can be seriously questioned, dramatically reconfigured, or thoroughly abrogated. This position is as disturbing as it is vexing. The perspective is particularly thorny when considering the freedom-limiting practices of civil commitment, criminal confinement, or both. After all, if sustained institutional care is part of the problem, what are its alternatives?

Punishing the Mentally Ill does not offer a detailed response to the dilemma it systematically identifies. While this is a worthwhile (policy-based) project in its own right, it is decidedly beyond the scope of the present endeavor. Instead, the focus of this book is on critique. Accordingly, I draw from a wide range of literatures and consolidate them so as to make, hopefully, a compelling and cogent argument about law, psychiatry, and punishment.

In order to accomplish my objective, the book is divided into two main sections: civil confinement and criminal confinement. Each section contains several chapters. The chapters address important and provocative controversies that have received considerable research attention, especially during the past twenty-five years. The presentation of this material is not exhaustive. Rather, each chapter discusses a notable psycholegal topic in order to illustrate a particular point about the penalty for mental illness.

In chapter 1, I address the issue of civil commitment. In particular, I trace the recent history of this practice, pointing out how related matters such as interpreting mental illness, defining and predicting dangerousness, and establishing a right to refuse treatment all have been plagued by "illness politics." This notion refers to the law's preference for liberty and psychiatry's penchant for treatment producing client/patient abandonment. I demonstrate how illness politics is linked to paternalism, and explore its three most prevalent forms: social control; custody; and treatment. I conclude the chapter by suggesting how law and psychiatry can help fashion a more humane civil commitment policy, and recommend that it be based on understanding and valuing the identity of the mental health consumer.

In chapter 2, I explore the ethics of advocacy for the mentally ill. Specifically, I question whether it is possible for the medicolegal community to know, define, and promote fully the interests of psychiatric citizens. To answer this query, I review the manner in which rights are routinely given to and taken from mental health consumers through the law. In this context, I assess the ethics of involuntary confinement and the ethics of advocating for the rights of the mentally disordered. I argue that psychological egoism or measured altruism underscore decisions made at the crossroads of law and psychiatry. In other words, I demonstrate how advocates incompletely (and selfishly) represent the consumer's interests, which is not the same as genuine client/patient advocacy. Given this distinction, I conclude by speculating on who the "real" benefactor is in the forensic decision-making process.

In chapter 3, I investigate the dilemma of community-based treatment for the mentally ill. I consider whether, and to what extent, the psychiatric citizen possesses a federal constitutional right to such treatment. To access this matter,

I canvass the precedent-setting case law on the issue and the political philosophy related to it. This investigation reveals how certain values (e.g., identity politics or the reduction of difference to sameness) govern forensic courtroom decision making. These values give rise to the mostly absent right to community-based treatment for psychiatric citizens. In response to these values and their marginalizing logic, I offer three counter arguments: a sociological analysis on the success of neighborhood-situated care; a legal analysis on the federal constitutional source of such a right; and a philosophical analysis on the limits of identity politics.

In chapter 4, I describe the social control thesis. This notion builds on Michel Foucault's work regarding disciplinary institutions. Given the analysis in the first three chapters, I argue that mental illness is "policed" and that this policing fills a social function; namely, the surveillance and control of difference. I explore how such monitoring is linked to specific disciplinary regimes (i.e., the psychiatric hospital, the correctional facility), and speculate on whether alternative conceptual approaches to disciplining difference exist that more completely advance our understanding of mental illness, dangerousness, and confinement. I conclude the chapter by asserting that the penalty for mental illness operating within and throughout psycholegal decision making is the policing of difference. I contend that this practice, although mostly unconscious, adversely harms or negatively impacts the identity of psychiatric citizens.

In chapter 5, I examine the phenomenon of transcarceration. This is a process whereby psychiatric citizens are alternately and repeatedly routed to and from the mental health and criminal justice systems. I argue that this is the effect of the social control thesis. I explore trancarceration both conceptually and ethnographically. Relying on constitutive thought, I demonstrate how users of mental health services both shape and are shaped by the discourse and logic of custody, control, and treatment. I speculate on how transcarceration therefore renders such citizens ideological "prisoners" of confinement.

In chapter 6, I investigate the psychiatric courtroom; specifically, the not-guilty-by-reason-of-insanity (NGRI) and the guilty-but-mentally-ill (GBMI) verdicts. I demonstrate how decision making in the forensic courtroom is the state-sanctioned vehicle by which the social control thesis is legitimized. I consider several unconscious, but deeply felt, forces that inform and circumscribe legal and psychiatric decision-making. Specifically, I argue that subjectivity and language are integral to the clinicolegal sense-making process. This phenomenon is defined as desire-in-discourse. I demonstrate how desire-in-discourse, particularly within law and psychiatry, creates and sustains symbolic violence that, knowingly or not, discursively punishes the mentally ill in social effect. I demonstrate how this occurs through NGRI and GBMI practices.

In chapter 7, I explore the correctional law and policy on executing the mentally ill. To ground the analysis, I rely on the interpretive tools of legal semiotics and deconstruction. I demonstrate how clinicolegal notions such as competency, treatment, or both embody hidden messages and concealed assumptions about the mentally disordered, confinement, and capital punishment. These messages and assumptions are latent, though semiotically and deconstructively discernible, and fail to find their way into the otherwise narratively coherent and socially constructed text on executing the psychiatrically disordered. I argue that revealing this unspoken text allows us to interpret what values are privileged and what values are excluded within forensic decision-making practices. I conclude by maintaining that the social control thesis and the penalty for mental illness entail the articulation of values that deny and repudiate difference. This is how desire-in-discourse functions at the conscious level.

In chapter 8, I present a provisional, though critically informed, theory of punishment situated at the crossroads of law and psychiatry. I explore additional features of desire-in-discourse by relying on several of Jacques Lacan's psychoanalytic formulations. I show how the unconscious mind of law and psychiatry operates, reproducing and sustaining language and thought that marginalizes and invalidates the mentally ill for their articulated and lived difference. This is how desire-in-discourse functions at the prethematic level. Following this analysis and based on the accumulated insights of each chapter, I describe, in postulate form, a theory of punishment. I conclude by tentatively discussing the justice policy implications of the theory in relation to the future of civil and criminal mental health confinement law.

Punishing the Mentally Ill provides a critical review of how law and psychiatry interactively function, impacting the every day lives and ongoing experiences of mental health consumers. Ultimately, this book wrestles with notions of citizen justice and social well-being, and the extent to which existing psycholegal practices sufficiently advance these important objectives. *Punishing the Mentally Ill* considerably challenges the wisdom of law and psychiatry, raising many troubling philosophical, societal, and policy questions as a consequence. While this is certainly not the final word on the topic, readers will have to decide whether this book provides a compelling critique, documenting where and how punishment is enacted at the crossroads of law psychiatry. Indeed, in the final analysis, readers will have to determine for whom justice is served as our system of mental health law responds to psychiatric disorder and renders judgments about civil and criminal confinement.

PART ONE

Civil Confinement

ONE

Civil Commitment and Paternalism

Legal and Psychiatric Dynamics

OVERVIEW. *The legal and psychiatric communities are largely responsible for fashioning social (and public) policy in relation to the mentally ill. The question, of course, is to what extent do these systems work in concert to affect meaningful outcomes that include the sensibilities of persons with diagnosed psychiatric disabilities. This chapter examines a full range of forensic issues that impact civil commitment determinations. How are involuntary hospitalization decisions made? In what way are treatment needs balanced against liberty rights? What are the aims of civil confinement? To what extent is justice for the mentally ill assured through institutionalization? What role, if any, does paternalism, punishment, or both play in the decision-making process? These and other similar questions are explored in the pages that follow.*

INTRODUCTION

The history of civil commitment and confinement law in general reflect long-standing attitudinal divisions among the psychiatric and legal communities, patients' rights advocates, governmental agencies, legislative bodies, and other invested constituencies (Deutsch, 1949; Grob, 1973, pp. 4–12; Scull, 1989, pp. 4, 10). At the center of this controversy are two well-established and, at times, competing social values that attempt to fashion appropriate mental health policy. On the one hand, involuntary hospitalization for mentally ill persons diagnosed as dangerous or otherwise disabled is encouraged. On the other hand, the slightest abridgment of personal autonomy and individual liberty for these citizens is discouraged. While the medical profession asserts its responsibility to treat dangerous (Chodoff, 1976, p. 496) and obviously ill persons (Treffert, 1985, p. 259) so that they are effectively controlled (Zusman, 1982, pp. 110–113), civil libertarians seek to challenge psychiatric judgments altogether. These advocates maintain that mental illness is manufactured (Szasz, 1970, pp. 1–15), that civilly confined persons are in fact prisoners (Ennis, 1972, p. 2) and that the "preciousness of liberty" doctrine demands that the practice of involuntary hospitalization be abolished (Morse, 1982a, pp. 54, 106).

The results of this and prior debates have produced large-scale reforms with disappointing consumer-oriented outcomes. From the introduction of the asylum and public intervention in the form of moral treatment (Morrissey & Goldman, 1984, p. 786); to the emergence of the psychopathic hospital and the mental hygiene movement (Grob, 1983, p. 144), to the more recent spawning of community mental health and its emphasis on deinstitutionalization (Bachrach, 1978, pp. 573, 574; Musto, 1975, p. 53; Talbott, 1979, pp. 621, 622), one reality has endured: "While cyclical patterns of institutional reform" have been the hallmark of America's response to the mentally ill (Morrissey & Goldman, 1984, p. 790; Morrissey & Goldman, 1986, pp. 12, 13), the politics of abandonment has been and continues to be its legacy (Rhoden, 1982, p. 375; Isaac & Armat, 1990, p. 250).

This statement is not so much an indictment of those forces that largely shape civil commitment laws or develop intervention strategies for effective treatment. It is, however, a recognition that although we have journeyed beyond the institutional "snakepits" of the past (Deutsch, 1948, pp. 3–21), the "right to rot" is not an acceptable path (Appelbaum & Gutheil, 1980, pp. 720–723). Our contemporary social landscape, especially over the last 25 years, poignantly reflects this theme of abandonment. Psychiatric facilities, viewed in the past as nightmarish warehouses servicing chronically mentally ill persons have been replaced by ill-conceived and poorly managed new "asylums" in the community (Goldman & Morrissey, 1985, p. 722; Lamb, 1979, p. 129). And while treatment regimens for persons committed against their will continue to evolve through psychopharmacological and other therapy-based discoveries, the best available evidence shows that these interventions are only minimally better than doing nothing at all (Brooks, 1987, pp. 339, 341; Durham & LaFond, 1988, p. 305).

Coupled with these disturbing realities are the commitment laws themselves (Perlin, 2000). No where else are the entrenched tensions that beset the psychiatric and legal communities more evident. Challenges to the scientific meaning of mental illness (Morse, 1978, pp. 527, 528; Scheff, 1984, pp. 1–3; Laing, 1969, pp. 7–10), pitfalls in predicting dangerousness (Morse, 1982b, p. 95; Shah, 1977, pp. 91, 98), debate over the promise and peril of involuntary outpatient commitment (Mulvey, Geller, & Roth, 1987, p. 571; Miller, 1985, pp. 265, 267; Hinds, 1990, pp. 346, 349), division over the patient's right to refuse treatment (Roth, 1986, p. 139, 142; Brooks, 1987, p. 339), disagreement about the efficacy of the least restrictive alternative doctrine (Arrigo, 1992b, pp. 1–31; Schmidt, 1985, p. 13; Hiday & Goodman,

1982, pp. 81–83), and other such matters demonstrate a woeful lack of consensus on how best to deliver much needed services to psychiatrically disordered citizens, while respecting the intrinsic dignity and right to self-determination these consumers possess. It is not surprising that in the wake of such acrimony over appropriate mental health policy, deinstitutionalization remains a dream deferred for the chronically disordered (Dorwart, 1988, pp. 287, 290), involuntary treatment for the homeless mentally ill continues to escalate (Belcher, 1988, p. 1203; Lamb, 1984, pp. 899–903), and an alarming number of mental health systems users find themselves displaced throughout the criminal justice system (Brakel, et al., 1985, pp. 1–15; Lamb, 1982, p. 17; Slovenko, 1977, pp. 817–818).

The purpose of this chapter is to examine critically the role that both law and psychiatry have played in casting mentally ill persons as deviants; citizen/outsiders caught in a crossfire of illness politics (Szasz, 1987; Grob, 1994). This examination will focus on those values protected and privileged by the medical and legal professions as reflected in confinement law and policy primarily during the last quarter of the twentieth century. The social, economic and political power these disciplines exercise in the lives of psychiatric citizens raises significant questions concerning the future of involuntary civil commitment both from a clinical and justice policy perspective. As such, these matters will be addressed as well. No attempt will be made here to detail the historical dimensions of abandonment in the care and treatment of the mentally ill. Similarly, assessing other environmental influences contributing to this phenomenon (e.g., urbanization, immigration, industrialization, transinstitutionalization) is beyond the scope of this chapter. While these factors are significant components in the development of civil commitment laws, they are decidedly more global in nature.

My aim is to provide a current account of how law and psychiatry, despite their respective calls to safeguard individual rights and to treat the sick, have fashioned an ineffective system of care. I begin with a brief history emphasizing the social, scientific, and legal developments that set the stage for present-day civil commitment policy. I then outline in what context law and psychiatry speak for the mentally ill, evaluate some controversial and significant areas where treatment, liberty, or both are sacrificed, and describe the inherent social values law and psychiatry promote through confinement practices. By carefully considering the manner in which involuntarily committed persons are simultaneously subjected to and repeatedly forced to choose among principles of freedom in the abstract and clinical interventions in the extreme, my intent is to identify the parameters of a debate that embody the ongoing climate of uncertainty in civil commitment matters. Along these lines, I conclude this chapter with several tentative recommendations for ameliorating the crisis in civil confinement practice and policy.

HISTORICAL BACKGROUND

The first half of the 20th century was marked by minimal activity regarding civil commitment laws or policy making (Appelbaum & Gutheil, 1991, p. 46). While state statutes reflected regional or even local interests in appropriate service delivery to the mentally ill, many states provided only modest procedural protections to these citizens (Deutsch, 1948, p. 215). In addition, some states recognized a practice of indeterminate commitment on the basis of what can only be described as vague statutory construction (i.e., the person was a "social menace" or "a fit and proper" candidate for institutionalization) (Myers, 1983–1984, pp. 367, 381).

Coupled with these lenient commitment standards was a belief on the part of many psychiatrists that institutional confinement was far more humane than the ravages of poverty or incarceration (Cohen, 1979, pp. 339, 340–351; Deutsch, 1948, p. 73). Through reliance on a "need-for-treatment" approach (Deutsch, 1949, p. 171), physicians were afforded a great deal of latitude in civil confinement matters. This latitude was indicative of a period marked by discretion rather than procedure in the care and treatment of the mentally ill (Mulvey, 1987, p. 575). In fact, the majority of the states adopted this standard for civil commitment from the 1930s through the 1960s (Myers, 1983–1984, p. 381). The net effect of these scientific and sociolegal practices was the swelling number of persons that found themselves involuntarily hospitalized. In 1955, for example, the average daily census of persons committed in state and county mental hospitals was a staggering 560,000 (Goldman, Adams, & Taube, 1983, p. 129).

The excesses of this period in civil confinement matters were substantially the result of the state's unbridled authority to impose involuntary commitment (Morse, 1978, p. 529). This authority is derived from two sources: the police power and the *parens patriae* power (LaFond, 1981, pp. 499, 502; Kittrie, 1972, p. 59). The police power accords the states "a plenary power to make laws and regulations for the protection of the public health, safety, welfare and morals" (Comment, 1974, pp. 1191, 1222). Moreover, this authority bestows on states the responsibility to commit involuntarily mentally disordered persons whose behaviors demonstrate that they are a danger to self or others. The other prong of authority vested in the states is the *parens patriae* power. Under this doctrine, states are entrusted with civilly confining persons against their will when they are unable to care for themselves. This is generally understood to include an inability to provide for one's basic needs (e.g., food, clothing, safety, and shelter).

What is most significant about the concept of *parens patriae*, is the historical value attributed to this practice of paternalism. It is deeply embedded in Western culture and thought. Indeed, the disturbing dimensions of *parens patriae* can be traced from Roman law to English law to colonial American jurisprudence (Grob, 1994; Holdsworth, 1966; Kittrie, 1972, pp. 12–40). Designed to protect "idiots and lunatics" while managing their estates (Blackstone, 1783, p. 426), these duties were abused by avaricious and profit-minded persons, leaving the mentally disabled all too frequently to their own devices (Meyers, 1983–1984, p. 403). Based in large measure on the law of property, the Crown protected the heirs of wealthy "idiots and lunatics" from disinheritance by invoking the right of *parens patriae* (*Hawks v. Lazaro*, 1974, p. 109). And, as for the impecunious, English law required that the Crown assume societal responsibility to care for those individuals unable to care for themselves (Comment, 1974, p. 1239).

With the independence of the American colonies, *parens patriae* was understood to be vested in the state legislatures (*Hawaii v. Standard Oil Co.*, 1972, pp. 251, 257). Later, this authority was generally (but explicitly) reaffirmed by the Supreme Court to be vested in the "[s]tate as [the] sovereign" (*Fontain v. Ravenel*, 1855, pp. 369, 394). Early appellate cases like *In re Barker* (Johns. Ch., 1816, p. 232) and *In re Oakes* (Law Rep., 1845, p. 122), firmly established the court's jurisdictional claim in matters pertaining to the protection of the psychiatrically disordered. All available evidence indicates that *parens patriae* was relied on as much for the protection of the mentally disordered as for matters of property and wealth (Myers, 1983–1984, p. 384). In 1890, for example, the U.S. Supreme Court described the state's parental power in the following manner: "[I]t is a most beneficent function, and often necessary to be exercised in the interests of humanity, and for the prevention of injury to those who cannot protect themselves" (*Mormon Church v. United States*, 1890, p. 57).

With the dawn of the 20th century, this *parens patriae* theme was renewed when a federal district court stated that "[a] state would indeed be derelict of its duty if it failed to make adequate provision for the care and treatment of the insane. The state is the *parens patriae* of the insane" (*Hammon v. Hill*, 1915, pp. 999, 1000). Soon thereafter, the Oklahoma Supreme Court reasserted the notion of *parens patriae* as a viable state mechanism for protecting the incapacitated and for overseeing matters of property and wealth (*McIntosh v. Dill*, 1922, pp. 917, 925). As the Court maintained, "[t]he doctrine . . . may be defined as the inherent power and authority of a Legislature of a state to provide protection of the person and property of persons *non sui juris*" (*McIntosh v. Dill*, 1922, pp. 917, 925).

In the late 1970s, Utah expressly upheld the *parens patriae* justification for civil commitment by declaring it to be a legitimate source of state power when hospitalizing mentally ill persons against their will (*Colyar v. Third Judicial Dist. Court*, 1979, p. 429). And finally, a New York appellate court relatively recently enunciated the state's *parens patriae* authority by declaring that a respondent's homelessness was the result of "serious mental illness" and not a "lack of housing for the poor" (*Boggs v. N.Y. City Health and Hosp. Corp.*, 1987, pp. 340, 365; see also, Williams & Arrigo, 2001).

What the foregoing discussion reveals is how deeply interwoven the *parens patriae* concept is in the fabric of American jurisprudence. In recent years, some commentators have staunchly criticized the medical profession's widespread reliance on it when involuntarily hospitalizing the mentally ill (Durham & LaFond, 1985, pp. 395, 397; LaFond, 1981, pp. 526–535; Morse, 1978, pp. 628–640; Perlin, 1999). Despite concerns for abuses in and sacrifices of personal liberties, other commentators find the doctrine's underlying theme of social responsibility for dangerous and gravely disabled persons to be sound (Appelbaum, 1984, pp. 133, 134). As I shall demonstrate shortly, however, it is precisely this valued notion of paternalism (in its police power and *parens patriae* form) that continues to underscore both the psychiatric and legal approach in matters of civil commitment; an approach that has resulted in casting the mentally ill as deviants, contributing to a legacy of abandonment. In other words, the historical value of paternalism, as currently expressed in the law, is responsible for the present climate of uncertainty that plagues the mental health system.

By the mid-20th century, it was evident that social reform in the care and treatment of the mentally ill was essential. Large state hospitals functioned as primary care-takers for the growing number of patients committed against their will (Grob, 1983, p. 189). Conditions in these institutions were abominable (Deutsch, 1949, pp. 448–449). Not only was understaffing rampant (*Wyatt v. Stickney*, 1972, p. 375), but the qualifications and skill level of many hospital employees providing basic services to mental health consumers was dangerously suspect (*Halderman v. Pennhurst State School & Hospital*, 1977, p. 1295). Soft shackle restraints and seclusion rooms were found in most psychiatric facilities (Scull, 1981, pp. 1–18). Long-term chronic patients deteriorated to a state of helpless institutional dependency (Goffman, 1961, p. 47; Rhoden, 1980, p. 403; Vail, 1966, pp. 22–23). Brutish attacks by residents and staff, at times resulting in death, were not uncommon (*Wyatt v. Aderholt*, 1974, pp. 1305, 1311). And the vision of social reform anticipated by the mental hygiene movement and the psychopathic hospital was reduced to obscurity, not unlike those involuntarily hospitalized persons whose promise of treatment translated into the perils of lifetime confinement (Scull, 1981, p. 171; Scull, 1989, p. 143).

These abuses signaled a need to alter significantly services delivered to mental health consumers. In 1946, the National Institute of Mental Health was founded, and funding for community mental health care was made available (Schoonover & Bassuk, 1983, p. 135). In 1952, the introduction of chlorpromazine, an antipsychotic medication, was hailed as a curative chemical agent for treating the symptoms of psychotic patients (Pepper & Ryglewicz, 1982, p. 389; Scull, 1984, p. 189). At the same time, a nascent humanitarian belief that long-term confinement of the profoundly ill produced warehousing, dehumanizing, and, therefore, harmful effects was popularized (Goffman, 1961, pp. 4–10; Pepper & Ryglewicz, 1982, p. 388; Scull, 1984, p. 189). Court cases decided during the late 1960s and early 1970s extended this awareness. Specifically, a number of landmark decrees, recognizing the fundamental liberty interests of the mentally ill were upheld, including community-situated treatment (*Lake v. Cameron*, 1966, p. 657); due process procedural protections (*Lessard v. Schmidt*, 1972, p. 1078); the right to treatment (*Rouse v. Cameron*, 1966, p. 451); medical and Constitutional minimal standards in treatment (*Wyatt v. Stickney*, 1972, p. 373); and the right to refuse treatment. In addition, state hospital administrators, alarmed by conditions of population overcrowding (Bardach, 1972, p. 52; Jones, 1972, p. 83) and structural decay (Bardach, 1972, p. 52), considered their hospitals "bankrupt beyond remedy" (Robitscher, 1975, p. 146). And finally, legislators, responding to the public clamor for institutional reform, adopted a series of statutory remedies. In 1963, the Community Mental Health Centers Construction Act (CMHC) was passed by Congress, making community-based mental health a crucial service available throughout the country (Myers, 1983–1984, p. 418). In 1965, the Medicare and Medicaid programs were enacted, providing relief for mental health consumers receiving community-based services and care (Lamb & Mills, 1988, p. 475). And, in 1969, California passed the Lanterman-Petris-Short Act; legislation that set a nationwide standard for civil commitment based on the criterion of dangerousness (Lamb & Mills, 1988, p. 475). Now, not only was the need-for-treatment approach essential to involuntary civil commitment decision making, but so too was the patient's demonstrated danger to self or others (Wexler, 1981; Perlin, 1999).

These events triggered the massive deinstitutionalization movement that occurred during the late 1960s (Grob, 1983, p. 121; Scull, 1984, p. 33). So sweeping were these measure that the per day number of residents in state and county mental hospitals reached a low of 138,000 in 1981 (Goldman, Adams, & Taube, 1983, pp. 129, 132). Deinstitutionalization brought with it an expanding array of neighborhood services for mental health consumers. Outreach, residential care, day programming, crisis intervention, and other maintenance-based strategies reduced general reliance on psychiatric facilities for many chronically mentally ill citizens (Goldman, 1983, pp. 129–134).

Notwithstanding these advances—measures promulgated by the social, scientific, and legal developments outlined above—deinstitutionalization possessed severe limitations. For example, community support was not immediately forthcoming (Rhoden, 1982, p. 431; Talbott, 1980, p. 47). Indeed, to this day, many mentally disordered persons find themselves unwelcomed residents or guests of board-and-care homes, single room occupancies, welfare hotels, and flophouses (Arrigo, 1994a; Hoch & Slayton, 1989, p. 189). Others filter through the criminal justice system, somehow surviving in local lock-up and detention centers or security prisons (Treffert, 1982, pp. 123–125). And still other psychiatrically disabled persons marginally exist on the streets where they sometimes die homeless (Lamb, 1984, p. 903; Lamb, 1989, p. 269; Arrigo, 2001b). These disturbing realities are exacerbated by bouts of involuntary rehospitalization or multiple hospitalization for the chronically mentally ill (Bachrach, 1983, pp. 73–91). Even when community placements are secured, the results are not always rewarding (Scull, 1984, pp. 99–101). The clinical, controlled, and predictable delivery of psychiatric services in these environments often echoes the familiar regimen of asylum practices (Torrey, 1997).

Many mentally ill lives have been punctuated by intrusive institutional confinement. This confinement has been replaced by a neglectful community care system, featuring ongoing cycles of short-term civil commitment, incarceration, or homelessness (Costello & Preis, 1987, p. 1538). Perhaps most troublesome is the woeful lack of effective community mental health services for mentally ill young adults (between the age of 18 and 35). Possessing limited social skills, complicated by persistent, and at times, severe psychiatric impairments, these individuals wander through life confronted by its stress and their own psychosis (Pepper & Ryglewicz, 1982, p. 389).

To be sure, the magnitude of society's failure to provide adequately for the needs of the mentally ill during the last 25 years is immense (Grob, 1994; Perlin, 2000). The devastating effects "in terms of human suffering is incalculable" (Pepper & Ryglewicz, 1982, p. 389). Driven by paternalistic intentions, current state civil commitment laws and policies bear out these unpleasant circumstances. Chronic patients are forced to choose between two dichotomous and altogether dissatisfying alternatives: total freedom from involuntary hospitalization or total confinement in the restrictive setting of a psychiatric facility (or its functional equivalent in the community) (Myers, 1983–1984, p. 381). Advocates from our legal and scientific professions have bequeathed to the mentally ill an uncertain future in civil commitment matters; a future where psychiatric persons remain citizen/outsiders (Arrigo, 1996b). This legacy of abandonment is directly linked to the specific areas in which both disciplines speak for the psychiatric consumer. Because these issues begin to disclose the values that law and psychiatry privilege, an examination of these topic areas is in order.

WHEN THE COURTS AND PSYCHIATRY SPEAK FOR THE CITIZEN/OUTSIDER

On the Meaning of Mental Illness

Scheff (1969, pp. 6–30; see also, Scheff, 2000) maintains that in the face of uncertainty both the legal and psychiatric communities strongly favor a presumption of illness when rendering decisions in the care and treatment of the mentally disordered. Nowhere else is this more evident than in their consideration of the meaning of mental illness. In most jurisdictions, the process leading to involuntary civil commitment initially requires a showing of the substantive standard of mental illness or a showing that the individual is suffering from a mental disorder (Reisner & Slobogin, 1990, p. 453). The inability on the part of most state legislatures to operationalize this construct has given the courts the role of "fashion[ing] a definition for the words "mentally ill . . . thereby fill[ing] the void in the statutory hospital law" (*Dodd v. Hughes*, 1965, pp. 540–542). This responsibility is complicated when considering the due process liberty interests of the psychiatric citizen protected under the 14th Amendment. Any law that impinges on these rights (e.g., rights pertaining to freedom of movement and freedom from bodily restraint), requires "reasonably clear guidelines" as to their reach (*Smith v. Goguen*, 1974, pp. 573; *Youngberg v. Romeo*, 1982, p. 307).

Confronted with the task of determining whether or not a person is mentally sane, courts typically rely on the expert testimony of physicians and mental health professionals (Reisner & Slobogin, 1990, p. 455; Warren, 1982, pp. 106–122). This diagnostic judgment by experts subjects the commitment proceeding and its outcome to the available medical evidence. Some important strides have been made to assess mental illness as more than deviation from the psychiatric norm in both Great Britain (Laing, 1967, pp. 1–50; Laing, 1969, pp. 33–69), and the United States (Szasz, 1963, pp. 1–15; Szasz, 1974, pp. 1–35). Additionally, other necessary efforts to construct commitment laws satisfying patients, doctors, and lawyers (Appelbaum, 1984, pp. 133–134; Roth, 1979, p. 1121; Stromberg & Stone, 1983, p. 275) have been attempted. Nonetheless, the greatest difficulty with psychiatric testimony is its unreliability in the courtroom (Ennis & Litwack, 1974, p. 712), especially when vague labels are relied on to describe mental illness (Haddad, 1974–1975, p. 439; Shell, 1979–1980, p. 6).

Despite the numerous studies and research protocols documenting the differences in diagnoses among psychiatrists and other mental health clinicians (Shell, 1979–1980, p. 6), courts encourage and depend on this testimony in civil commitment matters. The deferential posturing of most courts allows the meaning of mental illness to be shaped by the attending physician and treatment team. Charged with diagnosing and treating particular maladies (Scheff, 1984, p. 17), the psychiatrist defines mental illness as disease (Szasz, 1987, pp. 45–103). Given that the medical imperative is to presume sickness, this same logic is applied when rendering decisions for purposes of civil commitment, regardless of uncertainty (Kutner, 1962–1963, p. 383). In sum, then, the norms of cooperation and accommodation govern the commitment proceedings (Scull, 1989, pp. 130–189); a process in which both legal and psychiatric role playing have evolved into what one critic has coined a consensual and "commonsense model" of madness (Warren, 1982, p. 38).

Pitfalls in Predicting Dangerousness

A second substantive element required by most states in the wording of the civil commitment laws is the finding that some specified adverse consequence will follow if the person is not involuntarily hospitalized (Reisner & Slobogin, 1990, p. 460). This is generally understood to mean that the person is a danger to self, others, or both. While mental illness as the sole basis for commitment was first rejected by the U.S. Supreme Court in *O'Conner v. Donaldson* (*O'Conner v. Donaldson*, 1975, p. 563), this did not eliminate the inherent difficulties subsequent courts found in applying such a standard; specifically, there is an assessment of probability of dangerousness in every instance of civil commitment (Diamond, 1974, pp. 439–444; Wexler, 1981, p. 11). Despite both legal and psychiatric efforts to understand adequately and to apply consistently this standard, the practical results have not been promising. In short, this requirement is disturbing because of its propensity for over- and underinclusivity (Diamond, 1974, p. 111; Monahan, 1996).

A representative body of literature indicates that psychiatrists are inclined to prefer safety and caution in their predictions of dangerousness (Chambers, 1972, pp. 1107, 1153; Monahan, 1996), and that overinclusivity tends to be more common than its counterpart (Monahan, 1981, p. 112). More disturbing than these findings are studies that report the low rate of accurate predictions of dangerousness or studies that demonstrate how harmless persons are routinely diagnosed as dangerous (Ennis & Litwack, 1974, p. 693).

While the psychiatric profession's inaccurate predictions of dangerousness have fashioned a system of wrongful preventive detention (Morse, 1982a, p. 85), "both federal and state courts continue to sustain police power authority in involuntary civil commitment proceedings" (Haddad, 1974–1975, p. 225). The complicity of the legal community regarding the dangerousness criterion endorses the consensual values of cooperation and accommodation previously referenced. Despite empirical arguments advanced by legal and social science commentators documenting why psychiatric evidence should be significantly circumscribed (Ennis & Litwack, 1974, p. 733) or altogether eliminated (McCormick, 1972, p. 29), it appears that in matters of civil commitment it is "better to be safe than sorry."[1] Expert testimony is admitted into evidence because it is believed that it "will aid the trier in his search for truth" (Cleary, 1972, p. 30). The underlying presupposition is that experts can draw inferences from a set of circumstances that lay persons cannot. Whether or not psychiatric predictions of future dangerousness meet this general test of admissibility, given the unreliability of psychiatric judgments, does not appear to be particularly relevant from the standpoint of the courts.

The Gravely Disabled Criterion

A number of states allow for the civil commitment of nondangerous mentally ill persons by protecting those who cannot provide for their own physical needs

(Comment, 1974, p. 1223). The American Psychiatric Association's Guidelines for State Legislation on civil commitment of the mentally ill, has, in pertinent part, defined this criterion as follows:

> [The person] . . . is substantially unable to provide for some of his basic needs, such as food, clothing, shelter, health, or safety or [the person] will, if not treated, suffer or continue to suffer severe mental and abnormal mental, emotional, or physical distress, and this distress is associated with significant impairment of judgment, reason, or behavior causing a substantial deterioration of his previous ability to function on his own. (Schmidt, 1985, p. 29)

With such a criterion in mind, some commentators assert that the American Psychiatric Association is attempting to expand the scope of the state's *parens patriae* power (Schmidt, 1985, p. 29; Arrigo, 1993c). This "distress and deterioration" provision is targeted at the large numbers of second-generation mental health consumers; chronically ill patients living in the community, cycling in and out of hospitals, somehow surviving in abandoned buildings and alleyways (Stromberg & Stone, 1983, p. 278).

Coupled with these APA guidelines are efforts by some state legislative bodies to extend civil commitment to persons deemed obviously ill (Treffert, 1985, p. 260), or to generally broaden the statutory criteria for civil commitment (Washington Revue Code Ann., 1985). These measures are, in part, acknowledged as a response to libertarian critics of involuntary hospitalization. As one commentator opposed to restrictive commitment standards put it, "How real is the promise of individual autonomy for a confused person set adrift in a hostile world" (Bazelon, 1975, p. 907).

Patients' rights attorneys and other critics of this more recent trend in civil commitment matters are concerned with the justice policy implications for increasing the state's authority to involuntarily hospitalize people (Durham & LaFond, 1988, pp. 317, 330). While the psychiatric community and supporters of the psychiatric ideology favor commitment standards based on medical criteria (Treffert & Krajeck, 1976, pp. 283–294), albeit with constructive legal safeguards (Chodoff, 1976, pp. 499–501; Roth, 1979, pp. 1123–1127), civil libertarians believe such guidelines will only foster more unwarranted (Durham & Pierce, 1982, p. 216) and improper (Morse, 1982a, p. 54) commitments. In addition, these critics maintain that the practical assessment of the "distress and deterioration" criterion will subject mental health consumers to the increased and relative treatment discretion of psychiatrists (Rubenstein, 1983, p. 559; Ley & Rubenstein, 1996).

Perhaps most troubling for advocates is the potential loss of liberty interests secured during a flurry of mental health litigation during the late 1960s and early 1970s. For example, one of these cases (*Rouse v. Cameron*, 1966, p. 451), addressed why mentally disordered persons needed to be singled out as a special class deserving treatment, especially when the treatment typically resulted in institutional confinement (Ennis, 1972, p. 33; Comment, 1974, p. 1264). These objections are predicated upon what civil libertarians view as the psychiatric community's continued use of questionable and imprecise criteria regarding definitions of mental illness and crazy behavior (Morse, 1978, pp. 527–654). Although acknowledging the "scandalous conditions" in which many psychiatrically disabled persons live (Schmidt, 1985, pp. 11–15), these critics do not accept the suggestion that civil commitment criteria should therefore be expanded. As one analyst exploring this relationship has argued, too much discretion has already been given individual psychiatrists in commitment matters, thus arrogating what "is fundamentally a moral, social, and legal question—not a scientific one" (Morse, 1982a, p. 60).

The foregoing discussion demonstrates that both the legal and scientific communities contribute greatly to the policy formulation of substantive standards in civil commitment. While some psychiatrists perceive the intervention on the part of mental health lawyers as a "holy legal war" against state hospital psychiatry (Halleck, 1975, pp. 2–7) or as a "legal onslaught" (McGarry, 1976, p. 320), other psychiatrists regard the judicial involvement as a welcomed move toward shared decision making (Hoffman, 1977, pp. 84–87). Notwithstanding these opinions, some level of legal and mental health systems interaction is evident in civil commitment matters (Shah, 1981, pp. 219–259); specifically, in defining mental illness, assessing dangerousness and interpreting gravely disabled criteria. While some accommodation is operative in commitment hearings (i.e, the court's reliance on psychiatric diagnoses and predictions of dangerousness), this value does not appear to be as forthcoming in issues relating to increasing the state's *parens patriae* authority.

In both instances, however, it is clear that the courts and psychiatry speak for the mentally disabled citizen (Perlin, 2000). In this context, both disciplines exercise a level of paternalism, despite their apparent intentions to represent the best interests of the mental health consumer. It is precisely this value which places mentally disordered persons outside the normative social order, subjecting them to a neglectful system of care. This dilemma is magnified when strong adversarial and antagonistic situations develop. What follows are some selected areas of intense controversy.

CAUGHT IN THE CROSSFIRE: PSYCHIATRIC TREATMENT AND A PREFERENCE FOR LIBERTY

The Right to Refuse Antipsychotic Medications

Of particular importance during the deinstitutionalization movement, was hospital reliance on psychotropic drugs which facilitated massive patient discharge from public mental institutions (Scull, 1984, p. 171; Brooks, 1987, p. 345). These new medications were praised by psychiatrists and mental health policy makers because of their primary capacity to relieve psychotic symptoms; specifically, delusions, hallucinations, and agitation. Thus, persons previously unable to live in the community were now able to do so, sometimes with only minimal support or supervision. While the initial impact of antipsychotic drugs significantly helped to reduce patient assaultiveness and disruptiveness, a dark side to these medications surfaced in the 1960s and 1970s (Brooks, 1980, pp. 180–181; Brooks, 1987, pp. 342–345; Rhoden, 1987, p. 401). An alarming number of mental health consumers experienced physical, emotional, and mental side effects that diminished the person's quality of life (Conley, 1986, p. 64). While some hospital experts believed that the harms caused by these chemical agents were more damaging to the patient than the psychosis itself (Brooks, 1987), other psychiatric physicians minimized their unavoidable impact, insisting that the side effects could be controlled (Klein & Davis, 1969, p. 42).

Amid this climate of psychiatric uncertainty, civil libertarian attorneys, patients' rights advocates, and other concerned citizens began exploring the extent to which the administration of psychotropic medication was both unnecessary and avoidable (Klein, 1986, pp. 80–86; Tanay, 1980, p. 1; Winick, 1986, pp. 7–31). In some instances, courts found that medication reliance was administered strictly for staff convenience not patient treatment (*Davis v. Hubbard*, 1980, p. 926). In addition, inaccurate diagnoses subjected many mental health consumers to a forced regimen of harmful neuroleptics (Lipton & Simon, 1985, p. 369; Pope & Lipinski, 1978, pp. 825–826). Compounding these problems was the countertherapeutic use of antipsychotic drugs for purposes of punishment and control (Brooks, 1987, p. 352; Szasz, 1977, p. 12; Szasz, 1984, p. 86). All of these factors led a district court judge to conclude that the administration of antipsychotic medications by public hospital staff occurred in a "grossly irresponsible" fashion (*Rennie v. Klein*, 1979, p. 1301).

Despite increasing evidence detailing the harmful effects and inappropriate administration of drug treatment for psychiatrically ill citizens, most state mental hospitals continue to rely on this intervention believing it to be the most effective mode of treatment (LaFond & Durham, 1992; Levy & Rubenstein, 1996). In the wake of this controversy, the constitutional right of involuntarily committed mental patients to refuse antipsychotic medications was born (*Rennie v. Klein*, 1981, p. 836; *Rogers v. Okin*, 1980, p. 650; *Mill v. Rogers*, 1982, p. 291; *Winters v. Miller*, 1971, p. 65). The establishment of this liberty interest was based on a right to privacy which emphasized autonomy and self-determination (*Roe v. Wade*, 1973, p. 113; *Griswold v. Connecticut*, 1965, p. 479). This right does not pertain to persons either dangerous to self or others, in an emergency situation, or to those individuals unable to make a rational treatment decision (Doudera & Swazey, 1982; Roth, 1986, p. 139). The purpose of this right was originally drafted so as to place final refusal in the hands of the consumer not the clinician (Brooks, 1987, p. 358). The practical effect, however, has been to grant patients a right of objection and to insist that the hospital staff review the person's medication regimen (Roth & Appelbaum, 1982, p. 179). Final authority regarding treatment decisions continues to be vested with the psychiatrist and attending treatment team (*Youngberg v. Romeo*, 1982), provided their judgments correspond with the agreed on practices of the medical profession (Gutheil, 1980; Gutheil, 1985).

Although the right-to-refuse treatment doctrine was designed to curb psychiatric abuses in the care and treatment of the mentally ill, procedural safeguards ensuring this right have significantly hampered its effectiveness (Brooks, 1987, p. 341; Winick, 1997a). While the right to a due process hearing presided over by an independent psychiatrist not affiliated with the state mental health system ensures that the case is decided on the merits of the refusal, this private physician must consider issues of patient competence or dangerousness, must assess the side effects of the medication, and must evaluate the availability of a less intrusive treatment for the patient (*Mills v. Rogers*, 1982).

This process was made formidable with the decision in *Rogers v. Okin* (1984) (Isaac & Armat, 1990, p. 250). Here, the court ruled that a judicial hearing was required on the issue of competence and that the appointment of a guardian *ad litem* was necessary for refusing patients diagnosed as incompetent. As a result of the competency question, many mental health consumers declining medication returned to their previous chronically ill state (Gormley, 1984, p. 366; Hughes, 1984, p. 483; *In re Guardianship of Roe*, 1981, p. 40). Additionally, this latter guardianship protection raised important ethical questions involving the substitution of one's judgment for the diagnosed incompetent mental health consumer (Treffert, 1982, pp. 123–125), and the role that informed consent played in a patient's right-to-refuse decision making (Appelbaum & Gutheil, 1981, pp. 129–202). Psychiatrists criticized the legal system for abuses in competency hearing delays, and have drawn attention to what they regard as the real issue; namely, quality of care (Appelbaum & Gutheil, 1981, p. 720) not the "right to rot" (*Project Release v. Prevost*, 1983, p. 971).

Subsequent courts addressing the issue of a nondangerous mentally ill person's rights to refuse treatment have continued this focus on the matter of competence (*Mills v. Rogers*, 1982, p. 306). And, as I will subsequently explain in my discussion of the least intrusive means or least restrictive alternative doctrine, the shifting tensions in the psycholegal debate appear to be moving in the direction of the medical profession's preference for treatment. While the U.S. Supreme Court has declined to assess whether or not an involuntary committed mental patient has a federal constitutional right to refuse antipsychotic drugs (*Stensvad v. Reivitz*, 1985, p. 131), other federal district courts are addressing related matters (*Stensvad v. Reivitz*, 1985, p. 131). Their judgments reflect an ever-increasing erosion of the right-to-refuse treatment phenomenon established by earlier decisions. As one court concluded, "an involuntary commitment is a finding of incompetency with respect to treatment decisions. Nonconsensual treatment is what involuntary commitment is all about" (cited in Durham & LaFond, 1985, p. 434).

Notwithstanding these legal trends, it is clear that civilly committed persons exercising their right to refuse antipsychotic medications conjures up strong adversarial sentiment among psychiatric and legal commentators (Winick, 1997). Governed by values of providing treatment and safeguarding liberty respectfully, the results of their antagonism has alternatively fashioned a system of ineffective treatment (Isaac & Armat, 1990, p. 263; Levy & Rubenstein, 1996) and noncare for the mentally ill (*Lake v. Cameron*, 1966, p. 660; *O'Conner v. Donaldson*, 1975, p. 576). This dilemma is exacerbated by the controversial meaning and application of the least restrictive alternative phenomenon; a doctrine that not only challenges the quality of treatment but also the locus of care.

The Least Restrictive Alternative Doctrine

The central question posed by the least restrictive alternative doctrine in cases of civil commitment is whether or not the method of treatment is least intrusive (*Jackson v. Indiana*, 1972, p. 729; *Youngberg v. Romeo*, 1982, p. 317; *Thomas S. v. Morrow*, 1986, p. 375), and the locus of care least confining (Hermann, 1990, pp. 382–384). These matters challenge clinical judgments regarding what constitutes the most effective psychiatric intervention (Costello & Preis, 1987, p. 1551), and medical and legal decisions about where that intervention can best be administered (Keilitz, Conn, & Giampetro, 1985, pp. 703–710). The obvious and persistent tensions created by such considerations are designed to satisfy the patient's interest in being free from unnecessary and harmful treatment (Brooks, 1987, p. 351; Gutheil et al., 1983, pp. 7, 10; Zlotkin, 1981, pp. 375, 412).

In the involuntary hospitalization of the mentally ill, the least intrusive means analysis is an important consideration in right to refuse treatment cases (Brooks, 1987, p. 361; Gutheil et al., 1983, p. 10; Zlotkin, 1981, pp. 423–428). At issue is the careful balancing of the mental health consumer's interests to be advanced by the administration of antipsychotic drugs (*Rennie v. Klein*, 1981, pp. 845–847). Some commentators, suspicious of this approach, claim that rather than securing efficacious treatment, "legal advocates have imposed a system of noncare in the most restrictive alternative" (Isaac & Armat, 1990, p. 333). Others point to the swelling number of chronically ill persons who, for lack of treatment, find themselves either homeless (Lamb, 1984a, p. 902; Rhoden, 1982, p. 408), or filtered through the criminal justice system (Treffert, 1982, p. 132; Myers, 1983–1984, p. 403).

More recently, because of the fallout of the least restrictive alternative principal, courts are deferring to the medical community's agreed upon assessment of what treatment is least intrusive (*R. A. J. v. Miller*, 1984, p. 1322; *Rivers v. Katz*, 1986, p. 345). While some jurisdictions continue to recognize this doctrine on the basis of state statutes and common law (*Rodgers v. Commissioner of the Department of Mental Health*, 1983), this liberty interest is giving way to what the U.S. Supreme Court has called "the demands of an organized society" (*Youngberg v. Romeo*, 1982, p. 320). In short, state mental hospitals are deciding what is in the best interest of the psychiatric citizen; judgments that carry with them a presumption of validity.

The problem with this approach in civil commitment matters is the unlikely probability that professional psychiatric consensus will opt to forego drug therapy or hospital confinement when treating mental health consumers (Arrigo, 1992b, p. 26). Essentially, the medical establishment would need to admit that a treatment regimen of antipsychotic medication and involuntary hospitalization possessed only limited effectiveness (Durham & LaFond, 1988, pp. 346–351) and, therefore, was not consistent with reasonable professional standards in treating mentally ill persons (*Clark v. Cohen*, 1986, p. 79). Moreover, community-situated treatment would have to be consistent with reasonable professional standards, satisfying the "minimally adequate" treatment needs of the psychiatric consumer (Costello & Preis, 1987, pp. 1548–1549). This kind of deliberate departure from the medical model approach does not appear to be forthcoming (Levy & Rubenstein, 1996).

Aside from the problems of forced treatment and institutional care, are the disturbing consequences of the court's more recent wholesale support for psychiatric decision making in confinement matters. The deference afforded the medical profession's mode of psychiatric intervention presupposes that mental health consumers are persons lacking control and judgment, needing to be confined for their own good (Morse, 1982a, pp. 58–67). Some critics denounce psychiatric assessments citing what they believe to be the medical community's manufacturing of madness (Szasz, 1970, pp. 83–110). Other commentators resist judicial support for total psychiatric decision making in civil commitment and treatment matters, maintaining that "psychiatric opinions are essentially political judgments" (Pfohl, 1978, p. 229).

Whether opposed to heightened psychiatric authority in issues of patient treatment, or a firm believer that "the worst home is better than the best mental hospital" (Cumming & Cumming, 1957, p. 34), the results of the clinicolegal debate on the least restrictive alternative doctrine have only further stigmatized the mental health consumer (Scull, 1989, p. 218). The meaning of liberty for the involuntarily committed person is "social marginality, deprivation, and despair" (Warren, 1982, p. 203). Both the courts and psychiatry have fashioned a system which one observer woefully concludes, "harms and kills the sick" (Warren, 1982, p. 203). These outcomes are a product of the imposition of legal and medical values that unfortunately cast the psychiatric citizen as a social outcast (Arrigo, 1996b). One attempt to minimize stigmatization that provides for treatment while respecting legal safeguards, has been the suggestion of involuntary outpatient commitment. Amid a climate of flux and uncertainty in matters of civil commitment, this strategy ostensibly offers hope for a necessary balance between individual and state interests.

Involuntary Outpatient Civil Commitment

A logical extension of the right to refuse treatment and least restrictive alternative controversies is the issue of involuntary outpatient commitment (Hinds, 1990, p. 847; Keilitz et al., 1985, p. 693; Winick, 1997a). The mental health literature reflects that there is no standard definition, shared perception, or agreed on practice among states invoking this doctrine on what exactly it entails (Miller, 1982, p. 265). Quasi-experimental studies offer only limited information regarding outpatient commitment procedures (Hiday & Goodman, 1982, pp. 791–793) and patient types admitted with expanding commitment laws (Miller & Fiddleman, 1984, p. 149). This notwithstanding, legal commentators have relied on it to construct arguments outlining when state intervention in the lives of psychiatric citizens is beneficial or problematic. Some reviewers argue that compulsory community treatment is essential so that the state does not discriminate against the poor; consumers disproportionately committed to psychiatric facilities (Bleicher, 1967, p. 93). Others propose a more selective reliance on the practice of involuntary outpatient commitment, restricting its use to individuals committed under the *parens patriae* justification (Myers, 1983–1984, p. 412), or pursuant to conditional release or outpatient commitment statutes (Hinds, 1990, p. 381).

Despite differing views on its meaning and its use from both the medical and legal professions, compelling treatment in the community is increasingly recommended for chronically mentally ill individuals (Hinds, 1990, p. 381). The hope is that those persons with a history of failing to follow through on their treatment plans (voluntarily taking prescribed antipsychotic medications and consistently maintaining scheduled therapy appointments), can be prevented from future inpatient hospitalization by involuntary outpatient civil commitment (Bursten, 1986, p. 1256; Hiday & Scheid-Cook, 1987, p. 229).

A number of arguments have been put forth which address the advantages and disadvantages of compelling involuntary treatment in the community (Mulvey, Geller, & Roth, 1987, p. 571). Proponents argue that a population of some mentally ill persons cannot experience the full benefits of living freely and autonomously in our society without the imposition of some structure (Lamb,

1984a, p. 903). Involuntary outpatient civil commitment ensures this structure, protects mental health consumers from becoming disenfranchised and abandoned, and safeguards their liberty to the fullest extent that their disability will allow. Supporters also point to the possibility for greater comprehensive service delivery when treating patients in the community; avoiding the reactive, crisis-oriented approach that governs most state mental hospital systems (Caton & Gralnick, 1987, p. 860). Finally, advocates of this position maintain that psychological treatment in the community "introduces the patient to the experience of living . . . in a nonpsychotic state" (Mulvey, Geller, & Roth, 1987, p. 578). Therefore, involuntary outpatient commitment facilitates an ongoing process of stable rehabilitation in a community setting.

Critics of this intervention strategy are primarily concerned with what they believe to be another effort at coerced treatment under threat of state action for noncompliance (Hinds, 1990, p. 388). Concerns about the limited efficacy of available treatment, especially when forced, suggests that individual liberty interests will be sacrificed at the expense of mere social monitoring functions (Morse, 1982a, p. 74). This raises additional questions about the extent of governmental intrusion in the lives of mental health consumers. Intervention in the form of compulsory community treatment may lead to unwarranted intrusions elsewhere for an expanded group of mental health clients. Specifically, because the dangerous standard for involuntary outpatient civil commitment would necessarily be lower than the impatient standard, the need-for-treatment criterion would gain greater prominence. This could subject many mentally disordered persons to the same discretionary abuses psychiatry practiced prior to the inclusion of the dangerous criterion. In addition, the right-to-refuse treatment doctrine would not extend to cases involving compulsory community care. "By definition, a person cannot refuse treatment while being involuntarily committed on an outpatient basis" (Mulvey, Geller, & Roth, 1987, pp. 516–517). Another objection to the practice of involuntary outpatient civil commitment is the potential for abuse and the difficulty with ensuring quality control. The outpatient relationship occurs in a noncontrolled environment, between a patient and professional. Transactions are private and monitoring of actual service delivery, both in method and manner, are not easily verifiable. A final concern voiced by opponents of involuntary outpatient commitment is the harm caused to the therapeutic relationship. Reliance on coercion significantly jeopardizes the likelihood that consumers will positively and willingly accept treatment, no matter how efficacious the intervention may be. A system predicated on negative sanctions can only further stigmatize persons already suffering from acute alienation (Mulvey, Geller, & Roth, 1987, p. 577).

What the preceding analysis on involuntary outpatient civil commitment discloses, is how uncertain both the psychiatric and legal communities are when addressing issues of effective treatment that do not infringe on an individual's fundamental liberty interests. Once again, both camps assume to know what is best for the psychiatric citizen. Whether asserting a need for treatment or a right to liberty, these professions exercise a degree of paternalism that significantly distances the mentally ill from the rest of society. Although some courts have recognized the right of *competent* mental health consumers to refuse medication absent an emergency (*Rogers v. Okin*, 1980, p. 656; *In re Guardianship of Roe*, 1981, p. 55), and although arguments have been advanced that assert the right of a competent outpatient to refuse medication in a nonemergency situation (Hinds, 1990, p. 392), one thing is unequivocally clear: courts decide on the issue of competency (Weiner, 1985, p. 341), and clinicians treat consumers as patients that are sick (Scheff, 1984, pp. 8–12) and incompetent (Roth et al., 1977, p. 280). The point is not that the legal and psychiatric communities have no role to play in the lives of mental health clients. Moreover, the point is not that the mentally disordered need no care. *The real issue is understanding the implicit values that underpin clinicolegal decision making and then evaluating what consumer needs are being met by such an approach.* This undertaking will significantly help to contextualize the kind and quality of services provided to the mentally disabled. In addition, by comprehending just what values are protected by civil commitment and confinement laws, it may be possible to initiate a system that moves beyond the present climate of uncertainty and abandonment.

THE POLITICS OF ABANDONMENT

I have argued that existing psychiatric and legal decision-making practices in civil commitment matters foster a disturbing system of care for mental health consumers. Moreover, this system effectively treats these citizens as the outcasts neither profession necessarily intends them to be. One possible explanation for the failed service delivery system involves the social values that underpin psychiatric and judicial intercession. While reference to the historical dimensions of paternalism has been cited as a contributory factor, scant attention has been given to the various forms in which paternalism currently manifests itself in relation to the mentally ill. As a point of departure, I recognize that there is, ostensibly, a fundamental clash of interests operating in civil commitment matters (Hermann, 1990, p. 361); namely, the rights of an individual to engage in independent choice-making versus state interference justified on the basis of benevolently securing the happiness, welfare, and needs of the coerced party (Dworkin, 1979, pp. 78–90). Notwithstanding this tension, the intrusion into the lives of many mentally disturbed persons is significant and profound. In part, this is the product of law and psychiatry's commitment to paternalism, a social value that is recognizable by its three distinct forms.

THE THREE FORMS OF PATERNALISM

Social Control

The social control argument essentially posits that involuntary hospitalization is a necessary and acceptable response to a disabled person's lack of behavioral control (Zusman, 1982, pp. 118–125). This position further assumes that the individual mental health consumer, contrary to the ordinary citizen, lacks choice-making capacity and therefore cannot knowingly be deterred from engaging in violent or dangerous conduct (Treffert, 1985, p. 259).

The contribution of the legal system in deferring to and then regulating what psychiatry labels incapacity through dangerousness, grave disability, or both demonstrates how this profession esteems social control interests (Perlin, 2000). While many courts attempt to ensure that full disclosure of the risks and benefits inherent in a particular course of psychiatric treatment are made available to a consumer with sufficient faculties to reasonably understand what is being proposed (*Von Luce v. Rankin*, 1979, p. 448; *Truman v. Thomas*, 1980, p. 905), questions involving the voluntariness of the consent (*Aden v. Younger*, 1976, p. 662; *Price v. Sheppard*, 1976, p. 908) and concerns about the patient's ability to comprehend the impact of treatment, are part of the court's decision-making role (Gormley, 1984, p. 361). As previously mentioned, courts are increasingly relying on psychiatric expert testimony to ascertain whether or not individual mentally disturbed persons possess choice-making capacity to assume responsibility for their physical welfare (Reiser & Slobogin, 1990, p. 397). When an incompetency determination is made, the court may appoint a guardian to represent the interests of the consumer (*In re Guardianship of Roe*, 1981; *In re Colyar*, 1983, p. 738). When the psychiatric citizen is found incapable of rendering informed consent in matters of treatment or confinement, a substituted judgment must be made for the patient by the court (Gromley, 1984, p. 365).

There is a striking parallel that I wish to draw between the court's interest in protecting the welfare of mentally ill citizens and wards of the state; specifically minors. In fact, recent statutory language addressing guardianship law states the following: "[A] guardian of an incapacitated person is responsible for care, custody, and *control* of the ward. . . . [Such] guardian has the same duties, powers and responsibilities as a guardian for a minor" (Uniform Probate Code, 1990) (emphasis added). Moreover, massive support for the enactment of Adult Protective Service statutes (APS) has occurred during the past 15 years. This is evidenced by the majority of the states having adopted some sort of APS provision (Myers, 1983–1984, p. 416). These statutes, designed to provide necessary treatment for the mentally ill, are modeled after comparable statutes representing the needs of children and youths (Myers, 1983–1984, p. 416). Finally, while the U.S. Supreme Court has recognized that juveniles possess a panoply of procedural rights ensured to all citizens (*In re Gault*, 1967), the substantive liberty interests of involuntarily hospitalized minors are significantly circumscribed by parental judgments, provided they receive the medical profession's endorsement (*Parham v. J.R.*, 1979, p. 604). In short, the Supreme Court held in *Parham* that Georgia's voluntary commitment guidelines did not violate the procedural protections guaranteed to minors in the *Gault* decision. "Parents retain plenary authority to seek institutional care for their children, subject to a hospital physician's independent examination and medical decision" (Morris, 1986, p. 946). Regardless of the child's protest, if the parent's judgment is that their son or daughter is mentally ill, can benefit from institutional care, and is supported by a physician's assessment and diagnosis, then the child will be admitted involuntarily for psychiatric treatment. This sort of judicial decision making underscores the court's preference for socially controlling not just chronic psychiatric patients but minors *suspected* of mental illness.

Custody

The paternalistic value of custody bears an important relationship to the issue of suspicion of illness, probability of dangerousness, or both. As the preceding sociolegal history on civil commitment and paternalism disclosed, visibility of the mentally ill has often resulted in incarceration or other forms of confinement (Grob, 1994). These outcomes follow today despite differences in diagnoses among physicians and low rates of accurate predictions. Critics of this approach have likened these police power commitments to preventive detention (Herman, 1973, pp. 673, 688), and have dismissed the claim that a loss of liberty is warranted in order to prevent future possible harm (LaFond, 1981, p. 527). The American Psychiatric Association's guidelines on state legislation, regarding civil commitment of the mentally ill recommend limiting the police power function (Schmidt, 1985, p. 39; Stromberg & Stone, 1983, p. 383). By the same token, however, they encourage an expansion of the *parens patriae* commitment criteria. This would subject a greater number of mentally ill persons to custodial confinement for treatment purposes (Chodoff, 1976, p. 499), especially when they are considered to be obviously ill (Treffert, 1985, p. 259).

The legal system as well demonstrates its support for the paternalistic value of custody. Some observers have suggested that deinstitutionalization made the community the functional equivalent of the hospital (Bachrach, 1983, p. 83; Scull, 1984, p. 177; Torrey, 1997). Those services once availed in a psychiatric facility increasingly became the responsibility of the community (Pepper & Ryglewicz, 1982, p. 390). As several commentators have indicated, the conditions in which many mentally ill persons live in community settings is simply deplorable (Rapson, 1980, pp. 193, 243; Hombs & Snyder, 1982, p. 85).

Often, care and services do not extend beyond the administration of medication (Myers, 1983–1984, p. 29). Further, the influence of mental health lawyers and the courts in promulgating such a system is immeasurable and well documented (Scull, 1984, p. 125; Rhoden, 1982, p. 412).

Another aspect to the important social value of custody is the procedural standard of proof required at civil commitment hearings. Unlike criminal prosecutions where the state must demonstrate *beyond a reasonable doubt* (at least 90% certain) that the accused is responsible for the commission of a crime, the burden of persuasion in confinement proceedings is based on a showing of *clear and convincing evidence* (75% certain) (*Addington v. Texas*, 1979, p. 418). The implication is that psychiatric patients are afforded a procedural safeguard less than what is availed to criminal defendants (Morse, 1982, p. 98). It is therefore easier (and, thus, desirable) to confine mental health consumers who *may* be dangerous to self or others or who *may* be gravely disabled than it is to incarcerate alleged felons. The only justification for such a policy is that a temporary loss of liberty (preventive detention) is in the best interest of society and the individual psychiatric citizen (Zusman, 1982, p. 112; Treffert, 1985, p. 259; Chodoff, 1976, p. 497). In these instances, proponents argue, it is better to be safe than to be sorry.

Treatment

A third paternalistic value underscoring involuntary hospitalization, civil commitment laws, and confinement policies is a concern for treatment. From the perspective of psychiatry, this occurs not only because of the administration of antipsychotic medications and other clinical interventions, but because of the medical community's conscious effort to control "crazy" behavior (Morse, 1977, p. 610). This control is accomplished by identifying those activities which fall outside the boundaries of "normal" conduct. The American Psychiatric Association relies upon its Diagnostic and Statistical Manual to categorize behavior along a continuum of craziness (Arrigo, 1992b, p. 10). Of course, the impact of such classifications is to "treat" behaviors that psychiatry, as reflected by prevailing social norms, deems unbefitting (Szasz, 1963, pp. 11–88; Szasz, 1987, pp. 9–132). Judicial complicity in this scheme is evidenced by the court's deference to the medical community's professional consensus in psychiatric matters (*Youngberg v. Romeo*, 1982, p. 307; *R.A.J. v. Miller*, 1984, p. 1319). As I have argued, this deference is present not simply in appellate case law, but in the administrative proceeding as well.

Further evidence of paternalism-as-treatment in current civil commitment laws and practices comes from an administrative court's determination that a particular consumer is *not* "crazy" or psychiatrically ill. Consequently, involuntary hospitalization does not follow. In essence, courts, tribunal decision brokers, or both determine that an individual is "well," in the clinicolegal sense, and maintain that it is therapeutic to release the person from custody. This brand of treatment may include a discharge plan (a medication regimen and outpatient therapy). However, this plan, when disregarded by the mental health systems user, can and does produce symptom escalation, decompensation, acute psychiatric crisis, and eventual rehospitalization (Torrey, 1997).

To illustrate, a study of a model program in the state of Massachusetts found that the rate of repetitions for civil commitment, rehospitalization, or both was staggering. Even when funds were provided for community-based services and support, and even when the chronically disabled persons of this model program were believed to be capable of living in the community (some 90%), only 5% did not suffer any psychiatric setbacks. As the outcome study's primary investigator concluded, "life for [many] patients [became one of] decompensation in the residential setting, stabilization in the hospital, return to the residential setting, decompensation again, and the cycle repeated]" (Geller et al., 1989, p. 33). As the example suggests, when a person is discharged and treated on an outpatient basis, there is considerable doubt about the therapeutic and efficacious consequences of this action, especially when the anticipated result is "revolving door" institutional care.

RECOMMENDATIONS

Thus far I have provided a historical account of events during the past 25 years primarily responsible for present-day confinement practices, discussed the context in which law and psychiatry speak for the mentally ill, evaluated three controversial policies that magnify clinicolegal tensions in commitment matters, and outlined those core values underpinning judicial and psychiatric decision making. At this juncture, rather than rejecting outright the psychiatric and legal vision of treatment and liberty respectively, a more reasonable approach requires fashioning a policy that incorporates the salient contributions of both professions. Such an orientation is critical if a future directed policy in civil commitment matters is to be established.

Striking a proper balance between confinement and liberty is not an easy task. In the past, while clinical intervention left unchecked produced frightening asylum conditions (Rothman, 1980, pp. 17–40; Scull, 1984, pp. 117–133), legal remedies worshiping the treasure of liberty only applauded an ideal at the expense of real human suffering (Mulvey, Geller, & Roth, 1987, p. 575). A fair-minded position must accept the premise that limited psychiatric intervention for therapeutic purposes (including coercive treatment) is sometimes warranted. This holds true especially for persons so severely affected by their disorder that they are "no longer capable of making a rational choice whether to continue in (their) present state or to seek treatment for (their) mental illness" (LaFond, 1981, p. 526). The difficulty with this proposition is the tendency on the part of psychiatrists to overestimate the benefits of a particular treatment regimen and delimit the harm, while mental health lawyers may acknowledge the harm yet deemphasize the benefits (Brooks, 1987, pp. 344–353). These perspectives are understandable, given medicine's deterministic affection for more and better science and the law's rights-conscious esteem for more and better justice (Schmidt, 1985, p. 40).

In order to construct a civil commitment policy infused with the insights of both professions, understanding the essential needs of mental health consumers is a prerequisite to any future policy aimed at improving the mental health care system. Although this undertaking addresses only a limited aspect of involuntary hospitalization, the psychiatric and legal implications for such an approach refocuses critical attention on the mentally disabled citizen's heretofore misplaced interests. In what follows, I identify five consumer-based needs that require psychiatric, legal, and other constituency recognition before it is possible to move beyond the present climate of uncertainty and abandonment in civil commitment matters. Consideration of these issues could help reduce the mutual antagonisms that plague both professions by serving as the first step toward shaping a policy that is as well designed as it is well-intentioned.

Quality Care

The constitutional right to quality care is the most fundamental interest at stake for psychiatric patients in civil commitment proceedings. Although this issue has received some attention from psychiatric (Appelbaum & Guthiel, 1981, p. 199) and legal (Arrigo, 1993c) commentators, these investigations mostly address the right to such care in medication refusals (Winick, 1997a). A more general right to quality care recognizes the intrinsic dignity of human beings no matter how disabled or dysfunctional. It is a liberty interest that encompasses the right to be free from bodily intrusions (*Johnson v. Silvers*, 1984, p. 823; *Lake v. Cameron*, 1966, p. 657; *Davis v. Hubbard*, 1980, p. 916; *Dodd v. Hughes*, 1965, p. 540), the right to bodily integrity (*Project Release v. Prevost*, 1983, p. 962; *Jones v. Gerhardstein*, 1986, p. 2), and the right to autonomy and self-determinism (Hermann, 1990, p. 362). Each of these rights is directly linked to a more basic claim to person-hood. Given the past psychiatric abuses, a healthy skepticism regarding the role of mental health professionals to treat therapeutically rather than to control socially is certainly understandable. Nonetheless, allowing treatment discretion for the psychiatric profession is acceptable *provided:* (1); the quality of intervention is recognized by the established medical community in which civil liberties are fully respected, (2); the clinical team's accountability for treatment decisions is monitored regularly, and (3); the consumer, a peer advocate if requested, and other affected, nonhospital personnel are participants in the commitment/treatment process. This is not to suggest that a costly and time-consuming system be erected as much as it is to underscore the importance of fully exploring the manner in which quality care can, in fact, be administered. It is an ongoing process that requires an assessment by physicians, attorneys, community representatives, and the consumer.

Protection Against Unnecessary Harm

An extension of the right to quality care is the right to be protected from harmful interventions (Brooks, 1987, p. 350). Although the literature is voluminous on the adverse effects of institutional confinement, benevolent coercion for chronically mentally ill persons can be more than custodial and the administration of antipsychotic medication can be more than heuristic. Part of the solution lies in understanding how psychiatric facilities are both physically and socially constructed in ways that institutionalize the mentally ill. Some recent social-psychological literature is examining the community model as an appropriate paradigm for greater social cohesion and personal well-being in diverse organizational settings (Arrigo, 1994a, 1997c; McKnight, 1987, pp. 54–58). If the harm that is caused by commitment and the treatment course that follows is to be reduced, greater exploration in this area of social designing is necessary. Both physicians and patients' rights advocates need to demonstrate an increased sensitivity to how social and physical space can be configured in ways that benefit the mental health consumer (Lamb & Goertzel, 1977, pp. 679–682).

Safe, Supportive, and Affordable Housing

An evaluation of civil commitment raises important questions concerning alternative care that is as efficacious as hospital confinement but is as nonrestrictive as one's mental disability will allow (Keilitz et al., 1985, p. 692). An absence of affordable housing stock that is both structurally safe and interpersonally supportive, substantially narrows choice-making prospects for civil commitment parties. Nonetheless, for a system of involuntary commitment to be as effective in caring about the mentally disordered as it can be, pursuing the full spectrum of available treatment possibilities must be acknowledged as absolutely essential (Myers, 1983–1984, p. 425). Too often commitment proceedings are tainted by a dispassionate recounting of somatic symptoms and a detached verbalizing of adversarial rhetoric. Given that the goal of involuntary treatment is to return the consumer to a mental health state in which the individual can make an informed and rational decision about their acceptance of the prescribed intervention (Roth, 1979, p. 1122), and given that this intervention is to be the least restrictive upon one's liberty (Turnbull, 1981, p. 26), then evaluating the safe, supportive, and affordable housing options in a particular jurisdiction must be factored into the decision making equation that attorneys and physicians undertake. If the commitment hearing can delve into deeply personal renditions of human suffering and misery, then a deliberate evaluation of noninstitutional, efficacious treatment is quite reasonable.

Understanding the Consumer's World

A significant problem confronting both medical and legal parties in civil commitment matters is the version of truth/justice these individuals embrace as knowledge and understand as power. Advances in both the physical and social sciences have fostered a society in which people are normalized and depathologized (Foucault, 1980, pp. 7–31). This is especially the case with the mentally ill (Arrigo, 1996b). The locus of responsibility for caring for these citizens has shifted from the family and local community to a group of trained psychiatric professionals (Arrigo, 1993b, p. 13). These experts assert the informed capacity to understand and treat mental health consumers (Scull, 1989, p. 216). The result is that we have fashioned a system that esteems the psychiatric community's world view (Kittrie, 1972, p. 18). Social meanings and acceptable behaviors are governed by the moral treatment of those professionals who exercise treatment power. In a culture where respect is afforded science, scientific assertions are an exercise of power that reduce the merits of other knowledge claims as less rigorous and, therefore, less valid (Arrigo, 1993c). The implications for such a monopoly of power are far-reaching. Not only are the mentally ill left to the moral entrepreneurship of the psychiatric profession, but this profession's version of truth, of power, is crystallized through the formation of laws affecting the care and treatment of the mentally disordered.

The "science" of law and psychiatry is representative of a certain approach that reflects the interests and attitudes of only certain members in society (Arrigo, 1996b). It is an approach that relies on linear, rational, deductive thinking to arrive at truth (Young, 1990, pp. 107–120). There can only be one commitment outcome in a particular hearing. This outcome must be based on only well-established and time-tested scientific truths, honored by only universally applicable legal precedents. This logic reduces uncertainty, ambiguity, unpredictability, multiplicity, and difference to unity and sameness. Intuitively, such an orientation appears counterproductive. Clearly, psychiatric citizens do not easily fit this unidimensional worldview. The result is that they are often normalized and institutionalized to perpetuate "the demands of an organized society" (*Youngberg v. Romeo*, 1982, p. 302). The totalizing effect of this legal and medical perspective denies not only the heterogeneity of the mentally disordered as a class of people, but the individuality of those consumers within this group. Both law and psychiatry must be more open to an approach that is comfortable with the contradictions, inconsistencies, and complexities that are an important cornerstone of human existence. Adopting this point of view can only further our comprehension of the felt and lived needs of mentally disabled citizens.

Reexamining the Civil Commitment Hearing Process

On a practical level, successfully understanding the previous point entails reevaluating how the commitment process unfolds. One commentator suggested that the "court of last resort" functions as a consensual and commonsense arena in which psychiatric and legal decision brokers decide the fate of mental health clients (Warren, 1982, p. 162; see also, Holstein, 1993). My experience at these proceedings as advocate, researcher, or both supports this claim.

Indeed, deferential dialogue all too frequently anticipates the hearing outcome. The point is not that this result is unacceptable. Accommodation is essential but not at the expense of advocacy (Poythress, 1978, p. 8). Usually, the entire affair is audiotaped or a stenographer is present promoting an air of formality. The parties present include the attending psychiatrist, perhaps some members of the treatment team, an attorney representing the hospital, an administrative law judge, some hospital security if necessary, the petitioner, a defense attorney, and the consumer. There can be little doubt that such an atmosphere engenders limited patient warmth or comfort. This speaks to the sort of impersonal and perfunctory approach the legal and psychiatric professions typically rely on in these instances (Morse, 1978, p. 100). The belief that a sterile and antiseptic environment somehow makes for friendly and open client discourse is at best short-sighted.

Interestingly, the organizational dynamics demand a kind of perfection that can compel the psychiatric citizen to live out the "crazy" role that he or she obviously knows all too well. On occasion, my experience has been that when this performance is not forthcoming, there is some suspicion about whether the client is perpetrating a hoax. Of course, when the disordered person performs as expected, the audience is generally willing to grant what, after all, the behavior only serves to affirm; namely, that the person is mentally ill, dangerous, gravely disabled, or all of these, and requires involuntary hospitalization and treatment.

Not only is the commitment process questionable, but the hearing outcome is susceptible to greater risk of error and wrongful confinement (Morse,

1978, p. 100). Although the standard of proof required by the Constitution places a stricter burden of persuasion on the state than the preponderance of the evidence criterion does (*Addington v. Texas*, 1979, p. 418), determining whether commitment is warranted should require no less a procedural safeguard than the reasonable doubt measure afforded criminal defendants (Morse, 1982a, p. 103). While the clear and convincing standard does reduce possible hearing outcome error, some courts have recognized the importance of applying the reasonable doubt measure in matters of involuntary treatment (*Lessard v. Schmidt*, 1972, p. 1078). A consumer-conscious approach recognizes the need for a supportive, comfortable environment governed by rules of informality and relationship-building, in which service needs are emphasized and liberty interests are *fully* protected.

While I recognize that the foregoing comments represent the philosophy of community (McKnight, 1987, p. 57), it is precisely this orientation that urges people to communicate openly rather than to accommodate mechanically. The former is inviting and the latter is distancing. Other nonhospital staff, including a peer advocate or community residents affected by the proceeding's outcome, can offer valuable insight into the consumer's ongoing behavioral patterns. This testimony could make the difference between in-patient commitment or total discharge. Given this very real possibility, concerned citizens should be notified of the hearing date, encouraged to attend, and asked to participate in the process. In a very meaningful way, the civil commitment hearing is like a town meeting: a member is in distress and all interested parties must work together to resolve the problem. Unfortunately, the present system does not fully adopt this point of view and commitment decisions are all too often made by those with limited information and resources.

CONCLUSIONS

In the preceding analysis of civil commitment laws and confinement practices in general, I endeavored to demonstrate how the past 25 years have been marked by disappointing clinicolegal decision making specifically for the consumer. Influenced by a belief in treatment (Treffert, 1985, p. 259; Chodoff, 1976, p. 496; Appelbaum, 1984, pp. 133–144) and a preference for liberty (Morsea, 1982, p. 54; Szasz, 1974, p. 233; Szasz, 1970, p. 33), the paternalistic tensions created by such a polarity of positions has taken a substantial toll on the lives of many psychiatrically ill citizens. Not only has the stigma of mental illness been further advanced by psychiatric and legal commitment practices, but the entire system of care has fallen short of its responsibility to deliver much-needed services. While uncertainty and abandonment have more recently been the familiar catchwords in mental health law (Isaac &

Armat, 1990; Levy & Rubenstein, 1996), the possibility for improving the present apparatus is within reach.

My contention is that exploring the values that underscore the legal and medical approach to involuntary civil commitment helps to contextualize why antagonisms have been so intense and intervention has been so disappointing. Rather than dismantling the entire system outright, the first step to fashioning a well designed commitment strategy requires a synthesis of the inherent wisdom found in each position. To that end, the benevolence of coercive treatment is recognized in limited circumstances where the patient lacks sufficient judgment to make a rational choice about continuing or discontinuing the prescribed treatment regimen. In addition, I maintain that establishing a client-based assessment of what needs are in the best interest of the consumer is a preliminary but necessary component to improving the present policy. This process reveals that there are five compelling client interests that require further consideration by both legal and psychiatric decision-makers. A right to quality care; protection against unnecessary harm; decent, affordable housing; greater understanding of the consumer's worldview; and a reconfiguration of the hearing process itself, are matters that significantly restore the interests of the consumer to their proper position of priority.

Perhaps the greatest difficulty with such an approach is in its implementation. It is one thing to assert basic human needs or an alternative perspective from which to consider the meaning of commitment, but it is another to have these rights and ideas accepted as a more balanced account that respect treatment needs and liberty demands. The extent to which physicians, hospital personnel, attorneys, community advocates, consumers, and other invested constituencies participate in this process of debate and discovery, will determine the degree of success these recommendations will yield. The present crisis in civil commitment laws and practices is not an endless chasm filled with consternation and despair. The most reasonable solution seems to entail a recognition that law and psychiatry continue to offer insights that should not be readily dismissed. By starting from a position that affirms the consumer's needs and interests, this preliminary step initiates reform and invites resolution. To be sure, a system that values humane treatment and safeguards precious liberties can effect the type of change that will steer us away from abandonment, provided we remember that the fundamental needs of psychiatric citizens must always come first.

TWO

Medicolegal Advocacy for the Mentally Ill

A Question of Ethics

OVERVIEW. *The previous chapter concluded by suggesting that the mediocolegal establishment could avoid many of the pitfalls and problems associated with forensic decision-making by attending first to the experiences and perspectives of the psychiatrically disabled. This, of course, begs the question: Is it possible to know, define, and promote fully the interests of the mental health consumer? This is an ethical matter at the core of legal and psychiatric practice, impacting, perhaps dictating, the choices such decision brokers routinely reach. This chapter critically explores the philosophical contours of ethics governing decision making at the crossroads of law and psychiatry. What human rights do the mentally ill possess? How are they established and revoked? How are these fluid rights linked to the civil confinement and advocacy processes? Is it possible for a person to represent completely the interests of another, especially one who is psychiatrically disordered? Ultimately, if mental health advocacy fails to embody the wishes of the consumer, to what extent are psychiatric citizens represented in any forensic decisions? In other words, who really benefits from the intervention? These and related matters challenge our traditionally held beliefs about the functioning of law and psychiatry in the everyday, taken for granted world of medicolegal justice.*

INTRODUCTION: ON THE NOTION OF JUSTICE AND ETHICS IN LAW AND PSYCHOLOGY

The field of law and psychology emerged in the late 1960s with an avowed commitment to justice (e.g., Arrigo, 2001c; Fox, 1997, pp. 217–220; 1999, pp. 9–12; Haney, 1993, pp. 375; Melton, 1990). This emphasis on justice was a deliberate attempt to make the forensic domain "relevant" (Tapp & Levine, 1977a, p. 363) by "challeng[ing] and transform[ing] a prevailing 'judicial common sense' that had been used to keep the disenfranchised down so long" (Haney, 1993, p. 375).[1] The clinicolegal field, with its identified "ultimate purpose" [of] promot[ing] justice and assess[ing] the role of law in achieving a just social order" (Tapp & Levine, 1977b, p. 5) was institutionalized with the 1968 founding of the American Psychology-Law Society (APLS) (Fox, 1999; Arrigo, 2001a). Unfortunately, for the early pioneers of the APLS movement, the centrality of justice in psycholegal research mostly remains diverted (Fox, 1997).[2]

Today, in far too many research settings, psycholegal scholarship focuses on a limited and narrowly construed collection of topics (e.g., Small, 1993, 1997; Ogloff, 1992; Kagehiro & Laufer, 1992; Saks, 1986; Roesch, 1995; Weiner, 1993). For example, jury behavior, eyewitness testimony, sex offender treatment, and expert witness studies while certainly interesting, seldom, if ever, explore prospects for broad-based social or political change (Fox, 1993), or examine opportunities for advancing the interests of citizen rights, collective justice, or both (Melton, 1988, 1992).[3] Despite these shortcomings, the forensic field is, at its core, about justice (Arrigo, 2000a). This means that questions concerning medicolegal practices and the manner in which people are socially, politically, economically, and philosophically affected by them require careful and considerable scrutiny.[4]

One domain where law-psychology-justice research has yet to assess forensic intervention entails the ethics of advocacy for the mentally ill (cf. Williams & Arrigo, 2000a). Broadly speaking, the concept of "ethics" has increasingly assumed a more passive, perhaps trivialized, role within various academic fields where, nonetheless, it is thought to be a valuable dimension and necessary condition to ensure the humanity of people.[5] One subdisciplinary area where this is most troubling is the law-psychiatry domain (Arrigo, 1996b). To be clear, our relegation of ethics to its more pedagogical and sanitary status forfeits its very foundations; that is, it undercuts the significance of moral contemplation and the importance of justice in human social interaction. Modern science teaches us to understand the ethical sphere within the imposed, coercive confines of its jurisdiction (Arrigo, 1995a, pp. 101–104). That is to say, ethics is "built" on an edifice, a structure, of *abstractions* resting solely on the intangible underpinnings on which it is posed. What is "selected out" as defining ethical boundaries is that which can be reduced to abstraction (May 1983).[6]

In the fourteenth century, William of Ockham proposed a economic principle that has (indirectly) come to influence the fabric of our ethical edifice—a position that is most often associated with John Locke (1968). Ockham's Razor states that "entities are not to be multiplied beyond necessity." In other words, what is simplest is best. Thus, an abstract rule becomes a rule because it is simple to follow—*to obey*. And, equally, our identification of those whose behavior conflicts with or otherwise transgresses our rules becomes less ambiguous and less subject to debate. Indeed, codification intends absence of ambiguity and, by extension, the elimination of individual decision making. Consequently, decisions are produced by designated representatives—the select few who, by way of "expert" knowledge, are deemed competent and are bestowed power to speak for (presumably on behalf of) other constituencies. Again, as I will argue shortly, this is particularly disturbing in the domain of psychiatry and law where the mentally ill are routinely subjected to the expertise of clinicolegal decision brokers (Arrigo, 1993c, 1996b), whose choices all too frequently activate transcarcerative ends (Arrigo, 1997e).[7]

Those phenomena that are easily subjected to "degrees of control and analysis necessary for the formulation of abstract laws" (Spence, 1956, p. 112) are codified in such a way as to demand control. What is more amenable to the formulation of abstract principles than laws (or rules) themselves? Such is the constitution of *ethical codes*. Many systems—including the mental health and the legal apparatuses—have been constructed (codified) in terms of abstract laws that collectively comprise an intimidating structure rendering volitional subjects impugned objects who succumb to the will of the code in unreflective, subjugated obedience (e.g., Arrigo, 1996b, 1996c, 1996d).[8] Indeed, what person or group could, without fear of legal reprisal or sanctioned repercussion, brave the turbulent waters of defiance and resistance; that is, embrace individual reason? We seek an edifying structure in our impetuous escape from the anxiety of personal choice and responsibility. Rollo May (1983) refers to this as the "edifice complex" (p. 52). The "escape" is treated at length by Fromm (1947) in his work *Escape from Freedom*.

What all this suggests is that we, as practitioners, scholars, or both in the world of humanism and of human rights, have acquiesced to an unreflective existence within the preconfigured borders of (ethical) codes laid before us by our ancestors. This legacy does not imply that we (as individuals), necessarily, have made a choice to escape from the freedom of responsibility. What it does, in fact, suggest is that we no longer enjoy the power *to make* such a *choice*. Indeed, at some historical point, the representative powers that be concluded it was in our best interest to be subjected to constraints on moral discretion. One can only assume that our predecessors were unable to find liberating the possibility of such unbridled freedom. Perhaps a select few made choices that were not in the best interest of their clients, communities, or both and, consequently, such decision-making power was withdrawn from *their/our* possession. The result, of course, continues to be a circumscribed education in morality and justice.

To be sure, many of us regard ethics as the study of rules or codes of conduct that define professional choice and responsibility (e.g., Bersoff, 1995). Regardless of how one may feel about the presence of such rules, we have, undoubtedly, lost touch with what ethics really is. That is, we no longer deliberately regard ethics as that which embodies concepts such as good, right, virtue, freedom, choice, and the morality that constitutes an ethical mode of being. Perhaps we are aware that ethical rules or codes are presumably assembled on such conceptual underpinnings, yet we frequently take this for granted: the recipe that has become ethics is merely "taught" to us. As a consequence, too many students and practitioners memorize selected ethical precepts that apply to their potential or actual areas of specialization. What we often neglect, however, are the critical and philosophical bases upon which such rules are formed. In other words, there is a certain morality and a particular sense of justice that encompasses every rule that we are taught or, perhaps, are teaching. On too many occasions, we unreflectively abandon the theoretical (and ideological) explorations that must necessarily accompany such instruction.

I contend that ethics, in its relationship to morality and justice, is not something that should be taught. Rather, it is something that should be *explored*; something one comes to understand on one's *own* terms. As Schopenhauer (1970) duly noted:

> As the biggest library if it is in disorder is not as useful as a small but well-arranged one, so you may accumulate a vast amount of knowledge but it will be of far less value to you than a much smaller amount if you thought it over for yourself. (p. 89)

When we experience knowledge—a knowledge that one must come to *personally*—only then can our decisions or choices be regarded as truly ethical. The distinction between the human being and the automaton posing as human is found within this process of reflection, of exploration.

My intention in the present chapter is to explore or travel across the various paths that influence the often unquestioned choices we are impelled (by rule/law) to make, and those we may, at times, ponder. An exploration of ethics necessarily encourages us to understand why we make the choices that we do. From my perspective, a choice that is based merely on custom, convention, rule, and so on is not an ethical choice at all. And, without choice, the humanity we proclaim to hold so dear in our professional pursuits not only disappears, it becomes nonexistent.

In this chapter, I critically address several philosophical underpinnings of ethical decision making. Admittedly, I focus my attention on a limited target area. Indeed, I will canvass a select number of significant issues that pose unique problems for humanity. The purpose of these excursions is that of reflection. In brief, I speculatively examine: (1) the relationship between human rights and the law; (2) the relationship between mental illness and the law (i.e., the rights of the mentally ill); (3) the ethics of involuntary confinement (i.e., taking away and giving back rights to the mentally ill); and (4) the ethics of advocating for the rights of the mentally ill.[9] I contend that these obviously provisional remarks tell us something unique about the nature of justice in relation to the psychiatrically disordered and the practice of mental health advocacy. Thus, throughout this investigation, my intent is to encourage thoughtful reflection on some key issues that lie at the intersection of law, psychiatry, and justice. I conclude by assessing the implications of this exploration for mental health law, psychological humanism, and critical inquiry.

HUMAN RIGHTS AND THE LAW

The first issue that must be examined involves the "parasitic" relationship between the law and individuals that delineates their rights as human beings. In short, as citizens of a larger society we are *dependent* on the law for the rights we possess as human beings. The use of the word "possess" is intentional. It implies something that is always temporary; that is, something that can be taken away. Further, it implies the presence of some definable, delimited "object" that an individual currently enjoys as her or his own. The word "right" itself has come to mean something that is *given* (as in a gift) and, consequently, something that can just as readily and easily be taken away (Arrigo & Williams, 2000a). Thus, a right is certainly not a freedom: there is always a certain boundary imposed on one's right. In other words, one does not have the freedom to do what one pleases with a right. One's right is defined, as are its margins, by an exogenous, legally demarcated morality of which one has no direct input.

In this sense, then, rights are something that we are given by the law. Without the law, one has no rights, per se or a priori. One must look to (i.e., rely on) the law for the very rights that allow us to be human, to behave as human beings (Williams, 1999). Admittedly, one may ask the following: Do we not enjoy certain rights merely by being human, by being alive in this world? To answer this query, one need only ask: Are there rights that cannot be taken away? The answer is clearly no. In other words, the extent to which our rights can be taken from us when, for example, we abuse or misuse them, is the degree to which they are always rights provided to us by the law.

The contours of this debate were extensively investigated by 18th-century French Enlightenment thinkers including Charles-Louis Montesquieu (1989), Francois Voltaire (1980; 1961), and Jean-Jacques Rousseau (1950), among others. The Enlightenment thinkers were active in protesting the essential lack of rights that the majority enjoyed. They argued for "natural rights"; that is, rights that *all* human beings were entitled to simply by being human. Thus, they advocated, among other things, for the abolition of slavery, freedom of thought and speech, and more humane treatment of criminals and other "objectionable" persons. Interestingly, these same human rights often conflict with law. Indeed, it is the law which, metaphorically speaking, "strips" individuals of their natural rights at birth, only to subsequently *give* rights back to individuals in the form of legislatively defined privileges and protections (i.e., "gifts"). As Rousseau (1950) suggested, these rights were mere "frauds"; instruments of the powerful established as a means of maintaining, by deception, *their* chosen way of life. I will return to this point later when discussing the *parens patriae* and police powers of the state in relation to the mentally ill. For now, however, I conclude by restating the original thesis: human beings engage in a parasitic relationship with the law. Further, the law is that which gives and takes away rights; it is the edifice to which we must turn to ensure that our rights are protected and sustained.

THE MENTALLY ILL, RIGHTS, AND THE LAW

The mentally ill as one citizen group in contemporary society find that they are in an even more precarious position than the general population. Not only are they, similar to all other human beings, living under the rights provided to them by the law, but they also constitute a membership group that has had many of their (given) rights taken from them (e.g., Perlin, 1999; Isaac and Armat, 1990; LaFond and Durham, 1992). Thus, not only must they look to the law to uphold their rights as human beings (i.e., human rights), they must fight the law to reestablish those rights (i.e., given rights) appropriated from them. In this sense, then, the mentally ill become twice-removed from a state of true human existence. Of course, one of the key dilemmas with this situation is that many mentally ill persons are not regarded as competent enough to represent themselves. In such cases as these, advocates[10] are appointed to help them fight or, even, to fight *for them*.

The unique position of the mentally ill, however, is one that is historically contingent. Indeed, their position with regard to rights and the law has changed over time (Morrissey and Goldman, 1984, 1986). While many would agree that the status of the psychiatrically disordered in society (particularly their treatment and legitimacy as human beings) has substantially improved over the course of history (Grob, 1994), this progress has not been without its impediments. Similar to Nietzsche (1966), one must question our premature celebration of a Darwinian definition of progress and the devolution of humanity that often accompanies such growth. Consistent with the previous discussion on the individual's parasitic relationship with the law, the changes that have improved the lives of the mentally ill (and others) have been at the hands of the clinicolegal establishment and have not been prompted by progressive social awareness (Arrigo, 1996b). Thus, while the mentally ill have attained certain rights not previously enjoyed by them, their dependence on the law *for* these rights has remained. What we have, then, is a positive correlation between the dependence of the mentally ill on the law, and the enrichment of their lives (e.g., justiciable rights) as human beings. Again, this process makes sense only by understanding that such enrichment comes *through* or *by way of* the law.

Clearly, the reliance on the law for rights claiming by the mentally ill has produced certain effects. For example, invoking the right to refuse treatment or to receive treatment represents changes in mental health law (e.g., Winick, 1997a). However, the assertion of each right requires one to approach the law. That is, these are not rights that the mentally ill can simply exercise by act alone, they must find acceptance from the powers that constitute the law before acting. Typically, this entails an administrative hearing to determine if the person is competently invoking their legally sanctioned right. Mentally healthy citizens have the power to act alone—without direct permission from the law. It is assumed that psychologically well members of society are competent to make rational decisions regarding their actions and, thus, will often do so. The mentally ill, however, must seek permission from the legal apparatus to act. Even then they are often appointed a qualified overseer (i.e., an advocate) to champion their interests.

Thus, in a sense, each time the mentally ill (or their representatives) engage the law, they strengthen and bolster their dependence on it and, further, become somewhat disempowered because of it. The law assumes more control over their lives and the mentally ill reinforce the preexisting medicolegal notion that they are incapable of advocating on their own behalf.[11] This, then, is the profound paradox which psychiatrically disordered citizens confront: to endure without rights (as the law has taken them away), or seek rights from the law which, in turn, fortifies the power of the law. As with most paradoxes, there is no simple solution. In fact, there may be no solution. Ethically speaking, however, what is important here is that we give adequate attention to the underlying, often hidden, consequences of our actions and those of others, even when ostensibly acting in the best interest of subjugated and marginalized groups.

THE ETHICS OF CONFINEMENT PRACTICES

When we speak of the rights of the mentally ill, we generally refer to those individuals who lost their rights (i.e., were involuntarily committed and subjected to the structural constraints of an institution). As explained in chapter 1, this loss of liberty is justified under two separate but interrelated mental health law doctrines: police power and *parens patriae* authority (Reisner and Slobogin, 1997). Each embodies underlying ethical assumptions that serve to rationalize the ensuing action or choice making impacting the mentally ill person in question. The former of these state interests was alluded to in a discussion involving Socrates and Thrasymachus appearing in Plato's (1957) *Republic*.

The Republic begins with the concept of *dikaiosyne*, a term that embodies those conventions that one must respect in the interest of other people. We can think of *dikaiosyne* as morality. In other words, it is a term that signifies a certain morality that should be obeyed because the interests of others are at stake. Thrasymachus, however, claims that such standards in which moral conventions are embedded are to the interest of the powerful. Morality, then, consists merely of rules imposed by the political powers that constitute a calculated attempt to preserve the advantage of the ruling class. They are rules that can be manipulated by those creating them if their interest calls for it. Thrasymachus' response exemplifies the present-day antithetical concerns of the state regarding the mentally ill.

Thrasymachus argues that society's interests are, thus, not uniquely his interests. In fact, immorality would be to one's advantage because the "just man always comes off worse than an unjust man" (Plato, 1957, p. 25). In other words, the powerful (i.e., the unjust) gain advantage in every situation where the common person (i.e., the just) concedes to convention (conventions, of course, are codified in such a way as to be in the interests of the powerful). Thus, the injustice that is suffered by the just man at the hands of the law, will only encourage the continuance of the vicious cycle of injustice if one were to always obey.

Taking Away the Human Rights of the Mentally Ill

In the context of the present concern, we can think of *dikaiosyne* as embodied in the law (i.e., in the law's treatment of the unique concerns of the mentally ill). I recognize that the law is informed by social notions of what is moral. Conceptualizations of "good vs. bad" and "right vs. wrong" are, of course, based chiefly on Judeo-Christian teachings. At some unspecified historical junction, however, the law no longer was informed by morality; rather, morality was imposed on society through the administration of the law (e.g., Fuller, 1964). Our civic conception of what one should or should not do increasingly refers to the edified morality termed the law. Again, this reference may be regarded as an "edifice complex"; that is, an entangled fixation on the law as an escape from the choices that confront us as human beings.

With regard to confinement practices for the mentally ill, the underlying concern is the best interest of the community versus the best interest of the individual (Resiner and Slobogin, 1997). By Thrasymachus's own assertion—and I have no reason to believe that it is not, to some degree, present in contemporary society—we must regard community interests as being defined by those *re-presenting* the community's concerns. Community standards, then, under the facade of the conventional morality, can be manipulated by way of the law. That is to say, those mentally healthy individuals looking out for their own interests and fitting the psychiatrically ill into a social framework, relegitimize their own status while subjecting mentally disordered citizens to a marginalized and often criminalized existence (e.g., Lamb, and Weinberger, 1998; LaFond and Durham, 1992).

This social framework, however, often (historically) implies a concern for the interests of the community at the expense of the interests of the mentally ill. To be sure, the celebrated perspective that regards the mentally ill as "dangerous," "undesirable," "deviant," "monstrous," "diseased," "demonic," and so forth would naturally incline the community to establish, as their particularized interest, the containment and control of those persons identified as outsiders (Williams, 1999; Arrigo & Williams, 1999a). That is, community interests in this context have traditionally been concerned with keeping the mentally ill *away from* the mentally healthy (Arrigo, 1992b). Frequently, these community interests have been motivated by fear and ignorance. A persistent regard for the mentally ill as dangerous has encouraged the powers of the state to implement police power clauses that allow for the involuntary confinement of the mentally ill; that is, persons thought to be a danger to the community. The reality for the community, however, is that the psychiatrically disordered are, with relatively few exceptions, no more dangerous than the healthy and competent members of society (Monahan, 1996). Indeed, it may be said that the supposed rational decisions of the mentally healthy can be far more irrational, injurious, and, thus, dangerous than the choices made by their presumably ill and incompetent counterparts (Isaac & Armat, 1990; LaFond & Durham, 1992; Levy & Rubenstein, 1996). As Thrasymachus professed, the "just" are often led to suffer injustices by conforming to the codified form of "justice" engendered by the political (Plato, 1957).

A similar injustice is enacted by the *parens patriae* power of the state. While such power is afforded the state on the assumption that involuntary confinement is, at times, in the best interest of the individual, undoubtedly there is a historical element of morality attached to it (Szasz, 1974). Many of those involuntarily confined for their own benefit are persons whose chosen standards of living differ markedly from the community. In particular, I refer to those whose existential choices are vastly inconsistent with traditionally held and normatively accepted ways of being (e.g., the homeless mentally ill population) (Lamb and Mills, 1984). The literature concerning *parens patriae* provides ample evidence of the confinement of individuals whose only crime was difference (see, e.g., Kittrie, 1972; Scull, 1989; Szasz, 1977; Williams, 1998, 1999; Arrigo, 1996b; Williams & Arrigo, 2001a). Again, we must ask ourselves the following: Does the best interest of the individual truly receive suitable consideration, or does the interest of the community (i.e., those maintaining a position of political power) receive full attention?

I submit that in both cases (the state's police power and *parens patriae* authority), *dikaiosyne* exists as law imposed on members of the community which, under present conditions, is not necessarily in the interest of all people. Embedded within our moral standards of community decency and appropriate behavior, are those biases that favor majoritarian standards of living and prosocial conduct. By subjecting the mentally ill to involuntary confinement in the interest of the state (i.e., protection against harm to others) or in the interest of the disordered person (i.e., protection against harm to self), I contend that such citizens are subjected to ethical standards constructed on unjust foundations. They are unjust in the sense that they do not represent a respect for the interests of all people, but merely demand a respect for the interests of majoritarian rule. Thrasymachus, then, would stipulate that morals delimiting practices for involuntary confinement are not necessarily in the interest of the mentally ill; rather, they benefit the state and the community. In this context, the community's interests are esteemed only insofar as codified law (i.e., a political prescription), delimiting a set of moral standards for the community and providing the illusion (or deliberate misrepresentation) of dangerousness regarding the conduct of the mentally ill.

Giving the "Gift" of Rights to the Mentally Ill

As noted previously, the mentally ill are in a unique position in contemporary society. Having lost their human *and* legal rights, they all too often exist as "prisoners" within a confinement setting (Arrigo, 2001b; Ennis, 1972; Levy and Rubenstein, 1996). Further, having been civilly committed, criminally committed, or both against their will, they experience a pervasive struggle with institutional personnel to enjoy certain rights while detained (e.g., Wettstein, 1998; Steadman, et al., 1989). At the historical origin of the asylum, the mentally ill were not only stripped of the right to exist in society, but also the right to exist humanely within the institution that housed or, perhaps, warehoused them (Grob, 1994; Rothman, 1971; Isaac & Armat, 1990). Admittedly, agents acting on behalf of the mentally ill have succeeded in establishing a panoply of rights provided to individuals within confinement settings (e.g., Perlin, 1999). While many advocates of the psychiatrically disordered have been generally pleased with these developments, I submit there are certain ethical assumptions frequently neglected or overlooked when evaluating this progress.

On this latter point, I again turn to the notion of *dikaiosyne* for guidance. This time, however, I examine it in the context of rights *given back to* those whose rights have been appropriated. This process refers to morality that is established by the law, enacting and endorsing the liberty interests (rights) of the mentally ill. Once again, we must question whether these afforded rights are in the best interest of the mentally ill. Indeed, given Thrasymuchas' perspective on *dikaiosyne*, we must look within these established rights to what may be hidden within their explicit meaning. In other words, are the liberty interests availed to the mentally ill tainted by the concerns of those from whom the rights originate? At first glance, one can assume that these rights represent the prerogatives of the psychiatrically disordered. This is not to suggest that mental health consumers do not want these rights as much as it is to consider whether the bestowal of these legitimated rights truly reflects the unique interests of those to whom they are given?

Accordingly, I pose the question as follows: do we (i.e., the community) want what the mentally ill want, or *do we want what we want for them?* I shall return to this matter in the context of mental health advocacy. For now, however, I acknowledge the possibility that changes made in the way of rights for the involuntarily committed mentally ill are often informed by those granting such rights. For example, would the law truly provide rights for the psychiatrically disordered if it were not in the interest of the law or community that it represented? At the very least, the law is unlikely to give something to someone or some group that disturbs or challenges its comfortable, status quo existence (Arrigo & Williams, 2000a). Thus, confronted with the Court's inevitable interest-balancing model of weighing conflicting or competing constitutional rights, the question asked is not whether availing liberty safeguards is in the best interest of the mentally ill; rather, the question posed is how will such protections, if bestowed on the psychiatrically disordered, endanger the community's rights as expressed through the law? In other words, what can the (clinicolegal) system afford to *give* them?

Machiavelli (1985) recognized the fact that certain things provided to others can endanger or, at least, alter one's own existence. Accordingly, he presented an alternative that may be applicable to the present concern. Machiavelli echoed the sentiments of Adeimantus, another of Socrates' interlocutors in *The Republic*. Socrates's reply to Thrasymachus' announcement that happiness is best achieved through immorality, involves a formulation of *kinds* of good. The second kind of good that Socrates describes is contingent on the consequences of one's action. In other words, actions are good (i.e., moral) if the effects of those actions are beneficial. Adeimantus, in turn, professes that indeed actions are commendable for their beneficial consequences, but such commendation derives also from effects that *appear* to be beneficial. Thus, actions that are celebrated as moral and good for their beneficial consequences need only have effects that are *perceived* as beneficial. Machiavelli repeats this sentiment in asserting that the Prince need not possess superior qualities that encourage respect, he need only *appear* to personify such admirable qualities.

With regard to rights *re-presented* to the mentally ill, I previously noted that such gifts were generally not given if the assigner stood to lose something in the transaction. One possible way to circumvent this danger would be to appear to be giving gifts (i.e., rights) that benefit the mentally ill when, in reality, the rights merely embody the appearance of benefit. In this case, nothing real is lost by the giver, yet nothing real is gained by the receiver. A genuine facade is established. In fact, what ensues is that the position of neither party in the transaction is substantially altered, yet the public (society) assumes that such beneficial change has occurred because it has been presented to them in that way.

Consequently, providing rights to the mentally ill by way of gift-giving (i.e., endorsing rights claims) ensures the appearance of morality (and justice). This is an altered morality that would not have been necessary had the mentally ill not been exposed to the injustices and immoralities of the past (i.e., the loss of human and legal rights). Consider, for example, the homeless mentally ill population. What is introduced into society is the notion that the effects of involuntarily confining such persons are beneficial. That is to say, if one's chosen standard of living is not necessarily compatible with society's standard, then the individual will certainly benefit from forced or coercive confinement. Indeed, the individual will be depathologized, made functionally well, and corrected (Arrigo and Williams, 1999a). Again, what is important here is that such an assertion is merely an appearance. It is a dramaturgical facade (Goffman, 1961), repeatedly staged to ensure society that everything is being done to improve the lives of deviant and diseased people when, in reality, such lives may not need alteration at all (Arrigo, 1996b, pp. 104–115). This position is not a full-fledged endorsement of homelessness for persons identified as psychiatrically disordered. Rather, I question the ethicophilosophical conditions that give rise to confining such citizens and the particular interests that are advanced in the process. Thus, if a lesson is to be learned from Adeimantus and Machiavelli, it is that we must be wary of appearances: they are often deceiving.

A Note on Intention

An additional perspective worth noting before moving to the ethics of advocacy itself comes from Immanuel Kant (1959). In *Foundations on the Metaphysics of Morality*, Kant puts forth a decidedly nonconsequentialistic rebuttal to Socrates's "good contingent upon consequences" thesis. He establishes the concept of good will as the basis of morality. "Nothing in this world . . . can possibly be conceived which could be called good without qualification except a good will" (Kant, 1959, p. 9). When considering the morality of actions, we need not concern ourselves with the actual consequences of such actions. These are unforeseeable and often uncontrollable. Rather, what is important is the intended consequence or the motive of the action. If the intention that gives way to an action is immoral, than the act is immoral categorically, regardless of its effects and who and how many may benefit from it.

To amplify this point, recall the discussion of rights given to the mentally ill. If those bestowing such rights act fundamentally or exclusively in their own best interest, then the act of giving is immoral for Kant. Such an act would be absent referral to one's duty as a human being; that is, the moral duty concerning the oughts that are a priori universals. For Kant, the "good will" acts according to the moral law and not the law of the legal system. If the intention of the giver was to deceive society and the mentally ill into believing, through appearance, that they were the receivers of some good, the gift of rights would not be given for moral reasons. Even if the mentally ill were to benefit from such a gift, the intention behind the act of giving would render the act immoral.

Thus, Kant extends this ethical exploration of mental illness and the rights afforded to those so designated beyond the act of giving per se, and beyond the consequences of an action. The issue of intentionality becomes a decisive factor in the morality of giving and taking. I contend that intention—along with *dikaiosyne*, consequences, and appearances—underscore ethical considerations such as those thus far presented. With regard to the confinement of the mentally ill (i.e., taking rights away) and the bestowal of the gift of rights (i.e., giving rights back), I note the importance of questioning the underlying ethical motivations for our decisions and the decisions of others. As I subsequently demonstrate, these ethical issues are even more complex when considering individual actions, including those of the mental health advocate.

THE ETHICS OF MENTAL HEALTH ADVOCACY

As Lacan (1981) observed, "One feels good in the Good" (Lacan, 1981, p. 58). In other words, happiness is achieved in the long term by accomplishing good (well-being of self or others) which represents an index of the Good (Julien, 1994). For Aristotle (1956), every human pursuit is one that aims at some good. If Aristotle is correct, then we all adopt and pursue projects that will produce goodness (for Aristotle, this was measured by the pleasure that was produced by such goods), either for ourselves or for others. Pursuing good for ourselves or for others lends itself to ethical treatment in the sense that I question whether, in fact, it is possible to *ever* act solely for the good of another. This is historically captured by the philosophical debate concerning egoism and altruism.

Returning again to Plato's (1957) *Republic*, there is an ongoing assumption that is shared by both Socrates and Thrasymachus. Throughout most of the *Republic*, the two espouse opposing ethical viewpoints, though their convictions concerning individual interests related to individual action are somewhat harmonious. Though only implicit in the oration of Socrates, each seems to recognize that individuals would not act against there own interests (less they be ignorant as to what is in their best interest). In other words, individuals act in accordance with the interests of the self. This is the principle assertion of egoism's two forms: people are always motivated by self-interest (psychological egoism), and people ought to be motivated by self-interest (ethical egoism).

The polar opposite of egoism is altruism. Altruistic actions are those in which one appears to sacrifice the interests of oneself in order to achieve some good or benefit for another. If one adopts the egoistic perspective on humanity, altruism is not possible; that is, one would never act outside of one's own interest (see, e.g., Hobbes, 1950). Thus, following egoism, even an act that provides the appearance of altruism is, in some way, beneficial to the individual performing the act. In this sense, sacrificing one's interests in the name of another, is only conceivable if one considers the act of sacrifice to be in one's own interest. Thus, the sacrificial "good" is always already intertwined with self-motivations (Arrigo & Williams, 2000a).

Given these observations on egoism and altruism, what, then, is the role of the advocate? When one thinks of advocacy, one is immediately drawn to the interpretation that the person acts for the good of the client. In light of the egoist claim that one never acts beyond one's self-interest, we must question the intention of the advocacy act. Does the mental health proponent stand to gain from her or his actions? Or, as the advocate would state, does the client's interests outweigh whatever self-motivations the advocate may wish to accommodate? In light of these issues, we turn, briefly, to several insights found in psychoanalytic thought. Psychoanalytic thought serves to advance our understanding of both the origins of altruism and, further, its very possibility in forensic practice.

The Psychic Origin of Individual Altruism

Any act of altruism, be it pure or motivated by underlying self-interest, has its origin in some element of the actor's psyche. That is to say, behaving in an altruistic manner because it is consistent with the aims of one's society is not sufficient to explain such actions. There is always an intrapsychic component for the adoption of such motives or, perhaps, needs. Otherwise, where might this *desire* for action agreeable with the altruistic doctrine originate?

In order to assess adequately the source of altruism and its relation to mental health advocacy, we must briefly consider the infant's psyche. What is important here is the relationship of the newborn child to the primary care-giver (typically the mother). We must remember that the first satisfying object in the world for the infant is an object that is similar to the child. The infant's sole means of gratification and well-being is the object of the care-giver. Thus, the newborn child first learns to know, perceive, and recognize the outer world through an object that is similar (i.e., another human being) (e.g., Freud, 1954). As a result, there is a profound realization that the object on which the infant is utterly dependent is another human being. The infant must develop a successful relationship with this other for gratification, indeed, for life itself. Of course, the newborn is also aware that the other can deprive the child of gratification. Generally speaking, then, it is during the first years of the child's life that the infant discerns the gravity of other human beings, and the need to identify with them as objects to benefit the self.

The primacy of the newborn's relationship to the other is mostly unconscious over the course of one's psychological development. The significance, however, remains. What becomes of primary importance in subsequent years, though, is the role of memory. As Freud (1954) noted, "If the object screams, a memory of the subject's own screaming will be aroused and will consequently revive [one's] experiences of pain" (p. 123). Thus, the initial relationship that develops between the infant and her or his "similar object" fosters a bond shared among all human beings in which experiences of the other (often unconsciously) invoke memories of comparable events in one's own life. For example, when we observe another person suffering we feel his or her pain precisely as another human being. Through the repository of memory we store our own experiences of suffering and respond to the pain of others accordingly.

Thus, following Freud (1954), human beings are identified in two ways by the individual psyche: as an "other"; that is, a separate nonself that exists in the same world; and as a memory or part of the self. As a result, when we experience other human beings, we experience them both as *separate* from ourselves and as *part of* ourselves. Put differently, the other constitutes both a "them" *and* an "us" (Williams, 1999). Given these comments on the psychic origin of individual altruism and the psychoanalytic duality of our human existence, what, then, are the implications of these observations for purposes of mental health advocacy? To examine this question more closely, I provisionally address the ethic of "love thy neighbor."

Love Thy Neighbor (As Thyself)

It is a common conviction that morality has been, and is still, immersed in various philosophical doctrines. While this notion has some merit, we must understand that Christian dogma is itself relatively new. Further, the idea of altruism has no systematic conceptual place in the writings of the ancient Greeks such as Plato. The historical origin of altruism is often linked with Jesus the Nazarene who professed that one should "love thy neighbor." This connection, however, is a misperception. What is often overlooked or, perhaps, neglected in this precept is the remainder of the statement; that is, "love thy neighbor *as thyself.*" When the phrase "as thyself" is rightfully appended to the maxim, it assumes something of an egoistic character. In other words, "as thyself" draws attention to the self in the exchange of love. Loving one's neighbor, then, arguably implies that the self is more important than the other. We should love our neighbors, but only insofar as we love ourselves. Again, we are led to Hobbes's (1950) consideration of altruism as an impossibility. That is to say, it is something that can never occur purely outside the interest of the self.

Accordingly, I question whether it is even possible to want the good of the other (i.e., *velle bonum alicui*) (Julien, 1994), particularly in regard to advocacy in law for the mentally ill. Based on my cursory analysis of individual altruism, its psychoanalytic origins, and the dualistic nature of our humanity, one must ask at what cost/benefit? In other words, does the mental health proponent want the good of the other *for the other* . . . or *for thyself?* This question is of considerable import when contemplating the justice (and morality) of advocacy. Indeed, the good advocate (referring both to clinicolegal skill as well as personal ethic) is always interested in the needs of the client. The philosophy behind advocacy itself is to improve the existence of the mentally ill by brokering for and promoting certain qualitative changes (e.g., improved autonomy, self-determination, social standing) in the lives of mental health citizens (Bersoff, 1995). Thus, the advocate is a representative because the person wants the good of the other.

It follows, then, that the revised concern in the altruistic notion of love thy neighbor is both *my* good *and* the good of the other. The interplay of love thy neighbor and *velle bonum alicui* produces certain revelations in the ethical treatment of advocacy. The "good" *(bonum)* is often that which I desire for myself and, consequently and by way of myself, desire for the other. If, as Freud (1954) informs us, I see the other in myself (i.e., I feel the other in myself), then I must also see and feel myself in the other. Thus, what I wish for the other is what I wish for myself and what I wish for myself is what I wish for the other. The good of the other "is made in the image of mine" (Julien, 1994, p. 86).

Given these relationships, we must be mindful of the negative therapeutic reaction that Freud (1954) discusses. That is to say, we must be wary of desiring and acting (advocating) for the good of the other, when the other, perhaps, does not even want this good (i.e., this good does not necessarily belong to the other). The other's well-being is, at best, a mere reflection of our own sense of what is good (i.e., healthy and just), captured, albeit incompletely and falsely, in our advocacy for the other.[12] It is all too natural for human beings to move beyond empathy; that is, to actually see and feel the self in the other and the other in the self. Given this tendency, is it possible, in situations where the *bonum* of the other is of *prima solicitudo*, to extricate the image of oneself in the other, and advocate for the other as solely other?

In psychoanalytic circles, similar concerns arise in the context of the clinician maintaining the posture of a "reflective mirror." Psychoanalytic theory, in particular ego psychology, recognizes the impossibility of the emotionless, reflective therapist. Issues of countertransference (in addition to the unconscious ethical dynamic previously discussed) create significant impediments to the therapeutic process. What is unconscious here becomes critical as the process of seeing and feeling oneself in the other is largely latent and subliminal. Thus, the response to the question concerning the possibility of extricating oneself from the other's image is resoundingly answered in the negative (particularly if one were not aware of such unconscious dynamics). Perhaps the answer will always be no. And, much like the recommendations of ego psychologists on this matter, one can only hope to be *aware* of such forces and their consequent impact on personal ethics and the advocacy process (e.g., Bacal & Newman, 1990; Blanck & Blanck, 1974; Kohut, 1971).

Turning briefly to the egoist conception of act and self-interest in light of *velle* helps elucidate this matter. As Julien (1994) contends, the implications of *velle* are as follows: "I want it to be *me* and no one else who accomplishes your good" (p. 86). In the case of some disparity between what the other wants and what I want for the other, a critical choice arises. That is, does the advocate proceed with a measured altruism or, instead, does the advocate retain the self-interest that accompanies egoistic action and impose his- or herself on the other? The latter intervention is contained in such statements as, "You will have to acquiesce in light of my *velle!*" In this case, the well-being of the other is made to depend on the efficacy of the advocate. Thus, there is a denial of subjectivity: the client's desire is subjugated in favor of the advocate's (expert) knowledge/experience of what is in the mental health consumer's best interest.[13] Of course, as we discovered with *bonum*, this knowledge that one supposes often reflects an understanding of oneself (i.e., to the extent that self-knowledge is possible). In either case (i.e., altruism or egoism), it would appear that the advocate must consciously assess the motives behind her or his actions. In light of the problems thus far explored with regard to mental health advocacy, the only answer may consist of this process of assessment, awareness, and deliberation.

IMPLICATIONS

Thus far in this chapter I have very provisionally and critically traversed several philosophical boundaries within which ethical decisions concerning mental illness, rights, and advocacy take place. However, there are other ethical themes that fall within the scope of this investigation. While it is not my intention to canvass all of the intricacies related to this topic, there are, nevertheless, some additional matters that require cursory explication. These matters include the elitism and competence of the advocate, as well as the ethic of "ultimate ends" versus "responsibility." I maintain that these issues are quite significant for the nature of mental health law and advocacy, citizen justice, and the future of humanism in the psycholegal field.

The Advocate: Elitism and Competence

In response to Jeremy Bentham's (1961) "calculus of felicity," John Stuart Mill (1951) introduced the notion of quality into the conceptualization of good.

Bentham claimed that as all human beings pursue the pleasure principle, it could be measured quantitatively against unpleasure or pain. When considering the behavior of an individual, the pleasure or pain that such action produces can be measured against other alternatives. Thus, the "calculus of felicity" determines what action is good based on the good it produces. What Bentham contributes to this investigation is the notion that quantitative examination of alternatives can be employed in ethical decision-making processes to determine the best course of action.

Mill's (1951) recourse consisted of the introduction of quality into Bentham's quantitative schema. For Mill, different goods possessed different qualities, and the quality of these different goods required consideration before contemplating action. In other words, it was not merely enough to identify what actions produced good; rather, the *kind* of good produced mattered when determining the best course of action. According to Mill, there were both higher or cultivated desires and lower or uncultivated desires. What is important in this treatment of "good," are the persons measuring it. As Mill (1951) explained: "The uncultivated cannot be competent judges of cultivation" (p. 10). Thus, to measure the quality of good that action produces, one must retain a certain degree of competence; that is, one must be cultivated or knowledgeable enough to know what is a "better" good compared with other goods. He feared that if every individual had an equal vote in such matters—given that the majority of individuals were not cultivated—civilization would suffer.

In Mill's ideal scenario, only a small minority would have the right to express opinion regarding an issue. The best educated, the most powerful (in short, the societal elite) would retain decision-making power. As abhorrent and inhumane as this may seem, I submit it is, in some meaningful way, the philosophy under which present-day mental health law in the United States operates (LaFond & Durham, 1992; Levy & Rubenstein, 1996). The state assumes that most "uncultivated" citizens (e.g., the mentally ill, the poor, the disenfranchised) are largely incompetent to make decisions regarding matters about which they are not educated. Thus, this country functions under a representative democracy; that is, a government in which a select few competent individuals, whether appointed or voted in, are chosen to represent the interests of the people.

To what extent and, in what respect, are these notions found in the psychiatric and legal communities? The answer is far from inconspicuous. This elite status is one we often unquestioningly confer on attorneys, physicians and, clinicolegal advocates. Their specialized knowledge speaks *for* others. Under the present system, the mental health law advocate represents the interests of the psychiatric consumer. Of course, a "re-presentation" always loses something: it can never fully embody one's interests as initially experienced within the client's subjective being. This is a danger inextricably lodged within the current system of mental health law. Further, given my previous analysis on egoism, this re-presentation of interests potentially signifies the erosion of citizen justice and humanistic practices, even from the most well-intended of advocates.

Ultimate Ends Versus Responsibility: Weber the Untimely Advocate

The ethics of advocacy postulated by Max Weber (1958) proposed a difference between ultimate ends and responsibility. Ultimate ends implies that a set of values exists that is ultimately right, and that these values should be fiercely enacted and endorsed. The ultimate end is inconsequential in that it does not regard effects as a factor in determining action. According to Weber, the logic of ultimate ends requires that we live by these values without concern for the consequences they produce. Contrastingly, an ethic of responsibility recognizes and, perhaps, celebrates the numerous systems of value and perspective contained within a given society. Thus, the ethic of responsibility endeavors to maximize the values of all persons, irrespective of some ultimate ethical truth that is mistakenly proclaimed to exist.

For the advocate, the distinction between the ultimate ends versus responsibility models is of consequence, particularly in relation to one's own ethical values, the values of the medicolegal system, and the values of the client. For example, if one considers the advocacy role to consist of "fighting" for the rights of clients at all costs (e.g., preventing involuntary hospitalization, regardless of client repercussions because such confinement amounts to unjustified imprisonment that is the pinnacle of institutional inhumanity), one is acting from within an ethic of ultimate ends. However, as most would concede, it is, on occasion, in the best interest of the client to be hospitalized, medicated, treated, and so on as the person's well-being may very well depend on these interventions. If advocates made choices within such a narrowly construed ultimate ends perspective, they might fail to recognize that their actions were not consistent with their client's interests. If, on the contrary, they were willing to recognize that maximizing the good of all persons might entail action that advocates are not inclined to invoke (e.g., not involuntarily hospitalizing a homeless, mentally ill client who claims to prefer the outdoor chill of subzero degree weather to the comfort and warmth of temporary housing or shelter), their decision making would be governed by an ethic of responsibility. In both instances, however, the problem of egoism, as I described it, remains.

This dilemma in advocacy, based on Webarian ethical models, is complicated further when turning to the standards of professional organizations or the law itself for guidance. If we accept, at all costs, those standards delineated in the canon of ethics for psychiatrists, social workers, nurses, lawyers, and the like, or even the codified system of case and statutory law under which rules are established, we subscribe to preconfigured or *defined* values as ultimate ends to "goodness." This method is undesirable. It necessarily neglects the variable nature of being human: the differing needs of individuals; the differing necessities of situations; and the differing consequences and differing effects of action. As I have argued, this is the ethical model too many of us have come to adopt without sufficient reflection. There is something quite profound about our humanity (and the humanity of others), intrapsychically and interpersonally lost in the process. To embrace an ethic of responsibility, however, is similarly problematic. This course of action can be the basis of negligence suits, disbarment, suspended and revoked licenses, and other similar professional difficulties. Interestingly, Weber's (1958) position is to endorse an ethic of responsibility when faced with consequential situations. Regrettably, however, his thesis does not examine the matter of egoism as I have delineated it.

CONCLUSIONS

In this chapter, I raised questions about ethics, rights, mental illness, and advocacy, especially in the context of clinicolegal decision-making affecting the humanity and justice of those individuals involved in the process. I did not provide many answers. This was not my intention. Instead, the reader was asked to travel through a myriad of questions. The purpose of this exploration was to educate and to encourage thought, consideration, and introspection, and not to provide the solutions that many mistake as the ultimate aim of education. This excursion was meant to take the reader beyond the obvious; that is, beyond books and beyond conscious experience, to conceptual vistas one may not have immediate access to on an everyday level. These are the often uncharted places on the map of one's profession. Perhaps they do not even appear on the blueprints that our profession provides, indeed *gives*, us. These are the destinations of personal insight and social change; places that move human thought forward where previously it stood still and was stagnant.

To be sure, clinicolegal advocacy, as a institutional mechanism for advancing mental health consumer interests, produces a curious form of justice for the psychiatrically disordered. From its unsettling relationship with rights giving (i.e., psychiatric citizens legitimizing the hegemony of the clinicolegal establishment) and rights taking (i.e, psychiatric citizens experiencing civil/criminal confinement), to its problematic association with ethical egoism (i.e., advocates/experts presenting their own interests or incompletely re-presenting the concerns of consumers), mental health systems users are, at least, one step removed from advancing their own justice-based sensibilities. This conclusion may not appear problematic or troubling to most. After all, persons with diagnosed mental disorders are defined as variably sick, diseased, and unable to speak on their own behalf. Thus if follows that someone else, in particular a conscientious consumer advocate/activist, most likely would be best positioned to represent those psychiatric citizens who could not champion their own causes. As a critical and philosophical matter, I contend that this state of affairs, while certainly well-intended, remains deeply distressing.

If advocacy in mental health law is anchored by clinicolegal interpretations of rights, illness, competency, and the like, and if confinement decisions hinge, fundamentally, on an appeal to established structures of civil and criminal institutional authority, what room, if any, is legitimately left for the disparate voices of the psychiatrically disordered? Indeed, given these constructed realities, on whose behalf is the advocacy truly initiated?[14] Firmly lodged within these questions is a concern for how (and why) the system of mental health law substantially misses the mark with citizen justice and psychological humanism. This observation squarely returns us to the thesis entertained in this chapter; namely, providing a critically inspired and philosophically animated examination of the ethics of advocacy for the psychiatrically disordered.

I recognize that human beings are vulnerable. As such, the ethical standards that inform our everyday decision making should not be regarded as invincible or intractable. When too rigidly or dogmatically imposed, they dismiss, sanitize, diminish, or otherwise conceal the fragility of being human. If too artificially or abstractly wedded to the ebb and flow of human conduct and social interaction, ethical precepts eliminate the possibility that one may terrify another by illuminating his or her vulnerability. This is precisely the prism we all too frequently avoid. This light of innocence and uncertainty exposes the flaws, the ironies, and the absurdities of being human. But this glow is not cataclysmic. It is the light that makes growth and discovery possible. It illuminates the road that may, if we choose, lead us to another place, a better place, a more just and humane place. Identifying this juncture in the law-psychiatry arena is sorely needed. It is especially important for those ethical matters impacting society's approach to mental illness, confinement, and advocacy. Indeed, it may be the path that, one day, helps restore dignity to all those who are or will be institutionalized.

THREE

The Right to Community-Based Treatment

OVERVIEW. *The previous chapter concluded by suggesting that psychological egoism or measured altruism underscores decisions made at the crossroads of law and psychiatry. This means that the interests of disordered citizens are never completely realized. One important domain where the rights of persons with mental disabilities are particularly problematic involves the question of community-based care and treatment. This chapter assesses the dilemma of mental health consumer rights, focusing on whether the psychiatrically ill possess a fundamental liberty interest in mental health treatment, outside the context of institutional intervention. Does the Federal constitution guarantee a right to community-based care for psychiatric citizens? Do forms of neighborhood intervention for the mentally disabled produce better, more efficacious treatment outcomes than hospital care? Have sociological practice models offered any promising results? Aside from the ethical dynamics (discussed in chapter 2) undermining or abridging prospects for citizen justice, are there other philosophical bases that help explain the mostly absent right to community-based treatment for the mentally disordered? Questions such as these compel us to think about how the legal and psychiatric systems value persons with mental disabilities, and the extent to which we all regard them as vital members of society or casualties of social and public policy better left confined.*

INTRODUCTION

There is an obvious and persistent tension that exists when two conflicting and, ostensibly, countervailing social values attempt to determine prevailing constitutional law. This is most certainly the case with the involuntary civil commitment of the mentally disabled.[1] Liberty interests of the individual, guaranteed under the 14th Amendment of the United States Constitution, are balanced against the "demands of an organized society" (*Youngberg v. Romeo*, 1982, p. 320; see also, *Poe v. Ullman*, 1961). These conflicting interests are exacerbated when debating a constitutional right to treatment for mentally disabled persons in the community. Prior to the Supreme Court's ruling in *Youngberg*, proponents of community-based treatment supported a "least intrusive means" doctrine, maintaining that the state's interests in curtailing the psychiatrically disabled person's dangerousness could be achieved in the least restrictive environment (Chambers, 1972; Spece, 1979).

By extension, these advocates further argued that since involuntary confinement to a hospital posed a significant threat to the nondangerous mentally disabled person's 14th Amendment liberty interests, the state's 10th Amendment interests in treatment and protection could be satisfied in a nonhospital setting. Indeed, the absence of risk posed by nondangerous mentally disabled persons vitiated the state's 10th Amendment *parens patriae* or guardianship role, as well as its police power to prevent harm (Perlin, 1999). In time, this legal concept of "least restrictive alternative" became a household expression when referring to community-based treatment among service providers, mental health professionals, and other advocates (Turnbull, 1981; Miller, 1982).

However, with the *Youngberg* decision, it was less certain that such a constitutional protection afforded to the mentally disabled would prevail. In this case, the Supreme Court did not address the larger question of a general right to treatment, but instead focused on the particular issue of a right to treatment where such treatment was necessary to ensure the 14th Amendment liberty interests of personal safety and freedom of movement. Indeed, Romeo argued that further self-help programs were necessary to reduce his aggressive behavior and that the absence of such programs precipitated his violent outbursts. The Court of Appeals for the Third Circuit concluded that Romeo only sought treatment related to his interest in safety and freedom from restraint. Indeed, as Romeo asserted, his medical experts, if permitted to testify, would demonstrate that these training programs would curtail his aggressiveness (*Romeo v. Youngberg*, 1980, p. 159; *Youngberg v. Youngberg*, 1982, pp. 317–318).

Justice Powell, speaking for the majority, adopted the lower court position proposed by Chief Judge Seiz from the Third Circuit Court of Appeals. In his concurring opinion Seitz argued that Romeo sought *only* a constitutional right to "minimally adequate care and treatment" (*Youngberg*, 1982, p. 318), where such habilitation was necessary to sustain his liberty interests in safety and movement. The Supreme Court opted to consider only this reading of *Youngberg*, at the expense of the broader question of a general right to treatment in the least restrictive alternative. This decision signaled a conservatism that has had widespread implications for justice policy in the care and treatment of the mentally disabled (cf. *Olmstead v. L.C.*, 1999). Not only did *Youngberg* dispense with "the least intrusive means" doctrine, the doctrine that determined whether hospital confinement was necessary to provide minimally adequate treatment, but it substituted this standard by giving deference to accepted professional medical judgment that carried with it the presumption of validity.

A number of post-*Youngberg* courts have found support for the proposition that there is no constitutional right to a least restrictive environment (*Society of*

Good Will to Retarded Children v. Cuomo, 1984; *Lelsz v. Kavanagh*, 1987). Conversely, other post-*Youngberg* decisions have articulated a position that community-based treatment *is* "minimally adequate" and, thus, constitutionally required to protect the person's liberty interests. In these instances, however, professional consensus must assert that care and treatment in the form of community-based care is appropriate while hospital confinement is not (*Clark v. Cohen*, 1986; *Cohen v. Clark*, 1986; *Thomas S. v. Morrow*, 1986; *Kirk v. Thomas S. by Brooks*, 1986; *Childress v. Thomas S.*, 1986; *Woe v. Cuomo*, 1984; *Association of Retarded Citizens of North Dakota v. Olson*, 1982–1983; *Olmstead v. L.C.*, 1999). Given this standard's presumption of validity, it is unlikely that an unqualified constitutional right to community-based treatment will prevail.[2] Moreover, even if such a right were constitutionally guaranteed to the institutionally confined mentally ill and retarded, there is no evidence to suggest that such a ruling would apply to noninstitutionalized disabled persons (Rapson, 1980; Scull, 1989; Sedgwik, 1982; Kittrie, 1971). This further proves the claim that the conservatism of the Supreme Court in *Youngberg* poses significant justice policy implications in the care and treatment of the psychiatrically disabled.

This chapter explores these implications by critically examining the political philosophy of post-*Youngberg* decisions. Indeed, whether guided by substantive, procedural, distributive, restorative, or other models of justice, there is a system of ethics operating that underpins the Court's constitutional analysis. This ethicopolitical orientation makes certain value statements about the individual or group affected by the particular ruling. These values statements are based on widely shared democratic principles; including, impartiality, formal equality, a unitary moral subjectivity, and the therapeutic as just (e.g., Fraser, 1997). The problem with this approach, however, is that it presumes an homogenous public that rewards those who subscribe to the paradigm and oppresses those who do not (e.g., Young, 1990; Arrigo & Williams, 2000a). As a group excluded from decision making, the mentally disabled do not fit this normative framework (Arrigo, 1996b). The Supreme Court's deference to the established judgement of mental health professionals regarding minimally adequate treatment of the institutionally confined and the Court's unwillingness to address the more weighty issue of a constitutional right to community-based treatment for the mentally disabled in *Youngberg*, speaks to a particular posture toward the profoundly ill that has significant justice policy implications for this constituency.

In addition, a sociological analysis will be presented regarding a need for a right to community-based treatment for the mentally disabled. This is a broad reference to the deinstitutionalization movement which began in the 1950s. This movement was a response to a series of interrelated events; including, the introduction of chemical agents that addressed the symptoms of mental illness (i.e., antipsychotic medication) (Waldinger, 1986), the prevailing belief that long-term confinement produced warehousing, dehumanizing, and therefore, harmful effects (Herr, 1979), and a growing awareness among courts that persons with mental disabilities possessed fundamental liberty or civil rights (e.g., Comment, 1974).

Relatedly, the issue of a right to community-based treatment will be examined further by identifying the constitutional sources of that right. Accordingly, the due process interests guaranteed under the 14th Amendment and the protection against cruel and unusual punishment clause of the 8th Amendment will be considered. Finally, a critical theory of justice regarding the right to community-based treatment for the profound mentally disabled will be presented as a supplemental source to that right.

FEDERAL CONSTITUTIONAL ANALYSIS: POST-*YOUNGBERG*

Post-*Youngberg* courts fall into two classifications.[3] While the first group broadly dismisses all claims to a constitutionally based right to community-situated treatment for the psychiatrically disabled, the second group of cases equates minimally adequate treatment with community-based services. Both types of cases are explored below.

Group One Cases

A crucial aspect in these cases is the rejection of the "least intrusive means" analysis. Accordingly, courts ruling this way assert that there is no constitutional right to "community placement or a least restrictive environment under the Federal Constitution" (*Society for Good Will to Retarded Children v. Cuomo*, 1984, p. 1248; *Lelsz v. Kavanagh*, 1987, p. 1251). In these instances, because "least restrictive environment" is synonymous with "community placement," institutionalization, as a general matter, does not *deprive* one of their liberty (e.g., *Phillips v. Thompson*, 1983, p. 368). The emphasis on deprivation of liberty without due process of law is significant because persons who are institutionally confined receive mere custodial care, as distinguished from treatment designed to improve the conditions of the mentally disabled individual. This guardianship care is minimally adequate treatment and, therefore, does not violate the constitutional protection of personal safety and freedom of movement.[4]

According to courts favoring the group one analysis, institutional confinement of the mentally ill or retarded is permissible even where there is disagreement between plaintiffs and defendants concerning whether said confinement is minimally adequate.[5] Although there may be *credible* testimony proffered by plaintiffs' experts that state hospital confinement will not serve plaintiffs' *best* welfare, the presumptions of validity and correctness afforded a state mental health administrator's decision to institutionalize prevails.[6] For group one cases, it does not matter if community placement and service is the optimal treatment remedy for institutionally confined disabled persons, it must be the *only* remedy (*Lelsz v. Kavanagh*, 1987).

Group Two Cases

Similar to the first collection of post-*Youngberg* cases, group two advocates abandon the "least restrictive alternative" doctrine and rely on the consensus of the medical profession. Integral to this analysis is professional judgment, agreeing on the appropriateness of community-based services and the inappropriateness of institutional care (*Association of Retarded Children of North Dakota v. Olson*, 1982).[7] The holding in *Olson* serves as the watershed case, establishing this fundamental right. Following *Youngberg*, the federal district court in *Olson* reasoned that no specific analysis of a constitutional right to community-based treatment for the institutionalized mentally retarded could be entertained. However, the court maintained that *Youngberg* stood for the proposition that an absolute right to the least restrictive alternative should be rejected. Therefore, the federal district court concluded "that a constitutional right to the least restrictive method of care and treatment exists only insofar as professional judgement determines that such alternatives would measurably enhance the resident's enjoyment of basic liberty interests" (*Olson*, 1982, p. 486).

Other federal courts have followed the reasoning initiated by *Olson* (e.g., *Clark v. Cohen*, 1986; *Thomas S. v. Morrow*, 1986). At issue is whether community-based treatment is predicated on a clear consensus of mental health experts who believe that: (1) persistent hospitalization and treatment is *not* consistent with reasonable professional standards; and (2) community-based treatment is consistent with reasonable professional standards (Costello & Preis, 1987, p. 1548). "Minimally adequate" treatment, constitutionally protected under *Youngberg*, is understood to be synonymous with community-based treatment. Institutional confinement in the absence of such minimal care is not only unconstitutional, but must be substituted for community-situated treatment.

An additional feature to the group two cases is the interpretation of "professional consensus" employed by courts. The decision in *Lelsz v. Kavanaugh* (1987) suggests that courts are under no obligation to assert and enforce a right to community-based treatment unless the rights of an *individual* plaintiff are at issue.[8] Moreover, the judgment of mental health professionals must be in *complete* agreement that sustained institutional confinement is not "minimally adequate." Not only does such a standard deprive mentally disabled groups from relief they would otherwise be constitutionally permitted as individual plaintiffs, but arriving at uniform professional consensus in such cases seems unlikely.[9]

Political Philosophy

While post-*Youngberg* courts tend to be divided on the constitutional right to community-based treatment for persons mentally disabled, both groups of cases make certain assumptions about these persons (Young, 1990; Arrigo, 1996b). These assumptions convey a message largely fueled and substantiated by the mental health community.[10] Not surprisingly, these presuppositions are calculated into the "balancing of interests" test courts rely on when rendering a decision of constitutional significance. The traditional mental health community, through its established natural scientific approach, has devised an elaborate cataloging of mental disorders including criteria defining a particular disorder (e.g., APA, 1994). Similar to the holding in *Youngberg*, there is a "presumption of validity" attached to this diagnostic and statistical reporting.[11] This approach is especially troubling since the reliability and validity of these clinical assessments are, at best, questionable, and at worst, arbitrary (Morse, 1982b, 1988).[12]

Despite the tenuousness of traditional psychiatric diagnoses, the courts defer to the psychiatric community's understanding of the psychiatrically disabled. These disabled persons are labeled as diseased, deviant, and dangerous (Arrigo, 1993c). When determining a constitutional right to community-based treatment, dependent in large part on the medical community's professional consensus, balancing individual liberty interests against relevant state interests necessarily includes the above value-laden assumptions. In short, rather than being acknowledged as fully human, the implicit assumption and practical effect is that mentally disabled persons are deemed virtually, but not fully, human.[13]

While post-*Youngberg* courts adopt the medical community's professional consensus regarding the nature of the institutionally confined, there are also a number of assumptions courts rely upon when assessing the state's relevant interests (Cameron, 1988). Protecting the mentally ill and retarded from themselves and others, especially when diagnosed as dangerous, and guarding the health, comfort, and welfare of legally disabled persons, underscores a theme that the judgment of mentally disabled persons is subject to substitution.[14]

The concept of substituted judgment has been staunchly criticized by some commentators (Gutheil & Appelbaum, 1983). Interpreted as a faint-hearted effort to honor the wishes of a diagnosed incompetent, mentally disabled person, opponents charge that substituted judgment allows decision makers (the courts or state agents) to substitute their own psychiatric theories or preferences for those of an incompetent person. Notwithstanding such attacks, courts depend on this doctrine. This reliance is predicated on certain democratic principles presumed applicable to everyone in society. The moral reasoning engaged in by the courts is defined by the discourse of justice and rights (Fraser, 1997). Under this paradigm, moral reasoning is broadly and similarly applied to all people, ostensibly from an impartial and impersonal perspective (Young 1990, p. 96). Notions of formal equality, impartiality, order, logic and objectivity are distributive principles constituting a network of values that summarily represent the state's relevant interests (*Youngberg v. Romeo*, 1982).

Faced with these assumptions, a court is now prepared to engage in the process of constitutional deliberation regarding the right to community-based treatment for the institutionally confined mentally disabled. On the one hand, individual liberty interests are contextualized as the rights of disease-ridden, deviant-minded, and danger-prone outsiders (Arrigo, 1996b). On the other hand, relevant state interests are contextualized as the demands of impartial, orderly, rational, and impersonal state agents.

The ethical framework operating when such a balancing of interests is present (including the related assumptions), necessarily entails a utilitarian analysis (Bentham, 1879/1961; Mill, 1863/1951). The essential ethical consideration is whether an action (for our purposes not acknowledging a constitutional right to community-based treatment for the mentally disabled) contributes to the good of the majority. Given that the approach of utilitarianism is teleological, it looks to the consequences of an act to determine moral judgments. The utility of *not* acknowledging a constitutional basis for community-situated treatment regarding the mentally ill and retarded is weighed against the utility of acknowledging such a constitutional right. This balancing occurs in relation to a court's weighing of the relevant state interests. The utility of affirming order, unity, normalcy, and objectivity is balanced against the utility of not affirming such democratically based principles. When framing these ethical tensions this way, it is no surprise that the post-*Youngberg* courts' perspective on justice consistently fails to acknowledge the unconditional right to community-based treatment for the mentally disabled. To do otherwise would not only displace the reasoned consensus of the psychiatric profession, but would decenter the universal truth and power attributed to those fundamental concepts that constitute our system of justice.[15]

SOCIOLOGICAL ANALYSIS: FROM DEINSTITUTIONALIZATION TO RECOMMUNALIZATION

The need for a right to community-based treatment for the mentally disabled is most evident when examining our society's disturbing social landscape. Far too many persons remain institutionally confined when they could be better served in far less restrictive community environments (Kiesler, 1982a; Lamb, 1984b; Arrigo, 1993c). This position is equally applicable to chronically mentally ill and severely mentally retarded persons, provided requisite funding and support services are made available to them. The tragedy of excessive hospitalization is compounded by the inadequacy of community designed treatment and programming. The lack of treatment and support is substantially the result of government failure to reallocate mental health resources in the community (Levy & Rubenstein, 1996). Instead, this is where psychiatric institutions discharged ("dumped") the mental disabled (Mills & Cummins, 1982, p. 272; Rhoden, 1982, p. 376; Isaac & Armat, 1990).[16] As discussed in chapter 1, the devastating results are that incalculable numbers of people find themselves either marginally housed or on the streets without the support and care they need in order to survive.[17]

Deinstitutionalization was the public policy initiative designed to treat the psychiatrically disabled in community settings rather than institutional environments (Herr, 1979; Lamb & Mills, 1984). Not only did this strategy fail in implementation, but in far too many instances, mentally disabled persons were made worse off than if they had remained institutionally confined, albeit inappropriately.[18]

An additional matter related to the failure of deinstitutionalization is the phenomenon of multiple hospitalizations for the chronically mentally ill and the severely developmental disabled. Confronted by either inadequate community options or long-term institutional confinement, these persons routinely cycle in and out of local mental health facilities by way of involuntary, short-term civil commitments. This pattern of multiple hospitalization is known as the "revolving door" syndrome. Admitted to psychiatric facilities because of an acute crisis, these persons are typically stabilized on antipsychotic or antidepressant medication and released into the community with either no formal discharge plan or one that is not possible to monitor. In the absence of effective community support services and care, these profoundly disturbed citizens once again experience those symptoms (e.g., aggressiveness, paranoia, hallucinations) that escalate them to crisis. Their decompensation is so significant that involuntary rehospitalization is prescribed where the cycle of psychiatric care to living on the streets perpetuates itself (e.g., Stein, & Test, 1980; Lamb & Weinberger, 1998).

These sobering realities demonstrate that for many mentally ill and retarded people their lives have been marked by intrusive institutional confinement, a neglectful community care system, and have been punctuated by ongoing bouts of short-term civil commitment or incarceration via the criminal justice system (Costello & Preis, 1987, p. 1533; Myers, 1983–1984; Braddock, 1981; Arrigo, 1993c). These policy problems have lead some politicians and mental health administrators to call for less stringent state criteria regarding the civil commitment process.[19] The public has also responded to the abandonment of the mentally disabled by forming patient advocacy groups. These collectives are largely comprised of the families of the psychiatrically disabled. They are frustrated by the absence of adequate and compassionate care provided to their loved ones, and believe that the burden of caring for their relatives should be placed in the hands of the state.[20]

From excessive institutional confinement, to deinstitutionalization without requisite community supports, to current trends calling for greater state authority expanding involuntary civil commitment laws, the mentally disabled find that their liberty interests are continuously subordinated by the demands of powerful state agents. These demands represent the political will of the traditional psychiatric and medical communities, affirmed by the courts, at the expense of those disabled persons whose voices are silenced by an absence of negotiating power. Not only must the mentally ill and retarded endure the devastation of their debilitating illness and cope with the hardship of personal stigma, they must also succumb to the inadequate treatment choices laid before them, and accept the limits of their liberty.[21]

Some city planners and urban sociologists have advocated a move toward reintegration or "recommunalization" (Arrigo, 1994a, 1997c). This strategy essentially affirms the premise that when people are acknowledged for their competencies and encouraged to pursue them as a way of contributing to the stability of the overall community, other community members will be more inclined to accept the personality deficiencies of their neighbors. This communal tolerance is predicated on the understanding that identity is not constituted by the sum of one's deficiencies. Rather, identity is a product of competency and fallibility, activity and passivity, wellness and pathology. Additionally, by blending diverse groups of people in safe and supportive community environments (including the mentally disabled, the working poor, the frail elderly, the paraprofessionally employed, college-level and vocational students, the chemically dependent, etc.) and by inviting neighbors to create the cultural ethos of their community in a responsible manner, this peer-directed and empowerment philosophy will produce a reasonably self-governed community (Arrigo, 1997d).

Contrary to other initiatives designed to reduce the capacity of psychiatrically disabled persons to function in the community as autonomously as possible, this strategy seeks to avoid unnecessary institutional confinement and restore the eroding liberty interests of the mentally ill and retarded. Not only would such an approach reduce the risk of mentally disabled persons from being caught in the web of revolving-door hospitalizations, it would help enhance the likelihood that work, living arrangements, and friendships would be sustained (*Mental Health Association v. Deukmejian*, 1986). As long as the professional mental health consensus concentrates on treating the mentally disabled person's disability at the expense of acknowledging the fullness of their identity, the right to community-based treatment will remain an intellectual diversion. As long as a presumption of validity is afforded the psychiatric community's assessment of an individual mentally disabled person's condition, the rulings of most post-*Youngberg* courts will remain decidedly conservative. The only way to create a new progeny of post-*Youngberg* decisions is to establish a judicially enforceable right to community-situated treatment for the institutionalized mentally ill and retarded via the federal constitution.[22] Equally important and underpinning the formation of this right is the development of a critical theory of justice in regard to this constituency.

THE RIGHT TO COMMUNITY-BASED TREATMENT

Over the last several decades a number of scholars and courts have debated the constitutional question of a deprivation of liberty interests when assessing the right to treatment for the mentally disabled (Perlin, 1999; Levy & Rubenstein, 1996; Reisner & Slobogin, 1997). Their analyses have focused on both the cruel and unusual punishment clause of the 8th Amendment,[23] as well as a series of procedural and substantive due process concerns under the 14th Amendment.[24] The central problem with these constitutional arguments is that they lack the vitality necessary to sustain binding imperatives for the courts and, consequently, create no judicial obligation regarding right to treatment decisions (Durham & LaFond, 1988, p. 314), including the right to community-based treatment for institutionally confined, mentally disabled citizens.

Any success these positions have thus far achieved has been largely hampered by the Supreme Court's ongoing assertion that "need alone" is not sufficient to establish a constitutional right (*Youngberg v. Romeo*, 1982, p. 317). Equally burdensome has been the Supreme Court's opinion that a state is under no obligation to address all aspects of a particular at-risk group or some of those aspects at the expense of addressing another needy population (*Olmstead v. L.C.*, 1999). Strategically, the constitutional arguments mentioned above emphasize the preciousness of liberty (rather than the need for service) which is abridged when confinement to a psychiatric facility is ordered. The Supreme Court has looked favorably on this premise.[25] Additionally, there is one constitutional theory affirming the right to treatment that has withstood the rigor of courtroom debate and analysis. In essence, this theory asserts that if the state deprives a mentally disabled person of their liberty for purposes of therapeutic treatment, then the state is required to administer said treatment *Jackson v. Indiana* (1972).[26]

Building on these notions, establishing a right to community-based treatment for the psychiatrically disabled entails a recognition of the significant liberty interests jeopardized by institutional confinement. The *Youngberg* Court acknowledged that the basic liberty interests of personal safety and freedom from bodily restraint were guaranteed under the 14th Amendment. These fundamental rights were further understood to require "minimally adequate care and treatment," in order to preserve and exercise these liberty interests. Here, as in prior cases, the Supreme Court *assumed* that the mental health profession could provide *effective* treatment for mentally disabled persons seeking a right to treatment as involuntarily confined citizens (e.g., *O'Connor v. Donaldson*, 1975; *Rone v. Firemen*, 1979; *Woe v. Cuomo*, 1984). Indeed, if effective treatment was not the assumption, then why else would treatment be administered at all (Durham & LaFond, 1988, pp. 315–316)? This assertion, coupled with the minimally adequate care and treatment standard enunciated in *Youngberg*, form the basis of a constitutionally protected right to community-based treatment for the institutionalized mentally ill and developmentally disabled under the 14th Amendment's due process clause.

The failure of the medical profession regarding *inpatient* treatment for persons hospitalized against their will, overwhelmingly demonstrates the misplaced assumption of the Supreme Court (Durham & LaFond, 1988; Levy & Rubenstein, 1996). Time and time again, the empirical evidence reviewing the efficacy of drug and psychotherapeutic treatment for involuntary hospitalized, nondangerous mentally disabled patients does *not* establish treatment effectiveness (e.g., Eysenick, 1952; Meltzoff & Kornreich, 1970; Rachman, 1973; Parloff, 1978; Smith, et al., 1980). In fact, community-based *outpatient* services have offered outcomes equal to, if not superior than, hospital-situated treatment (e.g., Arrigo, 1994a, 1997d; Greene & De la Cruz, 1981; Kiesler, 1982; Straw, 1982).

The mental health profession is able to satisfy the *Youngberg* Court's assumption that neighborhood-based programs can provide effective treatment because community-situated treatment demonstrates a level of effectiveness that exceeds the hospital environment. This is true if we understand the mental health profession to include community-based providers, professional/paraprofessional staff, volunteers, and the like. But this is not to suggest that neighborhood-based organizations are synonymous with the hospital. Indeed, in some instances, community-based facilities are acknowledged as extensions or satellites of the psychiatric hospital. The latter emphasize institutional control while the former emphasize peer-directed autonomy. This difference gives rise to the minimally adequate treatment issue.

The state's curtailment of individual liberty interests of psychiatrically confined persons for a therapeutic purpose requires that minimally adequate treatment be provided to ensure that, while hospitalized, their 14th Amendment rights are, in fact, protected. If this provision is recognized as a fundamental right for mentally disabled individuals hospitalized against their will, it follows that mentally ill and retarded citizens living outside a psychiatric facility are entitled to the same treatment and care that would enable them to preserve and exercise their 14th Amendment liberty interests, albeit in the community (Costello & Preis, 1987, p. 1542).

This notion of "extended liberty" was first articulated in *Thomas S. v. Morrow* (1986). At issue was whether a behaviorally disordered individual, dependent on the state for care and treatment, could receive minimally adequate treatment in the community as opposed to the hospital. The court reasoned that liberty interests do not emerge for psychiatrically disabled plaintiffs when involuntarily hospitalized. The 14th Amendment's substantive due process protections afforded the mentally ill and retarded are fundamental and constant (*Thomas S. v. Morrow*, 1986, pp. 374–376). This analysis is not predicated simply on an individual's need for services, but rather on the preciousness of liberty fundamental to all citizens.

If the only place where the court's assumption of effective treatment is likely to be realized is in the community, then any argument favoring the constitutional right to community-based treatment for the institutionalized psychiatrically disabled must unfold with this premise in mind. The *Youngberg* court established a right to minimally adequate care and treatment for institutionalized mentally disabled persons. The *Thomas S.* court expanded this right by recognizing that the liberty interests of the 14th Amendment for the mentally ill and retarded exist *before* institutional confinement; that is, while in the community. If the one place where minimally adequate treatment is likely to be realized is in the community, as opposed to a psychiatric facility, then the one place where minimally adequate care and treatment will obtain is in the community. Hence, establishing a constitutional right to community-based treatment for the institutionalized psychiatrically disabled is really a matter of operationalizing what it means to acknowledge a constitutional right to effective, minimally adequate treatment.[27] Additionally, this is not merely a needs-based right to treatment; a position the Supreme Court has routinely frowned on (*Olmstead v. L.C.*, 1999). Rather, this is the establishment of a right triggered by the deprivation of liberty interests plus the only treatment response that satisfies the Court's preference for effectiveness.

While institutional confinement is permitted if therapeutic treatment is provided, hospital treatment for the mentally disabled has not been proven effective. Therefore, it is neither therapeutic nor minimally adequate. The hospital's constitutional authority to institutionalize (i.e., 10th Amendment) must give way to community-situated treatment that does satisfy these requirements. The failure of psychiatric facilities and other state agents to comply with minimally adequate treatment (effective, community-based treatment) raises an important question concerning Eighth Amendment protections; specifically, protection against cruel and unusual punishments. Given that effective, minimally adequate treatment is only constitutionally satisfied in community settings, does mere custodial care or, in the extreme, warehousing of profoundly ill citizens erode their Eighth Amendment liberty interests against such treatment?[28] This is most certainly the case if institutional confinement is presumably for a therapeutic purpose. In instances such as these, the intervention of hospital confinement bears no reasonable relationship to the goal of effective psychiatric treatment. Since effective, minimally adequate psychiatric care is not provided in the hospital environment, inpatient treatment of the profoundly mentally ill and retarded amounts to punishment, which is barred by the Eighth Amendment's proscription.

In the case of custodial care the results are similar. The state's interests focus on providing essential life supports to those unable to care for themselves or on those persons without the support of others who can assist disabled persons with these necessities in the community. Rather than emphasizing the provision of survival needs via the hospital, attention should be directed at the state's failure under its policy of deinstitutionalization to deliver such care and support as promised. If the community setting is where the mentally ill and retarded are afforded the greatest chance of realizing their potential in the face of their disability, then the state has an obligation to ensure that effective, minimally adequate care and treatment is made available to such citizens. These essential life supports can be administered in the community provided the political will recognizes that community systems are a more efficient and economic means of delivering necessary services (Eysenick, 1952; Meltzoff & Kornreich, 1970; Rachman, 1973; Parloff, 1978; McKnight, 1987; Arrigo, 1994a).

In the absence of such recognition, custodial care is no different than that which is provided to convicts of the criminal justice system.[29] The mentally disabled are punished via institutionalization for their severe and/or persistent retardation or illness (Ennis, 1972; Szasz, 1973), and this punishment is barred by the Eighth Amendment's cruel and unusual punishment proscription.

The foregoing analysis is not meant to suggest that psychiatric hospitals do not provide services (Klein, 1980). The essential challenge facing post-*Youngberg* courts is whether they are prepared to acknowledge that these services can more effectively and economically be administered in a more supportive environment, albeit in a community setting. Developing a critical theory of justice, predicated on the right to community-based treatment and care for the profoundly mentally ill and retarded, is a preliminary step integral to this endeavor. To that end, the following analytical framework is offered to assist the Supreme Court in confronting one of its most complex, controversial, and daunting challenges.

THE LOGIC OF IDENTITY AND THE POLITICS OF JUSTICE

In order to develop a critical, though somewhat provisional, theory of justice affirming the right to community-situated treatment for profoundly disabled psychiatric citizens, it is first necessary to discern the form of legal justice accepted as knowledge/truth and, therefore, power in American society.[30] In chapter 4, I will provide a more detailed assessment of this matter. For now, however, I wish to outline several of its core features.

The form of legal justice recognized as truth is not merely the result of oppressive forces forgoing a judicial right through restrictive laws (Foucault, 1965, 1977). If this were so, one could argue that the Supreme Court, in denying the mentally disabled the unqualified constitutional protection of effective, minimally adequate care and treatment in the community, has simply exercised its right to protect society from persons capable of harming themselves or others. In the modern era, the growth of new disciplines (e.g., epidemiology, psychology, criminology, forensics) has fostered a "disciplinary society" in which people are normalized and depathologized (Foucault, 1965). This control occurs through the instrumentation of science (e.g., the system of medicine), dictating what particular truths or knowledges are acceptable (and therefore privileged) and dismissing those that are not (Foucault, 1980). Thus, the discipline of science offers a constellation of truths by which people and their behaviors can be regulated. The power it exercises over individuals is inventive, technical, and productive. Indeed, rather than imposing retributive measures on norm violators, "modes of surveillance" are carefully implemented so that the individual can be transformed and treated.

The sociological history of the mentally ill and retarded in both England and the United States are excellent illustrations of this point (for England see, e.g., Parry-Jones, 1972; Scull, 1979; Showalter, 1985; for the United States see, e.g., Dain, 1964; Rothman, 1971; Grob, 1973; Scull, 1984). Today, the locus of responsibility for caring for the mentally disabled has shifted from the family and local community to a group of trained professionals who, on the basis of their expertise, assert the informed capacity to understand and treat these citizens (Freidson, 1970; Isaac & Armat, 1990). The result is that rather than forgoing a system of care predicated on punishing the mentally disabled for their particular maladies (Szasz, 1970), we have fashioned a "therapeutic state" that esteems the psychiatric community's worldview (e.g., Zilboorg, 1941; Alexander & Selesnick, 1966; Dain, 1964; Rothman, 1971; Scull, 1984; Grob, 1994). The consequence of such a system is that these trained experts negotiate reality for psychiatrically disabled persons and the rest of society (Scull, 1989). Social meanings and acceptable behaviors are governed by the moral temperament of those professionals who exercise treatment power. In a culture where science is afforded respect, scientific assertions are an exercise of power that render the merits of other knowledge claims (e.g., belief, experience, intuition) as less rigorous and, therefore, less valid.

The implications of such a monopoly of power are far reaching. Not only are the mentally ill and retarded left to the moral entrepreneurship of the psychiatric profession, but this profession's version of truth and power is crystallized through the formation of laws affecting the care and treatment of mentally disabled citizens (Arrigo, 1996b). Similar to science, the law's claims to truth are indivisible from the exercise of its power. Through the legal method, the law sets itself outside the social order presumably rendering sound, rational, impersonal, and objective judgments concerning complex and contradictory life circumstances occurring within this arena. In this way, our system of jurisprudence functions as a force, believing that it has the power to right wrongs (Arrigo, 2001c).

The problem with the law's apparent omnipotence, more than being elevated like esteemed science, is that its language system and thought processes are representative of a certain approach that reflect the interests and attitudes of only certain members in society.[31] While it is theoretically true that concepts such as impartiality, formal equality, objectivity, and others seem representative of society that seeks justice for all, such posturing in practice amounts to sociopolitical justice when considering an issue like the right to community-based treatment for the institutionalized mentally ill and retarded. Indeed, the moral reasoning that the courts engage in ignores, through its detached orientation, the needs of people in particular situations and social contexts. This restricted field of ethics is neither specific nor subtle, but general and indistinct. Therefore, those basic principles underlying most theories of justice (e.g., concepts like impartiality, formal equality, the therapeutic as just) are not adequate to address the interests of those whose styles of existence do not fit the ordered, logical, reasonable point of view that such principals promote (Fraser, 1997). The prevailing justice principals advocate the logic of identity, the logic of sameness; notions that seek to reduce differences to unity (e.g. Adorno, 1973; Derrida, 1976; Irigaray, 1985a; Young, 1990). The psychiatrically disabled do not fit such singularity of reason or understanding and, therefore, they are homogenized in the face of their diversity, succumbing to law's reductionism.

The problem with the logic of identity as reflected in the law, is that it only relies on linear, rational thinking to arrive at truth (Williams & Arrigo, 2001). The building blocks of legal knowledge are elemental facts that fit one on the other creating the one principle unity, the one universal truth, the one overarching law that mirrors the essence of the phenomenon under examination (Young, 1990). Through the logic of identity, legal thought aims to harness everything under its direction, eliminating uncertainty, ambiguity, unpredictability, multiplicity, and difference. The fact that the psychiatric community's primary treatment choice depends largely on the application of drug therapy, demonstrates this profession's desire to reduce the behaviors (styles) of the mentally disabled to more universally acceptable ways of comportment. Hence, the logic of sameness denies the plurality of particular psychiatrically disabled citizens their bodily experiences. These experiences, evaluated against the objectively sound standards of the reasoned and ordered medical profession, are then affirmed by our rational judicial system.

Following in the footsteps of science, the law's approach in rendering courtroom decisions is to adopt a universal perspective that is identically applied to all parties involved (Darwall, 1983). Understood and esteemed as the concept of impartiality, the law's quest for objective truth suffers from the same reductionistic dilemma found in the realm of science. The impartial judge remains detached and dispassionate. This individual *reasons* (rather then experiences) a specific holding built on previous case law that affirms a particular, universally applicable truth. In fact, the ruling must be universally applicable because it builds on other holdings that, when added together, create a unity that furthers the cause of order, reason, logic, and sameness. In this regard, impartial reasoning is transcendental: outside the realm of concrete situations and actors. It forges a unitary moral subjectivity: a unidimensional style of being that orders society's members to act only in certain ways or suffer the penalties for nonconformity.

The logic of identity permeated throughout the law and best represented in the concept of impartiality, denies difference in a number of ways. Situations are not contextualized and the particularity of experiences are afforded the same moral rules, regardless of circumstances.[32] Additionally, impartiality attempts to neutralize and discount any experience that cannot be reduced to law's normative framework (Arrigo, 199bb, 1995c). Finally, multiplicity is reduced to one unity. In its quest for objectivity, impartiality signifies a perspective that any and all rational subjects can adopt. Indeed, "[t]he impartial moral judge . . . ideally should treat all persons alike, according to the same principles, impartially applied" (Young, 1990, p. 101).[33]

Clearly, mentally disabled persons do not fit the unitary dimensions prescribed by science and the law and they are therefore both normalized and institutionalized to perpetuate the "demands of an organized society" (*Youngberg v. Romeo*, 1982, p. 320). The totalizing effect of the law's logic of sameness denies not only the heterogeneity of the mentally disabled as a class of people, but the individuality of those mentally ill and retarded citizens within this group. Confronted by the scientific and legal language systems—systems that represent the justice of rationality, normalcy, order, and unity—establishing a critical theory of justice for the psychiatrically disabled is essential.

Central to this theory is the politics of difference; a concept of justice that esteems individual and cultural heterogeneity, acknowledges the particularity of social situations, values the multiplicity of experiences, and affirms the ambiguities and inconsistencies of life. In order to accomplish this task successfully, it is necessary to redefine the very patterns of thought that structure psychiatry and law's construction of reality, truth, and power. This project of redefining both disciplines entails the use of imaginative discourse. Imaginative discourse is that very process whereby one carefully discerns the meanings situations hold for a person (Ricoeur, 1975; Murray, 1986, 1987). Rediscovering the signification of metaphor, symbol, and myth as ingredients of storytelling (the unfolding of one's life) help to inform this process as a meaningful expression of one's reality.[34] With regard to profoundly disabled psychiatric persons, uncovering the multiple meanings situations hold for them, with all their inconsistencies, contradictions, and unpredictabilities, is crucial to maximizing their potential to live as autonomously as their particular disabilities will permit.

The project of constituting a politics of difference by redefining the disciplines of law and psychiatry entails a dismantling of the prevailing symbols of unity, rationality, and identity that these intellectual domains hold so dear. The symbolic value of psychiatric facilities, civil commitment hearings, burdens of proof, scientific and legal evidence, and other such examples[35] convey a message of impersonal, dispassionate, and objective reality. These signifiers, however, do not reflect the interiorized experiences, needs, capabilities, interests, or aspirations of the individuals they so greatly effect. Community-based treatment does. It allows individuals with psychiatric disorders the opportunity to at least discover, on their own terms, what meanings situations hold for them without the imposition of normalizing psychiatry and impersonal law. The challenge that lies ahead for legal scholars and social commentators affirming the right to community-based treatment for the institutionalized mentally disabled, is to unpack these multiple meanings as a way of validating the politics of difference. Once this process is undertaken, the unitary imperative of both law and psychiatry can be sufficiently decentered, ushering in alternative styles of existence that defy and displace the logic of identity and the politics of justice.

CONCLUSIONS

This chapter demonstrated the need and the right to community-situated care and treatment for the institutionalized mentally ill and retarded. This project began by exploring those federal constitutional cases that examine the 14th Amendment liberty interests at stake, giving rise to such a consideration. The fundamental rights guaranteed to involuntarily committed psychiatric citizens necessarily include interests in personal safety, freedom of movement, and such minimally adequate treatment as might be required to preserve these liberty interests. Based on this position, interpretations of the minimally adequate treatment provision have largely fallen into two camps: those asserting no constitutional right to community-situated treatment; and those that do. In the former instance, proponents argue that there is no fundamental protection afforded the mentally ill and retarded regarding a "least restrictive environment." In the latter instance, advocates submit that community-based treatment is minimally adequate care. Both positions assume a particular political philosophy.

This philosophy gives deference to the established judgment of the mental health profession, regarding the nature of the confined person's psychiatric illness and the extent of their dangerousness. Typically viewed as diseased and deviant, the medical community relies on empirically unreliable and limited information when rendering pronouncements about the needs of the mentally disabled. The effects of their "scientific" method is to make certain value statements about individual patients or the psychiatrically disabled as a class. Similar to the mental health profession, the court carries with it these value-laden assumptions when delivering judicial decisions, affecting the constitutional rights of involuntarily confined persons. When balancing the interests of an ordered and rational society (or its state representatives like psychiatric facilities) against the seemingly unpredictable and unintelligible world of psychiatric outsiders, the utilitarian conclusions for the mentally disabled are inevitable.

The sociological history of the mentally disabled was considered as a means of demonstrating the need for a right to community-situated treatment for these persons. From the failure of deinstitutionalization to the growing numbers of mentally ill and retarded that find themselves homeless, incarcerated, or cyclically committed against their will, the erosion of adequate community support systems continues while our social landscape suffers the devastating consequences of abandonment. Some interesting initiatives have evaluated prospects for recommunalization for the mentally disabled. In these instances, however, the necessary political will acknowledging the cost effectiveness and efficiency of such models must be present to support and sustain these efforts over the long haul.

Having explored the present state of affairs both constitutionally and sociologically for profoundly disabled psychiatric persons, a judicial right to community-based treatment for these citizens was posited. This position acknowledged the court's preference for effective, minimally adequate care and treatment, arguing that the one place where such a standard was likely to exist in practice was in the community rather than in psychiatric facilities. Community-based treatment was understood as the only legitimate utilization of the minimally adequate treatment provision guaranteed under the constitution. This analysis was distinguished from the previous arguments affirming the right to such care and treatment by drawing attention to the symbiotic relationship between effective mental health care and minimally adequate treatment. Previous arguments addressing this issue rely on a balancing of interests: individual liberty interests versus the demands of an organized society. Additionally, the failure to acknowledge such a constitutionally protected right under the 14th Amendment raises important 8th Amendment concerns. Involuntary civil commitment of the mentally ill and retarded does not provide effective, minimally adequate treatment when the hospitalization is for a therapeutic purpose or when the confinement is primarily custodial. Hence, such institutional confinement amounts to a violation of the cruel and unusual punishment clause barred by the 8th Amendment.

Finally, a provisional theoretical analysis of both law and psychiatry was presented. The language system and thought processes of these disciplines presuppose a regime of truth and, therefore, power that effectively discounts and invalidates all other statements that do not fit their unitary, normalizing imperatives. Legal and scientific truths are understood as rational, orderly, sequential constructions that define one meaning, one perspective, and one reality that is objectively and impartially verifiable. These notions promote the logic of identity; a logic that dismisses difference. Inconsistencies, ambiguities, unpredictabilities, and indeterminacies are not the language of privileged law and science. Hence, for the institutionalized mentally disabled, their styles of being are normalized and depathologized, chiefly through drug therapy and cognitive-behavioral interventions. For those citizens who resist such curative measures, the legal system imposes sanctions (e.g., civil commitment), effectively forcing submission to the rule of order, the rule of law.

In order to break free from such unidimensional thought and language processes, a return to imaginative discourse was encouraged. Rediscovering the metaphors, myths and, symbols that more authentically describe the intimate and internal experiences of the mentally ill and retarded is vital to dethroning the normalizing power of law and science. This process affirms the multiplicity of experiences that constitute the plurality of meanings situations hold for people. This is not to suggest that a substituted reality, method, thesis, form, or unity should be privileged. On the contrary, the suggestion was that through discursive imagery we can come to value and validate difference; styles of being that defy sameness most significantly contextualized in the community.

FOUR

Policing and Disciplining Mental Illness

Social Control and Chaos in Confinement

OVERVIEW. *Chapter 1 provided a historical critique of legal and psychiatric decision-making, arguing that the abandonment of the mentally ill has been a function of paternalistic values and practices. I asserted that meaningful, sustainable reform could be enacted if the fundamental needs of mental health citizens were central to any agenda promoting change. Chapter 2 assessed whether this focus on consumer interests was possible, especially in the context of advocacy for persons with psychiatric disorders. I explained how psychological egoism or measured altruism underpins all mental health advocacy efforts, establishing an ethical practice that effectively displaces the psychiatric citizen from the process of genuine consumer representation. Chapter 3 examined how the right to community-based treatment symbolizes a particularly troubling domain where the interests of persons with mental disabilities are mostly denied, notwithstanding constitutional, sociological, and philosophical efforts to the contrary. The absence of a recognized fundamental liberty protection is suggestive for how the legal and psychiatric communities devalue different (i.e., nonhomogenous) identities.*

Chapter 4 situates the previous application studies within their relevant conceptual framework. In short, given the analysis in the previous chapters, I argue that mental illness is "policed" and that this policing (i.e., civil confinement) fills a social function; namely, the surveillance and disciplining of public hygiene. This perspective gives way to a host of questions. For example, how do the psychiatric and legal systems participate in the social control of public hygiene? How are the constructs "mental illness" and "dangerousness" interpreted such that certain disciplinary regimes (e.g., the psychiatric hospital) are identified as appropriate mechanisms to regulate and police "disordered" behavior? Can alternative conceptual approaches (e.g., the new science of chaos theory) contribute to our understanding of mental illness and confinement? If so, what do these approaches portend for the civil commitment of disordered citizens? Questions such as these compel us to reflect critically on the penalty one endures when identified as mentally ill, violent, in need of treatment, or any combination of these. These are matters that invite us to think discernfully about whether legal and psychiatric decision-brokers advance the interests of citizen justice and social well-being or whether they perpetuate and, therefore, legitimate a constellation of values that fully deny mental health consumers their right to be different, indeed, their right to be.

INTRODUCTION

As described in chapter 1, the legal and psychiatric communities continue to address, with some profound uncertainty, the matter of civil confinement for dangerous mentally ill citizens (e.g., Levy & Rubenstein, 1996; Arrigo, 1996b, 1993c; Isaac & Armat, 1990; LaFond & Durham, 1992). In short, proponents of involuntary hospitalization contend that a temporary loss of freedom, liberty, and right to self-determination is justified in order to protect society from the unstable and potentially injurious behavior of severely disordered psychiatric persons (e.g., Scull, 1989; Chodoff, 1976; Treffert, 1985; Roth & Kroll, 1986). This decidedly conservative and medical model perspective has dominated social, political, and economic practice since the Enlightenment (e.g, Szasz, 1987; Scheff, 2000; Sedgwick, 1982). Indeed, as chapter 2 explored, it is (unconsciously) embedded in the practice of mental health advocacy, and as chapter 3 explained, it is thoroughly lodged within the Supreme Court's interpretation of fundamental liberty rights (e.g., community-based treatment) for psychiatric citizens.

Critical social inquiry, however, articulates a potent rejection concerning the foundations of contemporary psycholegal theory and practice (Arrigo, 1996b). These criticisms converge on a number of arguably false, morally ensconced, and politically laden assumptions attributable to modern science: (1) that mental illness is a *real* difference necessitating censorship; (2) that the mentally ill present a greater identifiable threat to society than the mentally healthy; and (3) that science possesses the key to understanding and treating mental disease or defect (Arrigo, 1992b, pp. 9–12, 23–29).

One of the most influential and time-honored of criticisms is associated with Michel Foucault's social control thesis (e.g., Foucault, 1965, 1970, 1972, 1973a, 1976, 1977, 1980). Foucault's critique of institutions (i.e., psychiatric, penal) viewed confinement of the noncriminal as a method of controlling (or isolating) the socially undesirable. Consistent with other justice systems, Foucault (1965, 1977) reasoned that institutionalization was a means of policing public hygiene; that is, ridding society of *difference*. Whether intended public policy or the likely result of society's faith in the prophecies of modern science, Foucault (1980) argued that involuntary confinement of the mentally ill and dangerous productively and inventively advanced the state's regime of power in the name of privileged scientific truth.

Given Foucault's position, a number of important issues arise yielding alarming or, at least, troubling effects. Specifically, psychiatric and legal systems of control (e.g., the hospital, the prison) promote legitimate social welfare interests; however, these interests are based on questionable and, in some cases, inaccurate science (Arrigo, 1993c, pp. 142–157; LaFond & Durham, 1992). Thus, the existential condition of diverse mentally disabled citizens is normalized, depathologized, and homogenized, difference is corrected, indeed sacrificed, at the alter of medical knowledge, and the politics of psychiatric justice prevails (Arrigo, 1996b, 1997e).

This chapter examines the present-day vitality and utility of Foucault's social control thesis, as revealed in several enduring psycholegal controversies, specifically those discussed in previous chapters. In brief, I examine how the crossroads of clinicolegal science have produced problematic criteria for civil commitment by revisiting the meaning of mental illness and dangerousness. I demonstrate how these criteria effectively promote and maintain the state's realm of power while substantially undermining the right of vulnerable collectives, citizens, or both to be different (Kittrie, 1972).

The intent behind this theoretical analysis of confinement and its application to civil commitment practices is deliberately limited in both scope and depth. Unlike the more detailed assessment provided in chapter 1, here I merely wish to tease out several of the more salient conceptual insights contained in Foucault's work and strategically connect them to mental health civil law. This approach will allow me to then draw suggestive and, arguably, provocative linkages to subsequent sections of the chapter.

In subsequent sections, I contemporize the Foucauldian theoretical analysis by relying on the new science of chaos theory.[1] Chaos or complexity theory distinguishes the presence of social disorder from *order within social disorder* (Young, 1992; Milovanovic, 1997a; Williams & Arrigo, 2001). The notion of patterned regularities operating deep within the apparent randomness of dynamical systems (including the behavior of individuals as micrological systems), challenges the assumptions informing correctional, psychiatric, and/or legal practice. It draws attention away from modernist convictions of linear cause-effect inquiry, precise prediction, and rigid control, toward postmodernist notions of nonlinear causality, spontaneity, and chance that can exist simultaneously with order (see, e.g., Arrigo & Schehr, 1998; Arrigo, 1997b, 1994b for some diverse crime, law, and justice examples). I conclude my investigation by returning to the criteria of involuntary civil commitment. I demonstrate how the application of selected chaos theory principles represents a much needed post-Foucauldian assessment on the matter of confinement for the mentally ill. In order to situate this chapter, however, I begin with a review of Foucault's social control thesis.

FOUCAULT AND THE SOCIAL CONTROL THESIS

> [W]hen you look closely at the penal code . . . *danger* has never constituted an offense. To be dangerous *is not an offense*. To be dangerous *is not an illness*. It is not a symptom.

> And yet we have come . . . to *use* the notion of danger, by a perpetual movement backwards and forwards between the penal [legal] and the medical [psychiatric].
>
> —Michel Foucault, *Confinement, Psychiatry, and Prison*

The historically informed social theory of Michel Foucault was instrumental in developing a critique of the psychiatric institution, medical justice, and the means by which society disciplines difference (Foucault, 1965, 1977). A Foucauldian analysis of legally endorsed, involuntary civil commitment can be regarded as an exemplar of state-sanctioned social control. Foucault, both explicitly and implicitly, addresses the issue of confinement in considerable detail.

Foucault's purpose in *Madness and Civilization* (1965) and *Discipline and Punish* (1977) is to provide an account of the various, yet similar, roles institutions assume in society. In doing so, he systematically traces the development of social control, as linked to science or scientific truths, to demonstrate the expanse of disciplinary practices in contemporary society. The function of law, psychiatry, and confinement, as differing modes of societal surveillance, is to attain the same penultimate goal: control (Foucault, 1977; 1990; Garland, 1990).

Though *Madness and Civilization* is primarily concerned with psychiatry and the mentally ill and *Discipline and Punish* with penology and the criminal element, there is considerable promise for a social control thesis at their intersection. Indeed, their substantial overlap and interrelatedness contribute to an overall understanding of the social policing of difference. In the following sections, I elaborate on the constituents of Foucault's social control thesis. As I contend, this model, as a comprehensive critique, forms the basis of how justice is rendered today at the crossroads of law and psychiatry, criminal justice and mental health.

Psychiatry and the Hospital

Foucault's (1973, 1976, 1977) assault on the psychiatric institution described psychiatrists as "functionaries of social order." Thus, the practice of psychiatry was to police social hygiene and public health. In describing the evolution of this science into law, Foucault (1990) states: "If psychiatry became so important in the nineteenth century, it was not simply because it applied a new medical rationality to mental or behavioral disorders, it was also because it functioned as a sort of public hygiene" (p. 134). This bridge between the medical function of psychiatry and the management function of police enabled a new form of repression—namely, cleansing public morality.

One example of this repressive function arose with the advent of a different nomenclature for psychiatric institutions. Formally referred to as "asylums" and subsequently termed *hospitals*, public perception concerning the utility of these facilities was dramatically altered. Psychiatry drew attention to the "medical" role of the discipline; that is, to the reparative possibilities of an emerging science that could "make good" the mass of social problems afflicting everyday citizens (e.g., disorder in the street, at work, in the family) (Foucault, 1990, p. 180). Thus, the "true vocation of psychiatry" became a function of public hygiene (Foucault, 1990, p. 180).

Foucault also drew attention to the practices of reflexology, popular in Soviet psychiatry after 1945. This treatment method interjected public immorality and irrationalisms (e.g., homosexuality, criminality) into the disciplinary equation by exposing one to photographs while subjecting the individual to sickness-inducing injections. This Pavlovian approach was designed to fashion aversions to the foci of presumed irrationality and immorality. Arguably, the medicalized psychiatric and the clinicolegal apparatuses could "cure or correct" such maladaptations with simple therapeutic techniques. Similar positivism was observable in the United States with the invention of the lobotomy: a psychiatric intervention designed to fix problems of social hygiene. Here, too, the psychopathic hospital was the locus for corrective treatment.

The "Dangerous" Individual

> Legal justice today has as much to do with criminals as crimes. . . . [F]or a long time, the criminal had been no more than the person to whom a crime could be attributed and one who could therefore be punished, today, the crime tends to be no more than the event which signals the existence of a dangerous element . . . in the social body.
>
> —Michel Foucault, *The Dangerous Individual*

According to Foucault (1990), the arrival of psychiatry into criminality, provided a new direction for the examination of mental illness and crime. The attention could be focused on the *individual*; that is, the criminal, as opposed to the crime itself. The notion of "danger" would establish for itself a permanent role in social analyses. Foucault (1990) refers to this movement as the "psychiatrization of criminal danger" (p. 128). A series of motiveless, heinous offenses in the eighteenth and nineteenth centuries begged for an alternative explanation for these crimes (Foucault, 1975). More broadly, the question was why would someone engage in such horrid acts and inflict such deplorable suffering on society without any manifest logic? The answer was linked to psychiatry. More specifically, the answer was insanity; that is, the unreason or irrationality of the minds of "crazy" people (Foucault, 1965; see also Szasz, 1987).

This insanity, writes Foucault (1990), is "hidden"; it represents a danger in that it is beyond the actor's responsibility; beyond his control because he is frequently unaware of it. Nineteenth-century psychiatry "invented an entirely fictitious entity, a crime which [wa]s insanity, a crime which [wa]s nothing but insanity . . ." (Foucault, 1990, p. 132). Thus, psychiatric intervention into the causal explanation of criminality "created" a new crime. The unpredictable and latent danger of the insane constituted a crime in itself; it was uncontrollable and the *potential* danger to society was justification for its control. "Crazy" people could be regarded as criminal because of what they represented (Morse, 1978; Arrigo, 1997d, 1997e). It was the intervention of psychiatry into law that sanctioned, produced, and legitimized this causal link between insanity and crime.

In the wake of psychiatry's engagement with law, the notion of "dangerousness" was born. Foucault (1990) notes that psychiatrists regarded themselves as "civil servants concerned with public hygiene . . . their job was to supervise whatever was in a state of disorder, whatever presented a *danger*" (p. 188). In the end, this notion of dangerousness found itself in legislation. People were being confined because they had been dangerous, not necessarily because of an overt act of criminality. In fact, Foucault (1965, 1977) informs us that Soviet legislation reached a point where being *perceived* as dangerous constituted an offense in the penal code! Though falling short of this extreme in American legislation, the concept of dangerousness still governs the way society addresses mental illness. Indeed, "[the] police [and] psychiatry are institutions intended to react to *danger*" (Foucault, 1990, p. 188). When it cannot be proven that an individual is dangerous to others, the concept of dangerous to self is introduced. Thus, *any* form of danger becomes justification for involuntary (criminal/civil) confinement. Accordingly, psychiatry becomes a "social police."

The Social Police: Controlling Difference

Foucault (1965, 1977, 1990) was uniquely concerned with the prominence that the characteristics of dangerousness assumed in contemporary society. Legal confinement of individuals thought to be dangerous; that is, those who were *potentially* a threat to society, provided a device for neutralizing difference and for policing what was socially undesirable. Interestingly, the dangerous individual often did not commit an offense. If this criterion was met, the person was otherwise confined under penal law. For Foucault (1976, 1977), the condition of (civil) confinement, in the absence of legal harm, left unresolved the question of why society was so inclined to deprive dangerous, noncriminal citizens of liberty.

Foucault's (1980) later work concerned itself with the relationship between power and knowledge/truth (for applications to law and mental illness see Arrigo, 1993c, pp. 45–51, 135–140). He describes "apparatuses" of power-knowledge as "structure[d] . . . heterogeneous elements such as discourses, laws, institutions" (Sarup, 1993, p. 65). These apparatuses contained strategies for discipline and domination through the use of new technologies. As Foucault (1980) argues, power as power-knowledge/truth is monolithic "not because it embraces everything, but because it comes from every where" (p. 93). In Foucault's sense, psychiatry became an all-encompassing expression of knowledge/truth; that is, a legitimated form of disciplinary control through the instrumentality of scientific discoveries and medical breakthroughs. Our understanding of mental illness and its relationship to crimes of insanity was inventively transformed into clinical and psychopharmacological strategies of social control. This is what Sarup (1993) refers to as "weapons of attack and defense in the relations of power and knowledge" (p. 66). The more knowledgeable and powerful our "weapon of attack" (i.e., psychiatry) became, the more legitimate our justification for the deprivation of individual liberties became. As Sarup (1993) notes of Foucault:

> Whereas we might normally regard knowledge as providing us with power to do things that without it we could not do, Foucault argues that knowledge is a power over others, the power to define others. In his view knowledge ceases to be a liberation and becomes a mode of surveillance, regulation, and discipline. (p. 67)

Thus, following Foucault, psychiatry in all its evolution, does not, liberate or help the mentally ill; rather, it regulates such citizens and their difference. Indeed, as I have argued elsewhere (Arrigo, 1993c, 1996b), particularly in my assessment of involuntary hospitalization for the civilly committed and incarceration for the criminally insane, Foucault demonstrates how clinicolegal science "speaks a [certain] truth, exercises power accordingly . . . , and produces a disciplinary society in which people [a]re normalized and de-pathologized" (Arrigo, 1993c, pp. 49, 135).

This theme of fostering a disciplinary society is pronounced in Foucault's work. For example, in *Discipline and Punish* (1977), Foucault examines the prison as a generating milieu for modes of productive surveillance and inventive control. Clearly, this is a position consistent with his conception of psychiatric institutions as well. Similar to Castel, Castel, and & Lovell's (1982) analysis of psychiatry's embeddedness in society, Foucault (1976) maintains that the expansion of disciplinary powers enabled the psychiatric control of the underclass (see also Sullivan, 1996). No work better illustrates this notion than Bentham's (1962) assessment of the prison and jail. He notes that when the jail is used for custodial purposes, it "is not a punishment" (Bentham, 1962, p. 420). Thus, if a person has yet to be convicted of a crime by our justice system, he should not be punished (i.e., confined) (Sullivan, 1996, p. 455).

In relation to the institutionalization of potentially dangerous individuals, imprisonment is not justified unless a crime has been committed. According to Foucault (1976, 1977), the reformation of the psychiatric institution and its assumed "therapeutic" value was an attempt to justify the deprivation of one's liberty (technically, the imposition of a *punishment*). While prisons and hospitals may not be construed as equally depriving of fundamental freedoms, involuntary civil commitment of the mentally ill is, nonetheless, a confinement analogous to the deprivation of liberty notable in the penal environment (Arrigo, 1996b). For example, while the committee, similar to the jailee, may be thought to have engaged in a potential wrong (or actual wrong in the case of the latter), the committee is psychiatrically detained in the absence of legal proof of social harm. As I indicated in chapter 1, in these instances the state's exercise of control in the form of confinement is justified on the basis of its police and *parens patriae* powers.

According to Foucault (1980), the disciplinary power of the prison (and the psychiatric institution) is in its application of technical knowledge (e.g., epidemiology, forensic psychiatry) to penal and medical justice where the aims of scientific truth are extolled in the form of objectification, classification, and quantification (Arrigo, 1992b, pp. 23–29). All coercive (i.e., corrective) institutions discipline society in an effort to restore individuals to socially appropriate (acceptable or normal) patterns of thought and behavior. This normalization, through the imposition of scientific standards, is oppressive in every aspect. It is a dehumanizing method of domination (Garland, 1990, pp. 169–70). The institutionalization of the mentally ill, then, becomes a means of restoring, cleansing, and/or sanitizing one's pathologized cognitive-behavioral processes, one's existential difference, in accordance with societal norms.

We see this activity of de-pathologizing the person in, *inter alia*, police and mentally ill citizen encounters (Patch and Arrigo, 1998), the organization of prisons (Arrigo and Williams, 2000b) and in the behavior of those confined (Arrigo, 1997e; Thomas, 1988). Indeed, in correctional facilities, micropowers invade the soul of the individual rather than merely the body. As Sullivan (1996) notes, "by means of quiet punishments, mild but repeated, privately enacted, increasingly solitary, and systematically applied over prolonged periods, the state gradually gaine[s] access to the soul . . . and eventually gaine[s] control (p. 450). While the word *punishment* may appear to be a somewhat inappropriate term regarding the institutionalized mentally ill, the same systematic, thought-invading, and control-induced measures are undertaken to "correct" the psychiatric individual. In this instance, the clinicolegal apparatus, through productive power and in the name of scientific truth, endeavors to elevate the disordered individual to society's standards of wellness (Arrigo, 1996b, 1996c). If the techniques of medicine do not work, the individual is simply confined for a protracted period of time (Arrigo, 1997e, 1996a, 1996d).

Thus, Foucault (1965, 1977, 1990) concludes that it is not so much the actual danger that the individual represents, as much as his or her embodied difference. It is this difference that the state attempts to regulate through sustained intervention practices (e.g., drug therapy) during confinement. These practices are deemed appropriate given existing medical knowledge. Consequently, according to society, this episteme, as an expression of power embracing certain truths, is just. After all, the best medical evidence suggests that the psychiatric interventions are therapeutic. By definition, that which is therapeutic must, then, be in the best interests of the mentally ill. In this knowledge equation, the civil confinement of dangerous, noncriminal citizens serves the interests of everyone. This is how Foucault's social control thesis functions in psychiatry and in institutional decision-making. Medical science is the avatar of psychiatric justice (Arrigo, 1996b); the self-appointed police of public hygiene. In particular, psychiatry claims to possess privileged knowledge and, thus, to exert legitimate control. For these reasons, courts rely on the medical community to define the concepts of "mental illness" and "dangerousness" and, further, to *predict* the probability of noncriminal harm (Arrigo, 1993c, pp. 142–147). Even though questions remain about psychiatry's efficacy in such matters (Levy & Rubenstein, 1996; LaFond & Durham, 1992; Isaac & Armat, 1990), it nonetheless is presumed to have privileged knowledge and, thus, is granted the power to control.

SOCIAL CONTROL IN THE CONTEXT OF CONTEMPORARY SOCIETY

The usefulness of Foucault's critique for contemporary society in part rests in the conviction that "mental illness" is not historically situated; rather, it is an enormously fluid concept (Scheff, 1984). What is time-honored, however, is the activity of policing that the state employs. Though evolving through various regulatory means (Morrissey & Goldman, 1984, 1986), the end remains the same: controlling that difference socially and legally designated as psychiatric disease (Arrigo, 1992b, pp. 4, 9–12). The clinicolegal landscape of today deliberates on this difference in its search for exacting definitions for the constructs "mental illness" and "dangerousness." The preciseness and clarity of these definitions are perhaps no where more significant than in the context of civil commitment determinations. Indeed, psycholegal questions related to the efficacy of involuntary hospitalization have become one of the foremost controversies within the mental health law community (e.g., Williams & Arrigo, 2001; Holstein, 1993).

Foucault's social control thesis obtains to the extent that the state employs social order functionaries to maintain the status quo. The question, of course, is how does the state achieve this end? To put the matter differently, to what degree does the state, through the operation of law, separate the mentally ill from the mentally healthy for purposes of protecting society's interest in homogeneity, while, at the same time, tacitly supporting the psychiatric citizen's fundamental freedoms? As I have explained elsewhere:

> On the one hand, individual liberty interests are contextualized as the liberty interests of disease-ridden, deviant-minded, and dangerous-prone *outsiders*. On the other hand, relevant state interests are contextualized as the relevant interests of impartial, orderly, rational, and impersonal state agents. (Arrigo, 1992b, p. 12) (emphasis added)

What once was effected through such devices as communal ostracism and banishment (Foucault, 1965), is now achieved through the instrumentality of *clinicolegal* science; that is, regulation inventively realized based on the (conspiratorial) collaboration of psychiatry and law (Arrigo, 1996b). In the following sections, I examine more closely how contemporary psycholegal practices exemplify Foucault's social control thesis. To advance this argument, I revisit the concepts of mental illness and dangerousness in the context of current civil commitment law.

The Criterion of Mental Illness

The first substantive criterion for civil commitment is the presence of a mental impairment. Most jurisdictions delineate this as the existence of mental illness or a showing that the individual is suffering from a mental disorder (Reisner & Slobogin, 1997). Consistent with basic due process, the U.S. Supreme Court has held that an individual who is not mentally ill cannot be involuntarily committed for civil purposes (see, e.g., *Foucha v. Louisiana*, 1992). Given that the existence of mental illness is a necessary prerequisite for civil confinement, the primary issue is in accurately defining it.

The psychological community has generally used the term *mental illness* for purposes of diagnosis and treatment (Winick, 1995a). The legal construct, however, assumes a slightly different nature. In addition to facilitating appropriate civil commitment determinations, the meaning of mental illness is relevant in law for purposes of such clinicolegal matters as: insanity defense verdicts; competency to stand trial hearings; right to refuse treatment assertions; and competency to be executed findings (Winick, 1995, p. 554). Given the variety of legal contexts in which definitions of mental illness assume dispositive value, the need for accuracy in clinical diagnoses becomes much more pronounced. Regrettably, the legal meaning of mental illness has ominously and demonstrably established for itself anything but the embodiment of precision and clarity.

The legal meaning of mental illness. The abolitionist reformers of the 1970s vehemently argued that mental illness was a bankrupt and easily manipulated term (e.g., Melton et al., 1987, p. 217; Holstein, 1993, pp. 3–4; Arrigo, 1993c, pp. 19–23, 1996b, pp. 43–45). Indeed, legislative attempts to define and operationalize the term offered mostly vague and circular interpretations (Levy & Rubenstein, 1996). Over the years, the law has imposed only minimal limitations on the mental illness construct, often using broad and general definitions (e.g., Winick, 1995a, p. 554; Comment, 1983; Williams & Arrigo, 2001; see also *Dusky v. United States*, 1960). Melton et al. (1987), cite one of the most specific of legislative initiatives to define mental illness: "[m]ental illness" means a substantial disorder of thought, mood, perception, orientation, or memory, any of which grossly impairs judgment, behavior, capacity to recognize reality, or ability to meet the ordinary demands of life, but shall not include mental retardation (p. 221). This proposal is far more explicit than the tautological observation: "A mentally ill person means a person whose mental health is substantially impaired" (Melton et al., 1987, p. 221); however, the former definition lingers in ambivalence, relying on vague terms such as *substantial, grossly impaired*, and *ordinary demands of life*.

The legislature's obvious imprecisions and operational failures with defining mental illness, in effect, gave to the courts the role of "fashion[ing] a definition for the words 'mentally ill' . . . thereby fill[ing] the void in the statutory hospital law" (*Dodd v. Hughes*, 1965, p. 542). The capacity of the courts to assign meaning to this construct, however, is tempered, in part, by the limits imposed on governmental state power to commit involuntarily (Levy & Rubenstein, 1996; Winick, 1995). The Constitution's 5th and 14th Amendment protections establishing freedom from restraint, freedom of movement, and freedom from unwanted invasions of body and mind prohibit the government from arbitrary confinement decisions, thereby heightening the burden of justification (e.g., Winick, 1995a, p. 500; Arrigo, 1992b, p. 143). Infringement on these liberty interests requires "reasonably clear guidelines" (*Smith v. Goguen*, 1974, pp. 572–573; see also *Youngberg v. Romeo*, 1982).

Given that many state legislatures have effectively abdicated to the courts their responsibility to define precisely and clearly the meaning of mental illness, judicial tribunals (especially appellate courts and administrative decision brokers) have uncomfortably assumed the task of ascertaining the (non)existence of mental illness in relation to a particular plaintiff or petitioner in a given case (Arrigo, 1993c, pp. 23–25). To assist in this process, most courts have deferred to the professional judgment of mental health "experts" (e.g., Perlin, 1999, 2000; Reisner & Slobogin, 1997; Bonnie, 1993; Holstein, 1993; Melton et al., 1987). Typically, this includes the clinical wisdom of psychiatrists and psychologists. This *dependence* on the medical establishment in the decision making process persists, despite substantial research documenting the lack of consensus among professionals in matters of diagnosis (Monahan & Wexler, 1978; LaFond & Durham, 1992; Levy & Rubenstein, 1996). The lack of consensus among mental health professionals is, in part, a function of medicine's ineffective pursuit of a precise description for mental illness (Shell, 1980, p. 6).

What is perhaps most disturbing about the deference courts exhibit in matters psychiatric, is their overreliance on medical diagnoses. Indeed, expert forensic testimony is viewed as integral to civil commitment determinations. As other have shown, however, the medical community, when confronted with clinical uncertainty, favors a "presumption of illness" (Scheff, 1984, pp. 6–30, 91; Arrigo, 1996b, pp. 38, 118). Thus, it is not unreasonable to surmise that borderline cases are all too frequently identified as instances of persons experiencing mental illness for legal (i.e., involuntary commitment) purposes.

The Criterion of Dangerousness

The concept of dangerousness is pivotal to civil confinement matters. During the 1970s, in response to the inadequacies of the threshold finding of mental illness, many legislatures and courts began implementing dangerousness provisions (see e.g., *O'Connor v. Donaldson*, 1975). This added substantive criterion requires a showing that the individual poses a threat of serious harm to self, others, or both. Although initially touted as a well-intended and much needed psycholegal reform measure, the dangerousness criterion has spawned a host of mental health law controversies, challenging the overall legitimacy of state-sponsored civil commitment. Difficulties with defining dangerousness in a legal context, problems with the accuracy and reliability of dangerous predictions, and erosions of presumed unfettered civil liberties have generated much of this debate. These issues are briefly reexamined in the proceeding sections.

The meaning of dangerousness. The more rigid standards for civil confinement that developed out of the 1970s reform movement required that, in addition to a mental disability, the individual pose a substantial threat of serious harm to oneself or others (Levy & Rubenstein, 1996). Generally, this provision was interpreted to imply a real and present threat of harm (see, e.g., *Lessard v. Schmidt*, 1972), and clear and convincing proof of dangerousness (*Addington v. Texas*, 1979). The meaning of dangerousness refers not only to violence to oneself or others, but also to severe neglect where one is unable to survive in the community; that is, where one is "gravely disabled" (Comment, 1983, pp. 674–677; Levy & Rubenstein, 1996; *O'Connor v. Donaldson*, 1974).

The concept of dangerousness has been referred to as one of the most elusive doctrines in mental disability law (Perlin, 1999). Durham & LaFond (1985) describe agreed-on standards for dangerousness as "woefully lacking" (as cited in

Arrigo, 1996b, p. 55). Indeed, Shah (1974, 1977) and Wettstein (1984) regard the concept as malleable and clouded by incoherency.

Similar to mental illness, statutory construction of dangerousness is essentially minimal and, thus, convincingly vague (see, e.g., Simpson, 1984; Arrigo, 1996b), leaving the responsibility to define and operationalize the construct with the courts (Melton et al., 1987). This endeavor is confounded by their reliance on the mental health profession to "fill in the details" (Levy & Rubenstein, 1996, p. 29), Curiously, all available evidence suggests that the psychiatric community is itself vastly uncertain, purporting several contestable definitions of their own.

For example, Brooks (1974), in his analysis of the term dangerousness, isolated four components worthy of consideration: (1) the severity or magnitude of predicted harm; (2) the probability that the harm will occur; (3) the frequency with which the harm may occur; and (4) the imminence with which the harm will occur. By weighing each of these factors respectively, Brooks argued that a conclusion (judgment) could be reached regarding the dangerousness of an individual. Thus, a trivial and unlikely harm such as tossing rocks at automobiles would constitute less danger than a serious and likely harm such as a drug-related murder that would constitute more danger (Levy & Rubenstein, 1996).

The concept of harm has been further assessed by most states (Melton et al., 1987) and their respective courts (see, e.g., *State v. Krol*, 1975; *Matter of Harry M.*, 1983) as a threat of *physical* injury. In addition, a number of states allow for the commitment of individuals predicted to represent an emotional harm to others (Melton et al., 1987). Generally speaking, though, forecasting dangerousness to self or others can be regarded as the possibility of wrongfully doing physical harm to self or (an)other human being(s).

Though typically vague in nature, statutory definitions of dangerousness range from "mentally ill and likely to injure himself or others," to requirements of recent "overt acts," suggesting that the individual is dangerous. Pennsylvania, for example, requires a clear and present danger component as demonstrated by conduct occurring within the past 30 days (Paczak, 1989). This overt act requirement represents an issue where the courts are divided (Arrigo, 1996b, pp. 124–127). Here the question is whether civil commitment is justified by a "mere prediction of future harm, without evidence of an actual act, attempt, or threat of dangerous behavior" (Levy & Rubenstein, 1996, p. 31). According to some commentators, the overt act requirement is regarded as a remedy for the arbitrary and unreliable predictions of dangerousness made by mental health professionals (Perlin, 2000).

Proponents have received some support from courts on the overt act issue. Several courts have ruled that without an overt act requirement, a given state's commitment statutes would be "overly broad or unconstitutionally vague" (Levy & Rubenstein, 1996; see also *Lessard v. Schmidt*, 1972; *Lynch v. Baxley*, 1974; *Doremus v. Farrell*, 1975). More recently, however, courts have generally failed to require such evidence (e.g., *Project Release v. Provost*, 1983) and, despite the reform efforts, overt conduct is typically not a prerequisite for a finding of dangerousness (Melton et al., 1987, p. 223).

Predicting dangerousness. The controversy surrounding the addition of "dangerousness" as a criterion for civil commitment is acutely problematic. Empirical research repeatedly demonstrates that mental health professionals remain unable to predict accurately the dangerousness of any one individual (e.g., Monahan, 1996; Arrigo, 1996b: 66–68, see also *Barefoot v. Estelle*, 1983). Referring to Brooks's (1974) four considerations related to dangerousness, an assessment of the factors associated with a probability of adverse consequences is distinctly contingent on whether psychiatry, psychology, or both are sufficiently advanced in these diagnoses. As Arrigo (1993c, p. 144) notes, the practical results of such efforts have not been promising. Indeed, as one established expert in predictions of future violent behavior concludes: "When it comes to predicting violence, our crystal balls are terribly cloudy" (Monahan, 1996, p.107).

Despite the medical establishment's inability to predict dangerousness with any degree of accuracy, the testimony of expert witnesses remains a pivotal factor in civil commitment proceedings (Reisner & Slobogin, 1997). Further, states continue to sustain police power authority in issues of civil commitment (Perlin, 1999). Interestingly, most courts have yet to implement additional due process safeguards to defend against unwarranted commitments, instead accepting "remarkably low levels of predictive accuracy" to justify involuntary confinement (Levy & Rubenstein, 1996, p. 31). Rather than raising legal safeguards, courts have considered the psychiatric community's fallibility in predicting future dangerousness as justification for *lowering* due process protections (Perlin, 1999; Levy & Rubenstein, 1996).

Dangerousness and civil liberties. One example of how inaccurate predictions of future dangerousness changed the legal landscape for the mentally ill is the case of *Addington v. Texas* (1979). In *Addington*, the court rejected the proof-beyond-a-reasonable-doubt standard for civil commitment noting that "there is serious question as to whether the state could ever prove beyond a reasonable doubt that an individual was both mentally ill and likely to be dangerous" (p. 422). Consequently, the U.S. Supreme Court recognized the clear-and-convincing standard in commitment cases. Some critics have vehemently argued that applying the clear-and-convincing standard of proof (or any of the other currently utilized standards) to predict future dangerousness is nothing short of "futile" (Cocozza & Steadman, 1976, p. 1101). Given that the accuracy of psychiatric predictions of dangerousness is considerably lower than the minimally required 51% standard (i.e., preponderance of the evidence), applying a more stringent test would, at least, seem to be questionable clinicolegal practice.

A significant body of criticism converges on the mental health field's propensity for overinclusivity. The "better safe than sorry" climate of the medical community is responsible for ceaseless numbers of perfectly harmless individuals routinely being diagnosed as "dangerous" and consequently subjected to involuntary confinement (see, e.g., Ennis & Litwack, 1974; Arrigo, 2000a). Livermore, Malmquist, & Meehl (1968) elucidates psychiatry's over prediction as follows:

> Assume that one person out of a thousand will kill. Assume that an exceptionally accurate test is created which differentiates with 95% effectiveness those who will kill from those who will not. If 100,000 people were tested, out of the 100 who would kill, 95 would be isolated. Unfortunately, out of the 99,900 who would not kill, 4995 people would also be isolated as potential killers. In these circumstances, it is clear that we could not justify incarcerating all 5,090 people. If, in the criminal law, it is better that 10 guilty men go free than that 1 innocent man suffer, how can we say in the civil commitment area that it is better that 10 harmless people be incarcerated lest 1 dangerous man be free? (p. 84)

Livermore et al.'s analysis not only embodies the inherent contradiction in the civil versus criminal confinement process, but represents the further erosion of constitutional safeguards for disordered citizens. In matters of civil commitment, the "better safe than sorry" approach directly opposes the "better sorry than safe" sentiment of the criminal justice system (Arrigo, 1996b, pp. 75–79). Clearly on this matter, the liberty rights of the mentally ill do not equate with the liberty rights of the criminally accused.

The controversy surrounding the dangerousness criterion for civil commitment in most states is conspicuously discernable. The predictions of dangerousness that courts rely on, based on the mental health field, are as unreliable as the meaning of dangerousness is vague (Williams & Arrigo, 2001). Indeed, the process of predicting one's likelihood for engaging in future harm is responsible for the unnecessary confinement of innocent and harmless individuals (Morse, 1982b). Further, it is responsible for a failure to confine several who are truly a danger to social welfare (Morse, 1988).

The criticisms of dangerousness as vague in connotation and inaccurate in prediction, are equaled only by charges that mental illness definitions are arbitrary, imprecise, and unclear (Perlin, 1999). Consistent with Foucault's social control thesis, the application of his critique to contemporary civil commitment practices seems evident: involuntary confinement of the dangerous, noncriminal mentally ill person is a sustained effort to discipline difference.[2] Indeed, the mental illness and dangerousness criteria, as the imperfect and incomplete criteria of civil commitment determinations, function as clinicolegal justifications for policing public hygiene; that is, for correcting, sanitizing, and depathologizing one's unique, though nonhomogenous, subjectivity. To be sure, current civil commitment practices, informed by the knowledge of medical science and, thus, operating as an inventive mode of surveillance, police nonnormalizing thought-behavior and productively contain it (e.g., through drug therapy) in order to advance the truth of psychiatric justice. This is a truth that discounts those differences constitutive of the divergent and embodied realities experienced by various mentally ill citizens (e.g., Arrigo, 1996b, 1996c, 1996d).

CHAOS THEORY AND THE SOCIAL CONTROL THESIS

However cogent Foucault's thesis is in and of itself, more recent insights into social behavior provide a logical and necessary extension. I contend that Foucault's social control argument, as applied to contemporary psycholegal practice, leaves room for advancement. Though the utility and vitality of Foucault's critique, as employed thus far, resonates quite distinctly, the inroads provided by chaos theory, nonlinear dynamics, or both move the critique still further. Indeed, the emerging paradigm of chaos/complexity theory contributes to an enhanced understanding of the social control thesis and its consequent implications for medical justice in society. Similar to my initial analysis on Foucault and civil commitment, I begin with an overview of the relevant theoretical points and then provide a sustained application. At issue in this analysis is how the policing of public hygiene becomes the penalty that psychiatric citizens must endure for their felt and embodied differences.

The Chaos Paradigm: Modernity versus Postmodernity

Chaos theory is a conceptual and practical approach, enabling the researcher to better comprehend the complex and turbulent behaviors embedded within disorderly phenomena (e.g., Abraham, Abraham, & Shaw, 1990; Hayles, 1990; Porter & Gleick, 1990; Prigogine & Stengers, 1984; Briggs & Peat, 1989). The "noise" in systems traditionally disregarded by modern science in the pursuit of prediction and control is the source of considerable inquiry by postmodern investigators (Bütz, 1997; Williams & Arrigo, 2001). Indeed, what was once regarded as irrelevant in the quest for knowledge, is now an object of inquiry itself. The modernist pursuit of cause and effect explanatory rationales and its accompanying linear method of social inquiry, are supplanted by the new "orderly disorder" equations of chaos theory.

Nonlinear dynamics (chaology) challenges orthodox propositions regarding the search for universal laws, global Truths, or both. It recognizes the innate characteristics of change, variation, unpredictability, and difference in the behavior of physical and social systems. As a model of discovery, chaos theory portends an epistemological break from the modern scientific world. Chance, randomness, inconsistency, and flux are key components to how systems (including the clinicolegal apparatus) behave. Thus, while Foucault's genealogy takes issue with the operation of psychiatry, the role of the institution, and medical justice, chaos theory moves beyond mere critique. Indeed, nonlinear dynamics further explains why socially policing public hygiene is the product of the modern episteme, and suggests how society might function under different circumstances—that is, behave without the stifling control imposed by coercive clinicolegal regimes of disciplinary surveillance.

The behavior of natural and social systems is demonstrably nonlinear. In contrast to modern conceptions, nonlinearity in human affairs is not processed as irrational, imperfect, or deviant; rather, it is viewed as the inherent consequence of social relations (e.g., Young, 1991a, 1991b). The assumptions of modern inquiry—that the world is an orderly whole, capable of systematic reduction revealing functional parts, each causing discernable, logical, and predictable behavior—are subject to many extraneous, anomalous interferences (Milovanovic, 1997a; Pepinsky, 1991). Though certainly logical and intuitive, the notion that the world is akin to a "machine" cannot account for the seemingly random disorder existing within it. Nonlinear analysis relieves modern science of its futile search for precise order or explanatory formulae (Arrigo, 1995b).

Goerner (1994), for example, alludes to the classical (modern) view of linearity and order as the baseline of society, with nonlinearity and disorder representing deviation. He argues that this model is being supplanted by the postmodern notion that disorder is, in fact, the baseline, and that order is deviation. When linking these sentiments to Foucault's social control thesis and its application to civil commitment, a change in the clinicolegal perspective necessarily follows: efforts to impose productive order would be replaced with technologies of disorder. This is the point at which Foucault's insights are considerably advanced by the contributions of chaos theory.

Chaos in Social Systems: A Necessary Transition

Chaos theory informs us that no one state can be regarded as a normal, natural, inevitable pattern of social life toward which all individuals or systems converge (Young, 1992, 1997a, 1997b). Contrarily, society and its constituent segments must be examined in light of the disorderly, divergent, and nonlinear dynamics that define them. Chaos theory claims that these dynamics are propelled by changes in key parameters that can incite a stable, linearly progressing system into a state of chaos (i.e, orderly disorder). These diverse social parameters consume the society around us. Consuming variables such as economic inequalities, political privileges, power relations, and other social forces are all critical factors that, under severe conditions, become catalysts for the chaotic dynamics inherent in all systems. Controlling these parameters has traditionally been regarded as integral to the containment of unpredictability; a condition viewed mostly in modern science as unacceptable. Containing the presence of disorder (e.g., through the disciplinary power of medicine and law), neutralizes the prospects for society to assume its potentially chaotic nature. As Foucault (1965, 1977, 1990) reminds us, this clinicolegal endeavor has historical significance. Indeed, the critical examination of contemporary civil confinement practices undertaken in previous portions of this chapter reveals just how profound the containment of chaos can be.

Society consciously manages those parameters considered excesses of order (e.g., redistribution of wealth, increases or decreases in the assault on crime, institutionalization for dangerous, noncriminal mentally ill). In addition, through its systems of regulation (e.g., hospitals, courts, schools), society keeps these excesses within predefined boundaries (Young, 1991a; 1997b). The chaos principle of *negative feedback loops* demonstrates this management function at work.

As Young (1997b) asserts, negative feedback loops "defeat flexibility and change; thus end[ing] in death for society which uses them as logic for social control" (pp. 77–84). The "death" of society to which Young refers results from a lack of growth or the reproduction of only equilibrium conditions. Chaologists believe that "healthy" systems need chaos (e.g., Pool, 1989; Van Eenwyk, 1991). Adaptation to changing social conditions requires a flexibility which, in turn, depends on choices. Homoeostatic or equilibrium conditions achieved by way of social control negate choices and, thus, the possibility of growth through adaptation.

Chaos theory's idea of *order out of chaos* describes a new, more complex state that emerges from chaotic conditions. It is a spontaneous, self-organizing phenomenon in which a more adaptive order materializes (Williams & Arrigo, 2001). Order out of chaos necessarily fills the role of compelling an orderly, but antiquated, system into a reconstituted (dis)order, critical for accommodation in an evolving social system (e.g., Bütz, 1997; 1992; see also Kauffman, 1991 on *anti-chaos* and the necessary transitory stage of chaos between periods of order). Thus, nonlinear dynamics maintains that disorder and periods of chaos are *necessary* in all social systems (Williams & Arrigo, 2001).

Returning to Foucault's thesis, we note the *means* by which historical suppression (physical) and repression (psychical) of this necessary disorder has occurred within the clinicolegal apparatus, thereby muting the possibility for any liberating social transitions (i.e., self-organization). The disciplines of psychology and psychiatry, as regimes of knowledge/power, have forcibly neutralized and sanitized this natural growth process (e.g., coercive treatment, civil commitment). As a result, society has endorsed a certain truth reflected in its time-honored position; namely, to police disorderly and disorganized noncriminal, though potentially dangerous, behavior on the basis of medical (i.e., psychiatric) justice (Arrigo, 1996b).[3] This containment of self-organizing potential is observable on an even more invidious level in the form of psychotropic medication. Indeed, psychoactive drugs, dispensed for purposes of appropriate "corrective" therapy, normalize thought and depathologize behavior. They also suppress the potential for natural growth and development. Indeed, as Barton(1994) cautions:

> If one [administers] a psychopharmacological agent and it does stop chaotic patterns, have we not also wiped out the seeds of a more adaptive psychological order—an order that may have taken days, weeks, months, or even years to develop in the complex electrochemical organization of the brain? (p. 695).

The Medical Justice System: From Linear to Nonlinear Management

As Foucault's (1965, 1976) discourse on mental illness and psychiatry reveals and as my contemporary assessment of civil commitment practices discloses, disordered psychiatric citizens are socially policed and hygienically managed to further the episteme of medical justice. In addition, the deference availed to the mental health community by the legal system in matters psychiatric establishes a new instrument of control. Behaviors that were formerly governed by the criminal justice apparatus are diverted to the medical justice system. What was once difference in the form of deviance, is now difference in the form of disease. This alternative articulation of disorder is subject to treatment rather than punishment. With continued neuropsychological and psychopharmacological discoveries, crimes of alterity are less criminal and more medical (i.e., more effectively addressed by controlling the *soul* not just the *body*). Thus, the psychiatrization or medicalization of crime assumes a political dynamic (Sedgwick, 1982; Guattari, 1984). It entails disciplining those disease-ridden and dangerous-prone segments in society (Arrigo, 1992b, pp. 9–12) in the most humane of fashions (see e.g., Szasz, 1974, on the *myth of mental illness*).

The preceding observations describe a linear model of management. Chaos theory argues that the way to regulate any phenomena in society is through nonlinear control (Williams & Arrigo, 2001; Milovanovic, 1997a; Pepinsky, 1991). Thus it follows that the method by which mental illness ought to be approached is through (dis)order. Again, according to chaos theory, absolute, tight, rigid control is detrimental to the growth of any social system (including the self as a complex, adaptive organism). Accordingly, I contend that mental illness can no longer be regarded as a crime or a disease; rather, it must be viewed as *a corollary to the "illness" of society* in general. Indeed, mental illness is not a necessarily controlled critical parameter inducing chaos; instead, it is a reaction to the existing perturbations of larger key parameters (e.g., the economic and social inadequacies of deinstitutionalization, the absence of affordable, decent, and safe housing, the devastation of poverty, the spiraling costs of health care, the victimization that comes with crime). Nonlinear management does not promote a radical absence of control; rather, it is a dialectic in which freedom and control are extolled.

If, as chaos theory claims, social dynamics are inherently nonlinear, then they cannot be regulated (as currently practiced) through linear methods (i.e., negative feedback loops). Changes in key parameters can "push" society beyond the brink of stability or equilibrium conditions. Given society's inability to control significantly these parameters through its sundry systems (e.g., criminal justice, medical, social welfare), continued linear management, on its own, will be futile. I maintain that the prevailing condition of society is beyond the scope of linear organization. Society as a chaotic system (i.e., as a system of [dis]order), where key parameters remain unstable, requires a different set of guiding principles. In such a system, I recognize that only chaos can cope with chaos (Bütz, 1997). Thus, a requisite degree of nonlinearity in management is needed.

In the remaining two sections, I examine more closely how such nonlinearity would affect the issue of civil commitment and the behavior of the clinicolegal system. Two principles of chaos theory help illuminate this project. These include the notion of *attractors* and *fractal space*. While chaos theory is replete with many other principles, it is my position that these two concepts are uniquely suited to further the post-Foucauldian analysis on the policing of mental illness through the management practice of confinement, as entertained in this chapter.

Attractors: The Strange Route to Social Difference

Attractors are patterns of stability that a system settles into over time (Goerner, 1994, p. 39). The trajectories of nonlinear systems tend to converge or situate themselves into one of four patterns (Abraham, Abraham, & Shaw, 1990). Thus, attractors in nonlinear systems are analogous to a magnet, pulling the system toward it (Briggs & Peat, 1989, p. 36). They function to produce an orderly behavior in dynamical systems. The *quality* of order, however, is paramount.

One type of attractor that chaos theory identifies is the *point* attractor. It is also termed the *fixed-point* or *single-point* attractor. The point attractor encourages a system to approach a stable end state (Davies, 1989). It functions to maintain a systemic state of equilibrium. Bütz (1997) refers to the point attractor as depicting a system whose "dynamics represent a . . . movement toward rest" (p.

27). If all natural and social systems are chaotic (constituted by [dis]order), how, then, do fixed-point attractors function in practice?

The diversity of a system, notwithstanding its natural inclination toward disorder, is attracted to a point of stasis; that is, a convergence of trajectories that produces a stable, homogenous end state (Barton, 1994). Consider, for example, the manner in which victim offender mediation (VOM) sessions move to resolution (Arrigo & Schehr, 1998), or the manner in which administrative psychiatric tribunals adjudicate a petitioner's request for release from institutional confinement (Arrigo, 1996b). There are many perspectives, bits of information, interpretive meanings, expressions of sentiment, and so on that *could* inform these different sessions/hearings. Instead, however, the discourse is monitored, controlled, cleansed, producing a homeostatic outcome: restitution or release respectively. Without such point attractors, the VOM session is termed a failure and the civil commitment proceeding ends in continued institutional confinement.

I note, though, that the more natural, spontaneous, fluid activity of these two systems (i.e., the VOM hearing and mental health law tribunal as ancillary justice apparatuses), embodied by its actors and agents, is quashed by the point attractor. Behavior that would otherwise symbolize the diversity and heterogeneity of social life is displaced by the fixed attractor. The fixed attractor harnesses diversity into a single categorical representation, endeavoring to create homogeneity with inherently heterogeneous groups.

This same notion can be loosely traced to Foucault's (1965) archeology of madness. Foucault's critique of the modern institution accentuates the role of the mental hospital in confining difference until such difference is "repaired" and one is able to rejoin society. Extending this observation to present-day confinement practices, the civil commitment of the mentally ill and dangerous signifies a disciplinary effort to normalize such individuals. Thus, the point attractor employs psychiatric confinement both to draw all difference to it and, subsequently, to channel all difference into a healthier end state. As a result, the depathologized citizen is reinstated; he or she returns to the homogeneity of the whole.

The mechanism of social control functions to ensure the magnetic effect of the point attractor. It aspires to limit human (social) interaction to a given attractor (i.e., a specific "way of being" or a particular "socially appropriate" behavior). The apparatus of control attempts to identify the system's key parameters; that is, those pivotal disturbances presumably causing chaos (irregularity, disorder) in society, and endeavors to keep them "in check." Thus, the parameter of social behavior is attracted, through coercive means, to a specified, predetermined and morally motivated end state: psychological normalcy, wellness, health. Any deviation from this end state quickly subjects the system (and persons within it), to control inputs such as withdrawal or stabilization. In medical justice, this is accomplished through involuntary commitment (a withdrawal input designed to fix the anomaly), involuntary medication (a stabilization input designed to arrest the disorder), or both. Thus we see that stifling difference (i.e., psychiatric disorder) precludes systemic transitions to more natural periods of chaos. Healthy mental functioning is the point attractor through which social-psychological control is sustained.

In addition to the contention that eliminating difference is toxic to societal growth, other factors undermine the logic of the point attractor when medical and psychological control efforts operate. There are extraneous variables that often encumber mental health compliance, perhaps rendering it altogether impossible. As Young (1997a) notes: "[i]t's no good telling people to behave one way if critical variables make it difficult to comply" (p. 85). Thus, exercising control over social behavior by regulating mental health; that is, by defining and coercing psychological normalcy, wellness, and health, yields conformity with defined norms *provided* individuals have some conscious control, meaningful control, or both over their own emotional well-being. To demand such adherence would necessitate the elimination of many unpredictable and uncontrollable influences (key parameters) on individual mental functioning (e.g., poverty, crime, divorce, unemployment, death, and other so-called crises). When medical and psychological control mechanisms are active, the individual is *punished* for reacting naturally to external and uncontrollable stimuli. Indeed, the system proceeds to reprimand humans for simply being human!

I maintain that chaos theory advances Foucault's social control thesis by explaining how and why the medical justice system behaves as it does in relation to the civilly committed, given the concept of the point attractor. However, there is another attractor within nonlinear dynamics that represents the potential for liberating growth and change. This is the *strange* attractor. The strange attractor offers a vision of what society could be without the regulatory limits imposed by the fixed attractor (i.e., strict control of difference). The notion of the strange attractor, then, allows us to move beyond a mere critique of the point attractor and disciplinary practices, toward a more emancipatory orderly disorder dynamic, governing social affairs and civic life. In this section's remaining paragraphs, I sketch the operation of the strange attractor and link it to the post-Foucauldian analysis of involuntary hospitalization for the mentally ill.

Chaos theory insists that strange attractors are more conducive to the presence of social well-being (e.g., Bütz, 1997). The strange attractor, most often depicted as the butterfly attractor, governs the chaotic, far-from-equilibrium conditions of complex, adaptive systems. The system's movements or tendencies never completely repeat themselves, never totally trace the same path twice. This is particularly apparent at the micro-interactional or situational level where a great deal of unpredictability prevails (Williams & Arrigo, 2001). Over time, however, with repeated behavior something of a macro-interactional or global explanatory pattern emerges. Elsewhere, (Arrigo, 1996b) I described this phenomenon in my assessment of chaos theory and the criminally insane:

> The ostensibly unintegrated ramblings of a serial killer include the repetition of dissociative themes. The horrifically-inspired activities of a pedophile include a series of iterative rituals. The seemingly crazed thoughts of a cannibal include recurring images consistent with his/her desire to digest human flesh. (p. 199)

The significance of the strange attractor is in its capacity to embrace fully nonlinear and apparently uncoordinated local behavior, while, at the same time, to plot out the parameters or boundaries toward which the system tends more globally. Thus, the strange attractor essentially permits endless and undefined movement within the *naturally* emerging limits of a given system.

As my previous comments on the point attractor demonstrated, linear control of the mentally ill, perpetuated by the system of medical justice, denies the more inherent, nonlinear dynamics governing a disordered person's behavior. In addition, however, this containment fails to acknowledge the key social parameters beyond the control of the individual that tend toward chaos. Both impede societal growth. The organic presence of unpredictability and unmanageableness necessitates the emergence of strange, less defined parameters for social functioning. Social behavior must not be limited to a precisely demarcated notion of appropriateness; rather, it must "accept variations around a theme" (Young 1992, pp. 448–460).

When applying the strange attractor phenomenon to civil confinement, several observations are worth noting. The point attractor, operating under psycholegal mechanisms of direct control, draws social behavior *to* a stated theme (involuntary commitment as an outcome). The organic tendencies of disorder (difference) in society, however, tend more toward a strange attraction. Indeed, we are not identical to one another, at best we are only similar. At the same time, though, the strange attractor in the medical justice system draws human behavior, by way of a natural tendency, *around* a macro-interactional theme (e.g., mental health, wellness). Thus, local variation coupled with global organization is what is meant by chaos in the form of the strange attractor in relation to the psychiatrically disordered.

Consider the notion of dangerousness. It some jurisdictions it is represented by the threat of overt action (e.g., Paczak, 1989). Although these perilous expressions of dangerousness may be similar, there is always some degree of differentiation between any two individuals or circumstances. At the local and everyday level, mental health law experts regard this degree of variation as clear grounds for insisting on more precision in defining and predicting future possible harm. Instruments of psycholegal control, as represented by a point attractor, disregard traces of difference. Indeed, in the face of medical uncertainty psychiatrists find mental illness and tend to make overinclusive determinations of dangerousness. Thus, civil commitment obtains. I contend that the *meaning* of such diverse threats, over time and with careful plotting of behavior, could produce a strange attractor effect. In actuality, the threats are variations around a theme of dangerousness, signifying different realities for diverse individuals. Some threats are likely to produce harm and others are not. The "strange" form of social control would allow *difference to be difference* within a self-ordered social system. Arguably, as a result, fewer noncriminal and presumed to be dangerous mentally ill citizens would be wrongfully subjected to institutionalization.

The Fractal Geometry of Social Control

Foucault's (1965, 1976, 1990) genealogy also confronts, though sometimes only implicitly, the structural component of the psycholegal system. In other words, there is an enduring tendency to regard social and individual phenomena as organized around binary oppositions such as good-evil, reason-unreason, mentally healthy–mentally ill. These oppositions are particularly relevant to a critique of the very meaning of mental illness and dangerousness in relation to civil confinement determinations. Thus, as Foucault (1965, 1976) systematically demonstrates, the very identification of persons as mentally ill, dangerous, or both provides us with considerable room to engage in critical reflexive analysis.

Geometry and chaos theory describe fractals as irregular forms (Wegner & Tyler, 1993, p. 16; Series, 1992, p. 139), infinitely detailed and undifferentiated. A fractal is confined to a finite area, yet on closer evaluation, the area becomes increasingly vast and immeasurable as a result of the complexity of its form. In other words, they are bounded by definite size, yet they can be infinitely complex (Bütz, 1997, p. 94). Consequently, the application of fractals to social systems permits an endless possibility of movement and measurement within the given system.

Let us consider the clinicolegal apparatus and its civil commitment decision-making processes in relation to the concept of dangerousness. The system is bounded by certain forms; that is, it functions to produce definable meanings. Persons can be found: (1) dangerous and mentally ill, requiring involuntary confinement; (2) dangerous and non–mentally ill, requiring possible criminal incapacitation; (3) nondangerous and mentally ill, requiring no hospitalization; and (4) nondangerous and non–mentally ill, again requiring no civil confinement. The potential forms associated with that element of the system (here defining dangerousness in relation to civil commitment matters) are useful only in so far as the structured, defined forms allow. Thus, there is absolutely no room for meaningful interpretation of dangerousness outside of those forms that the clinicolegal system permits.

However, if the system was constrained by alternative fractal forms (e.g., different nonclinicolegal meanings for the construct dangerousness), the complexity of the form would yield greater possibility for diverse understanding. These different forms would provide opportunity to find meaning outside of that which the established fractals deem permissible. Essentially, a more inclusive realm of possible meaning would materialize. Indeed, given similar events concerning a question of dangerousness, more than one social reality would exist; that is, more than one perspective would be heard. In order for the construct of dangerousness to be imbued with greater relevant meaning, boundaries of social definition must be loose and open to varying interpretations.

Chaos theory asserts that the value of any truth has a fractal nature. Instead of labeling a behavior or meaning as right-wrong, just-unjust, normal-abnormal, the fractal quality of any thought or behavior requires its disposition to be "a matter of degree" (Arrigo, 1997b, p. 185). The socially condoned categorization of reality into absolutes, dismisses the more logical assumption that reason, truth, health, normality, and the like, are the product of intersubjective and interpretive practices (Holstein, 1993). Elsewhere, I have alluded to this indeterminacy in stating that in many situations, "a more honest and complete reading of the circumstances suggests that interpreting reality is about shades of meaning, degrees of accountability" (Arrigo, 1997b, pp. 185–186). No two people respond identically to changes in personal or social parameters.

For example, if we observed only the outcome (i.e., different, nonnormal behavior), and not the fractal realm of diverse possibility that exists within individuality (i.e., multiple ways of being), it would be easy to identify the end state as requiring the social policing of public hygiene. If, however, we perceived the differently abled individual as only one of many citizens whose difference (i.e., mental illness) was of no more consequence than any other distinguishing characteristic, our stance might change. We might then focus on the larger social parameters or conditions that give rise to the realities we observe. Further, we might then comprehend how chance, randomness, variety, and the nonlinear progression of small differences in situational misfortunes produce certain results for *everyone* (Williams & Arrigo, 2001). The personal effect is a matter of degree. Some will live out these conditions psychotically, antisocially, depressively, some will experience these parameters less problematically, and still others will not be significantly affected at all.

Thus, the value of any reality assumes a fractal nature. I maintain that the system of law and psychiatry must be prepared to embrace this fractal, as opposed to linear and binary, logic. With no clear distinction between conditions that give rise to mental illness, dangerousness, or both and those that do not, the medical justice system's interests in socially policing public hygiene, through the instrumental activity of civil commitment determinations, cannot justifiably assign a binary label (i.e., mentally ill vs. mentally well) to individuals.

Chaos theory, then, consistent with Foucault's social control thesis, suggests a more nonlinear, nonconfining approach to regulating difference. Where Foucault's archeology of madness accounts for the proliferation of productive disciplinary regimes based on scientific knowledge, the orderly disorder notion of fractals, explains how society could effectively manage (and why it should) the nonlinearity of human existence. These observations are an important extension of Foucault's enduring social philosophy.

According to chaology, fractal forms of management and control are essential. This approach assumes a more open nature; one that allows for a certain amount of diversity and individuality within a specified domain of inquiry. Thus, chaos theory would require a more widely constructed interpretive schema for defining "mental illness," "dangerousness," or both than what presently exists. In fractal forms, both order and disorder are found. Thus, it logically follows that tighter, more rigid control is not necessary for an overall sense of order. The system of social control can accommodate nonlinearity (i.e., individuality, diversity, difference), yet maintain some degree of regulation. Again, the group subject to control (i.e., noncriminal, though potentially dangerous, mentally ill citizens) is not manageable by confined forms; variation must be considered as a response to that difference which society and its members embody.

CONCLUSIONS

In principle, the goal of any democratic society is to maximize the quality of life for all, while limiting the extent to which its members are subjected to social control measures. Foucault (1965, 1976, 1990) provides extensive historical evidence that, in fact, psychiatry, the role of the institution, and medical justice are the very antithesis of this goal. In this chapter, I argued that this realization forms the basis for his social control thesis. In addressing the origins of the demarcation and marginalization of psychiatric difference, Foucault's analysis represents a compelling argument for the reconstitution of the current system of confinement. Not only are the mentally ill regarded as different, they are socially policed and hygienically regulated on the basis of what medical science purports to know about mental disease or defect. As Foucault reminds us, it is this disease, as difference, that is systematically normalized, depathologized, and homogenized in the pursuit of scientific (power and) knowledge. Indeed, this policing is the penalty psychiatric citizens must endure for their articulated and felt difference.

This analysis led me to consider how the social control thesis operates in the mental health law arena, especially given contemporary civil confinement practices. Revisiting the definition of mental illness and dangerousness were pivotal to this assessment. As I suggested, what remains clear is that despite various neuropsychological and psychopharmacological discoveries, a host of conceptual, definitional, and predictive problems plague the clinicolegal system. Notwithstanding these dilemmas, the courts continue to rely on the best available medical evidence; evidence that is, by all accounts, imprecise, incomplete, and unclear. Thus, I concluded that not only is difference regulated and cleansed, it is managed and sanitized in the furtherance of psychiatric justice.

Admittedly, the presentation of Foucault's thesis and its relevance for contemporary mental health law was limited. This choice, however, was calculated. Indeed, I also considered whether Foucault's critique could be advanced in light of the new science of chaos theory. Along these lines, I was more interested in exploring several possible linkages between Foucault's archeology of madness and selected principles of chaology. Chaos theory or nonlinear dynamics claims that a mixture of both order and disorder is more consistent with how natural systems, social systems, or both function. Further, chaos theory argues that so-called anomalous occurrences, "noise" in the system, or other unexplained irregularities are not insignificant for mapping out the organization of phenomena. I conceptually suggested how both principles represent a dramatic break from modern science and its commitment to order, predictability, and control. While I recognized that Foucault's thesis was somewhat consistent with these notions, it was clear that nonlinear dynamics represented an important ideological backdrop from which to articulate a post-Foucauldian analysis of contemporary civil commitment practices.

In order to advance this assessment, I broadly addressed how chaos naturally operates in social systems. I examined how nonlinear dynamics exist among phenomena, thereby more organically promoting flexibility, adaptability, and the possibility for heightened societal growth. I also identified the processual shift needed in order to move easily from linear to nonlinear modes of managing behavior in complex social systems.

This exposition was significant for applying two central chaos theory principles to the problem of civil commitment for the noncriminal, though potentially dangerous, mentally ill citizen. These key concepts included attractors and fractal space. In particular, I demonstrated how the strange attractor and the fractal form challenge the social control model of medical justice.

As a general statement, chaos theory asserts that individual differences must be allowed to exist; that is, that tolerance for individual, nonlinear behavior does not dispose a social system (i.e., people) to unmanageable disorder. Indeed, the fractal nature of human existence tends toward a strange attractor: a naturally occurring order within the disorder of a system. Excessive regulation at the personal or local level does not ensure stability at the societal or global level. I concluded by suggesting that concern must be directed toward those key parameters that are loosely and unstably constructed (e.g., poverty, unemployment, crime), giving rise to the presence of mental illness. In the context of civil commitment criteria and the clinicolegal system responsible for the adjudication of such matters, efforts to arrive at precise definitions and exacting science will necessarily be compromised, given the unpredictability that is the human condition. This is not to suggest that it is impossible to manage chaos. Indeed, it is possible. However, it is not possible to control chaos by means that defeat variation, change, and flux. In short, it is not possible to manage chaos by rigidly policing difference. Once again, I noted that these observations were broadly consistent with Foucault's thesis; however, I argued that they considerably charted a new and worthwhile direction by which to extend his critique.

PART TWO

Criminal Confinement

FIVE

Transcarceration and Mentally Ill "Offenders"

Prisoners of Confinement

OVERVIEW. *The first section on this book examined several important aspects of civil confinement for mental health citizens, emphasizing the values underscoring legal and psychiatric decision making. The respective chapters moved from very practical concerns (e.g., dangerousness, involuntary commitment) to very theoretical matters (e.g., identity politics, the social control thesis). From this analysis I drew one provisional and striking conclusion: the penalty for mental illness (i.e., psychiatric difference) is the policing of public hygiene.*

Left unexplored, however, was the extent of this disciplinary surveillance. In other words, while the social control thesis was identified in the civil arena of mental health law, no attempt was made to assess its prevalence (or its operation) in the criminal realm of psychiatric justice. The chapters in this section systematically address this matter.

Chapter 5 provides a necessary transition, exploring how users of psychiatric services are frequently routed to and from the mental health and criminal justice systems. If, as I argue, the social policing of public hygiene produces this effect (i.e., transcarceration), several enduring questions remain. For example, how do psychiatric citizens interpret and define their everyday reality? How do the agencies of which they are a part interpret and define the reality of mentally ill "offenders?" Does the language and logic of transcarceration make psychiatric citizens ideological prisoners of confinement? If so, what are its implications for law, psychiatry, and punishment? By exploring several of the individual, organizational, and structural forces governing the civil and criminal divide of confinement, we deepen our regard for mental illness and the pervasiveness with which it is pathologized, regulated, and corrected. Ultimately, we learn something more about society and ourselves, and the complicitous role both assume as we manufacture madness.

INTRODUCTION

The psychiatrically disordered are a distinct (and growing) subgroup within the penal system (e.g., Steadman et al., 1989; Lamb & Weinberger, 1998; Wettstein,

1998; Arrigo, 1996b). For many of these citizens a process called *transcarceration* pervades their lives (Arrigo, 1997e; Isaac & Armat, 1990). Transcarceration entails the ongoing routing of mentally ill offenders (MIOs) to and from the mental health and the criminal justice systems. When persons with psychiatric disabilities are perpetually and alternately housed in the civil and criminal systems of institutional control (e.g., hospitals, jails), they become prisoners of confinement; that is, the process of transcarceration substantially restricts the capacity of MIO individuals to vary their role performances or to renegotiate their identities. They live out their deviantly defined (i.e., "mad" or "bad") statuses and are largely powerless to alter them. Mentally ill offenders, then, are "silenced" through the activity of transcarceration (1996b), and they assume their oppressive position as a marginalized and captive group.

In my own penological scholarship, I have emphasized how the mental health and criminal justice communities work in concert to exclude the voices of (Arrigo, 1994b) and ways of knowing for (Arrigo, 1996a) persons confined, producing both social repression (Arrigo, 1996c) and psychological punishment (Arrigo, 1995d, 1996d). Moreover, in much of this research, I have relied heavily on the critical potential of postmodern criminological theory in an effort to advance our understanding of how intrapsychic pain and interpersonal violence are enacted for MIOs through the "expert" forensic decision making of the medicolegal establishment (e.g., Arrigo & Williams, 1999a, 1999b). Missing from these investigations, however, has been any significant contextualizing or ethnographic data that could confirm (or deny) the theoretical conclusions reached. The following chapter fills this gap in the literature.

This chapter is divided into four sections. First, selected elements of constitutive criminological thought are presented. This perspective represents an important strain of postmodern analysis conducive to the enterprise outlined above. Second, three distinct case studies of persons with identifiable mental illness subjected to civil confinement, criminal confinement, or both are then described. These life stories dramatically reveal how transcarceration uniquely impacted their everyday experiences. Third, the selected principles of constitutive criminology are applied to the three representative case studies.[1] This level of inquiry demonstrates where and how transcarceration functioned for these disordered citizens and the extent to which each person was a prisoner of confinement. Fourth, the chapter concludes by speculating on the future of confinement practices in relation to psychiatrically disordered offenders. This commentary is useful because it enables us to see how the penalty-for-mental-illness thesis fluidly operates in ongoing, real life civil and criminal contexts. Moreover, the final section is significant because it demonstrates the degree to which clinicolegal decision brokers, and those psychiatric citizens subject to confinement, unconsciously legitimize and reinforce the very process that punishes people for their articulated and lived difference.

CONSTITUTIVE CRIMINOLOGICAL THEORY: AN OVERVIEW

Constitutive thought has firmly established itself as an important and leading postmodern orientation accounting for major developments within the sociology of law (Hunt, 1993) and criminological theory (Henry and Milovanovic, 1996). Selected application studies have addressed such diverse matters as sociolegal studies and their "critical" discontents (Hunt, 1987), psychoanalysis and the constitution of crime (Arrigo, 1998), the coproductive forces of law in American history (Salyer, 1991), media images in crime (Barak, 1993), and an integrated theory of social justice (Barak and Henry, 1999). Moreover, two recently released anthologies by Henry and Milovanovic (1999) and Henry and Lanier (2001) spell out a number of areas in crime and justice where the conceptual tools of constitutive theory are prominently and aptly displayed.

Several noteworthy schools of thought inform the constitutive perspective. Foremost among them are existential phenomenology, labeling theory, social constructionism, and poststructuralism. The intellectual history of constitutive theory also includes the post-Foucauldian investigations of Fitzpatrick (1984) and Coombe (1989), the structuration analysis of Giddens (1984, 1990), the social control taxonomy of Cohen (1985), the sociology of knowledge formulations of Bourdieu (1977, 1987), the symbolic interactionism of Blumer (1969), and the political economy of Marx (1967). Clearly, the "constitution" of constitutive theory represents an eclectic orientation to understanding society and social phenomena, and this is certainly the case with constitutive studies in law and criminology (Arrigo, 1997a).

As with any substantive theory, there are a number of central principles comprising constitutive thought. For purposes of this chapter, four concepts integral to the composition of the theory will be enumerated. These concepts include: (1) the decentered subject; (2) the recovering subject; (3) the social structure as deconstructive and reconstructive; and (4) the definition of crime (Lanier & Henry, 1998). The selection process is not arbitrary. These four tenets were chosen because of their unique capacity to advance our awareness of mentally ill offenders, transcarceration, and punishment. In what follows, I briefly describe each of these constitutive principles.

Decentered Subject

Constitutive theory's reliance on the notion of a decentered or "divided" subject stems from the psychoanalytic semiotics of Jacques Lacan (e.g., 1977, 1981; for various applications in law and criminology see Milovanovic, 1997b). Lacan

(1977, p. 166) argued that identity (agency) and meaning (knowledge) are intimately connected to the language we use to convey our thoughts, impulses, feelings, attitudes, judgments, and so on. However, the language that we use typically speaks *through* us; that is, it represents a stand-in for the "real" subject whose identity, regrettably, remains dormant, silenced, oppressed (Lacan, 1977, pp. 193–194, 310–316; 1988, p. 243; Henry & Milovanovic, 1996, pp. 28–34). This posturing by discourse can be traced to the implicit values and hidden assumptions embedded in words, phrases, or both that, unwittingly, are conveyed in the activity of speech production.

Elsewhere, I have shown how this process operates in civil (Arrigo, 1993c) and criminal (Arrigo, 1996b) forensic settings. Words or expressions such as "dangerous," "incompetent to stand trial," "psychotic," "guilty but mentally ill," "diseased," "in need of treatment," "criminally insane," and the like, are used by medicolegal decision brokers to render judgments about the confinement of disordered citizens. These terms, however, as part of a coordinated and specialized language system (i.e., psycholegal discourse) represent a "master (juridical) narrative . . . produc[ing] a circumscribed knowledge understood [to be] *psychiatric justice*" (1997e, p. 32). Indeed, the joint operation of the medical and legal establishment fills in these terms with selected contents, consistent with their unstated values, effectively reducing the otherwise multifarious meanings of these terms to limited possibilities (Arrigo, 1996b, pp. 174–175).

For example, to define a person as "diseased" or "in need of treatment" is to imply that the individual is not well and is not able to care for him- or herself. The hidden value unconsciously at work with these descriptors, then, is that the person is a passive, rather than an active, architect of their life and, therefore, is not in control of it. Corrective action is necessary so that the individual can normatively function and be made well (Arrigo & Williams, 1999b).

What is troubling about this conclusion is that alternative interpretations for persons with mental disabilities do not find their way into psycholegal discourse. Words or expressions such as "consumer," "mental health systems user," "psychiatric survivor," "disordered citizen," "differently abled," and their corresponding assumptions and values, are denied affirmative recognition within mental health law circles. Indeed, as a practical matter, in order for persons with psychiatric disabilities to petition for release from civil custody, criminal custody, or both they must adopt the preexisting parameters of meaning that already define them. To resist these linguistically structured medicolegal categories of sense-making is to risk sustained confinement in the prison or in the hospital (Arrigo, 1994b, pp. 25–31; Arrigo, 1996c, pp. 151–173). In this context, disordered subjects contribute, knowingly or not, to the very victimization of self and denial of identity they seek to renounce.

According to Lacan (1977, 1981) this struggle in discourse is how the concealment of one's true or authentic self occurs. It is the presence of hegemony (Laclau & Mouffe, 1985) assuming a discursive linguistic form (Henry & Milovanovic, 1996, pp. 158, 160–162). The subject in speech is therefore *unstable* rather than stable, *decentered* rather than centered (MacCabe, 1979, p. 153). The mentally ill offender, then, is "the embodiment of multiple, overlapping, and contradictory expressions of desire, representing discordant voices [that are] temporarily unified by way of a dominant grammar and language system" (Arrigo, 1996c, p. 168)

Recovering Subject

Although language, as a stand-in, speaks *for* the subject (e.g., Silverman, 1983; Pecheux, 1982; Deleuze & Guattari, 1987), it does not follow that human agency is without implication in the activity of naming or defining reality. Indeed, the divided or decentered subject confronts the dialectics of (linguistic) struggle (Henry & Milovanovic, 1996, pp. 170–177). For example, while structural forces (e.g., the criminal justice and mental health systems) announce the humanity of MIOs, disordered citizens can and do contribute to that which defines them (e.g., participation in consumer self-help groups). As Bourdieu & Wacquant explain (1992) "Social agents are knowing agents who, even when they are subjected to determinisms, contribute to producing the efficacy of that which determines them in so far as they structure what determines them" (pp. 167–168). Thus, subjects help develop or produce the very social forms of which they are a part.

Recovering subjects, however, are not necessarily cognizant of the world that they coshape. Indeed, "the world produced by human agency is only episodically perceived as the outcome of its own authorship: much of the time we are forgetful producers of our world" (Henry & Milovanovic, 1996, p. 37). This forgetfulness returns us to the power of those social and structural forces that define our existences and mark our realities, in ways that are never neutral, saturated as they are in cloaked values and concealed assumptions that inconspicuously convey something more, or something other, about our identities. The stock of our cultural and personal experiences, the expanse of our philosophical, political, and religious alliances, the magnitude of our institutional, organizational and corporate allegiances all constitute our "habitus" (Bourdieu, 1984; Rosenau, 1992, p. 59). "The substance of being human must, therefore, entail what preceded us as biography, what looms ahead as prospect, caught in the contingent moment of the here and now, plowed by the discordant strands of unconscious processes" (Henry & Milovanovic, 1996, p. 36).

But in this scripted process of being decentered, the subject can be retrieved. Without ongoing, active engagement from individuals there would be no world, no cultures, no social conditions, and no habitus. "Human agency is connected to the structures that it makes, as are the human agents to each other in making those structures" (Henry & Milovanovic, 1996, p. 39). Discourse is pivotal to how agents recover from their historically mediated, discursively constituted, and structurally situated existences. Recovering agency and being, then, involves reclaiming one's affirmative place in the dialectical play of speech. As Freire (1972) observed: "To exist, humanly, is to *name* the world, to change it. Once named the world . . . , [it] reappears to the namers as a problem and requires of them a new *naming*. Men [and women] are not built in silence, but in word, in work, in action-reflection" (p. 76).

The constitutive challenge for the recovering subject is to resist the organizing parameters of meaning that "speak" the person; that is, through discourse, human investment in the linguistic (and therefore social) reproduction of established structures must be displaced. To effect this end, human agency and, thus, one's potential liberation, must be in flux, mutable, in process (Kristeva, 1984). Transformation for the recovering subject necessarily includes the development of alternative vocabularies of meaning. These are "replacement discourses" (Henry & Milovanovic, 1996, pp. 41, 214–229) that embody the disparate voices of and ways of knowing for those marginalized by the prevailing language system in use (e.g., medicolegal discourse). Through these alternative vocabularies, "the aim is to [replace] an inchoate life narrative [with] a congruent one, and [to] transform . . . [the] meanings that previously blocked the person's story with new ones" (Omer & Strenger, 1992, p. 253). This approach acknowledges that people are "their own authors and can become [their own] poets" (Parry & Doan, 1994, pp. 47). Thus, reclaiming one's rightful place as the architect of one's life, means that people must be given the requisite (reflective) space within which to speak "true words" (Freire, 1972, pp. 56–67) about themselves, about their interpersonal exchanges, and about the social world humans develop.

Social Structure as Deconstructive/Reconstructive

While the decentered subject can be retrieved, and while the recovering subject struggles in speech to fashion new or alternative vocabularies of meaning in which one's identity is more completely embodied, agency is inexorably connected to the material world in which it exists. But the constitutive position on structure or form does not subscribe to an objective, reductionistic, or historically fixed characterization for social order. Indeed, "social structure is a cluster of ideas and images about order and its maintenance, a collection of humans oriented to uphold their version of these images, the reality of the outcomes that follow from actions they take to bring this about, and the potential to transform these images, actions and outcomes" (Henry & Milovanovic, 1996,

p. 65). Thus, the construction of social reality is a *coproduction* in which "structure (the individual-social) and agency (active-passive) are mutually implicated in any production of knowledge" (Henry & Milovanovic, 1996, p. 65; see also, Giddens, 1984).

Constitutive theory acknowledges that the principle means by which structural or organizational forces are defined as such is through language, and it is through the spoken or written word that the dialectical play of meanings (and their differential effects) embedded in these phenomena are given expressive form (e.g., Derrida, 1973, 1978). Thus, for example, execution of the mentally ill who invoke a right to refuse treatment (Arrigo & Tasca, 1999) is intimately linked to how the *prison system* and its *agents* interpret competency, treatment refusal, and mental illness (Arrigo & Williams, 1999b). As a constructed text or narrative, the structural response (i.e., execution or stay of execution) is laden with a multitude of meanings anchored in a coordinated language system (i.e., medicolegal discourse), producing circumscribed images about MIOs on death row (prisoners as diseased, deviant, and dangerous) taken to be de facto reality. These are summary representations (Knorr-Cetina, 1981, pp. 36–37) in which spoken meanings become everyday constructions, given the behavior organized around them (e.g., forensic psychiatrists assessing competency and predicting dangerousness, approaching mental ill as a disease, and testifying in court as "experts" about both). As a result, these images and selected meanings establish themselves as concrete entities; that is, "real" categories of classification, notwithstanding the provisional, relational, positional, and thus, unstable nature of social forms and structures (Arrigo, 1995b, pp. 452–454).

The preceding analysis, then, anchors our understanding of how social structure can be deconstructed and reconstructed. Indeed, the discursive coproduction of reality leaves open the door to possible transformation. Constitutive theory allows us to comment critically on what is and to suggest reflectively what could be. Organizational and social conditions, once constituted as summary representations, depend on the investment of humans to sustain these constructions in everyday discourse, with their implied values and hidden assumptions (Henry & Milovanovic, 1996, p. 68). But these constructions, particularly those that are marginalizing and alienating, can be exposed, reversed, destabilized, or dismantled. The activity of deconstruction (e.g, Derrida, 1973; Balkin, 1987) allows us to decode the meanings embedded in the words or phrases used to name the very oppressive forms or images we help to create. In addition, a re-identification with nonterritorialized modes of communication (Deleuze & Guattari, 1987), more fully affirming of the speaking being, is possible provided we accept the "relative autonomy of structures and subject as well as their dependence in the co-production of social reality" (Henry & Milovanovic, 1996, p. 69). This is what Giddens (1984) means when describing the *duality* or mutuality of structure and agency. Both have meaning apart from and because of one another. Thus, in relation to the deconstructive/reconstructive possibilities for structure we conclude that "the social properties of social systems are both medium and outcome of the practices they recursively organize. Structure is not 'external' to individuals . . . it is in a certain sense more 'internal' than exterior to their activities. Structure is not to be equated with constraint but is always both constraining and enabling" (Giddens, 1984, p. 25).

The Definition of Crime as Power to Harm

An important facet of constitutive criminology is its explanation of crime. Both the passive (decentered) and active (recovering) subject dialectic, along with the deconstructive/reconstructive dynamics of social structure, substantially inform the constitutive understanding of crime. As a summary statement, crime is more than "symbolic violence" (Bourdieu, 1977, p. 192), or the will to harm others where overt and acknowledged domination psychically fosters power differentials in which autonomous subjects become objects of control, victimization, and oppression (Bourdieu & Wacquant, 1992, p. 167). Constitutively speaking, "crime is the expression of some agency's energy to make a difference on others and it is the exclusion of those others who in the instant are rendered powerless to maintain their humanity. . . . Crime then is the power to deny others their ability to make a difference" (Henry & Milovanovic, 1996, p. 116). This is expressed in one of two ways: harms of reduction or harms of repression (Henry & Milovanovic, 1996, p. 101; see Henry & Lanier, 1998, p. 622 for a more visually dynamic overview; see Lanier and Henry, 1998, pp. 27–33, for an expanded view).

Harms of reduction refer to the denial of a person's overall identity or to the loss of a distinct quality constituting the individual. Thus, as a discursive construction, the offended party is somehow restricted from being who he or she is because of the actions of another. For example, when psychiatrically disordered citizens are thwarted in their request to be found not guilty by reason of insanity (NGRI) because of their difference (Arrigo, 1994b), or are found guilty but mentally ill in spite of their difference (Arrigo, 1996a), then they experience a loss because of who they are. Harms of repression refer to the denial of a person's potential to be other or more than who the individual is (Tifft, 1995, p. 9). Thus, as a discursive construction, the offended party is restricted in or prevented from "achieving a desired position or standing" (Henry & Milovanovic, 1996, p. 103). For example, when persons with mental disabilities are denied access to community-situated housing because their speech, thought, and behavior is appreciably different from others in the neighborhood, then they suffer a loss given their restricted access to a desired position (Arrigo, 1992b).

Both harms of reduction and harms of repression are committed by "excessive investors" in power (Henry & Milovanovic, 1996, p. 220; Henry & Lanier, 1998, p. 615). Excessive investors place considerable energy in the control of others, conveyed through language, where the "victim of crime is . . . rendered a non-person, a non-human, or a less complete being" (Henry & Milovanovic, 1996, p. 116). Harms of reduction and repression, then, are exemplars of power where difference is territorialized, criminalized, and vanquished.

THREE CASE STUDIES ON CONFINEMENT: AN ETHNOGRAPHY

Between the years 1984 and 1991 I had occasion to work as a mental health outreach worker in Pittsburgh, Pennsylvania. Much of my time was spent in soup kitchens, sandwich lines, psychiatric facilities, abandoned buildings, deserted alleyways, welfare hotels, chemical dependency units, and prisons. The people with whom I worked were homeless, marginally housed, or soon to be discharged from psychiatric hospitals or released from criminal custody. Much of my time was spent in the communities in which they lived. My contact with them was mostly informal, unstaged, but streetwise. Many, though not all, of the people I met experienced bouts of depression, addiction, unemployment, while others had been civilly and criminally confined. All of them lived on a social margin (Stonequist, 1934), and struggled to survive day-to-day (see Arrigo, 1997c for some "criminal" subgroup applications exploring this phenomenon).

During the period of time that I worked as a mental health outreach worker, I attempted to establish rapport with people and to assist them, both socially and psychologically, in coping with their life circumstances and changing them if they so desired. Most individuals spoke of wanting to alter their lives; few were successful (cf. Arrigo, 1994a for a model of successful community reintegration). This was particularly the case for persons who had been civilly confined, criminally confined, or both. In what follows, I briefly recount the stories of three persons whose lives were dramatically, though differentially, connected to the phenomenon of transcarceration. The ethnographic comments that follow are drawn from my previous field research (1996b, pp. 104–115), exploring the impact of mental health laws that produce "casualties of confinement" (Arrigo, 1996b, p. 104).[2] Missing from these findings, however, was any targeted assessment of social structure and human agency and their interactive capacity to coproduce the reality of transcarceration, rendering subjects prisoners of institutional control. Accordingly, I provide background on how three, typical mental health citizens defined themselves, how they spoke about the civil justice and criminal justice systems of which they were a part, and what became of them in the wake of both.

On Being Mentally Ill: The Case of Edith

Edith lived in Pittsburgh's notorious Hill District. The "Hill" was well known for its urban poverty, drug culture, housing projects, and civic unrest. In many ways, the Hill District was an abandoned community, devastated by the transition from the city's manufacturing-based steel and iron industries to its service-based health and human service economies. When neighborhoods are ignored, the people in it are similarly forgotten. They succumb to the ravages of social disorganization. This was certainly the case for many people who lived in the Hill.

By her own admission, Edith was loud and obnoxious. She was a confirmed alcoholic who drank daily, often to the verge of passing out. Edith was also prone to depression and had attempted to take her life several times. "When I'm shit-faced I don't feel so bad about things. . . . It's this drinking or I die." The connection between alcohol abuse and chronic depression pervaded Edith's life. When she spoke, her speech was alternately slowed and pressured. She was prone to outbursts of anger, sometimes even rage, only to quiet herself suddenly in a fist full of tears and self pity. "*(Screaming)* Look at me! Look at *me!* What do I have . . . nothing! *(Crying)* I ain't no good, damn it. I can't do nothin' 'bout my life, now. It's over for me."

Edith lived alone except for an unnamed cat in a basement flat of a deserted apartment building. Her living quarters were festooned with debris, tattered clothing, jarred food (take-out meals from the nearby soup kitchen), and several stacks of assorted newspapers and magazines. I visited her weekly and we spoke mainly about drinking and death. On one occasion, Edith described how she had jumped from a seven-story building, shattering a number of bones in her left leg, leaving her an invalid. "I just did it, ya know? I had to. I couldn't take being this way (referring to depression) any more and I was tired of the booze." She spoke about her "emotional problems" but never articulated the source of her obvious pain.

> Maybe this is it for me. Maybe I'm suppose to be like this . . . stupid, depressed, and drunk all the time. *(Laughing)* I'm a real fuck-up and I have to deal with it, ya know? I have to accept my shit. *(Angrily)* It's *my* shit. . . . It's me and my life and that's all there is to it. Why can't I get over it? Why?

Edith had been involuntarily hospitalized in the past. She believed she needed to be permanently hospitalized. She spoke about being civilly committed and felt it was an answer to much of her mental anguish.

> I've got an illness, a disease. It's not my fault. I can't stop myself from thinking. I can't stop myself from thinking. *(Holding her head with her hands firmly and crying)* Look at me. I'm nothing. I'm already dead.

> The drinking, it's about being dead. I need to go to the hospital. I'm dead. *(Crying)* I'm *all* dead! If they put me away at least I can die like the crazy fool that I am. At least I can die there with my illness.

On one particular occasion, in the midst of Edith's fierce depression, I drove her to a psychiatric facility for possible inpatient treatment. The attending physician diagnosed her as mentally ill and chemically addicted. The hospital stipulated that before any intensive psychiatric care could be extended to Edith, she would have to go through a 72-hour alcohol detoxification program and participate in a 28-day rehabilitation plan. The community mental health hospital was not in a position to ensure that Edith would be placed in an alcohol recovery unit, and encouraged her to pursue this course of action on her own. Indeed, hospital staff made clear that scarce financial resources and long waiting lists would delay prospects for immediate intervention and sustained services any time in the near future. However, following successful completion of an alcohol rehabilitation program, psychiatric treatment would then be reconsidered.

Edith was faced with a profoundly frustrating dilemma: on the one hand, she was not "mentally ill" in the clinicolegal sense and, thus, could not receive psychiatric attention; on the other hand, she was an alcoholic but could not address her chemical abuse problem because of inadequate subsidies and limited placements. The hospital did not believe that drinking to death was, on its own, sufficient to diagnose Edith as a chronic depressive personality with extreme suicidal tendencies. As a result, she found herself stuck in a seemingly endless cycle of drinking to deaden the depression and feeling suicidal when sober because of the alcohol abuse. Trapped in and tormented by these restricted roles, neither the mental health nor the chemical dependency systems offered her much respite or relief. She died two years later, alone in her apartment. Although eventually Edith had been prescribed the alcohol inhibitor antabuse, she nonetheless drank, causing uncontrollable convulsions to her body that resulted in a fatal heart attack.

The Cycle of Psychiatric Treatment: The Story of James

James lived in Pittsburgh's downtown YMCA at a time when the facility housed a vulnerable tenant population (e.g., the mentally ill, the frail elderly, the chemically addicted) without offering the requisite support services many residents needed. The building was structured as a single room occupancy (SRO): living quarters included basic amenities (e.g., bed, walk-in closet, night stand, chair); semiprivate bathroom facilities on each of the facility's floors were shared. Although the YMCA provided affordable housing, tenants remained mostly unknown to each other. Some preferred their anonymity, others, like Jim, suffered quietly because of it.

I first met James after some concern was expressed by building management that a tenant had been locked away in his flat for some time. After repeated attempts over a few days to gain access to his room, Jim unbolted his door and allowed me to enter. As I stepped into his living quarters, the stench of spoiled food and urine-stained clothing filled the air. Papers, books, clothing, and other paraphernalia cluttered the space. A large, color television filled much of the room and was playing loudly as an episode of a soap opera unfolded. James moved about slowly, awkwardly, listlessly. His speech was barely audible. His voice was expressionless. He was a mass of unmet needs: his hair was matted and unkempt, his shirt and pants were torn and frayed, his thoughts were incoherent and disorganized, his face was unwashed and unshaven, his body was limp and emaciated.

Following some preliminary discussions with James about his background, I eventually realized that he was partially paralyzed. This explained the motor difficulties and the organic impairment. I also discovered that he was a veteran and a frequent inpatient at the VA's local mental health hospital. A severe cardiac arrest, before his arrival at the YMCA, along with a history of depression and chronic organic brain syndrome (OBS) had all been diagnosed and treated there.

After a series of limited exchanges over a several week period, I asked James about his television and why the channel was always set to a day-time drama. On each prior visit, regardless of the time we met, James' TV was turned on and he intently watched one soap opera program after another. "I like the doctors." He said this a few times and smiled until his voice gave way to silence. I pressed him for more information and then he told me: "I'm a doctor."

It was hard to imagine how this man, seemingly lost, forgotten, and confused as he was, could ever have been a physician. The truth is, he was. Piled deep within a stack of papers scattered across his desk, Jim pulled out his college and medical school diplomas, his honorable discharge papers from military service, and several pay stubs documenting that he had worked at Pittsburgh's Allegheny County Morgue as a forensic pathologist. With this information in hand and with his permission, I was able to track down Jim's complete medical and psychological history.

Of particular significance were the number of involuntary commitments for which he had been treated. On four separate occasions within an eight-year period, Jim was involuntarily hospitalized for depression. Three of these commitments lasted 28 days, while the remaining civil confinement lasted 90 days. In each instance, hospital admitting staff determined that Jim was gravely disabled (i.e., deteriorating to the point of not eating, not sleeping, or generally not caring for himself). The hospital eventually discharged Jim following each episode of institutionalization. According to mental health law, when a person is no longer a danger to oneself (i.e., caring for one's physical well-being), the person must be released from confinement (Comment, 1983, pp. 674–677; Perlin, 1999, p. 127). In James's case, after some initial medical intervention and drug treatment, he agreed to frequent the veteran's hospital for subsequent medication monitoring and periodic therapy. In time, given the nature of his illness, hospital contact became more infrequent until it stopped altogether. Returning to his single room at the YMCA, Jim would retreat into the privacy of his living space. The prescription drugs would run out, the psychiatric symptoms would resurface, the decompensation would run its course again, and he would suffer alone in his anonymity.

This was the cycle of James's mental health treatment. The system of which he was part and the system of which he spoke, did little to ensure that ongoing, noncrisis care was made available to him. "This is where I live. I'm a doctor and sometimes I go to the hospital but I don't stay. I can't stay. It's not possible for me to stay." James negotiated his limited identity as a sick patient receiving "revolving door" treatment (Arrigo, 1996b, pp. 100–101). He was caught in a cycle of hospital care that restricted his ability to remain there as an inpatient and did not make it possible for him to thrive in the community as an outpatient. In the end, given the degree of sustained deterioration to his physical and mental condition, James was hospitalized on a psychogeriatric unit at the veteran's hospital where he passed away some five years later.

The Mentally Ill "Offender": The Case of Larry

Larry was a young man in his early 30s, small of stature but sturdy of frame who lived alone on the South Side of Pittsburgh. He frequented the city's soup kitchens and sandwich lines, collecting a modest subsidized income from the government. His head was completely shaved except for a thick batch of long brown hair that flowed from his crown to the small of his back. His ears were multiply pierced. His body was appreciably tattooed. He wore a goatee and fashioned a patch over his left eye. A colorful bandanna was carefully placed around his head.

I first met Larry at a downtown sandwich line. He had difficulty standing still and paced incessantly. He spoke to himself, sometimes shouting obscenities, sometimes muttering compliments. When I addressed him, he would modulate his personality without provocation or inducement: at times he was polite and overly gracious, and at other times he was enraged and extremely abrasive. When I asked Larry about this he would say, "It's like I'm always different, thank you. *(Angrily)* I'm a fuckin' asshole! Yep, I am. *(Smiling)* I am. Please don't get pissed-off at me. Sorry! *(Screaming)* Please don't get pissed off at me. Thank you!"

I had enough educational training and field exposure to realize that Larry comported himself as a schizophrenic. He worked incredibly hard to contain his "demons" but was not always as successful as he wished he could be. His behavior and demeanor were problematic for another reason. Typically, people were offended by his more hostile comments and this led to intense verbal altercations, occasional scuffles, and full-fledged brawls.

Larry had been criminally incarcerated and civilly committed. Usually, he was placed in the county jail following a fist fight where police were called in to resolve the dispute. Unfortunately for Larry, his more violent tendencies surfaced while in the local lockup, resulting in the filing of additional criminal charges. Jail personnel were aware of Larry's psychiatric condition (he had been similarly incarcerated numerous times), and police personnel would transfer him to a community mental health facility for immediate psychiatric care. His schizophrenia was treated through forced medication. Once the symptoms that gave rise to his violent outbursts dissipated, he was discharged and released so that he could return to his South Side apartment.

On several occasions, I asked Larry about what happened to him and how he felt about being confined. It was during these instances that I came to realize just how tormented he was and how angry his transcarcerative experiences made him. In one of his more lucid moments, he summarized his feelings as follows:

> They put me away, man. It's not right. That's all I mean to them. I'm someone to put away to rot. I'm not an animal, no sir. You can't put me away like that, can't treat me that way. Sure I get upset. Everybody gets upset. Then I'm supposed to take this medicine *(Showing me a pill container)* and be good. I *am* good, right? They put me in the hospital with crazy people. I know I'm sick but I'm not crazy, right? I don't think I'm crazy. *(Laughing)* Crazy people can't think straight. Look at me. I got a place to live. I get my money and eat and take care of myself. And then they lock me up in the jail. *(Angrily)* I'm *not* a criminal? I get upset. I get upset, that's all. People get on my nerves sometimes, that's all. They don't understand me. I'm just a little sick but you can't tell me I'm crazy, and I'm not someone who, like, robs a bank or something. That's not me.

Larry continued on his course of clinical decompensation and criminal misconduct, with intermittent placement in his low rent apartment. He negotiated his identity through the alternating role performances of the diseased-minded and dangerous prone characterizations implied in the responses offered to him by the mental health and criminal justice systems. Ultimately, Larry found himself sentenced to a prison for a protracted period of time. The accumulation of criminal charges, coupled with failed inpatient psychiatric treatment, resulted in long-term confinement on a forensic unit of a correctional facility. With this placement secured, Larry became the embodiment of transcarceration: he assumed his socially structured and psychically inscribed role as both the "mad" and "bad" offender.

CONSTITUTIVE THEORY, THE MENTALLY ILL OFFENDER, AND TRANSCARCERATION: AN APPLICATION

The three ethnographies differentially demonstrate the power of language, constitutively produced through agency and structure, to define the respective realities of Edith, James, and Larry. Each subject uniquely became a prisoner of confinement. In what follows, I provisionally demonstrate how the selected principles of constitutive theory apply to the three cases presented. In this process, I describe as well the relationship between mentally ill offenders and transcarceration.

Revisiting the Decentered Subject

The decentered subject experiences a lack in discourse; that is, one's essential being and one's interiorized meanings are silenced through language. Discourse "speaks the subject." The stories of Edith, James, and Larry reveal how words and expressions convey (unconscious) intents that alienate and oppress people. Edith's dilemma involved the definition of mental illness. James's predicament centered around the explanation for psychiatric treatment. Larry's problem entailed the meaning of violence.

Edith 's forced choice (i.e., become "ill" in the clinicolegal sense or endure as a chronically depressed alcoholic) left her little room to rearticulate her identity. She was so thoroughly consumed by this choice that her persona was unmistakable: "I'm no good," "I'm nothing," "I'm dead." Indeed, so powerful was the established medicolegal meaning of mental illness that it stripped Edith of even this desired identity.

James's condition gave rise to a cycle of institutional treatment. His obvious and understandable identification with physicians resulted in repeated voluntary and involuntary hospitalizations that constituted and reaffirmed him as a "sick" patient. His listlessness, emaciation, expressionlessness, and so forth, were all exemplars of his lack, conveyed quietly through seclusion and anonymity. James disappeared in thought and action. Words escaped him. He vanished in discourse. It spoke, as a stand-in, for him.

Larry's identity was linked to the fluctuating roles he assumed as a criminal and as a schizophrenic. These statuses collapsed into one when he was placed in a correctional forensic setting. Violence (both verbal and physical) engulfed Larry's reality. From the way he dressed and kept his hair, to the pierced ears and eye patch, to the body tattoos and ferocious outbursts, Larry assumed the character of a menacing, conflicted, and troubled figure. He became the quintessential mentally ill offender and this defined his everyday existence.

Revisiting the Recovering Subject

The recovering subject attempts to transcend, through language, the preconfigured parameters of meaning that symbolize the person's identity. Retrieving one's identity involves an active engagement with discourse. Subjects must resist alienating and marginalizing words, phrases, and language systems (i.e., medicolegal discourse), and replace them with vocabularies of sense-making that restore their humanity and liberate them from oppression. Edith was unable to emancipate herself through speech, reflection, and action. James struggled, mostly unsuccessfully, to recover his identity. Larry actively resisted the assigned meanings embedded in the descriptor "mentally ill offender," and was punished for his opposition.

Edith wanted to be civilly confined. She made clear that she had an "illness, a disease," and that she wanted "to die" in a hospital because her life was "over." Edith felt as if she was already "dead," and that she had "nothing." Even when she questioned her existence, her words and thoughts returned her to the de-centered state in which she suffered. "Maybe this is it for me. . . . Maybe I'm supposed to be like this [i.e., depressed, suicidal, and alcoholic]? Why can't I get over it? Why?" Edith could not retrieve her humanity even in words. This inability contributed to her death. She was imprisoned by her thoughts numbed as they were with alcohol, confined by the depression that spoke her identity.

James, too, sought and valued confinement. Where Edith longed for institutionalization as a means of quieting her suffering, James dreamed of involuntary hospitalization as a way of rediscovering his previous identity. James said very little; however, he made clear he was a physician. The power of the statement, "I'm a doctor," stood in stark, seemingly unimaginable contrast to the manner in which he lived. But it was in uttering this phrase that Jim, disheveled, incoherent, and emaciated as he was, struggled desperately to liberate himself from his deteriorating existence. His fixation with day-time dramas and actors who portrayed physicians was a constant reminder of who he had been and what he might be yet again. These words and actions, as the locus of potential transformation for James, were not enough. His identity, as a gravely disabled, organically dysfunctional person, consumed him as he cycled in and out of mental health hospitals.

Larry did not want to be civilly or criminally confined. He wanted to live without regulation from systems of institutional control. He wanted to be "good." He feared being "crazy." He did not believe he was a "criminal." Larry's resistance in words and actions was a continual struggle to keep at bey his violence. Often, he overcompensated by being polite, almost to the point of being disingenuous. This was a deliberate attempt at being a "good" citizen. After all, Larry, like most ordinary, decent people had "a place to live," and he had "money and [ate], and t[ook] care of [him]self." Larry's outrage at being "put away" and his resistance to the labels "crazy" and "criminal" were efforts to resituate himself as someone who was merely a victim of circumstances. "I get upset. I get upset, that's all. People get on my nerves sometimes, that's all. They [the mental health and criminal justice systems] don't understand me. . . . That's not me." The more that Larry defined his own reality and the more that Larry insisted on who he was, the harder it became for him to control his fierce temper. His steadfast refusal (verbally and physically) to accept his predefined status as a mentally ill offender was *the* source of his confinement. The language and logic of transcarceration rendered him a prisoner. He was captive to a process that restricted him from being anything more, or anything other, than the very contained "animal" he said he would not be and could not be.

Revisiting Social Structure as Deconstructive/Reconstructive

Human agents are inexorably connected to the social and organizational structures that they define and of which they are a part. In this context, the naming of social forms and organizational images are both independent of and linked to the subjects who constitute them. Sustaining the mental health and criminal justice systems and the manner in which they operate, then, depend as much on how they are defined as they do on the continued investment of humans to endorse these very identifications. This structure (individual-social) and agency (active-passive) duality makes possible the deconstruction and reconstruction of images and forms, especially those that are alienating, marginalizing, and oppressive. The structure of civil confinement for Edith was that she actively constituted the mental health system as a psychopathologized place in which to die. The structure of civil confinement for James was that he passively defined the hospital as a restorative place in which to live. The structure of civil and criminal confinement for Larry was that he actively constituted the mental health and criminal justice systems as punitive places in which to suffer.

The psychiatric hospital was where Edith wanted to die. She believed she belonged there. "If they put me away at least I can die like the crazy fool that I am. At least I can die there with my illness." The system to which she professed such intense allegiance, however, refused her long-term admission. Much like Edith believed, the mental health facility existed to hospitalize and treat people with "an illness, a disease"; however, the system did not define Edith as someone who needed immediate psychiatric attention. Indeed, the hospital staff determined that, in her case, drug detoxification and rehabilitation were warranted. Edith was not interested in redefining her reality or the psychiatric system's role in her life. Instead, she vehemently maintained her investment in being mentally ill (i.e., depressed), and endorsed the psychiatric hospital as a place in which sick people could end their emotionally troubled lives.

The mental health hospital was where James wanted to live. He believed that his place was with other physicians. He vicariously experienced this sentiment while watching day-time soap opera dramas in his room. "I'm a doctor," he said. "I'm a doctor." But Jim suffered quietly, mostly in seclusion, anonymously. He passively pronounced his identification with the hospital. He (James the doctor) disappeared in his silence. The psychiatric system defined its role as one in which to treat people like James; however, intervention could only be short-lived. After all, he recovered while hospitalized and became well enough to be discharged. Once in the community, James would return to the privacy of his flat. The medication would run out, the symptoms of decompensation would return, and the depression would intensify. In his quiet but powerful way, James decidedly maintained his investment in "revolving door" psychiatric treatment and passively endorsed the hospital as a place in which to retrieve his past. The system of which he was a part willingly, albeit incompletely and temporarily, availed him of institutional services.

Larry resisted civil and criminal confinement. "I'm not crazy. . . . I'm not a criminal." The more intensely he renounced these descriptors (and systems), the more he became a part of them. Ultimately, he was fused to them. The mental health community defined its role as treating psychiatrically disordered people. The criminal justice community defined its role as handling overtly violent citizens. Larry was identified as both diseased and dangerous. His words, thoughts, and behaviors became synonymous with the meaning for the mentally ill offender. Although he actively resisted this characterization, his resistance was interpreted as an indication that he was, indeed, both diseased and dangerous. He was a schizophrenic and a menace. Larry actively maintained his opposition to civil and criminal confinement, alleging that they were places for "animals," places to "rot." For Larry, being "put away" was like a punishment; it was a place in which to suffer. The more that Larry spoke of transcarceration this way, the more it became the very structure of despair and imprisonment that he so forcefully rejected.

Definition of Crime as Power to Harm

The constitutive power to harm denies one of their ability to make a difference (Lanier & Henry, 1998). It denies one of their given humanity. This repudiation in discourse occurs through harms of reduction and repression. Harms of reduction restrict a person from being who one is through the actions of another. The person is treated as somehow less than one's identity would otherwise allow. Harms of repression thwart a person in his or her efforts to be something more or something other than the individual already is. The subject is prevented from reaching a certain objective or particular standing in life. Edith was the victim of crime. The mental health system presented her with a forced choice that denied her difference. Thus, the harm perpetrated against her was one of reduction. James was the victim of crime. The mental health system refused to accept him indefinitely for psychiatric treatment until it was too late. Thus, the harm perpetrated against him was one of reduction. Larry was the victim of crime. The mental health and criminal justice systems denied him of the potential to live as he chose. Thus, the crime perpetrated against him was one of repression.

The psychiatric community refused to accept Edith for immediate inpatient treatment. It defined her as a dual diagnosed (i.e., mentally ill and chemically addicted) client. But the implicit meaning of the dual diagnosis compelled Edith to confront an unreasonable dilemma: become psychiatrically disabled in the medicolegal sense *or* admit drug dependency and receive alcohol treatment. The problem was that Edith was both and she articulated her reality accordingly. The only system to which she could turn refused to embrace her spoken difference (i.e., simultaneously addicted and depressed). This denial of difference was the expression of state-sponsored power that reduced her humanity.

The psychiatric establishment subjected James to repeated institutional confinement, while typically ignoring prospects for chronic care. Although the system acknowledged that James was gravely disabled, it did not adequately support him once he returned to the community. While the medicolegal community embraced his mental illness, it did so partially and impermanently. As long as James fit the gravely disabled description he received psychiatric care. The problem was that James's illness extended beyond the limits of revolving door institutional treatment. His dysfunctional and debilitating life as an SRO resident (e.g., without food, companionship, socialization), traceable to his forgotten past as a doctor, was similarly a part of his identity. The mental health system ignored (or dismissed) this dimension of his articulated reality and, at best, interpreted it as symptomatic of his cycle of decompensation. Thus, James was forced into the limiting role of an occasionally depressed patient. He was not perceived as more or less mentally ill than this, and his identification as a forensic pathologist was ostensibly disregarded. James was denied his existence and quietly suffered because of it. This denial of difference was the expression of state-endorsed crime that repudiated the fullness of his humanity.

Larry refused to accept that he was mentally ill or criminally dangerous. He struggled to be neither, managing to secure an apartment and living independently. For Larry, these were clear indicators of being a "good" person. Larry's efforts to maintain this standing and thrive in the face of it were restricted by both the mental health and criminal justice systems. Larry cycled in and between the psychiatric hospital and the county jail. His transcarceration, and the unstated values embedded in this ongoing process, significantly prevented him from rising above the restricted role performances he was compelled to live out. Eventually, not only was he hindered from returning to his autonomous existence on Pittsburgh's South Side, he was precluded from redefining himself as anything other than a mentally ill offender. Larry was denied the potential to be free and self-sufficient. He was denied the possibility to be other than "mad" and "bad." This articulated refusal was the power of state-regulated crime to quash, through words and actions, the dignity and humanity of another.

IMPLICATIONS AND CONCLUSIONS

Transcarceration is a process by which persons with psychiatric disabilities are repeatedly and alternately contained in the mental health system, criminal justice system, or both. Thus, it is the product of the social control thesis, sustaining and legitimizing the policing of public hygiene. This chapter explored how transcarceration differentially impacted the lives of three disordered citizens, uniquely rendering them captives of disciplinary control. The method of analysis relied heavily on constitutive theory, informed by the ethnographic reporting of the researcher. What we discovered is how language, and the agency-structure duality implicated in the coproduction of reality, limited the role performances of the subjects investigated, leaving them little room to renegotiate their identities. Edith, James, and Larry were caught in a process that consumed and defined their existences. They distinctively invoked the discourse of "disease," "dangerousness," or both (with their implicit values and hidden assumptions) to specify their experiences, and the psychiatric and penal institutions of which they were a part responded accordingly. Edith and James died because of it. Larry suffered in the face of it.

Future research in the area of constitutive theory and mentally ill offenders would do well to examine how additional facets of agency and structure contribute (or not) to the activity of transcarceration. For example, this chapter did not consider the contextualizing variables of family history, political economy, religion, or the media. Indeed, it is easy to imagine how a history of mental illness in a subject's family might contribute to the articulation on one's own reality, the structural and organizational forces the person coshapes, and the interpersonal exchanges the individual coconstitutes. The same may be said for other variables not directly or indirectly examined in this study.

In addition, constitutive theory is replete with a number of interrelated concepts and principles (e.g., transpraxis, social judo, COREL sets) (Henry & Milovanovic, 1996). Given these limits, the application in this chapter can only be described as provisional at best. Accordingly, it follows that future scholarship in the area would do well to assess more systematically the utility of constitutive theory in relation to the psychiatrically disordered and transcarceration.

Finally, the conclusions reached from this chapter might lead one to assume that all mentally ill persons are prisoners of confinement. This is an oversimplification and an overgeneralization not intended by the analysis. The expressed purpose of this chapter was to demonstrate how the process of transcarceration worked in the lives of some psychiatrically disordered subjects, such that the penalty-for-mental-illness thesis could be made more evident and its effects more clear. What is disturbing about the conclusions reached is that, in the three cases examined, the effects of transcarceration were, without question, devastating.[3] Future investigators need to examine how agency and structure coproduce victimization in words and behavior, and how, if at all, replacement discourses (e.g., MIOs as "psychiatric *survivors*," "mental health *consumers*," "differently *abled*") reduce prospects for harm in speech and action.

With these research observations in mind, I acknowledge the shortcomings of my field work and the limited implications that follow. This notwithstanding, the chapter is suggestive on a number of fronts. First, language was significant to how Edith, James, and Larry defined their identities, and it was integral to how the civil and criminal systems of institutional control were interpreted and functioned in their lives. The selection of words, phrases, gestures, and silences, and so on (and the meanings embedded in them and the meanings subjects attached to them), illustrates the power of discourse to considerably shape reality.

Second, the language explored in this chapter draws our attention to how people were harmed and how crimes were enacted. Edith, James, and Larry were victims of disciplinary forces because of their spoken differences. The systems to which they turned (or attempted to resist) coshaped their identities. Edith's insistence on being mentally ill (and chemically addicted) was repressed by the psychiatric system. James's desire to be confined permanently as a chronically ill, rather than occasionally depressed, patient was (largely) repressed by the mental health system. Larry's potential existence as a free and self-sufficient citizen was so reduced by the criminal and civil confinement systems that he became the "mad" and "bad" person he so vehemently renounced.

Third, the descriptor "mentally ill offender" signifies something more than psychiatrically disordered persons who are incarcerated. Based on the analysis contained within this chapter, the meaning of the MIO label is threefold: (1) it refers to psychiatrically disabled persons who are so offensive to society, because they are different from their non–mentally ill counterparts, that they are civilly confined; (2) it refers to psychiatrically disordered persons who are so offensive to society, because they are different from their non–mentally ill counterparts, that they are criminally confined; and (3) it refers to psychiatrically disabled persons who are so offensive to society, because they are different from their non–mentally ill counterparts, that they are civilly and criminally confined. These conclusions suggest that being an "offender" has as much to do with one's articulated mental illness as it does with one's criminal conduct.

Fourth, transcarceration, constitutively interpreted, is the process that figuratively and literally condemns individuals to restrictive role performances (i.e., "bad," "mad," or both). Transcarceration renders subjects prisoners of confinement discourse. The result is that mentally ill citizens succumb to the marginalization, alienation, and victimization structurally embedded in the civil and criminal systems of institutional control, and linguistically reenforced by the very words and expressions subjects use to define and sustain them.

While certainly limited in application, the three subjects ethnographically investigated in this chapter participated in transcarceration. Their felt pain was real; their articulated suffering was deep. As victims of the language and logic of a restrictive process, their lives were unmistakably and dramatically altered. Edith, James, and Larry became prisoners of confinement, and they could do little to change their marginalizing and alienating identities. Indeed, the discourse and behavior of law and psychiatry, situated at the crossroads of civil and criminal mental health containment practices, made manifest the centrality of punishment within and throughout the everyday policing of madness.

SIX

Ideology in the Psychiatric Courtroom

Not Guilty by Reason of Insanity and Guilty but Mentally Ill

OVERVIEW. *While transcarceration represents the effect of the social control thesis, decision making in the psychiatric courtroom is the state-sanctioned vehicle by which the latter is established. In other words, the penalty for mental illness (i.e., the policing of public hygiene or difference) is identified, endorsed, and reenacted within a particular interpersonal and organizational context. Previous chapters exploring the civil side of mental health law provided some tentative, though useful, commentary along these lines. In short, I explained how involuntary psychiatric hospitalization was that mechanism designed to "correct" or "repair" (i.e., treat) one's mentally ill condition, and how such intervention was consistent with the social control thesis. Missing from this analysis, however, was any sustained effort to assess critically the ideological forces under which such determinations occur, mindful of how and why these judgments manifest themselves in the psychiatric courtroom. Moreover, while chapter 5 directed our attention to the individual and structural dynamics through which transcarceration is interpreted and defined, I did not consider how the domains of law and psychiatry are discursively constructed, giving rise to various confinement outcomes.*

This chapter addresses both of these matters. I examine two controversies within the criminal forensic arena. These include the non-guilty-by-reason-of-insanity (NGRI) and the guilty-but-mentally-ill (GBMI) verdicts. At issue are those unconscious, but deeply felt, forces that inform (and circumscribe) legal and psychiatric decision-making in the forensic courtroom. How is knowledge both constructed and articulated by clinicolegal decision brokers? What role does subjectivity play in the formation of this knowledge? How is language integral to the constitution of both? What is the relationship among discourse, subjectivity, and knowledge, and how is it relevant to the critique of law, psychiatry and punishment? These questions invite us to consider the subtle ways in which mental illness is policed, resulting in criminal confinement and the disciplining of difference. In addition, though, these questions challenge us to reassess the confinement process altogether, resulting, perhaps, in the realization that not only does the state-sanctioned mechanism of the psychiatric courtroom produce an absence of citizen justice but, more insidiously, it ensures the sustained presence of ideological oppression.

INTRODUCTION

The intersecting categories of crime and behavior provide many relevant examples that demonstrate just how important law and psychiatry are for setting social policy or for shaping forensic practice. The illustrations of officer styles and police personalities, scientific jury selection, the probative value of eyewitness testimony, prisoner rights, and lie detection through use of polygraphs represent only a few of the many controversial and contemporary topics in which we find the clinical forensic community assuming a crucial role in the legal system.

Despite these and other examples, very little is known about the bond which the systems of criminal justice and mental health share, particularly when producing outcomes predicated on the joint effects of law and psychiatry. Precisely because there is such a close relationship between these two disciplines, exploring how they behave interdependently during instances of thematic convergence is especially worthy of investigation. In other words, learning about how the clinicolegal apparatus interprets, for example, the evidentiary value of testimony from a person who is severely developmentally disabled, may give us more fruitful information concerning the operation of law and medicine and, thus, may tell us something more or something other about their shared likelihood for promoting psychiatric justice (e.g., Arrigo, 1993c, 1996b). It is this very information which helps to inform us; information which explains how the structure and process of clinicolegal decision making is conceived and how it functions.

Clearly, then, there is something to be said for a study exploring the overlapping effects of law and psychiatry and how these effects are organized and activated, particularly with themes of import for criminal justice and mental health. Although it is important to acknowledge the need for such an undertaking, it is also essential to identify specifically the context within which the analysis in this chapter will proceed. In brief, I want to present a largely theoretical assessment of the psychiatric courtroom, mindful of how decisions are fashioned therein, especially when confronted with possible criminal confinement matters.

One access point for this investigation comes from postmodernism. In chapter 5, I offered some limited observations about postmodernism as linked to constitutive theory and transcarceration. Here, however, some general observations about what this heterodox strain of analysis represents for purposes of truth, knowledge, reason, and the like, are in order.

In recent years, the social sciences have been subjected to a series of critiques under the broad banner of "postmodernism" (e.g., Dews, 1987; Giddens, 1984, 1990; Lyotard, 1984; Sarup, 1989; Rosenau, 1992). Essentially, this perspective claims that no essential or objective reality exits, that certainty and precision in scientific pursuits is nothing more than a privileged social construction, and that all assemblages of human social behavior originate through the language (i.e., speech ideas either written or uttered) we select to communicate our meanings. Therefore, according to postmodernists, the discourse we employ ultimately represents a constellation of subjective values.

In Europe, various scholarly associations inspired largely by the textual and nontextual contributions of Michel Foucault (e.g., 1965, 1977) have incorporated many of his ideas on power and knowledge to advance a postmodern psychology (Cooper, 1967, 1978), and to fashion some resistance to conventional mental health practices (Deleuze & Guattari, 1977, 1987; Guattari, 1984). On the American continent, however, some work in philosophical psychology is only now just beginning to address the relevance of postmodern thought. Selected topics include such investigations as: self and identity (Gergen, 1991, 1999); feminine ways of knowing (Gilligan, 1982; Gilligan, Lyons, & Hanmer, 1990; Silverman, 1988); systems theory (Abraham, Abraham & Shaw, 1990); the psychotherapeutic process (Bütz, 1992, 1997); and quantum psychology (Wolinsky, 1991, 1993).

In the field of criminal justice, we find a similar trend. A small, albeit growing, body of scholarship is also utilizing the tools of postmodern thought. Isolated studies in the United States have examined such themes as policing (Manning, 1988), images of crime (Young, 1996); punishment and penology (Howe, 1994) feminist jurisprudence (Cornell, 1991, 1993), and prospects for social justice and social change (Milovanovic, 1997a, 1997b).

Thus, on the American front we see that the contributions of postmodernism for both disciplines, although represented in the literature, have been rather slow in developing. It follows, then, that not only is little generally known about the relationship that criminal justice and mental health share—especially when investigating social problems on which they intersect (e.g., the psychiatric courtroom)—but scant attention has been given to (1) what the postmodern critique may offer that is relevant to each field and (2) how, at thematic points of convergence, clinicolegal practices therefore operate.

Notwithstanding the preceding commentary, this chapter will utilize several core ideas identified within the postmodern perspective to advance a provisional assessment of the intersecting categories of criminal justice and mental health. For purposes of exemplification, I will consider how the not-guilty-by-reason-of-insanity (NGRI) and the guilty-but-mentally-ill (GBMI) verdicts are conceived of and implemented through the instrumentation of both law and psychiatry. My postmodern focus will mostly rely on the psychoanalytic conceptualizations of Jacques Lacan (1901–1981). The emphasis on Lacan is deliberate. Many prominent figures identified as the architects of French postmodern thought were known to have attended Lacan's infamous Parisian seminars. Such notables as Jacques Derrida, Luce Irigaray, Roland Barthes, Michel Foucault, Julia Kristeva, and Jean Baudrillard are recognized today as having incorporated many of Lacan's conceptualizations into their own work (Arrigo, Milovanovic, & Schehr, 2000).

In the context of my theoretical inquiry, I will broadly explain how Lacan provides useful information pertinent to subjectivity or "desire-in-discourse" in the creation of (clinicolegal) knowledge. I will demonstrate, as well, how this information helps account for the specific construction of the NGRI and GBMI verdicts. I will conclude by speculating on the extent to which the behavior of law and psychiatry, through discourse, punishes the disordered defendant prior to the actual trial and before the administration of the forensic sentencing outcome (i.e., the NGRI or GBMI verdict). Throughout the exposition, I will limit the analysis to the most essential components of Lacan's otherwise complex and idiosyncratic conceptualizations. In order to help situate the chapter, however, I begin with some brief background on both the NGRI plea and verdict and the GBMI option. This is followed by important commentary on Lacanian psychoanalytic thought, understood as embracing the postmodern enterprise.

THE INSANITY DEFENSE AND THE GUILTY BUT MENTALLY ILL VERDICT: A PRELIMINARY BACKGROUND

In the United States, contemporary Insanity Defense Reform has undergone some considerable state statutory change (Steadman et al., 1993). According to most commentators, the course of this change is related to the 1982 acquittal of John W. Hinckley, would-be Presidential assassin of Ronald Reagan (Steadman et al., 1993, pp. 35–39; Mayer, 1987). Indeed, having successfully invoked the NGRI defense, Hinckley's acquittal fueled a massive reform, designed to limit the constitutional (especially due process) protections of insanity acquittees. During the 1980s, legislative rhetoric and public debate were rampant and both undoubtedly fueled the climate of revision throughout several mental health legal circles (Boyce & Jackson, 1982; Callahan, Myer, & Steadman, 1987).

In the wake of this clamor for reform, some states (e.g., Montana, Utah) implemented legislation effectively abolishing the insanity doctrine as an affirmative defense in all criminal cases (Arrigo, 1997d; Heinbecker, 1986). Notwithstanding these statutory efforts, empirical (Steadman et al., 1993, pp. 125–137) and legal (Bender, 1984) studies indicate that mental illness is continually invoked at the time of plea. "Indeed, the plea rate in which attorneys raise mental illness on behalf of their criminal clients [remains] the same whether before or after the reform" (Arrigo, 1997d, p. 192).

In the context of this chapter, the importance of the NGRI defense stems from its association with the GBMI verdict. Thus, in order to appreciate the development of the GBMI doctrine, it is important to position it in relationship to NGRI determinations. In part, this positioning requires some review of the precedent-setting case and relevant statutory law on the NGRI option. As I previously indicated, the Hinckley case is notable especially for the reforms it subsequently spawned. These reformist measures reached their apex with the decision in *Jones v. United States* (1983), and with the Insanity Defense Reform Act (IDRA), passed by the U.S. Congress in 1984. It is to these matters that I now briefly turn.

The Case of *Jones v. United States* (1983)

On September 9, 1975, Michael Jones was arrested for attempting to steal a department store jacket. Some 6 months later he was found not-guilty-by-reason-of-insanity. In accordance with the law, an administrative hearing was conducted 50 days subsequent to the verdict to determine if involuntary civil commitment should be continued. The burden of persuasion fell to the petitioner (Jones via his attorney) to demonstrate that he was no longer a danger to himself, to others, or both. Meeting this burden would enable the petitioner to be released form custody. Petitioner Jones failed to provide such evidence and, thus, his commitment was continued. One year later, a second release hearing was held. Jones's counsel argued that Jones had been civilly confined for a period longer than the one he would have received had he been criminally convicted of and sentenced for the original offense. Jones's counsel therefore challenged his involuntary civil commitment, claiming that it was unconstitutional.

The ensuing legal debate reached a climax in November, 1983, when the U.S. Supreme Court, having heard the case, offered its ruling. The Court held that an insanity acquittal is adequate justification for automatic commitment when the defense has the burden of proof. Furthermore, the Court held that petitioner's "maximum sentence" argument was not determinative. Indeed, although an insanity acquittee may be involuntarily detained for a period greater than if the acquittee were criminally incarcerated, such institutionalization has no bearing on the decision to grant petitioner's request to be released from civil confinement.

The Insanity Defense Reform Act of 1984

Another watershed measure which responded directly to the public's plea for change following the Hinckley case was the IDRA of 1984. This legislation was significant for two reasons: (1) for the first time there was a federal legislative code for use in insanity cases, and (2) a new balance was struck between the public's right to protection against harm and the disabled defendant's right to liberty safeguards that were based on the Constitution. In short, the test established by the IDRA provided more assurances to society at large, protecting it against the possible harm caused by insanity acquittees. As an affirmative defense strategy, the burden of proof shifted from the prosecution to the defense to show, based upon clear and convincing evidence, that the defendant's mental disease at the time of the criminal act was so severe that the defendant was unable to appreciate the wrongfulness of his or her conduct. As Mayer (1987) noted, "the public's overwhelming fear of the future acts of insanity acquittees produced [a] reform . . . that clearly reflected the overriding interest in public safety to the near exclusion of concern for the due process rights of acquittees" (p. 27; see also Simon & Aaronson, 1988). Thus, following *Jones*, the IDRA further advanced an attitude toward the (noncriminally culpable but) mentally ill, suggesting that such citizens required careful monitoring and surveillance, given their propensity to engage in unspecified, though likely, acts of future dangerousness and violence (Arrigo, 1994b, 1996c).

The Adoption of the Guilty-but-Mentally-Ill Verdict

The case of *Jones v. U.S.* (1983) and the 1984 IDRA were the impetus behind the adoption of the guilty-but-mentally-ill verdict (Singer, 1985; Steadman et al., 1993). As previously stated, the GBMI determination is a relatively recent development in law and psychiatry. Defendants found GBMI are sentenced as if they had been found guilty of their charge, with available psychiatric care and treatment provided by the correctional system (Calahan, Mayer, & Steadman, 1987; McGraw, Farthing-Capowich, & Keilitz, 1985). Thus, the GBMI verdict is an attractive sentencing alternative for juries dissatisfied with the NGRI option. The GBMI alternative is designed to both "curb the use of the insanity plea and verdict, [and] prevent . . . the early release of dangerous individuals" (Keilitz, 1987, p. 307).

In an effort to more accurately characterize the intent behind the GBMI option, several commentators have maintained that a more precise phrase for the doctrine would be "guilty and mentally ill" (Petrella, Benedek, Bank, & Packer, 1985; Smith & Hall, 1982; Steadman et al., 1993). Critics of the GBMI option charge that an unintended, though implicit, message communicated in the verdict is the presence of some diminished capacity on the part of the defendant. On the contrary, the GBMI outcome is structured to both acknowledge one's criminal culpability and one's mental deficiency, necessitating incarceration in a secure, albeit psychiatrically oriented, setting. The GBMI verdict currently exists in 12 states. Three states adopted it during the Hinckley case (April, 1981–June, 1982), and 11 states adopted the GBMI determination in the period immediately following Hinckley's acquittal (July, 1982–December, 1985) (Steadman et al., 1993).

Thus, we see that while the *Jones v. U.S.* case legitimated indefinite civil confinement for insanity acquittees, and while the IDRA guaranteed a more prohibitive standard for defense attorneys invoking a NGRI strategy, the GBMI verdict regards psychiatrically disordered defendants as both "bad" (criminal) and "mad" (mentally ill). Clearly, then, the not-guilty-by-reason-of-insanity and the guilty-but-mentally-ill options are very appealing topics, particularly when investigating the intersecting behavior of law and psychiatry, desire-in-discourse, and knowledge construction.

LACAN, POSTMODERNISM, AND PSYCHOANALYTIC THEORY: AN OVERVIEW

The significance of Lacanian theory for psychoanalysis rested on his insistence that the unconscious was structured much like a language (Lacan, 1977). Accordingly, in order to understand our internal (intrapsychic) thoughts and our interpersonal (intersubjective) exchanges, Lacan attempted to identify and ponder the inner workings of that discourse located within the primary process region (i.e., the unconscious). For Lacan, this sphere was understood to be the repository of knowledge, power, agency, and desire.

Another way to appreciate Lacanian psychoanalysis, particularly within the context of postmodern thought, is to situate his insights within that division of linguistic analysis termed semiotics (Milovanovic, 1992a). Semiotics is the study of language and the evolving meaning(s) communicated by and through discourse (Arrigo, 1995b). More specifically, the term implies that all communication, whether verbal, nonverbal, or extraverbal, represents a collection of signs. Thus, all words (written or spoken), gestures, or cues signify something more or something other than the words, gestures, or cues themselves. As a semiotician, Lacan emphasized the essential place that desire assumes in our choice of speech and the combination of words we use to communicate meaning. This semiotic focus is especially relevant because the selection process, although unconscious, telegraphs a certain (subjective) regard for human actors and the social order.

The following illustration demonstrates the significance of the latter point. In conversational speech, if an individual refers to a mentally ill person as "diseased" or as a "consumer of psychiatric services" we understand that the metaphorical references tell us more than one might gather from the explicit dialogue (i.e., that the individual in question is psychiatrically disabled). The first image invokes the language of treatment and illness. It is a figurative utterance which arguably objectifies the person as someone experienced most especially as a collection of symptoms, as a composite of his or her deficiencies. The second image relies on the language of economics. In this instance, we conjure up an awareness of the individual based on his or her participation in the (psychiatric) marketplace (e.g., outpatient treatment, drug therapy, institutional confinement). Thus, we see that both expressions are encoded; that is, they embody desire. It was this encoded, unexamined regard, and its careful elucidation, which was to figure prominently in Lacan's psychoanalytic formalizations during the course of his career.

Returning to the NGRI-GBMI verdicts, clinicolegal behavior, and the psychiatric courtroom, we see how Lacan's exploration of desire-in-discourse might be especially useful. The subject-in-law (the disordered defendant) appearing before a medicolegal tribunal is understood through a specialized speech lens; namely, those linguistic parameters defining psychiatric justice. In other words, any attempt to communicate meaning or knowledge from outside this sphere, any offering of a replacement grammar (including the more uncommon use of alternative forms of discourse such as psychotic utterances) is cleansed (i.e., relanguaged) and made compatible with those coordinates advancing the lens of "legalese" (Arrigo, 1993c, 1996c).

The implications for this provisional Lacanian critique as applied to the NGRI-GBMI options and, more broadly, criminal justice and mental health are profound. Indeed, the significance of this preliminary postmodern analysis raises some question about the nature of punishment and how violence through dominant speech ideologies (Henry & Milovanovic, 1991; Schwartz & Freidrichs, 1994) manifest themselves in justice systems. Recalling Lacan's notion of desire-in-discourse, it follows that disciplinary practices originate in our selection of language. Thus, the voice (i.e., the language) of the disordered defendant is first and foremost linguistically silenced. Put another way, following Lacan, even before the trial/hearing concludes, even before the "crazed" subject-in-law is fully exposed to the cumbersome justice process itself, it would seem that punishment is exhibited in the insidious form of linguistic oppression.

Of course, the same argument could be leveled against the court apparatus in general. Indeed, as others have demonstrated, the psychoanalytic conceptualizations of Lacan provide fruitful analysis relevant to the dynamics of "lawspeak" and courtroom practices for the disenfranchised masses (Milovanovic, 1992a). Thus, investigating the behavior of law and psychiatry relevant to the NGRI-GBMI options may be no more than an important exemplar of previous research in this area—one that establishes a base for testing a multitude of presumably innovative hypotheses. For example, one area of research significant to the psychiatric courtroom and therefore relevant in the context of Lacanian analysis would be any gender, race, age, or class differences among the actors in this setting, influencing the process and the specific language in use. In this chapter, however, the scope is decidedly more narrow. Through the instrumentation of the NGRI-GBMI options, I focus on those linguistic connections, if any, operating between law and psychiatry used to promote forensic justice (i.e., meaning, desire, knowledge) at the expense of the disordered defendant's linguistic reality (i.e., being, alternative desire, replacement knowledge) (Arrigo, 1994b, 1995d, 1996d).

LACAN AND DESIRE-IN-DISCOURSE: RETHINKING KNOWLEDGE AND THE NGRI-GBMI VERDICTS

Lacan's emphasis on desire-in-discourse calls into question the voice of the desiring subject (Milovanovic, 1992b, 1994a, 1995). In the context of the NGRI-GBMI verdicts, we recognize that this voice is saturated with the knowledge or sense-making claims of the clinicolegal establishment (Arrigo, 1993c, 1996b). Accordingly, it follows that in order to understand the construction and operation of the NGRI-GBMI options, some review of the interrelationship between discourse and knowledge, as examined by Lacan, is warranted. The most useful place in which to engage in this enterprise includes an assessment of Lacan's 1969–1970 seminar on the four discourses. In the following sections, I rely heavily on the translations and commentary of several Lacanian followers to advance our understanding of the more relevant components of the four discourses (e.g., Bracher, 1993; Lee, 1990; Melville, 1987; Milovanovic, 1992b, 1993; Ragland-Sullivan, 1986; Salecl, 1988). Along the way, I demonstrate their particular application to the NGRI-GBMI verdicts.

The Four Discourses, the Four Positions, and the Four Factors

Lacan's four discourses include those of the master, university, hysteric, and analyst (Lacan, 1969–1970, 1991). Lacan was interested in explaining how all forms of speech always embody desire and, thus, already convey a uniquely encoded (i.e., circumscribed) knowledge that tends to structure that subsequent discourse in a similar way. For our purposes, I consider the discourses of the master and the hysteric. Lacan's schematization for these two discursive structures can be depicted as follows:

Discourse of the Master	*Discourse of the Hysteric*
S1 → S2	\$ → S1
\$ ← a	a ← S2

For each Lacanian discourse, there are four corresponding critical positions and four factors. Each position locates the communication role that each factor assumes in the respective discourse. The four positions are as follows:

$$\frac{\text{agent}}{\text{truth}} \qquad \frac{\text{other}}{\text{production}}$$

Each factor identifies the elements of Lacanian intersubjective communication. Depending on their arrangement, one of four discourses is produced. The four terms (or factors) are as follows:

S1: the master signifier
S2: knowledge
$: the divided subject
a: *le plus-de-jouir* (that beyond excess)

Before proceeding with an examination of the discourses of the master and the hysteric, and their utility for comprehending clinicolegal knowledge with respect to the NGRI-GBMI verdicts, some summary statements regarding the four positions and the four factors are required. With respect to the four positions, the left-hand structure (agent-truth) is occupied by the sender of the message. It represents what factors (S1, S2, *a*, $) are active or dominant in the person sending a message. The right-hand structure (other-production) is occupied by the receiver of the message. It represents what factors (S1, S2, *a*, $) are activated in or elicited from the person accepting the message. In both structures, the positions above the bar (i.e., agent and other) are the more conscious and overt factors in communication. The positions below the bar (i.e., truth and production) are the more unconscious and covert factors in communication.

Lacan also provides us with information concerning the meaning of the individual positions. The upper-left-hand position (agent) is the place most active when communicating. It is from here that the message is generated. The lower-left-hand position (truth) represents what factor supports, albeit in a hidden way, the generation of the message sent by the agent. The upper-right-hand position (the other) represents the receiver of the message, or alternatively, what is activated in the listener, stemming from the message sent by the agent. The factor occupying this location presupposes a certain receptivity or openness to what is communicated in the message sent by the agent. The lower-right-hand position (production) represents the result following the other's receptiveness to the generation of the message. By this, Lacan means what knowledge or sense has been constructed following the operation of the factors in their specialized positions. Remember that, according to Lacan, depending on the location of the four factors (i.e., S1, S2, *a*, $), a certain discourse is in use (i.e., the discourse of the master, hysteric, university, and analyst).

The four factors also can be briefly explicated. S1 stands for master signifiers. These are foundational, though illusory, ideals (i.e., words or phrases) which symbolize our sense of fulfillment, our sense of identity, our sense of personhood. In law, for example, notable ideals would include "due process," "the reasonable wo/man standard," "equal protection," and "fairness." In democratic societies, such notions as "freedom," "proprietorship," "self-determination," and "equality" may have a similar function. Lacan was to employ the word *jouis-*

sance (that excess which is beyond) to convey the meaning and power such words and phrases convey for us in our daily lives. What makes master signifiers illusory is that they are neither similarly experienced by all people nor are they necessarily representative of everyone's *jouissance*. More on this point will be provided in my review of the master and hysteric discourses as applied to the NGRI-GBMI options.

S2 is the knowledge term. For Lacan, knowledge is always embedded in a battery of signifiers mediated by language. Thus, knowledge is always of a certain type. It is self-referential. Knowledge is generated within a particular language or mode of communication where it finds support. For example, in order to engage in the practice of law and to be effective at it, one simultaneously situates oneself within and is inserted into that discourse defining the linguistic parameters of "good" lawyering; namely, legalese or lawspeak. The same may be said of other systems of communication (e.g., medicine, sports, engineering). Furthermore, Lacan's view of the development of sense-making was unique. Opposed to mathematical knowledge, he pursued a form of mythic knowledge or narrative awareness for individual persons, one more in tune with their unique desire and sense of *jouissance* (Bracher, 1988; Lacan, 1985; Lee, 1990). Thus, some have suggested that Lacan must be read as offering a more descriptive and intuitive construction of knowledge, rather than a prescriptive and scientific understanding of it (Bracher, 1988; Laclau, 1989; Lee, 1990; Milovanovic, 1993).

The subject (or person) in Lacanian psychoanalytic theory is symbolized as $; that is, the slashed, divided, or decentered subject. Lacan (1977) examined the construction of the subject in both static and dynamic forms. For purposes of simplification and introduction, the speaking subject is defined as one who is not in control of speech (i.e., not in control of what one says and how one says it). The "discoursing" person is more the product of unconscious forces at work which regulate the selection of words and phrases one employs to communicate meaning as well as regulating the choice of how those words and phrases will be arranged to form a coherent narrative (Lacan, 1977). Thus, as MacCabe (1979) maintained, the subject when communicating is unstable, decentered, divided. It is this speech, uttered by the subject, which embodies desire; desire which represents a specialized knowledge endorsing a certain manifestation of *jouissance*.

The final factor is the *a*, *le plus-de-jouir*. In Lacanian psychoanalytic semiotics, the *a* has different functions, and he instructed his translators to allow readers to interpret and translate it in context (Milovanovic, 1993). Again, for purposes of simplification and introduction, the *a* is that fulfillment in communication *(jouissance)* which is left out, the *pas tout*, the not-all (Lacan, 1985). In other words, this lack of fulfillment can be traced to the divided subject ($) and what is left out in the articulated exchange between one's master signifiers (S1) and one's knowledge (S2).

On the "Master" Discourse and Clinicolegal Knowledge

We are now ready to examine the discourses of the master and the hysteric. Bracher (1993) has shown how the discipline of philosophy is an illustration of the discourse of the master. Milovanovic (1992b) has demonstrated how law can be seen as an example of the master discourse. Lacan, too, has examined science, arguing that it is an expression of the discourse of the master (1991, 1977). In each of these cases, the manner in which communication unfolds, desire is announced, and knowledge is conceived are similar. I submit that the same can be said of the intersecting categories of criminal justice and mental health (Arrigo, 1994b).

In the "master" discourse, S1, or master signifiers, are in the position of agent. Master signifiers representing the clinicolegal establishment related to the NGRI-GBMI verdicts include such words or phrases as "dangerousness," "diminished capacity," "treatment," "knowingly," "capacity to form criminal intent," "mental disease," and "incompetency." These and other expressions represent a constellation of ideals which receive further crystallization as master signifiers when codified as legislative or case law. These master signifiers, and their ideological content, are the substance of psychiatric courtroom communication. Prosecuting and defense litigators alike speak, know, interact, and represent their respective clients with these key linguistic constructions in mind. They endeavor to arouse or activate certain effects in the receiver of their messages (e.g., judges, jurors).

S2, the knowledge factor, is in the position of the other. The other or receivers of these master signifiers and all that they imply, include the judge, jury, plaintiff, court personnel, other attorneys, witnesses, and the (disordered) defendant. They are the recipients of that discourse uttered by the attorney. Again, counsel communicates through the master signifiers representing the forensic courtroom. Thus, the listener of such discourse receives a certain form of knowledge. This knowledge is circumscribed. It embodies the desire of those master signifiers representing only clinicolegal science or psychiatric justice. Absent from this knowledge are nonmedicolegal constructions.

The *a,* or *pas tout,* is in the position of product. Recall that positions below the bar are more unconscious, covert, and hidden. The fact that only a certain (medicolegal) knowledge has been transmitted to the receiver of the message means that much understanding is missing. Alternative constructions of "the what happened" in the psychiatric courtroom context are repressed. Replacement narratives remain dormant. Indeed, to invoke other master signifiers representing a different manifestation of *jouissance* is to expose them to objection by opposing counsel and to find them declared nonjusticiable by the bench (Arrigo, 1993c, 1996b). Even the activist or rebel attorney, endeavoring to adhere fully to the requests of the disordered defendant must re-present such solicitations so that they are compatible with justiciable dialogue (e.g., Milovanovic, 1996). Again, according to Lacan, something is left out in this process.

The decentered subject, or $, is in the position of truth. In the example above, we see how even the activist attorney, as promulgator of master signifiers and enactor of clinicolegal discourse, might find her or himself unfulfilled. Moreover, we see how the disordered defendant (i.e., the subject-in-law) is divided. Failing to find fulfillment in a battery of master signifiers representing psychiatric justice, the subject's truth, the subject's reality, remains concealed, repressed, silenced. Notwithstanding such denial of being and alternative sense-making, the divided subject, in the position of truth, turns to and supports those master signifiers in law and psychiatry that make possible the continued generation and circulation of those ideals that ultimately fail to encompass the citizen's essential reality. Thus, much like a feedback loop, the cycle continues to perpetuate itself.

On the "Hysteric" Discourse and Replacement Knowledge

In order to appreciate the limitations of clinicolegal knowledge within the intersecting categories of criminal justice and mental health, it is important to consider the discourse of the hysteric. In this formation, the slashed subject is dominant and endeavors to convey his or her despair or suffering to the other. At the same time, the divided subject disidentifies him- or herself from established master signifiers that cannot reflect the hysteric's desire. As the subject is located above the bar, his or her longing is overt, vocal, and dominant.

The hysteric's discourse is most prominent when the prevailing communication (here, medicolegal speech) does not include the parameters that give meaning to the desiring subject's being. In other words, the divided subject, as agent, attempts to locate a master signifier in the other's knowledge, sufficient to satisfy the hysteric's search for personal harmony or potential fulfillment. However, although the other's production of knowledge, promulgated by established (clinicolegal) master signifiers, ostensibly satisfies the agent's longing for personhood and identity, the agent quickly learns that such *jouissance* will not be forthcoming. The result is that the hysteric's truth, as his or her lack or *pas tout*, remains silenced and repressed. Thus, in this discursive structure we see how the *a*, with its *plus-de-jouir* character, is both the source and the product of the agent's desire.

In the psychiatric courtroom, particularly with a determination like the NGRI or GBMI verdict, the discourse of the hysteric is indeed evident. The disordered defendant turns to the court apparatus through her or his legal counsel for representation. The coordinates of the medicolegal sphere are constituted by a battery of master signifiers that are highly specialized and known only to the legally trained or the well-initiated. The subject-in-law, as decentered, is in search of meaning consistent with his or her desire in the plethora of master signifiers promulgated by the grammar of law and psychiatry. The other (here, the advocate), relying on the machinery of the clinicolegal system, attempts to incorporate, to embody, the disordered citizen's *jouissance* in the courtroom process. In this regard, the disordered defendant's quest for personal fulfillment is seemingly realized; after all, the attorney is advancing the client's desire for zealous counsel.

Notwithstanding this initial sense of identity fulfillment, the litigator's representations only minimally incorporate the disordered citizen's longing for stability, meaning, and coherence (i.e., the embodiment of the hysteric's desire). Even when the rebel attorney delivers on the promise that the case will go to court or that the outcome will advance the defendant's interests, the circumscribed knowledge of the other, of law and psychiatry, as uttered by the client's "mouthpiece," fails to embrace the discourse of the mentally ill defendant. The attorney, situated within and being constituted by the clinicolegal apparatus, re-presents the ostensibly unintegrated storytelling of the disordered citizen so that it is compatible with medicolegal jargon. All of the inconsistencies, contradictions, ambiguities, incompletenesses, and the like, are removed, are purged, by the advocate from the "what happened" in the case. However, these may be crucial moments of knowing from the psychiatric citizen's perspective. The result is that the fact-finding process in criminal mental health confinement law is consistent with master signifiers, perpetuating what is understood to be "good" forensic law, "good" psychiatric justice.

In this scripted process, however, an essential feature of the disordered citizen's interiorized reality (being) is conspicuously left out from courtroom consideration. The integrated system of communication symbolizing the clinicolegal apparatus is superimposed on (oppresses) the discourse of the psychiatric citizen. The result is that trial outcomes addressing confinement issues (e.g., the NGRI or GBMI verdict) for the psychiatrically disabled are nothing more than the affirmation of medicolegal science. As Pfohl (1984) argued, assigning meaning to words and phrases such as "mental illness," "dangerousness," "criminal insanity," and the like is simply the privileging and re-affirmation of a well-defined linguistic perspective, a social construction, of medical and legal reality.

DESIRE AND PUNISHMENT: DISCOURSE ON THE NGRI AND GBMI VERDICTS

Following the Lacanian analysis above, we see how the pivotal issue under consideration is not what legal strategies are articulated (e.g., NGRI defense) or what trial outcomes are realized (e.g., GBMI verdict). Rather, the critical matter under review is the territorialization of desire (Deleuze & Guattari, 1987), implicated within the interplay of language, subjectivity and knowledge. This position challenges us to rethink the conceptions of sense-making unconsciously activated by and ideologically anchored within the NGRI and GBMI options, when employed in the psychiatric courtroom.

The suggestion was made that the NGRI and GBMI verdicts are exemplars of how the intersecting categories of criminal justice and mental health behave. As I demonstrated, the operation of law and psychiatry, particularly in their overlapping construction of knowledge, produces a circumscribed (clinicolegal) reality that simultaneously advances its own system of communication while marginalizing all other discourses. This is the presence of linguistic oppression (i.e., symbolic violence or punishment). Medicolegal speech, as the manifestation of Lacan's discourse of the master, denies as justiciable any and all speech which does not advance the knowledge claims of the clinicolegal system. Following the case of *Jones v. U.S.* (1983) and the IDRA of 1984, the most extreme courtroom illustration of this phenomenon is the GBMI option.

The speech coordinates which define the courtroom communication of law and psychiatry represent the interests of order, reasonableness, objectivity, predictability, stasis, and sameness. These coordinates embody that desire which often fails to encompass the discourse symbolizing the disordered defendant's *jouissance*. Indeed, as I have shown elsewhere, and as this book increasingly makes evident, those speech coordinates most compatible with psychiatric citizens include contradiction, ambiguity, inconsistency, incompleteness, incoherency—in short, difference (Arrigo, 1993c, 1996b).

Notwithstanding the disordered defendant's lived and felt difference, according to Lacanian psychoanalytic theory any articulation of it falls below the bar of consciousness in the forensic courtroom. It represents Lacan's *pas tout*, or lack. Disordered defendants can either be psychologically "well" or "ill," as determined by medical knowledge and testimony, and, thus, can be either subjected to institutional confinement (criminal or civil) or altogether released/discharged. The sense-making claims of the NGRI option indicates that a psychiatric citizen is disordered and therefore is not criminally culpable. The sense-making claims of the GBMI verdict indicates that a psychiatric citizen is disordered and, notwithstanding such disability, is criminally responsible. Both clinicolegal constructs privilege a certain way of thinking, feeling, acting, and, ultimately, being that denies or quashes difference, based on ideologically embedded and unconsciously articulated clinicolegal values.

As this chapter has shown, the penalty for mental illness in the psychiatric courtroom is the construction of knowledge that gives voice and legitimacy to certain styles of comportment and ways of being while dismissing all others. It is this knowledge which structures the behavior of law and psychiatry. It is this knowledge, conceived of through clinicolegal discourse and desire, which informs decision making in the forensic courtroom.

To be clear, I am not suggesting that all persons who are "mentally ill" are not capable of "criminal" behavior. What I challenge, however, is the system of communication used to reach this conclusion. In other words, whose subjective system of communication is used to render persons NGRI or GBMI? In the context of such existing determinations, a circumscribed knowledge is used; one which advances only medicolegal discourse and, therefore, only its desire, only its sense of reality. Indeed, despite the growing and widely respected literature advancing an empowerment philosophy for the mentally ill (e.g., see chapter 3), nowhere in the psychiatric courtroom process is there reference to such persons as "consumers of mental health services," "psychiatric citizens," "the differently abled," and so on. Although these expressions may sound odd, perhaps even humorous, such references to them are the very sentiments that dramatically demonstrate the power of language to shape thought, to communicate desire, and to reflect knowledge.

CONCLUSIONS

This chapter broadly explored the intersecting categories of criminal justice and mental health. At issue were the overlapping effects (behavior) of law and psychiatry in the context of the NGRI-GBMI verdicts, as rendered in the psychiatric courtroom. The conceptual backdrop for this investigation focused on several core ideas contained in Lacan's postmodern psychoanalytic theory. Of particular interest was how desire announces itself in speech, yielding a circumscribed knowledge.

As a provisional critique, this chapter found that the NGRI and GBMI options amply demonstrate the joint effects of clinicolegal science. Clinicolegal discourse privileges its own system of communication in the forensic courtroom while simultaneously invalidating any alternative construction. By declaring psychiatric citizens not guilty by reason of insanity or guilty but mentally ill, these adjudicatory outcomes promote meaning at the expense of the defendant's being. This is the presence of oppression (i.e., punishment) as manifested in discourse.

I recognize that some people, despite psychiatric problems, commit criminal acts and need to be held legally accountable. However, before this conclusion can be reached, the imposition of language as a variable influencing, perhaps determining, trial outcomes must categorically be given further attention. In other words, only law and psychiatry, at their intersection, tell us who the criminally culpable and mentally ill are. Only law and psychiatry tell us what these expressions mean. This is circumscribed knowledge. It is incomplete. Thus, Lacan's postmodern psychoanalytic formalizations enable us to understand how the joint effects of medicolegal speech concurrently announce the desire/knowledge of some and quash the desire/knowledge of others. Clinicolegal discourse endures precisely because the voice of the psychiatric citizen is first and foremost silenced. Indeed, the GBMI verdict (i.e., defendants as both "bad" and "mad") is the most vivid example of this phenomenon. Clearly, then, such determinations as these in the psychiatric courtroom are the embodiment of punishment assuming an insidious linguistic form.

SEVEN

Executing the Mentally Ill

On Semiotics and Deconstruction

OVERVIEW. *The previous chapter argued that ideological forces underpin the criminal confinement process in the psychiatric courtroom. These forces are unconsciously constructed and linguistically coordinated to embody the voice of and way of knowing for legal and psychiatric decision brokers. As a consequence, the policing of public hygiene entails the corralling of speech, thought, and desire, consistent with the parameters of meaning representing psychiatric justice. The penalty for mental illness is the silencing of difference: the sense-making claims of mental health consumers and the deeply felt desire that breathes meaning into such utterances are pathologized, sanitized, delegitimized, or any combination of these.*

While the previous chapter explained several psychosemiotic dynamics at work (e.g., desire-in-discourse) giving rise to the behavior of law and psychiatry in the forensic courtroom, no detailed application study was presented. Relatedly, while Lacanian postmodern psychoanalytic theory was useful for exposing the manner in which language and subjectivity interdependently function to establish circumscribed clinicolegal knowledge, no systematic assessment of how these forces concretely operate was provided. This chapter addresses both of these matters.

As an ongoing clinicolegal practice, the silencing of psychiatric difference is perhaps no more disturbing than when a decision is made to restore an individual to mental competency for purposes of execution, notwithstanding the person's objection to it. Indeed, one's right to refuse treatment and one's competency to make such decisions while a death row prisoner are significantly called into question with this criminal confinement controversy. What is the state of the federal constitutional law on executing the mentally ill? How do legal deconstructionist principles and other semiotic insights inform our understanding of competency determinations and treatment refusal rights for mentally disordered death row prisoners? In what way are these matters relevant to this critical investigation of law, psychiatry, and punishment? If, as we discovered in chapter 6, the policing of mental illness always and already occurs through the overlapping effects of language and subjectivity producing circumscribed knowledge, then how can the practice of competency restoration for purposes of execution ever ensure the mentally disordered death row prisoner any semblance of due process? These are complicated matters that invite us to rethink the fundamental values of clinicolegal decision making and logic. These are vexing matters that challenge us to reconsider criminal confinement practices altogether. These are disturbing matters that draw our attention to those punitive forces at work in psychiatric justice, even when confronted with a person's imminent death.

INTRODUCTION

The behavioral and social sciences have recently reexamined competency to be executed decisions, especially in the context of their implications for mental health law and policy in general (Winick, 1997a) and psychiatrically disordered death row prisoners in particular (Arrigo & Tasca 1999; Winick, 1992). The essential debate focuses on those conditions wherein the state may, without abridging an inmate's constitutionally protected liberty interests, terminate the life of a citizen awaiting execution (Arrigo & Tasca, 1999, p. 319).[1] This is an extremely contentious matters and, as a result, the debate remains mostly unresolved by the United States Supreme Court. For example, questions persist as to whether the execution of a convicted mentally ill offender is, under particular circumstances, in the best interest of the state and, thus, society,[2] or whether it is the quintessential expression of judicially sponsored inhumanity (Abu-Jamal, 1995; Bedau, 1984, 1987; Dicks, 1990; Johnson, 1998).

Although doctrinal legal analyses and classical legal reasoning are useful approaches by which to assess this question, other more nontraditional methods of legal inquiry can provide compelling insight into the implicit social forces that influence the courts and the legislature (Arrigo, 1993c), as well as the unconscious clinicolegal processes that underscore psychiatric justice (Arrigo, 1996b). One way to investigate whether the execution of mentally disordered offenders serves the interests of society or advances legal harm comes from discourse analysis. The pivotal feature of discourse analysis is that all language *is* method (Arrigo, 1995b),[3] and that hidden assumptions and implicit values within a text (e.g., a state statute, an appellate transcript, a legal brief) can be deciphered, much like a coded message. Indeed, discourse analysis reveals something more or something other about the unconscious intent of the text, its author, or both. This additive feature in not detectable through standard legal accounts (Arrigo, 1993c, pp. 128–140).

Thus, it is through this discursive method of critical inquiry that the ideology embedded in the law, often concealed through and masked by a myriad of holdings, *stare decisis*, dicta, and the like, becomes increasingly transparent (see, e.g., Kairys, 1982; Tushnet, 1986; Unger, 1986; Hunt, 1986; Altman, 1990; Balkin, 1987). For purposes of this chapter, then, discourse analysis is helpful in that the language of confinement law is placed "under the microscope." The central issue considered is as follows: what does the United States Supreme Court "really" intend when, in certain instances, endorsing the execution of incompetent mentally ill prisoners on death row who invoke a right to refuse treatment? Put another way, what values, assumptions, and meanings are privileged through the legally sanctioned act of capital punishment for psychiatrically disordered offenders?

It is important to note that unlike the previous chapter's assessment of ideology in the psychiatric courtroom, this chapter directly examines the *spoken word* and the meaning(s) contained within the operative clinicolegal language on execution for those mentally ill citizens who refuse medical treatment, impacting prospects for competency restoration. In other words, the Lacanian critique of chapter 6 investigated the unconscious dynamics at work (e.g., desire-in-discourse), giving rise to circumscribed knowledge. An obvious extension of this critique is to examine actual speech production at the crossroads of law and psychiatry. Accordingly, the discourse analysis approach of this chapter micrologically explores selected words/phrases employed by the U.S. Supreme Court in regard to incompetent mentally disordered offenders who, in the face of imminent death, exercise their treatment refusal rights.

To focus the investigation, I offer a standard, though brief, assessment of the precedent-setting mental health case law on the execution of psychiatrically disordered convicts. This commentary considers the evolution of related issues such as the mentally ill prisoner's right to refuse drug treatment and the conditions under which a finding of incompetency does or does not mitigate capital punishment. I then provide a detailed overview of two methods for engaging in discourse analysis: structural semiotics and deconstructionism. These are not the only two approaches representing discourse analysis but, as I contend, each provides unique insight into the unconscious intent of the Court, consistent with Lacanian psychoanalysis as previously developed. The overview lays the necessary theoretical foundation for the application that follows it. Next, I consider how discourse analysis, based on principles found in structural legal semiotics and legal deconstructionism, furthers our understanding of the United States Supreme Court's more covert meaning when sustaining capital punishment for incompetent mentally ill offenders on death row. In this context, I specifically consider the words "incompetency" and "treatment" as linguistic artifacts (i.e., coded messages) that signify implicit values and hidden assumptions for the Court regarding mentally ill and disordered death row inmates. I conclude by speculating on the implications of this analysis in relation to the social control thesis, and for the execution of psychiatrically disordered offenders.

EXECUTING THE MENTALLY ILL: LEGAL ANALYSIS

Mental Illness and Capital Offenders

A substantial number of incarcerated individuals suffer from mental illness in one form or another (see e.g., Steadman et al., 1989, pp. 3–87; Alexander, 1992, pp. 119, 122; Lamb & Weinberger, 1998, pp. 483–492; Wettstein, 1998; Ogloff et al., 1994, p. 109; Metzner, 1998, pp. 107–115). Thus, it is not surprising that mental illness is a significant factor affecting the legal system's response to serious crimes whose punishment can and does amount to a death sentence (Arrigo & Tasca, 1999, p. 17; Shultz-Ross, 1993, pp. 426–428; Cohen, 1992, pp. 339–346; Liebman & Leibman, 1991, pp. 19–20). In this section, I am interested in whether an individual's mental illness effects, under the law, his or her future as a death row prisoner. This concern draws specific attention to the matter of one's psychological competency and legal right to treatment refusal (Arrigo & Tasca, 1999). Indeed, outside of competency to be executed determinations, death row prisoners have little opportunity of forestalling the inevitable execution that awaits them (see e.g., *Nebraska Press Association v. Stuart*, 1976; *Gannett Co. v. DePasquale*, 1979; *Press-Enterprise Co. v. Superior Court*, 1986; *Powell v. Alabama*, 1932; *Gideon v. Wainwright*, 1963; *Argersinger v. Hamlin*, 1972; *State v. Perry*, 1992; see also, Winick, 1997a, 299–300). Thus, the situation for the mentally disordered offender on death row is quite profound. The prevalence of psychiatric illness that predated sentencing and imprisonment, the exacerbating conditions of incarceration and impending execution, and the legal assertion of incompetency to be executed as a "last chance" for circumventing capital punishment, represent a complex clustering of variables significantly impacting the life or death of criminally confined individuals (Johnson, 1998, pp. 70–71; Heilbrun et al., 1992, pp. 596–597).[4]

The Case of *Ford v. Wainwright*

The 1986 case of *Ford v. Wainwright* addressed whether the Eighth Amendment's prohibition on "cruel and unusual punishment" applied to the involuntary administration of mental health treatment for patients and offenders (Winick, 1997, p. 223; *Estelle v. Gamble*, 1976; *Robinson v. California*, 1962, pp. 401–402). The critical question examined in the *Ford* (1986) case was whether "intrusive treatment administered essentially for reasons of punishment (to enable a state to carry out a death penalty) would offend contemporary standards of cruel and unusual punishment in violation of the Eighth Amendment" (*Ford v. Wainwright*, 1986, p. 408; Winick, 1997, p. 299). In the *Ford* (1986) case, the administration of medical treatment (drug therapy) gave rise to his competency to be executed. Thus, the Court considered whether said treatment amounted to "medical punishment" (see e.g., *Bee v. Greaves*, 1984; see also *Nelson v. Heyne*, 1974; *Mackey v. Procunier*, 1973).[5]

In response to this matter, the Court recognized the "ancestral legacy" of prohibiting the execution of the mentally ill, noting its historical regard as "savage and inhuman" (*Ford v. Wainwright*, 1986, p. 406). To support this contention, the Court cited Blackstone, and the English common law roots of stay of execution for the insane:

> Idiots and lunatics are not chargeable for their own acts, if committed when under these incapacities. . . . Also, if a man in his sound memory commits a capital offence, and before arraignment for it, he becomes mad, he ought not be arraigned for it: because he is not able to plead to it with that advice and caution that he ought. And if, after he has pleaded, the prisoner becomes mad, he shall not be tried: for how can he make his defence? If, after he be tried and found guilty, he loses his sense before judgement, judgement shall not be pronounced; *and if, after judgement, he becomes of nonsane memory, execution shall be stayed: for peradventure, says the humanity of the English law, had the prisoner been of sound memory, he might have alleged something in stay of judgement or execution* (emphasis added). (*Ford v. Wainright*, 1986, pp. 406–407; Blackstone, 1783, pp. 24–25).

While stay of execution for the incompetent death row prisoner had been generally practiced as common law prior to the *Ford* (1986) decision, the Court reaffirmed this notion in regard to medical treatment of a prisoner awaiting execution. As the Court explained:

> the various reasons put forth in support of the common-law restriction have no less logical, moral, and practical force than they did when first voiced. For today, no less than before, we may seriously question the retributive value of executing a person who has no comprehension of why he has been singled out and stripped of his fundamental right to life (*Ford v. Wainwright*, 1986, p. 405).

Thus, *Ford* (1986) was the first case in which the United States Supreme Court held that a prisoner had constitutional safeguards prohibiting execution while the person remained incompetent (Winick, 1992, pp. 319–321). Indeed, the Court concluded that the Eighth Amendment prohibits a state from carrying out a sentence of death on a prisoner who is insane (Winick, 1992, pp. 319–321; Appelbaum, 1986, pp. 682–684; Miller, 1988, pp. 67–90; Wallace, 1987, pp. 265–281; Ewing, 1987, pp. 175–185). This prohibition against executing an incompetent prisoner has since been adopted by the majority of states (Winick, 1997a, pp. 299–300; see, e.g., *Gregg v. Georgia*, 1976; *Proffit v. Florida*, 1976; *Ford v. Wainwright*, 1986, pp. 417–417).[6]

While *Ford* (1986) addressed the larger issue of protecting the Eighth Amendment rights of an incompetent death row prisoner who refused medical intervention, it fell short of offering viable standards for determining competency (Winick, 1997a, p. 349, 1995, pp. 30–33; Appelbaum, 1995, pp. 111–118). Moreover, the U.S.

Supreme Court in *Ford* (1986) did not consider the more complex question of whether a state could *coercively* treat a psychiatrically disordered death row inmate for purposes of competency restoration and eventual execution. In addition, it did not determine whether medical intervention and antipsychotic drug therapy were necessary in those cases where an incompetent prisoner, who refused treatment, was found to be dangerous to other inmates and correctional staff. This latter issue was squarely addressed in the case of *Washington v. Harper* (1990).[7]

The Case of *Washington v. Harper*

Harper (1990) is the watershed decision on the matter of treatment refusal for prisoners suffering from mental illness (Winick, 1997a, p. 3; see, e.g., *Mills v. Rogers*, 1982; *In re Guardianship of Roe*, 1981; *Rogers v. Commissioner*, 1983; *Rogers v. Okin*, 1984). The primary issue before the United States Supreme Court was whether the involuntary administration of medical treatment for a psychiatrically ill and dangerous prisoner violated the prohibition on cruel and unusual punishment guaranteed under the Eighth Amendment.[8] Further, the Court considered whether respondent *Harper* (1990) possessed a "significant liberty interest" in "resisting such unwanted treatment" (*Washington v. Harper*, 1990). The Court found that the police powers of the state to forcibly medicate outweighed the prisoner's constitutionally protected liberty interest from such intrusiveness, *provided* the administered treatment was necessary to "maintain . . . the security of the prison" (Winick, 1997a, p. 3; Arrigo & Tasca, 1999, p. 27), and was in the convict's medical interest (*Washington v. Harper*, 1990, p. 226). This concern for institutional security extended to the safety of correctional personnel, as well as other prisoners (1990, p. 227, p. 248 n. 18).

The significance of the *Harper* (1990) decision cannot be underestimated. For the first time, the United States Supreme Court made expressly clear that the state has a compelling and superseding interest in controlling and treating mentally ill prisoners who resisted drug therapy. The decision in *Harper* (1990) is consistent with prior and related rulings in which the Supreme Court demonstrated a preference for institutional policy, extending considerable deference to such facilities as legitimate agents of the state (see e.g., *Youngberg v. Romeo*, 1982; *Parham v. J.R.*, 1979; see also Arrigo, 1992b, p. 23). Further, *Harper* (1990) endeavored to balance treatment needs against liberty demands within a prison context, suggesting that the incompetency of the inmate expressed through an implied or actual risk of danger was the most dispositive on the issue of forced medication.

Consistent with the holding in *Ford* (1986), *Harper* (1990) examined what was in the best interest of the prisoner in relation to the state (i.e., the correctional facility, its constituency groups, and society in general). Where the *Ford* (1986) case found unconstitutional the execution of an incompetent death row inmate without further, though unspecified, justification, *Harper* (1990) determined that unwanted medical intervention for mentally disordered offenders was similarly unconstitutional, *unless* compelling state interests could be articulated. The Court concluded in *Harper* (1990) that when a prisoner poses a dangerous threat to others in the correctional facility and when the convict's treatment is in his or her best medical interest, then coercive intervention is constitutionally permissible. Left unresolved, however, was whether the logic of *Ford* (1986) and *Harper* (1990) applied equally to incompetent death row inmates who invoked their right to refuse treatment. This matter was addressed in *Perry v. Louisiana* (1990).

The Case of *Perry v. Louisiana*

The case of *Perry v. Louisiana* (1990) is significant for purposes of scrutinizing and ascertaining the government's interests in requiring that the psychiatric intervention forcibly administered to incompetent prisoners be medically appropriate (Winick, 1997a, pp. 272–273). In other words, the *Harper* (1990) decision did not address the full context in which a right to refuse drug therapy could be successfully asserted within the correctional milieu, although it seemed to imply it. In *Perry* (1990), the particular correctional context was death row. At issue was whether an incompetent mentally ill offender enjoyed the right to refuse drug treatment, as secured under the 8th and 14th Amendments, when said treatment was administered for purposes of competency restoration and execution (Winick, 1997, p. 273).[9]

Although the Court granted *certiorari* to hear the constitutional question raised by *Perry* (1990), resolution of the matter was avoided following oral arguments, given the intervening decision in *Washington v. Harper* (1990) (see also Winick, 1997a, p. 299). Thus, the case was remanded to the Louisiana State Supreme Court. Relying on the *Harper* (1990) ruling, the Louisiana Supreme Court found that an incompetent death row prisoner could not be forcibly medicated for the *primary* purpose of restoring competency for execution (Arrigo & Tasca, 1999, pp. 23–26; Winick, 1992, pp. 328–232). Indeed, the Court argued that *Perry* (1990) was distinguishable from *Harper* (1990) in that coercive medication of the inmate awaiting execution neither improved prison safety and staff welfare nor served the best medical interest of the psychiatrically disordered offender (*State v. Perry*, 1990, pp. 751–752). Thus, while *Harper* (1990) acknowledged coercive treatment for incompetent prisoners under constitutionally legitimate and clearly specified conditions, *Perry* 1990 essentially limited such intrusiveness (*State v. Perry*, 1990, p. 747).

We note, however, that the *Harper* (1990) versus *Perry* (1990) distinction does not reflect substantial difference in approach to treatment, competency, and execution issues regarding the mentally ill as originally developed in *Ford* (1986). Instead, there is a more consistent line of legal thought at work with theses three cases. Indeed, the holding in *Perry* (1990) merely *limits* the scope of execution for incompetent death row offenders who invoke their treatment refusal rights. In other words, the applicability of *Perry* (1990) only extends to those cases in which the state admits its purpose: medicate to execute. Under these conditions, treatment administered for the sole purpose of competency restoration and execution is medical punishment, ostensibly prohibited under the Federal constitution (Winick, 1997a, p. 300, 1992, p. 330; see also, *State v. Perry*, 1990). Forcibly injecting dangerous mind-altering drugs into a prisoner, in order to make a death row convict competent, circumvents the holding in *Ford* (1986). Interestingly, though, this does not guarantee that mentally ill prisoners awaiting execution and asserting a right to refuse treatment would, in all instances, be protected from capital punishment, despite 8th and 14th Amendment safeguards. Indeed, consistent with the holding in *Harper* (1990), to the extent that one presented a dangerous risk to other prisoners, to correctional staff, and to oneself, forced drug therapy could be constitutionally ordered. This result could follow, notwithstanding an inmate's liberty interest in refusing involuntary psychiatric treatment and in avoiding medical punishment. This weighty matter has yet to be addressed by the U.S. Supreme Court.

While the decisions in *Ford* (1986), *Harper* (1990), and *Perry* (1990) collectively represent the state of the constitutional law on treatment refusal for (in)competent inmates, they provide a somewhat uncertain legal standard regarding the execution of mentally ill offenders. This uncertainty is directly linked not only to whether the U.S. Supreme Court would concur with Louisiana's decision in *Perry* (1990), but whether it would, consistent with *Harper* (1990), forcibly treat violent and aggressive death row prisoners suffering from a mental disorder. In the latter instance, while the convict would no longer pose a risk of danger to self or others, his or her renewed competency would give rise to execution in contravention of the prisoner's right to refuse unwanted medication (Winick, 1992, pp. 319–321; Appelbaum, 1986, pp. 682–684; Miller, 1988, pp. 67–90; Wallace, 1987, pp. 265–281; Ewing, 1987, pp. 175–185).[10] I contend that answering these matters is, in part, related to how the United States Supreme Court understands the meaning of competency and treatment in relation to the psychiatrically ill offender and the death row prisoner. In order to assist the Court in evaluating its implicit assumptions and hidden values on these important issues, I rely on several insights contained in critical legal theory and discourse analysis.

THEORETICAL DEVELOPMENTS: ON STRUCTURAL LEGAL SEMIOTICS AND LEGAL DECONSTRUCTIONISM

Semiotics, Structuralism, and Structural Legal Semiotics

Critical theory building in law has developed considerably during the past two decades, and its growth has been particularly appreciable in the area of discourse analysis (see Milovanovic, 1994b, pp. 141–184). One expression of discourse analysis is semiotics (see, e.g., Sebeok, 1986; Saussure, 1966; Whorf, 1967; Rossi-Landi, 1977; Peirce, 1956, 1965; Eco, 1979; for applications in law and psychiatry see, Arrigo, 1993c, pp. 135–140, 1996b, pp. 151–174, 203–204).[11] Semiotics contains a variety of forms as developed and applied in the legal sphere (see e.g, Tiefenbrun, 1986; Kevelson, 1987, 1988, 1990; Jackson, 1991; Milovanovic, 1992, 1997a; Caudill, 1997). The particular brand of legal semiotics to which I draw attention is the *structural* form (DeGeorge & DeGeorge, 1972; Hawkes, 1977; Sturrock, 1979; Berman, 1988).

The term *structure* derives from the Latin *struere* which means "to build" or "to contrive." Structuralism, then, denotes the act or process of building, and structural semiotics refers to the search for identifiable *foundations* embedded in all language systems (Greimas, 1990, pp. 3–10). Structuralism is based, in part, on the linguistic work of Ferdinand de Saussure (1966). It also draws from Russian formalism and literary criticism inspired by Roman Jakobson, the anthropology of Claude Lévi-Strauss, and the narrative analyses of Roland Barthes and Algirdas Greimas (Berman, 1988, pp. 114–222; see also Tiefenbrun, 1986, pp. 113–147; Ogden & Richards, 1926; Culler, 1981; Arnaud, 1973).

The search for essential stabilities, underlying truths, and fundamental "laws" of human existence are found, for example, in the 19th- and 20th-century structuralist accounts of the mind (Freud, 1927), of culture (Lévi-Strauss, 1962), and of society (Marx, 1967). According to the structuralist tradition, every object of inquiry must necessarily be conceived as a structure or as a whole (e.g., Sartre, 1956; Kaufmann, 1956; Heidegger, 1958; Marcel, 1950/1951).[12] This wholeness was a search for order within the cosmos. As Barthes (1964) explains, "[the] aim of all structuralist activity, in the fields of both thought and poetry, is to reconstitute an object, and, by this process, to make known the rules of functioning, or "functions," of this object. Th[is] structure . . . brings out something that remained invisible, or, if you like, unintelligible in the natural object" (p. 213). Thus, this sense of completeness gives order to an otherwise fragmented and uncertain future (Barthes, 1964). The subject, and all of our unsubstantiated claims to autonomy, efficacy, causality, are supplanted by scientific rigor, totalizing truths, objectivist knowledge (Best & Kellner, 1991, p. 19).[13]

As previously noted, structuralism extensively employs Saussure's linguistic model. Thus, language is an essential determinant of structure. Structuralists maintain that language shapes the world, and the world, in turn, is known and determined by the nonreferential language system in use (Lévi-Strauss, 1963; Althusser, 1971): it is a closed system of communication. Language, understood semiotically, then, implies that it is possible to uncover the structural meanings (hidden values or implicit assumptions) conveyed in a system of communication. Law is one example of such a coordinated language system (Milovanovic, 1986, pp. 285–296, 1988, pp. 455–475), and the intersection of law and psychiatry (i.e., medicolegal discourse) is a more specialized variation of it (Arrigo, 1993c, pp. 135–140, 1996b, pp. 47–93). Given this appreciation for semiotics and structuralism, I therefore note that structural legal semiotics is the study of legal language, understood to be a collection of "signs" (Sartre, 1956; Kaufmann, 1956; Heidegger, 1958; Marcel, 1950/1951; Jackson, 1991; Best & Kellner, 1991, p. 19; see also Saussure, 1966, pp. 120–22).[14] The two particular medicolegal signs investigated is this chapter include "treatment" and "competency."

The model of structural legal semiotics I appropriate is borrowed from Bernard Jackson (1985, 1991, 1995). His model utilizes the "semiotic square" (Greimas, 1987, 1990, pp. 108–114) or the semiotic grid that is designed to tell us more about the process of meaning creation and the various interpretations that attach to the grouping of words/phrases specifically selected to convey our thoughts (Jackson, 1985, pp. 104–163, 1995, pp. 74–110, 117; Milovanovic, 1994, pp. 114–118). As applied to law, his schema is referred to as the narrative coherence model (Jackson, 1985, p. 93). This model allows one to uncover the "underlying, non-verbalized narrative (deep) structure" cloaked by the superficial structure of legal discourse and decision making (Milovanovic, 1994, pp. 117–118). This deeper level of signification reveals an "unconscious rationality which transmits cultural values and which is expressed in cultural products [e.g., U.S. Supreme Court rulings], albeit in an often transformed manner" (Jackson, 1995, p. 93). Methodologically, then, the semiotic square is helpful to legal inquiry in that it allows one to chart and lay out some of the discernible, though concealed, meanings lodged in the more formalistic language of law (Arrigo, 1997d, pp. 197–198). Thus, as a research tool, the grid permits one to discover, in a novel and creative way, something more about the unconscious intent behind what jurists say and what they mean.

As Diagram 7.1 indicates, the semiotic square is fashioned around binary oppositions and the interplay of meaning at work in these relationships. These include contraries (strong oppositions) and contradictions (clear negations). Examples of binary oppositions that are contraries include "day versus night," "right versus wrong," "healthy versus ill," "good versus bad." Examples of binary oppositions that are contradictions include "not day versus not night," "not right versus not wrong," not healthy versus not ill," "not good versus not bad." By

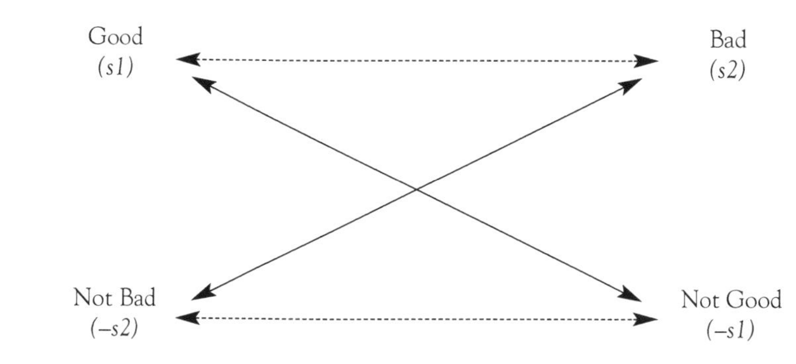

DIAGRAM 7.1. Semiotic Square

indicating the dominant term in the binary opposition (e.g., "day," "right," "healthy," and "good"), the negations are immediately implied ("not day," "not right," "not healthy," and "not good").

There is a built-in logic to this structural model of legal analysis demonstrating the subtlety of language and producing coherence in thought where semantical differences are examined closely for what they communicate (Arrigo, 1997d, p. 198). To illustrate, the term *not good* includes something other than bad (e.g., problematic, difficult, troubling), and the term *not bad* includes something other than good (e.g., marginally acceptable, satisfactory, okay). Operationally, the semiotic square is designed in such a way that the identification of one term in the grid makes possible the discovery of the other three terms, given the function of contraries and contradictions (Jackson, 1985, p. 77).

In a subsequent section of this chapter, I rely on the logic of the semiotic square, as the method for conducting structural legal semiotic analysis, to discover the deeper, unconscious meanings for the signs "treatment" and "competency." I contend that this particular form of legal inquiry tells us more about the U.S. Supreme Court's understanding of psychiatrically disordered prisoners and their death row executions. However, before commencing with this process, let us consider how the theory of legal deconstructionism can also assist in our overall evaluative task.

Post-Structuralism, Deconstruction, and Legal Deconstructionism

Poststructuralism emerged as a critical rebuttal of the structuralist assumptions regarding mind, culture, and society (Best & Kellner, 1991, p. 20; Berman,

1988, pp. 199–200). Where the aims of structuralism included a search for foundational truths, absolute certainty, objectivist knowledge, and systemic wholeness (Best & Kellner, 1991, pp. 51–52), poststructuralism waged "war" on all totalizing forms of reason, logic, and rationality" (Arrigo, 1995b, p. 450; Best & Kellner, 1991, pp. 20–21). Poststructuralists alleged that such structures were illusions of science and contrivances of politics because of the intervening variable of language. Unlike the structuralists who advocated the importance of discourse within narrowly confined parameters of meaning (i.e., the code of speech in use as nonreferential), poststructuralists celebrated the essential undecidability of meaning inherent in what we say or in what we write (Derrida, 1973).[15]

One explanation for the convictions of poststructuralist thought is contained in the deconstructionist work of Jacques Derrida (1973, 1976, 1981, 1982; see also Landau, 1993, pp. 1895–1909). Derrida offers a substantial critique of Western philosophy and thought he terms the "metaphysics of presence" (Balkin 1987, pp. 746–751; Culler, 1982). The metaphysics of presence is an effort to expose hierarchical oppositions implied or embedded in words or phrases used to convey meaning (Balkin 1987, pp. 746–751). Examples of hierarchical oppositions include "objective/subjective," "real/appearance," "straight/gay," "positive/negative," "normal/abnormal." In each instance, the former term is valued and privileged as presence, while the corresponding latter term is devalued and relegated as absence (Milovanovic, 1994, p. 101). These value positions are troubling because they connote certain shared and unstated beliefs in the primacy of the first term *over and against* the second one (Balkin, 1987, p. 747–748; Derrida, 1976, p. 3). Potentially, this is extremely problematic, particularly in relation to what gets defined as acceptable forms of human social interaction, appropriate modes of sense making, and customary ways of being. Ultimately, this can lead to the "privileging of certain *ideas* over others" (Balkin, 1987, p. 746–751; Arrigo, 1999a).

Deconstruction[16] then, can expose the biases or preferences contained within the simplest of notions (i.e., hierarchical oppositions) (Best & Kellner, 1991, p. 229; Berman, 1988, p. 204–208; Fuchs & Ward, 1994, pp. 483, 486–488). This is not to imply that deconstructionism functions as a totalizing proscription for social change. It merely reveals and decenters, although incompletely and temporarily, how legal arguments often disguise ideological positions.[17] Derrida's insights are important to this chapter's purpose because several of his major philosophical tenets direct our attention to the unconscious intent of the U.S. Supreme Court on such matters as treatment refusal for incompetent mentally ill prisoners awaiting execution. In order to demonstrate where and how legal deconstructionism is useful in this regard, I briefly review three Derridean concepts. These three concepts include: (1) the reversal of hierarchies; (2) *differance* and trace; and (3) arguments that undo themselves.

Reversal of hierarchies. By inverting privileged value positions, Derrida does not intend that one create new and permanent power relations. The logic of reversal is simply to ascertain what additional insights might be contained in the value positions and their newly articulated or scripted arrangement, once having switched them (Balkin, 1987, pp. 746–751). In addition, however, this deconstructive activity is quite revealing because it shows how *mutually interdependent* the two value positions are. Consider, for example, the term *sanity* as used in the mental health criminal and civil law context (see e.g., Reisner & Slobogin, 1997). Deconstructionists argue that, in the first instance, *insanity* is a derivative concept based on the other value or term. Thus, we have a binary opposition. On closer inspection, however, we note that the sanity of person "A" depends on the insanity of person "B" and vice versa. The meanings we assign to one are dependent on the meanings we assign to the other. What we thought was the privileged value (i.e., sanity) is itself dependent on the concept it was privileged over (i.e., insanity). Thus, not only is neither term foundational, but both mutually rely on each other to express thought and action. This leads us to ponder what replacement forms of logic would present themselves if the hierarchical arrangement was indeed reversed.

Differance and the trace. The concept of mutual interdependence, given the two terms in a binary opposition, is important to Derrida's notion of *differance* (with an "*a*"). The use of the word *differance* intends always and already three separate but related meanings (Derrida, 1981, pp. 39–40, 1982, p. 3). As Balkin (1987) describes it,

> *Differance* simultaneously indicates that (1) the terms of an oppositional hierarchy are differentiated from each other (which is what determines them); (2) each term in the hierarchy defers the other (in the sense of making the other term wait for the first term); and (3) each term in the hierarchy defers *to* the other (in the sense of being fundamentally dependent upon the other. (p. 752)

Let us return to our example of "sanity versus insanity" for further explication. *Differance* signals how the two value positions are different, how, given the metaphysics of presence and absence, the spoken or written term postpones, suspends, or represses the other, and how both values are mutually interdependent on one another for their identities (Arrigo, 1999a; Milovanovic, 1994, p. 101). Again, the play of differences and dependencies described here operate simultaneously.

Differance, however, is significant to the deconstructionist agenda for a related reason. Derrida's idea of trace implies that the two values in the binary opposition rely for their clarity and cohesion on the differentiation between them (Balkin, 1987, p. 752). In other words, each term (i.e., "sanity" and "insanity") contains the vestige of the other within it, and it is this lingering trace which anchors *differance* making the deconstruction of hierarchical oppositions possible (Derrida, 1976, pp. 46–47; Milovanovic, 1994, pp. 101–102).[18] The task of a legal deconstructionist analysis, then, is to identify the play of differences and the mutual interdependencies between terms in a hierarchical opposition, as a way of demonstrating the positional, relational, and provisional nature of all phenomena. I note, too, that the concepts of *differance* and trace are not *essentialist* terms in Derrida's epistemology. This thinking is antithetical to the deconstructionist project. Indeed, as Rorty (1978, p. 153) contends, such notions cannot be "divinized." Instead, '*differance*' and trace fleetingly capture the "foundationless, provisional . . . , or reversibl(e)" nature of meaning in human affairs (Balkin, 1987, p. 752).

Arguments that undo themselves. Inverting hierarchies in binary oppositions can be quite illuminating. One of the things this activity can point to is that the arguments supporting the privileging of the dominant term may be the reasons for endorsing the other value. There is a logic of justification that is undone or ungrounded through this deconstructive agenda (Derrida, 1976, pp. 30–44).[19]

Consider, for example, the values assigned to being mentally healthy versus being mentally ill (e.g., Arrigo, 1993c, 1996b; Foucault, 1965, 1976; Scheff, 1984; Warren, 1982; Szasz, 1963, 1987). The logic of psychological health implies that one behaves appropriately, thinks rationally, speaks coherently, feels naturally, lives ordinarily, and simply *is* normally. There is a certain predictability, routinization, control, homogeneity, and order implied in this model; however, some degree of deviation is availed to all individuals. Interestingly, we endorse appreciable departures from psychological health, even some forms of extreme dysfunction, *provided* the pathology produces meaningful results. The elite athlete who engages in intense physical training in order to play better, run faster, jump higher is not diagnosed with an obsessive-compulsive disorder. The actor or model who carefully monitors all caloric intake in order to maintain the fashionable waifish image portrayed on film or in print is not diagnosed with acute anorexia nervosa. The artist who paints hauntingly surreal images in order to convey the shocking and astonishing conditions of our times is not diagnosed with paranoid schizophrenia. The musician who suffers through atypical sleeping patterns in order to craft beautiful and deeply personal love ballads is not diagnosed with depression.

Each of these examples is an argument that undoes the dominant value position of being mentally healthy. In addition, each illustration demonstrates how psychological wellness (i.e., optimal success at sports, entertainment, art, and music) is really a kind of mental illness. And, finally, each instance shows how the limitations of psychological illness also represent the inadequacies of emotional wellness.[20]

EXECUTING THE INCOMPETENT DEATH ROW PRISONER: CONTRIBUTIONS FROM STRUCTURAL LEGAL SEMIOTICS AND LEGAL DECONSTRUCTIONISM

The previous section identified two nontraditional models of legal inquiry. I contend that both structural legal semiotics and legal deconstructionism, as distinct methods for engaging in discourse analysis, inform our prior case law assessment of treatment refusal for mentally disordered prisoners awaiting execution. In order to demonstrate the utility of each model's analytical tools, I first present an assessment of the signs "treatment" and "competency" from a structural legal semiotic perspective. I then examine these signs from the standpoint of legal deconstructionism.

Structural Legal Semiotics and the Sign of Treatment

Diagram 7.2 provides a structural representation of the sign "treatment." The four corners of the semiotic grid are mapped out on the basis of binary oppositions, consistent with the model's emphasis on contraries and contradictions. The *s1* term is *receiving treatment*. Its opposite value (the *s2* term) is *refusing treatment*. The negation of refusing treatment is "not refusing treatment." This is the *-s2* value. The negation of receiving treatment is "not receiving treatment." This is the *-s1* term.

I also note that Diagram 7.2 includes the semantical relationships generated from the contraries and contradictions. The sum of these various associations constitutes the deep structure of meaning (Jackson, 1985, pp. 102, 86–99; Milovanovic, 1994a, pp. 115–117)[21] at work in the U.S. Supreme Court's evaluation of treatment refusal for mentally disordered prisoners on death row. The individual relationships formed by the interplay of particular binary terms are also revealing. They tell us more about the Court's preference for certain juridical meanings at the expense of certain others. Thus, we are able to comment on those hidden assumptions and implicit values endorsed by the U.S. Supreme Court and those that are not.

In the analysis that follows, I begin with the more obvious associations and move on to those that are less conspicuous. The connection between "receiving treatment" and "refusing treatment" is receiving *coerced treatment*. In this relationship we understand that the effect of resisting that which one would otherwise receive can only produce some form of unwanted, though forced, intervention. The right to forcibly medicate mentally disordered prisoners was precisely the constitutional question at issue in the *Harper* (1990) case (Winick, 1997a, p. 3; Arrigo & Tasca, 1999, p. 27; see also, e.g., *Mills v. Rogers*, 1982; *In re Guardianship of Roe*, 1981; *Rogers v. Commissioner*, 1983; *Rogers v. Okin*, 1984;

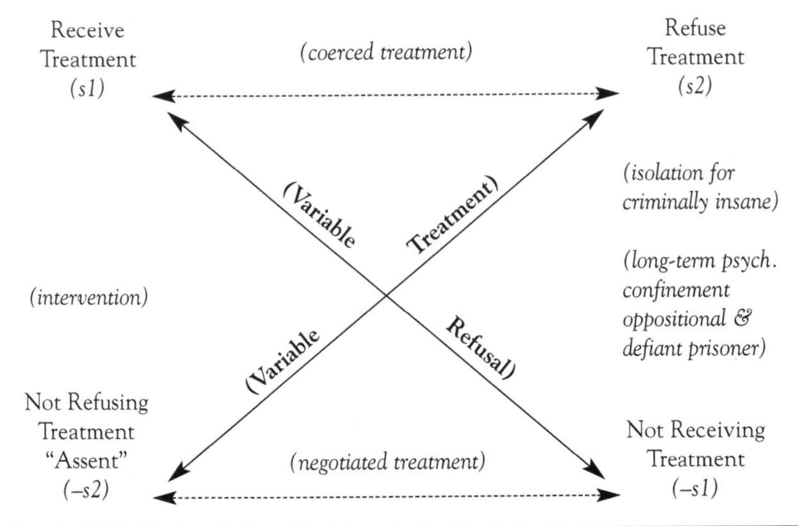

DIAGRAM 7.2. The Sign of Treatment and the Semiotic Square

Youngberg v. Romeo, 1982; *Parham v. J.R.*, 1979). Recall, however, that while *Harper* (1990) acknowledged the use of coercion under certain circumstances, it did not address forced treatment for incompetent *death row* convicts. This matter was subsequently examined in the case of *State v. Perry* (1992) (Arrigo & Tasca, 1999, pp. 23–26; Winick, 1992, pp. 328–232, 1997, pp. 272–273).

In addition, it is worth noting that while the Court's constitutional analysis in *Harper* (1990) and *Perry* (1990) hinged on the Eighth Amendment's prohibition of cruel and unusual punishment, the semiotic square and the semantical tension of receiving and refusing treatment enables us to locate this same meaning (i.e., coerced treatment *as punishment*) without expressed reliance on the constitution. This is an example of how nonlegal language (i.e., the jargon of treatment) gets translated into legal discourse (Jackson, 1995, pp. 80–86; Milovanovic, 1994a, pp. 114–117).[22]

The relationship between "receiving treatment" and "not refusing treatment" (i.e., "assent") is *intervention*. Treatment assent or, in the less extreme semantical form, treatment allowance is not equivalent to receiving treatment. The former value (assent) is a more active signifier connoting some meaningful participation in or agreement with the decision-making process. The latter value (allowance) is a more passive signifier, connoting general acquiescence to, perhaps submissiveness with, the medical intervention. In the context of an incompetent prisoner awaiting execution, the tension that is drawn out by the interplay of binary values is the administration of drug therapy (i.e., *intervention*) where the result is capital punishment. Similar to my previous semiotic inquiry, doctrinal legal analysis of constitutional law is largely unnecessary for arriving at this stated meaning. I note, though, that the intervention (legally constituted as *medicate to execute*) was precisely what the Court rejected in *Perry v. Louisiana* (1990). In this ruling, the Louisiana Supreme Court found unconstitutional the termination of a mentally ill prisoner's life where the state's interest was made clear: treat to punish. Thus, we see once again how the grammar of treatment (i.e., *intervention*) is transformed into legal discourse (i.e., medicate to execute), consistent with the U.S. Supreme Court's concern for weighty constitutional matters (i.e., the cruel and unusual punishment clause of the Eighth Amendment).

The remaining relationships found among the various contraries and contradictions are not so easily discernible. Given that the space limitations of this chapter render the analysis mostly provisional and exploratory,[23] I focus on only two of the remaining four semantical interplays in binary opposition.

The discursive connection between "refusing treatment" and "not receiving treatment" is twofold. In both instances, the association requires a judicial outcome (a meaning) that is less than affirming one's constitutional right to treatment refusal but more than not receiving any treatment at all. On the one hand, the product of the oppositional values suggests *isolation for the criminally insane*. This is not the same as endorsing treatment refusal and it is more than not receiving treatment. Indeed, it is a "type" of treatment in which medication refusal is acknowledged. On the other hand, the effect of the oppositional terms implies *long-term psychiatric confinement for the oppositional and defiant prisoner*. Again, this is less than constitutionally upholding one's right to refuse treatment and it is more than not receiving any medicolegal response. Validating this form of confinement is not as extreme as the semantic option of isolation.[24]

Both semiotic results suggest a number of things regarding the unconscious intent of the U.S. Supreme Court. Most especially, as a constitutional safeguard, treatment refusal is identified as such a fundamental freedom that any possible judicial recommendation or ruling short of endorsing it completely or requiring compulsory drug treatment (provided *Harper* (1990) justifications are in place) is not constitutionally enforceable. In other words, "middle ground" solutions generated from the semiotic square and the binary terms at issue are not within the scope of discursive possibility in correctional law. In addition, the semantical tension underscores an ongoing polemic in mental health law circles. In short, this polarized tension pits the psychiatric community's need for patient treatment (Chodoff, 1976, pp. 496–501; Treffert, 1985, pp. 259–264; Zusman, 1982, pp. 110–133) against the legal profession's demand for individual liberty (Morse, 1982a, p. 106). And finally, given the ostensible division between psychiatry and law on such matters (Arrigo, 1993c, pp. 8–23), the more essential value at stake in treatment refusal deliberations is the configuration of *paternalism* in psychiatric justice (Arrigo, 1993d, pp. 131–167, 1996b, pp. 129–174).

The relationship between "not refusing treatment" and "not receiving treatment" is also worth noting. The semantical possibilities at this intersection include *contemplated treatment* or, more likely, *negotiated treatment*. The latter option is more probable given that the binary value "assent" implies some active engagement with the process of drug therapy intervention. Identifying negotiated treatment as the meaning between the two values in binary opposition is based on locating a value that is less than assenting to treatment but more that not receiving any treatment at all.

Similar to the previous analysis, what is striking about the oppositional terms and the deeper structure of signification embedded at their semantic intersection is that the logic of negotiation conveys a certain positive appreciation for the parties involved. To negotiate with someone is to accept their competency or, at the very least, to recognize their capacity for the self-representation of interests. The absence of such an acknowledgment is to convey, implicitly, that the party in question is not able to bargain or arbitrate on one's own behalf.

As the holdings in *Washington v. Harper* (1990) and *Perry v. Louisiana* (1990) reflect, competency is an important marker for adjudicating the rights of mentally ill prisoners, including their possible execution (e.g., Appelbaum, 1986, pp. 682–684, 1995, pp. 111–118; Arrigo & Tasca, 1999, pp. 18–23; Winick, 1992, pp. 319–321, 1995, pp. 30–33, 1997, pp. 299–300). What I underscore, however, is that by teasing out the deeper structure of meaning in the "not refusing treatment" and the "not receiving treatment" binary opposition, we can locate the conspicuous disappearance of this significant matter. Indeed, what we notice is that while the U.S. Supreme Court contemplates one's constitutional right to exercise treatment, there appears, on an unconscious level, a conviction that the prisoner's competency does not exist and that, therefore, one's capacity to negotiate treatment is not even a justiciable possibility. Again, the proof of this statement stems from the absence of *negotiated treatment* as a viable consideration in right to refuse treatment deliberations (e.g., Arrigo, 1993c, 1996b; Grob, 1973, 1983; Isaac & Armat, 1990; LaFond & Durham, 1992; Myers, 1993/1994; Rothman, 1971, 1980; Scull, 1989).

Structural Legal Semiotics and the Sign of Competency

Diagram 7.3 provides a structural representation of the sign "competency." I note that the four corners of the semiotic square include specific values in binary opposition as contraries or contradictions. Starting with the upper-left-hand corner, the *s1* value is "competent." The opposite of competent is "incompetent," identified in the upper-right-hand corner as *s2*. The negation of incom-

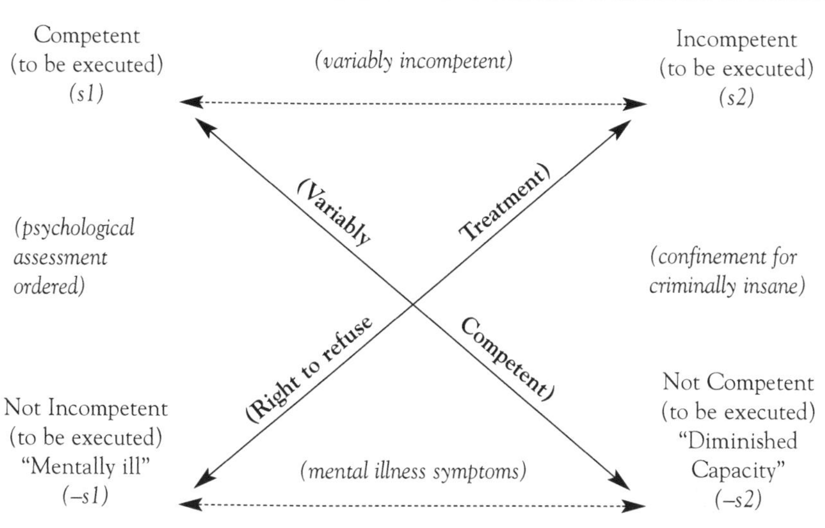

DIAGRAM 7.3. The Sign of Competency and the Semiotic Square

petent (the *-s2* term) is "not incompetent," located in the lower-left-hand corner. One who is not incompetent is still less than competent to be executed. The person is simply mentally ill. The negation of "competent" is "not competent," situated in the lower-right-hand corner as the *-s1* value. One who is not competent is less than incompetent; the person's capacity is merely diminished. There are a series of semantical relationships produced from the interaction of the contraries and contradictions. Similar to my structural legal semiotic investigation of the sign "treatment," I consider the more evident associations and then address those connections that are less apparent.[25]

The effects of joining the term *not incompetent* (i.e., mentally ill) with the value *incompetent* generates the *right to refuse treatment* outcome. In this binary relationship, we understand that something more than mental illness and something less than incompetency is required to fill the semantic chain of meaning. In the context of mentally disordered death row prisoners who might be found incompetent, the only plausible outcome is the invocation of treatment refusal. This semantical meaning is consistent with the holding in *Ford v. Wainwright* (1986), where the Court concluded that psychiatrically disordered prisoners had a right to refuse drug therapy (i.e., treatment), given the Eighth Amendment's prohibition on cruel and unusual punishment.

The association between the value "competent" and "not incompetent" provides additional information regarding the Court's understanding of mentally disordered prisons on death row. The identified semantic possibility must reflect something more than mental illness while not aligning itself entirely with the competency to be executed term. One plausible interpretation is the request for a *psychological assessment* to review competency. Again, we see how the semiotic grid produces meanings that naturally follow from the play of language contained within the semiotic square. In this particular instance, we see how the "unconscious rationality" in law is made manifest by returning to the logical play of oppositional values. The deep structure of clinical intervention (i.e., psychological assessment) materializes in the manifest structure of legal discourse (i.e., a competency evaluation) (Jackson, 1995, pp. 110–111). Indeed, what is identified in the semiotic square as a clinical matter (psychological discourse) becomes a juridical matter (legal discourse) when the semantic meaning of assessment is translated into the grammar of competency.

The relationship between the oppositional terms *not incompetent* and *not competent* produces some interesting results as well. The exchange of values here indicates that the semantical interpretation must generate something less than (full-blown) mental illness and something more than diminished capacity. Given that the context for utilizing the semiotic square focuses on the potential death row execution of psychiatrically disordered prisoners, one possibility is *mental illness symptoms*. This meaning obtains because characteristics of illness are not synonymous with a diagnosable disorder. Further, what is typically subsumed under the legal construct of diminished capacity is a specified cataloging of clinical traits.

The hidden assumption at the crossroads of this binary opposition is the esteem afforded clinical judgments by legal decision brokers. Indeed, although in recent times the U.S. Supreme Court has demonstrated ongoing deference to the wisdom of psychiatry and mental health practitioners in matters related to criminal and civil mental health law (see e.g., *Youngberg v. Romeo*, 1982; *Parham v. J.R.*, 1979), such consideration comes at an appreciable price for prisoners and patients (Arrigo, 1992b, pp. 10–11, 1997e, 2001b).[26] In short, many persons cycle in and out of institutional settings without appropriate care (Arrigo, 1992, p. 14; Isaac & Armat, 1990),[27] receive inadequate placements in the community (see, e.g., Arrigo, 1993d, pp. 151–152; Hermann, 1990, pp. 382–384; *Lake v. Cameron*, 1966), or succumb to bouts of chronic and persistent homelessness (Arrigo, 1996b, pp. 102–104; Isaac & Armat, 1990, p. 1; Lamb, 1984b), resulting, on occasion, in death (Arrigo, 1996b, pp. 104–108).

Once again, I note that this deep structure of meaning is brought to the fore by working within the parameters of the semiotic grid. Psychological discourse (i.e., symptoms of mental illness) gives rise to legal discourse (i.e., the jargon of clinical judgment as presumptively valid) (Arrigo, 1992b, p. 11; Jackson, 1995; see also, *In re Quinlan*, 1976; *In re Richard Roe III*, 1982; *In re Storar*,

1981). Further, as I indicated, the practical effect of this unconscious semiotic activity has been the spawning of a panoply of civil and criminal dilemmas in mental health law and policy (Arrigo, 1996b, pp. 47–94).

Legal Deconstructionism and the Sign of Treatment

While the structuralist approach employs binary oppositions to understand how meaning is *generated* from within nonreferential parameters of discourse, legal deconstructionism exposes the free play of differences and dependencies within hierarchical oppositions. Similar to the structural legal semiotic inquiry developed in this chapter, I address the sign of treatment and competency independently. Along the way, I comment on where and how legal deconstructionism offers insight not contained in a more doctrinaire analysis of (mental health) law.

Reversal of hierarchies. In the context of incompetent prisoners on death row, the sign of treatment includes the binary values *receiving treatment* and *refusing treatment*. To "treat" someone or something means to look on another in a particular manner. It is to hold oneself out to another in a specified way. To receive treatment, then, implies that the one who confers such an offering does so from within a unique perspective. But to treat someone is also to consign a reward; it is to regard the recipient as special or worthy of some *gift*. We convey this sentiment in such expressions as, "*How about I treat you to lunch.*" In medical discourse, however, the one who receives attention is regarded as ill (Scheff, 2000). Thus, the treater comports him- or herself as a manager of illness; that is, as the one who treats the sick party to relief, to comfort, and to cure. It follows, then, that the dominant value *(receiving treatment)* assumes its position because medical intervention is understood to give the gift of reparation: repairing, remedying, correcting illness and disease.

In the instance of psychiatric treatment, the same logic applies. The person who receives medical care and drug therapy is regarded as diseased (and dangerous) and in need of special care (Arrigo, 1992b, pp. 11–12, 1999a). The gift of treatment intends the elimination of suffering and pain. But here the treater makes an erroneous leap on two fronts. First, the logic of the gift is built around the discourse of reciprocity (e.g., Batailee, 1988; Caputo, 1997; Emerson, 1983; Mauss, 1990; Wolff, 1950; Nietzsche, 1995).[28] Second, the one who bestows treatment does so on the basis of presuming to know what gift is in the recipient's best interest (American Psychiatric Association, 1994; Scheff, 1984, pp. 163–174; Szasz, 1987).

What is troubling about the first misstep is that the treat or award of drug therapy creates, intended or not, a debt of gratitude or reciprocation in the recipient. We convey this sentiment in such expressions as: "*Since you treated me to lunch yesterday, let me treat you to lunch today*" (Caputo, 1997, p. 147). In addition, the giver of the gift is heartened by the bestowal of the treat; "consciously and explicitly" pleased for his or her display of generosity (Caputo, 1997, p. 141). Indeed, although offered without expectation of explicit gratitude (Nietzsche, 1996), the gift of treatment simply fortifies and nourishes the narcissism of the giver (Schrift, 1997). Thus, we come to the first paradox of conferring and receiving treatment: the one who treats, instead of giving, receives, and the one who is treated, instead of receiving, is in debt (Arrigo & Williams, 2000a).

What this exchange produces is the circular economy of reappropriation and reciprocation. Treatment, as a gift, serves a purpose. It signifies narcissism disguised by the pretense of generosity ("*let me treat* you!"), or it represents the anticipation of exchange masked by the facade of beneficence *(I can treat you if you let me)*. In both instances, the implication is the same. The person who gives believes he or she has something of currency: an award the other desires. Indeed, the consignor harbors the conviction, implicit or otherwise, that the offering, much like any present, is a gift worth possessing.[29]

This conviction gives rise to the other mistaken, or at least questionable, belief. When the justification for the gift of treatment is that the recipient's interests are best served by the award, the one who gives exercises power (Caputo, 1997).[30] The presumption is that the receiver of the award will be treated to mental health pain relief and to the reparation of psychiatric illness (Winick, 1977, pp. 813–814, 1997a, pp. 320–321; see also, *Riggins*, 1992, p. 540).[31] Under these conditions, refusing the gift of treatment ostensibly makes no sense.

Rejecting the gift of treatment, however, is not so much a constitutional exercise of one's right (Brooks, 1987, pp. 339–376; Winick, 1979/1980, pp. 331–420, 1993, pp. 205–237), as much as an existential statement about the will to forfeit receipt of an unwanted gift. This waiver of the award not only destabilizes the exercise of the giver's power over the receiver, it relinquishes the would-be gift recipient from the possibility of indebtedness and reciprocity. Thus, the giver's treat is returned not because it fails (potentially) to serve the best interests of the individual, but because even if it did, it still fails to have the same currency for the receiver that it does for the giver. This, then, is the second paradox of receiving and refusing treatment: the giver, instead of offering something of benefit for which the receiver is obliged, gives something that is unwanted for which the receiver is defiled.[32] In short, according to the gift recipient, treatment is not a gift worth possessing. Behind the presentation of the treat is an absence that the receiver recognizes and, therefore, rejects.

Differance and trace. The deconstructive interplay of the signs *receiving treatment* and *refusing treatment* demonstrates how mutually interdependent these values truly are in hierarchical opposition. The gift of drug therapy depends on its refusal in order for the award to convey its value. Conversely, the rejection of the offering takes on meaning only in relation to what the oppositional term signifies. Thus, neither value position can be foundational or privileged; rather, the terms can only express thought and action through the co-emergence of meaning situated in their intrinsic mutuality. It is this mutuality that gives the terms their identity, and it is through this mutuality that one meaning of Derrida's notion of *differance* appears. Put simply, each value defers to the other "in the sense of being fundamentally dependent on the other" (Derrida, 1981, pp. 39–40, 1982, p. 3; Balkin, 1987, pp. 752, 764–767).

The inversion of hierarchies, then, deconstructs the metaphysics of presence (i.e., *receiving treatment* as the dominant value). What is given is devoid of substance for the receiver and, thus, rendered an absence. But here, too, I note that this activity of decentering the gift of treatment does not elevate its refusal to a position of status. Indeed, while the two terms are differentiated from each other (a second meaning of Derrida's *differance*), precisely because we articulate one of the values in hierarchical opposition, we announce the other. That is to say, when we speak of refusing treatment we always and already speak of receiving it and vice versa. In deferring the unspoken term, we still, unconsciously and prethematically, make its absence present.[33] This is the third meaning of Derrida's concept of *differance*.

I note further, however, the relationship between *differance* and the trace at work in the sign of treatment. Through the performative dependencies and differences contained within the sign, each term not only contains the trace of the other within it, but the remnant of the other is that which makes possible the deconstruction of the hierarchical oppositions (Derrida, 1976, pp. 46–47; Balkin, 1987, p. 752). As previously explored, the concealed, though lingering, trace of *receiving treatment* in *refusing treatment* and of *refusing treatment* in *receiving treatment* demonstrates the *undecidability* of meaning in legal discourse and decision making (Derrida, 1973, pp. 157–162; Sarup, 1989, p. 36; Cornell, 1992, pp. 68–91).

Arguments that undo themselves. Supporting the dominant value of *receiving treatment* is an argument that undoes itself on two fronts. First, the value specified for this sign (i.e., the receipt of psychiatric illness reparation as a gift worth possessing) is really not a reward at all. If anything, it is an encumbrance for the one who rejects it. Moreover, that which does not benefit the recipient, even if it is believed to do so by the giver, is really not a gift worth giving. At best, it can only narcissistically satisfy the one who does the giving. Indeed, the receiver of treatment is indebted and must give, and the giver of treatment is aggrandized and must receive. Thus, the justification of treatment (as a gift of pain management or relief) is undone because it can never convey or accomplish what it intends. Forcibly medicating, as a gift, becomes an act of refutation. The giver refuses to accept the other's right to reject treatment. As an act of resistance, we see, then, that the limitations of giving treatment are much like the limitations of refusing treatment. Both are expressions of nonacceptance: neither party welcomes the other's point of view.

The second logic of justification that is ungrounded with the sign of *receiving treatment* is that it is better to refuse that to receive. By refusing unwanted drug therapy one is not indebted to the giver. By resisting uninvited medical intervention the economy of exchange, of reciprocation and reappropriation, is not mobilized. By averting the obligation of gratitude, one destabilizes the power the giver would otherwise have over the course of the recipient's future. Exercising treatment refusal, then, is a gift waiting to be received. The refuser longs for it to be embraced by all those willing to acknowledge the refutation. In particular, the treater is invited to accept the refuter's gift of autonomy and self-determination. Of course, like all gifts, it is better to refuse than to receive. Once again, this activity returns us to Derrida's notion of *differance*, trace, and the inversion of hierarchies.

Legal Deconstructionism and the Sign of Competency

Reversal of hierarchies. In the context of right to refuse treatment matters for death row prisoners, the sign of competency includes the values *competent to be executed* and *incompetent to be executed.* The dominant term assumes its position because it endorses and generally implies that one makes a choice knowingly (Appelbaum et al., 1987), rationally (Meisel & Roth, 1983, p. 284), and reasonably (Appelbaum & Roth, 1982, pp. 951–953; Grisso, 1986; Schwartz & Roth, 1989, p. 415). I note, however, that the mechanisms or *standards* by which competency is defined, operationalized, or both vary enormously (Winick, 1997a, p. 349). Thus, to be competent under the law is to be qualified or to be fit. It is the capacity to make one's own decisions, regardless of how ridiculous the choices appear (Winick, 1997a, p. 348).

But such competency is itself undecided (Derrida, 1973, pp. 157–162; Cornell, 1992, pp. 68–91; Sarup, 1989); that is, there is no guarantee when one objects to medical intervention that the refusal itself might not get interpreted as a display of incapacity or unfitness (Winick, 1997a, p. 351). Indeed, although the medicolegal community may classify a particular request as "grossly incompetent" (Winick, 1997a, p. 352), the plea can be deemed permissible in other mental health treatment contexts (cf. *Zinermon v. Burch*, 1990, p. 118). Competency, then, is already, and to some extent, incompetency. It is, in part, the absence of qualification and authorization to make knowing, reasonable, rational decisions. Interestingly, this is what gives incompetency its specialized and differentiated meaning.

Similarly, however, the binary value *incompetent to be executed* is not a privileged term, given the limits of its hierarchical opposition. To be incompetent does not preclude the articulation of certain desires (e.g., the refusal of unwanted or forced drug therapy). The resistance is, presumably, a comment on the invasiveness of the medical intervention. Moreover, it is clear that some mentally disordered people exercise this right, receive forced treatment over objection, and, once restored to "competency," still adamantly profess disapproval with the coerced medication in the first place (Meisel, 1979, p. 425). This returns us to the fuzzy logic distinguishing competency and incompetency in treatment refusal matters for death row prisoners. In short, when a person says no to forced treatment both before and after competency restoration, can it be said that the individual was ever really incompetent? The interpretation most favorable to coerced treatment proponents is that the person was, to some extent, competent and incompetent simultaneously. Indeed, the patient *was at least* sufficiently fit and qualified to make a choice about refusing treatment.

In addition, I note that the refutation, if truly made incompetently, can only proceed from some measure of competence.[34] Here, then, we see the discursive feedback loop embedded in the *competent to be executed* and *incompetent to be executed* values. In law, the significations we assign to one term mutually depend on the meanings we specify for the other term. What we take to be a dominant value (i.e., *competence*) is itself dependent on the concept it was privileged over (i.e., *incompetence*). But this value *(incompetence)* can only take on social use and value if based on its binary opposite *(competence)*. Neither term is foundational. The mutuality of both values is what makes thought and action pertaining to death row execution matters possible.

Differance and the trace. Given the mutuality of reliances situated within the binary terms for the sign of competence, we see how Derrida's notion of *differance* demarcates the oppositional relations. *Competent to be executed* and *incompetent to be executed* defer to one another in that the presence of one value makes the absence of the other manifest, and vice versa. This represents one meaning for *differance*. In addition, the force of the terms in the mental health law arena signals their differentiation. For example, an incompetent individual who asserts a right to treatment refusal given impending execution can, under certain circumstances, still be sentenced to death (*State v. Perry*, 1992, pp. 751–752). This is the second reading of *differance*. And, finally, the two values retain identity only because of the performative nature of differences and dependencies unconsciously activated through a deconstructive critique. Again, situated within each term is the trace of the other. In other words, given that each value contains the remains of the other within it, the logic of *differance* and the deconstruction of hierarchical oppositions is discoverable. This is the third interpretation of *differance*.

Arguments that undo themselves. Ungrounding the justification for the dominant value "*competency to be executed*" is not difficult to discern. Indeed, arguments for endorsing the privileged term really amount to supporting, albeit temporarily and incompletely, the value that is absent. As I have already indicated, to be competent is also to be incompetent; that is, to not act knowingly, rationally, and reasonably in all instances. I come to this conclusion because: (1) the standards by which competency is defined remain somewhat inconsistent and variable; (2) there are times when the courts endorse requests that border on or may be acts of incompetence (*Zinermon v. Burch*, 1990; Winick, 1997a, p. 352); and (3) there are times when restoration of competence through forced treatment over refusal, does not alter the patient's desire to be free from unwanted medication in the first instance (Meisel, 1979, p. 425). In each instance, the presence of *competent to be executed* as the dominant value is eroded by what it directs us to; namely, the value of *incompetent to be executed.* Once again, though, the logic of deconstruction in relation to arguments that undo themselves is not to privilege that which heretofore was absent. Indeed, the inversion of the hierarchy is possible only because incompetence is a value that can be measured against, although momentarily and provisionally, its binary opposite. Thus, we have the play of differences and dependencies at work revealing mutual interdependence.

CONCLUSIONS

The preceding application exposed the principles of structural legal semiotics and legal deconstructionism to the matter of treatment refusal for incompetent prisoners awaiting execution. The results of this assessment point to a number of implications for theory, policy, and practice. The comments that follow are limited. They merely reflect my overall concern for the plight of psychiatrically disordered prisoners awaiting execution and, therefore, should not be interpreted beyond this scope in mental health correctional law.

The observations described below are also provisional. The preceding analysis theoretically addressed only two dimensions of treatment refusal for mentally ill death row inmates: the sign of treatment and the sign of competency. In order to present a more detailed evaluation of implications, other signs (e.g., mental illness, dangerousness, informed consent) would require a careful and systematic exploration. Here, too, I would need to utilize the techniques of discourse analysis as previously described.

Of primary importance in my assessment of criminal mental health law is the power of language to shape both thought and action. It would be easy to dismiss the manner in which language modifies, regulates, obfuscates, or transforms decision making. After all, discourse is merely about words and, short of hate speech, words, in and of themselves, do not give rise to harm. I disagree. Language structures thought in ways that are not neutral (Arrigo, 1993c, 1996b; Tiefenbrun, 1986, pp. 91–93; Tushnet, 1991, p. 1517). Word are value-laden and they privilege certain perspectives at the expense of others. Whether written or spoken, there is always something more that "insists" in discourse. At times, the insistence is a subtle, but forceful, realization that we have failed people, intentionally or not, because their lives remain deeply marred; caught in the crossfire of illness politics (Arrigo, 1996b, pp. 148–157; Isaac & Armat, 1990). On many fronts, the dilemmas that plague criminal (and civil) mental health systems users are a constant and vivid reminder of how society has abandoned or forgotten them. But words are all we have—incomplete and unsatisfying as they are or can be.

Although philosophically based on different presuppositions, both structural semiotics and deconstructionism return us to the power of words. In the context of treatment refusal for prisoners on death row, the pain experienced through the text of mental health law is real and the harm is equally deep. This is not to imply that there is a concerted institutional effort to undermine constitutional safeguards; rather, it is an observation about the insidious nature of language that often *speaks through* the one who communicates (Lacan, 1977, pp. 25–29), functioning from within the preconfigured confines of a specialized grammar like the law, psychiatry, or their discursive coproduction (Arrigo, 1996a, 1997e).

Incompetent persons suffering from mental illness asserting their treatment refusal rights can, under specified provisions, be executed. This very sentence alone is both illuminating and frightening. What is provocative about the statement is that the United States Supreme Court has, in its unique way, attempted to fashion a public policy that balances competing institutional and individual interests. What is troubling about the assertion is that the Court's response to date has been anything but satisfying. This is not a knee-jerk response built around a healthy dose of liberal outrage. Rather, it comes from understanding that signs such as "mental illness," incompetence," and "execution," are saturated and cloaked within a multitude of complex and nuanced meanings that ultimately, when decoded, reveal the vast array of hidden contradictions, ambiguities, inconsistencies, dependencies, and differences contained within their usage. As a result, I seriously question the apparent rush to end life through the public policy initiative of capital punishment.

I note, too, that when addressing matters of treatment refusal for incompetent death row inmates, mental health law is considerably informed by ideology (Milovanovic, 1994a, p. 101).[35] This is a specific reference to unconscious values and unstated assumptions concerning the Court's regard for mentally ill prisoners, their imminent executions, and the systems of which they are a part. The foregoing structural semiotic and legal deconstructionist investigations demonstrated where and how the line between law and politics (i.e., ideological viewpoints) is not so clearly demarcated. For example, by relying on structural legal semiotics I explained how ideology informs the Court's dismissal of degrees of meaning for the binary tension "not refusing treatment" and "not receiving treatment." Embedded within the semantical play of differences, given the discursive constraints of the semiotic square, was the Court's inability to locate "middle ground" solutions (e.g., *negotiated treatment* or *contemplated treatment*). Indeed, one the core values I located in this semiotic assessment was paternalism. Interestingly, this notion is consistent with the commentary provided in chapter 1 and implied throughout subsequent chapters. While I recognize that identifying the value of paternalism is certainly not knew, the degree to which it is critically situated *first and foremost through language*, is relatively underdeveloped in the pertinent literature.

A similar argument about ideological decision making is traceable to how the United States Supreme Court interprets the sign of treatment. Deconstructively speaking, the gift of coerced intervention is anything but a precious reward or esteemed value for the recipient. Indeed, the gift of treatment creates an economy of reciprocity. If not derailed by the receiver, it renders the presenter a glorified recipient and the receiver an indebted giver.

Given the structural and performative power of language to unearth concealed meanings, and given the ideological core of mental health law on matters of treatment refusal for incompetent prisoners awaiting execution, it is increasingly evident that the penalty one endures for mental disorder (i.e., the policing of difference) is fundamentally activated deep within the uncharted mind of law and psychiatry. Language and subjectivity unconsciously interact, giving rise to certain meanings for the signs "incompetency," "mental illness," "execution," and the like. These preferred meanings embody the desire of the clinicolegal establishment, seemingly dismissing or quashing all other possible or alternative interpretations. As a result, punishment covertly manifests itself first in clinicolegal discourse and then in correctional practice.

It remains to be seen how the unconscious is mobilized, leading to the articulation of a circumscribed clinicolegal grammar on matters of civil and criminal confinement. In other words, what psychic forces are activated deep beneath the emotional soul and body of law and psychiatry, and how are they prethematically organized such that a certain (limiting, marginalizing, and alienating) grammar is generated and sustained in mental health civil and criminal law? In the final chapter I assess this very matter, providing a critically informed theory of punishment at the crossroads of law and psychiatry.

EIGHT

Law, Psychiatry, and Punishment

Toward a Critical Theory

OVERVIEW. *The previous chapter concluded by suggesting that structural semiotics and legal deconstructionism are helpful when decoding the ideological forces at work giving rise to decisions in which mentally ill persons, exercising their right to refuse treatment, are sentenced to death. As I explained, embedded within these judgments are a host of covert meanings, interpretations, or both that are dismissed by users of clinicolegal discourse. These concealed notions, when made manifest, disclose how punishment in law and psychiatry occurs first through the performative power of language with its subsequent and corresponding effects (e.g., executing the psychiatrically disordered). Missing from chapter 7, however, was any sustained attempt to explore more deeply how the unconscious "mind" of law and psychiatry functions. In other words, how is it mobilized such that the grammar of psychiatric justice is routinely invoked, thereby producing circumscribed civil confinement determinations, criminal confinement determinations, or both?*

To some extent, chapter 6 identified and explored important components of this question, utilizing a Lacanian semiotic framework for conceptual guidance. In short, I relied on the not-guilty-by-reason-of-insanity and the guilty-but-mentally-ill verdicts for exemplification, and explained how what one says (i.e., speech) is intimately connected to who one is (i.e., subjectivity), and that their overlapping interdependence yields limited meanings and partial truths in the psychiatric courtroom. This notwithstanding, several additional facets to discourse and agency require further explication, and the psychoanalytic insights of Lacan are instructive. For example, how is the "desiring subject" (e.g., lawyers, psychiatrists, patients) understood through speech, and how is one's meaning and *being embodied in the spoken word? Relatedly, what are the psychic forces that represent the unconscious, and how do they engulf and direct the production and recreation of clinicolegal discourse? These Lacanian notions inform our understanding of the desiring subject, activated and sustained when decisions are made at the crossroads of law and psychiatry. Indeed, these psychic forces situate the penalty for mental illness within the topography of the unconscious, drawing attention to the articulation of punishment based not on what one does nor on who one is but, more insidiously, on how one is defined. As I subsequently describe, this conclusion, substantiated through selected Lacanian theoretical formulations, along with the conceptual and practical insights developed in previous chapters, contributes to the articulation of a critically inspired theory of punishment at the intersection of law and psychiatry.*

INTRODUCTION

The purpose of this chapter is twofold: explore the contours of psychiatric justice lodged within the unconscious; and present a provisional theory of punishment. These aims are related to but go beyond the ideas entertained in the previous chapters. The first notion extends the conceptual analysis on Lacan and the not-guilty-by-reason-of-insanity and the guilty-but-mentally-ill verdicts, as presented in chapter 6. There I explained how discourse and subjectivity operate interdependently to produce circumscribed knowledge in the psychiatric courtroom. Therefore, the NGRI and GBMI options always and already reflect the assumptions and values of clinicolegal science at the expense of other ways of knowing, other ways of being.

In order to ascertain how this partial reality in law and psychiatry gets spoken, legitimized, and re-created, it is necessary to describe the inner workings of the unconscious. At issue here are the following: (1) at the spoken level, explain how the desiring subject functions; and (2) at the unspoken level, explain the composition of the unconscious. With regard to the former point, it is important to distinguish between the subject *in* speech and the subject *of* speech. With regard to the latter point, it is important to explain the psychic forces which sustain the production and circulation of (clinicolegal) discourse. In part, Lacan (1977) referred to these forces as the Symbolic, Imaginary, and Real Orders. Both of these matters allow for a more deliberate assessment of how intrapsychic and interpersonal speech are unconsciously produced, re-created, and legitimated.

Admittedly, these observations ask the reader to consider how prethematic dynamics give rise to intersubjective thoughts and exchanges. These notions are decidedly outside the scope of conventional or even mainstream liberal crime and justice studies, and the logic employed may be somewhat difficult to follow. Indeed, I recognize that relying on the insights of Lacan may be foreign even awkward for some; however, unlike any other social theorist before or since his time, Lacan understood the significance of agency in the articulation of thought and the construction of knowledge (Milovanovic, 1992a, 1997b). Thus, it follows that exploring the unchartered mind of law and psychiatry is important to describing not only its psychic configuration but also its power to produce harm in symbolic form (i.e., marginalizing and alienating language) and, therefore, in social consequence (e.g., confinement, execution).

Following my commentary on the unconscious and its relationship to clinicolegal decision making, I then address the second purpose of this chapter. In short, I revisit the practical and conceptual observations entertained throughout this book and incorporate them into a statement about punishment and mental illness. On this score, I explain how paternalism, psychological egoism, identity politics, the social control thesis, constitutive thought, desire-in-discourse, narrative coherence, the metaphysics of presence, and the psychoanalytic unconscious represent important markers in law, psychiatry, and their systemic intersection. As components of a critically informed theory of punishment, they delineate what the penalty for mental illness is and how it is maintained within and throughout ongoing clinicolegal practices. Given this analysis, I conclude the chapter by rethinking mental illness, particularly in the context of penal (and psychiatric hospital) abolition, and the justice-policy implications that stem from such a position.

THE UNCONSCIOUS MIND OF LAW AND PSYCHIATRY

The more algebraic formulations of Jacques Lacan (e.g., 1977, 1981, 1985, 1988, 1991) are often cumbersome and cryptic to decipher. This notwithstanding, located within his intricate mathematical notions are clues to understanding more about the subject's intrapsychic (internal) and intersubjective (interpersonal) thoughts and communications. Both are essential constituents in the sense-making process and fundamentally deepen our understanding of complex phenomenon, including decision making in civil and criminal mental health law. In the next three sections, aspects of Lacanian psychoanalytic semiotics are presented and then linked to clinicolegal decision-making. The first section reviews Lacan's notion of the desiring subject. The second section explains the psychic configuration of the unconscious represented by the Three Orders. The third section describes the interpenetrating forces that re-create the production and circulation of speech. Overall, these sections deepen our understanding of the ideological dimensions of punishment in law and psychiatry.

The Desiring Subject

As previously outlined in chapter 6, Lacan's (1977) insights center upon the operation of the unconscious, designated by him as the "Other" or *Autre*. In order to more fully grasp meaning in the act of speech production, the activities of the unconscious require careful and thoughtful attention. Indeed, for Lacan, meaning (i.e., sense-making) and being (i.e., subjectivity) are inextricably wedded to the discourse one employs. Thus, deliberately exploring this relationship allows us to access the often taken-for-granted variable of language as the embodiment of one's identity, unconsciously shaping the construction of knowledge.

This interdependence of self and language can also be described as the *desiring subject*. In Lacan's conceptual topography, the desiring subject is understood on the basis of two interactive dimensions (Benveniste, 1971). Diagram 8.1 depicts their interdependent effects. One dimension is the subject-*of*-speech *(le sujet de l'énonce)*. This is the self as grammatical "I." To illustrate: "*I* am going

Subject-*of*-speech	I act	I feel	I need	meaning	discursive production
Subject-*in*-speech	self?	self?	self?	being	discourse (it)self

DIAGRAM 8.1. Lacan's Speaking-Being

to the theater," or "*I* hope you enjoy your trip," or "*I* want something to drink." In speech, we give our identities meaning; that is, we fill in our identities with substance or content.

In the examples above, the "I" is someone who *acts* (i.e., goes to the theater), *feels* (i.e., experiences hope/anticipation), *needs* (i.e., craves liquids). This version of the self makes possible the concealment of the other dimension. The subject-of-speech represents the "presence of an absence" (Lacan, 1981, pp. 131–139; Derrida, 1973) What is present in speech is the grammatical "I." What is absent is the fact that someone is responsible for producing the uttered statements; someone whose complete spectrum of desires (e.g., longings, fears, aspirations) are silenced through language. This is the subject-*in*-speech *(le sujet de l'enonciation)*; that is, the fullness of the person in speech. This dimension is unconscious; it resides in the repository of the Lacanian Other. The combinatory effects of the two dimensions produce the speaking-being (Lacan's *l'être parlant*, or *parlêtre*).

The problem with the two-dimensionality of the speaking-being is that meaning is created (the subject-of-speech) at the expense of being (the subject-in-speech) and vice versa (Lacan, 1981, pp. 211–218). On the one hand, the subject-of-speech (the "I") is a stand-in for the absent subject in speech (Lacan, 1981, p. 139; Smith, 1988, p. 76). On the other hand, the subject-in-speech gives form in discourse to the grammatical "I" by filling in the "I" with content (Lacan, 1981, p. 218; Borch-Jacobsen, 1991, pp. 169–196). Thus, "the two subjects are never reducible to each other; they are forever separated by the barrier of . . . [meaning and being]" (Milovanovic, 1992b, p. 48).

In the context of civil and criminal mental health law, there is a more overt, active, and conscious regard for the rights of the public versus the rights of psychiatric citizens. This is embodied in such clinicolegal practices as paternalism (i.e., police powers and *parens patriae*), mental health advocacy, defining mental illness, predicting dangerous, confinement, and execution. In addition, however, there is also a more covert, passive, and unconscious language (i.e., the subjectivity of the mental health consumer). This remains concealed, dormant, and repressed. Each (overt and covert) discourse is fully dependent on the other yet equally responsible for the other's incompleteness. At the level of discursive semiotic production, meaning slips and stumbles forever dependent upon the desiring voice of the speaking-subject who "*insists*" on more. This insistence, this experience of slippage (i.e., the plane of discourse [it]self) is the subject-in-speech longing for a more complete articulation of his or her being.

Consider the example of civil commitment explored in chapter 1 and capital punishment entertained in chapter 7. In both instances, attorneys representing the interests of the disordered client are retained. The litigator's task is to ensure that sustained institutionalization and imminent execution are temporarily or indefinitely averted. This is what zealous representation entails. However, as subjects-in-speech, their only legally endorsed mechanism for expression is an appeal to the psychiatric courtroom and the circumscribed logic and parameters of meaning through which it functions. In other words, requesting the release of an involuntarily hospitalized citizen or invoking a right to treatment refusal on behalf of a death row prisoner can only proceed through a language consistent with the subject-of-speech. Indeed, the clinicolegal meanings of "mental illness," "danger to self, others, or both," "competency," "wrongful," "voluntary," "gravely disabled," and so on represent the only enforceable and legitimized source through which a psychiatric citizen's rights can be articulated. Any other speech code (and the sense-making claims that attach to them) is objected to by opposing counsel and declared by a judge to be irrelevant, immaterial, inadmissable (Arrigo, 1993c, 1996b). Thus, for these attorneys (and their clients) juridical meaning (through the subject-of-speech) is privileged and personal being (through the subject-in-speech) is denied. Clearly, then, understanding the dichotomous repository that is the Lacanian speaking-being provides us with deeper insight into the nature of discourse, subjectivity and desire, and offers us additional information regarding the process of speech production.

The Three Orders

In addition to the operation of the speaking-being and the manner in which it informs clinicolegal practices, is the psychic configuration of the unconscious. According to Lacan, the unconscious is composed of three main Orders. These Orders include the Symbolic, the Imaginary, and the Real. The interactive effects of these three discursive forms are responsible for the manifestation of the speaking-being and, thus, account for one's appreciation of all social phenomena,[1] including decision making in law and psychiatry.

The *Symbolic Order* is the sphere of established language and culture. It is also represented by the idea of the Other (the unconscious). This Other is where signifiers (words), unique and integral to one's being, are located.[2] The Symbolic Order is primordial; that is, it *is* always and already. As children, we are born into the Symbolic Order. Our initiation into this Order enables us to locate identity through a (shared) language that embodies desire. However, the child also is alienated and removed from all directly lived, phenomenal experiences. In other words, the Symbolic Order privileges (communal) meaning at the expense of (personal) being. Thus, we can once again speak of the Lacanian subject as the presence of an absence. This absence represents a loss establishing a fundamental *lack-in-being*. The matheme used by Lacan to designate this condition is the slashed or divided subject *($)*.

The *Imaginary Order* is the sphere of specular images *(imagos)*. It is the outcome of the mirror stage of development; a point in time (between 6–18 months) when the child initially sees itself in a mirror and constructs a fantasy, an ideal likeness, of the unitary subject, of the subject in relation to others, and of objects in the world *(objet petit [a])* that potentially fill the subject's desire. For Lacan, these primordial specular images are illusory and remain with the child throughout its lifespan as manifested in the subject's everyday interactions and constitution of self.

The *Real Order* is the natural, sensory, and biological sphere. It is beyond knowledge. It is in excess of words. It defies accurate symbolization through speech production. The subject's experience of alienation, of symbolic castration felt through the Symbolic Order, is the experience of separation from the Real Order. It is this felt lack which mobilizes desire. The Real Order is the desiring voice of the subject whose interiorized identity dwells in an uncultivated language awaiting articulation and legitimation.

According to Lacan, the interactive effects of these three Orders identify how the speaking-being is *decentered* ($). In other words, contrary to Cartesian epistemology that affirms the stable, unitary, self-regulated, rational, determining subject (Milovanovic, 1992b, pp. 44–51), Lacan suggests that the desiring subject is more unstable, disunified, regulated, irrational, and determined (Lacan, 1977, p. 166). Rather than embracing the plenary "I," a Cartesian subject who freely produces discourse and action, the Lacanian version of subjectivity has it that we are represented in discourse by signifiers that speak *through* us.

The creation of sense and the activity of speech production, then, represent a moment in which our desire is given expressive form. In other words, we embody desire (i.e., agency) through language precisely when we attempt to respond to that felt lack in being or, when we attend to the gaps in our being *(manque d'être)*. As Lacan has it, we *suture* or mend the gaps by locating objects of desire *(objet petit [a])* (Lacan, 1977, pp. 112–132). This suturing returns us to the three Orders. The Symbolic Order provides a treasure chest of signifiers (words/phrases) that potentially can embody desire for us. The Imaginary Order offers only fantasy constructions of self, others, and objects in the world. In other words, these illusory manifestations are an incomplete source for filling in the lack-in-being. The Real Order, always insisting, always awaiting anchorage *(capitonnage)*, slumbers in the distance yet makes its presence felt.

The mobilization of desire in the psychic apparatus makes possible the constitution of meaning. It is this meaning that overcomes our gaps-in-being.

Lacan refers to this experience as *jouissance* (i.e., that excess; that which is beyond enjoyment; enjoyment in sense). Remember, however, that such occasions as these are phantasmic in nature; that is, there is always and already something missing in the creation of sense (i.e., a more complete sense of one's being). Lacan was to depict this experience as follows: $ < > *a*. The arrows "< >" represent movement. The subject "$" disappears into its objects of desire "*a*."

Returning to the examples of civil commitment and execution for the mentally ill, psychiatric citizens (and their attorneys) experience a loss, a surrendering, of their selves (of their being) when invoking the forensic psychological language of involuntary confinement and capital punishment. In other words, the discourse of law and psychiatry speaks for and through them. In this respect, the language is oppressive. Subjects in a (psychiatric) courtroom cannot speak true words (Freire, 1972) about themselves. Their identities must always pass through and be mediated by clinicolegal discourse. This notwithstanding, the grammar of psychiatric justice temporarily, although incompletely, closes (sutures) and consolidates (anchors) the person's inherent lack-in-being. It is part of the coordinated language system constituting medicolegal thought. Thus, the preferred, though circumscribed, clinicolegal meanings that attach to "confinement," "dangerous," "insanity," "treatment refusal," "competence," and the like, are consistent with what courts take to be "good lawyering." In this respect, the discourse is liberating. After all, zealous representation necessitates that one be well-schooled in the full parameters of conventional legal thought and action.

However, psychosemiotically speaking, what is lost in this process of client advocacy is much more profound than the mere articulation of selected words and assembled phrases. In short, as the only juridically acceptable language available through the Symbolic Order, clinicolegal discourse offers the greatest possibility, although illusory, for one's identity fulfillment. As a consequence, psychiatric citizens (and their litigators) as divided subjects ($), disappear into the discourse of involuntary confinement or capital punishment *(objet petit a)*, unwittingly reproducing only those marginalizing and alienating meanings sanctioned in the courtroom. In other words, all of the fears, longings, inconsistencies, anomalies, contradictions, and absurdities of one's humanity and being are sanitized and cleansed, and made compatible with the coordinates of meaning representing psychiatric justice (Arrigo, 1996b). The silencing or reconstitution of being, activated at the unconscious level, is the manifestation of punishment assuming a discursive linguistic form.

Re-creating the Production and Circulation of Speech

In the previous two sections, I explained the dilemma with the speaking-being; namely, the privileging of meaning at the expense of being. In addition, I described the operation of the Three Orders, pointing out how the realm of the Symbolic represents prevailing culture, thought, and language. Both of these matters signal how speech unconsciously encodes reality in ways that give rise to circumscribed (clinicolegal) discourse.

Lacan's (1977) psychoanalytic formulations are also instructive in that they account for the more repressed, prethematic, and interpenetrating forces that re-create the production and circulation of speech. Identifying these psychic forces is important because they explain the unconscious process through which language, situated in the Symbolic Order, is called on to fashion and disseminate established meanings for all phenomena, including decisions made at the crossroads of law and psychiatry.

Others have explored, in varying degrees, these pre-articulated effects located in the repository of the unconscious (e.g., Jakobson, 1971, pp. 69–96.) For example, as explored in chapter 7, I explained how structural legal semiotics was useful when deciphering the operation of contradictions (i.e., clear negations) and contraries (i.e., strong oppositions) for the sign of "competence" and "treatment." By engaging in this analysis I was able to determine some of the unconscious rationality (i.e., ideology) informing the United States Supreme Court's decision making on such matters as the execution of mentally ill death row offenders who exercise their right to refuse treatment. What we discovered is that while the Court articulated a coherent legal narrative, it was steeped in unspoken and concealed cultural values (Jackson, 1995, p. 93).

For our purposes, however, the question in this section entails getting underneath the narrative of civil and criminal mental health law. In other words, how does the story of confinement get structured and spoken through the unconscious mind of law and psychiatry? Relatedly, how does this text get re-articulated, reproduced, and relegitimized through the dynamics of ongoing clinicolegal decision making? These matters explain why the policing of mental illness, as delineated throughout the preceding chapters, always and already assumes the form of symbolic violence producing punitive effects.

Diagram 8.2 depicts a Lacanian interpretation for how discourse is conceived of as such in the inner workings of the unconscious. The paradigm-syntagm sphere represents the most overt and conscious plane of speech production. Paradigm refers to the selection, choice, and substitution of words. Syntagm refers to the combination, ordering, and contextuality of words. It is at the paradigmatic-syntagmatic level that speech is uttered. In order for there to be an utterance, the subject unconsciously selects out words (paradigms) that are inserted into phrases/sentences, forming a somewhat organized and coherent chain of speech (syntagms). The chains of speech are consistent with the coordinated language system in use (e.g., clinicolegal discourse). Again, structural theorists have significantly explored the interpenetrating effects of these semiotic axes as applied to law (e.g., Jackson, 1985, 1991).

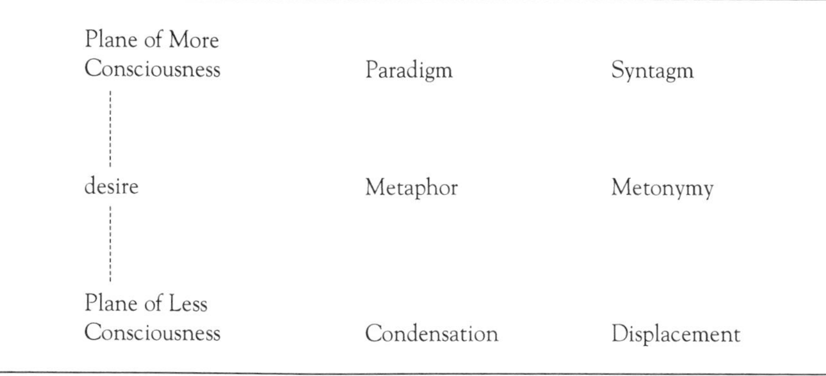

DIAGRAM 8.2. The Semiotic Grid

Notwithstanding the structural contribution, it is Lacan who extends the analysis to a deeper, more prethematized level. Both the condensation-displacement plane and the metaphor-metonymy plane are the covert and unconscious dimensions of speech production. The condensation-displacement axes does not figure prominently in Lacan's psychoanalytic semiotics. It is more consonant with a conventional Freudian (e.g., 1954, 1965) reading. The metaphor-metonymy sphere, however, represents an important addition to the psychoanalytic semiotic literature. This axis mediates and facilitates the other two paired axes (Silverman, 1983, p. 110).

In the constitution of sense, metaphors are structuring mechanisms. One word/phrase is substituted for another word/phrase in an imaginary space producing a coherent thought or a chain of speech. With the use of metaphor two entirely different signifieds are reduced to a shared signifier. Metonymy is the naming of an object and the object's completeness by referring to its parts. It is a reductive process which creates an equivalence between the thing itself and the constituents of the thing itself.

Both metaphor and metonymy figure prominently in clinicolegal discourse. For example, referring to a person diagnosed with a psychiatric disorder as "childlike," "diseased," "insane," "incompetent," "actively psychotic," "in need of mental health treatment," and the like are metaphors. Depending on situation and context, these words, phrases, or both substitute for the term *mental illness*. However, each of these expressions (including mental illness) conveys somewhat different thoughts and sentiments about the person with a diagnosed disorder. This notwithstanding, these differences are reduced to one shared meaning (Arrigo, 1993c).

In addition, metonymical expressions are found within the discourse of law and psychiatry. To illustrate, such terms as *auditory hallucinations*, *diminished capacity, substituted judgment, flight of ideas, fanciful thinking, criminal mind,* and the like are metonyms. Each of these expressions creates an artificial equivalence between a person diagnosed with a psychiatric disorder and aspects of that individual (e.g., hearing, thinking, judging). What makes these equivalents artificial is that the fullness of a person can never be reduced to one's parts, including persons diagnosed as psychiatrically ill. Thus, metaphor *represses* the fullness of the subject-in-speech and metonymy *reduces* the fullness of the subject-in-speech. Both deny, through prethematic language, a more complete sense of who the speaking-subject (i.e., the psychiatric citizen) is.

In Lacanian psychoanalytic theory, the significance of the three axes is in how they recreate the sphere of linguistic production and circulation. Of particular interest are the psychic forces within the unconscious mind of law and psychiatry that repeatedly give rise to circumscribed clinicolegal discourse in civil and criminal mental health law. Through the Semiotic Grid images, emanating from the Other, are given temporary psychical clarity within narrowly defined and circumscribed parameters of meaning. These images, as prespoken coordinates of sense-making, produce a *visée de conscience*; that is, a uniquely encoded awareness toward some aspect of reality (Metz, 1983, pp. 104–1143). This *visée* represents the argot of psychiatric justice which, in its very syntactic and psychic construction, rules out the possibility of explaining crime, behavior, and law in any other terms than its own (Arrigo, 1996b, pp. 175–202). Again, the Symbolic Order, as a facet of the unconscious, is composed of prevailing and privileged language, thought, and culture removed from the Real Order that embodies the authentic and untapped voice of the subject-in-speech awaiting legitimacy. Thus, what is selected out and spoken to convey unconscious desire is that grammar that fills in, although incompletely and temporarily, the subject's (i.e., the psychiatric citizen's) inherent lack-in-being. It is this prethematic selection process that dismisses the idea that human beings are often situated in contradictory, competitive, and inconsistent grammars seeking the embodiment of alternative desires.

Enactors of clinicolegal discourse (e.g., lawyers, psychiatrist), when speaking through the grammar of psychiatric justice, knowingly or not find themselves engaged in the reproduction of that sedimented speech constituting the medicolegal establishment (Arrigo, 1997e). Integrating all that has been suggested thus far on the three semiotic axes, we now see that there is an additional feature relevant to Lacan's notion of subjectivity. Desire arises from individuals and it is always unique to a person's life experiences. Thus, primordially, the desire of subjects is polyvalent, amorphous, and diversified. It floats amidst a sea of signifiers in the repository of the unconscious and awaits anchorage. Desire is eventually mobilized and embodied in words. The subject insists (i.e., seeks *jouissance*) but must navigate, unconsciously and prethematically, his or her psychic identity through the three semiotic axes. This movement produces words that are transformed into conventional meanings, consistent with a particular system of communication (e.g., law and psychiatry) and expressed through the paradigmatic-syntagmatic axes.

The Semiotic Grid and its corresponding axes show us that the intrapsychic and intersubjective sphere of speech production and circulation entails an unconscious process of linguistic structuration. Deep within the psychic apparatus, desire is mobilized as a response to a lack-in-being. In other words, desire begins to be embodied through words which speak the subject or speak through the subject. The signifier, as the locus of desire, must endure further manipulation, direction, reconfiguration with the metaphor-metonymy semiotic axes before it is spoken. Again, the spoken word is always and already of a certain language or of a particular discourse.

In the context of civil and criminal mental health law, the clinicolegal meanings that attach to mental illness and the assorted psycholegal issues pertaining to it always and already convey limiting (i.e., repressive and reductive) connotations. This is because the discourse of law and psychiatry unconsciously seeks to affirm values consistent with its own internal logic. As described in previous chapters, this is a logic that esteems unity, homogeneity, stability, and order. It is a logic that cleanses, sanitizes, and corrects difference.

As embodied in the psychiatric citizen, difference becomes a spoken category through which symbolic and then structural inequalities are produced, sustained, and legitimized. Indeed, mental health systems users, among other things, succumb to paternalism, limited advocacy rights, an absence of constitutionally ensured community based treatment, transcarceration, discursive constraints in the psychiatric courtroom, and death row executions. As exemplars of how the mentally ill are policed, we understand that these practical and ideological effects obtain because the unconscious mind of law and psychiatry is linguistically structured to encompass only that discourse reflecting its unitary, normalizing, and homogenous voice. All speech, thought, and behavior falling outside this sphere is dismissed and silenced. Such utterances, cognitions, or actions as these cannot find recognition and legitimacy in the unconscious terrain of psychiatric justice. Indeed, to do otherwise would displace and de-enter that system of communication that breaths meaning into the emotional soul and body of law and psychiatry. As a consequence, desire is territorialized (Deleuze & Guattari, 1987), being is denied, and the psychiatric citizen is punished.

TOWARD A CRITICAL THEORY OF PUNISHMENT

This chapter examined several ideological components germane to the policing of mental illness. In conjunction with the conceptual and practical observations developed throughout this book, it is now possible to present a provisional theory of punishment at the crossroads of law and psychiatry. Preliminarily, it is instructive to point out that the description of this disciplinary theory rests, in large measure, on the perceived and felt oppression promulgated by discourse, mobilized and activated at the level of the unconscious.[3] This approach does not discount the punitive effects of psycholegal decision making; rather, it situates these effects within their appropriate ideological and conceptual framework. This framework is coordinated within the psychic apparatus. Moreover, the theory presented here does not dismiss the political economy of law and psychiatry. These dynamics, although not systematically reviewed throughout this text, received some attention in previous chapters (see especially chapters 1 and 3).

Diagram 8.3 visually depicts the process through which the penalty for mental illness is activated, sustained, and legitimized. In this schema the salient features of each chapter are brought together. In order to disclose how punishment operates within and throughout psycholegal decision making, some general observations on the mechanics of the diagram are warranted. Following these comments, a series of postulates will be enumerated. These postulates represent the outline for a provisional and critical theory of law, psychiatry, and punishment.

The Penalty for Mental Illness: Understanding its Mechanics

Located at the left and right hand margins of the diagram are the spheres of more and less consciousness. Jointly, these domains constitute the pivotal divide by and through which desire is spoken or unspoken, present or concealed, mobilized or repressed. Depending on the position of the speaking-subject (e.g., as clinicolegal decision broker, as mental health advocate, as disordered citizen) the frequency, duration, and intensity of the person's desire is embodied in clinicolegal speech. However, regardless of one's subject position, desire-in-discourse anchors how the other elements of the diagram interactively function. Accordingly, the speaking-subject is the locus of all speech, thought, and action.

There are two intersecting axes that pass through the speaking-subject. These axes include the plane of meaning and being, and the plane of the real and the symbolic. The plane of meaning and being reflects the struggle the psychiatric citizen encounters when seeking identity fulfillment and interpersonal legitimacy through an established system of communication (i.e., clinicolegal discourse). The plane of the real and the symbolic specifies the dilemma the unconscious mind of law and psychiatry confronts when circulating and reproducing only certain meanings and values, consistent with its own internal and prethematic logic. Both of these axes interactively extend from the sphere of the conscious to the sphere of unconscious.

The plane of meaning and being and the plane of the real and the symbolic pass through the speaking-subject. This occurs because both axes are mediated by

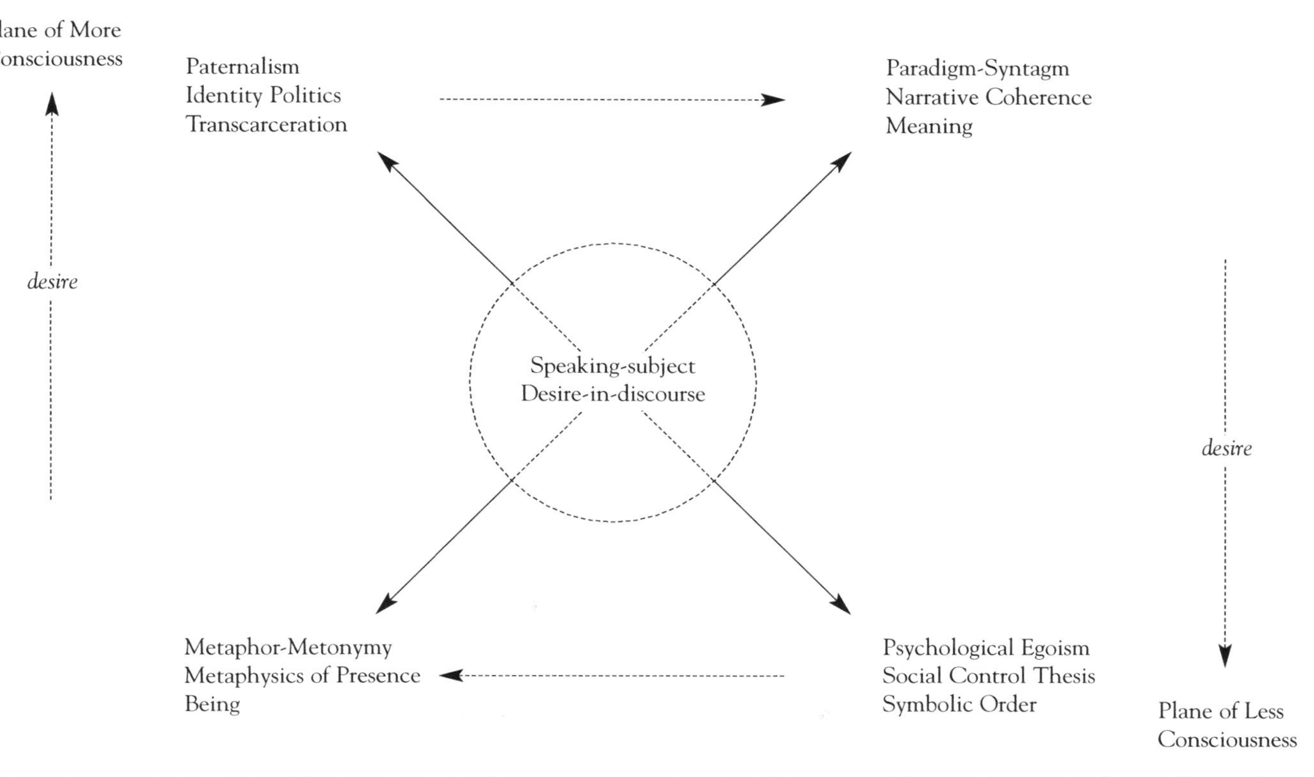

DIAGRAM 8.3. The Penalty for Mental Illness

the desiring subject. Relatedly, these two axes intersect and cross-over at the point of the speaking subject. This dynamic draws attention to the psychic and ideological forces that always and already encode reality for the psychiatric citizen.

There are two horizontal arrows identified in the diagram. The arrows represent movement. The arrow crossing from the upper left to the upper right conveys conscious activity. This is the behavior of law and psychiatry embodying values (e.g., paternalism) and locating them in narratively coherent speech chains (e.g., civil commitment). The arrow crossing from the lower right to the lower left signifies unconscious activity. What the conscious movement affirms are certain phenomenal forms, situated in the Lacanian Symbolic Order (e.g., psychological egoism, the social control thesis). As both source and product of psycholegal decision making, these phenomenal forms repress (i.e., metaphor), reduce (i.e., metonymy), or otherwise silence the humanity of psychiatric citizens. Indeed, their felt difference is made into an absence. This notwithstanding, as divided and decentered subjects, mental health consumers reify the language of law and psychiatry through their engagement with transcarceration. They shape and are shaped by its logic. This engagement gives rise to the articulated value and established meanings of paternalism. Thus, the penalty for mental illness endures and the cycle repeats itself much like a feedback loop.

The Penalty for Mental Illness: Understanding Its Postulates

Given the above observations on the mechanics of diagram 8.3, I now present, in postulate form, a heuristic and critical theory of law, psychiatry, and punishment. There are eight (8) premises to the theory. Each of them summarizes the most notable points raised in the respective chapters. Thus, for example, postulate 1 reflects the insights of the first chapter, postulate 2 reflects the insights of the second chapter, and so on, and so forth. After the presentation of each postulate, I then offer some brief observations on how the premise contributes to my overall thesis.

1. *The clinicolegal community endorses the value of paternalism (i.e., police powers and parens patriae), expressed through social control, custody, and treatment practices. Paternalism underscores all psycholegal decisions, including, among others, the meaning of mental illness, the definition and prediction of dangerousness, and civil and criminal confinement.*

Chapter 1 explored the recent past (i.e., past 25 years) on matters of confinement as understood by legal and psychiatric decision brokers. At the core of this history is the long-standing value of paternalism, expressed through social control, custody, treatment initiatives, or any combination of these. This is a spoken value embraced by the clinicolegal community. Paternalism necessitates that the rights of mental health citizens be balanced against the demands of an organized society. Given this tension, many contemporary psycholegal issues are fraught with uncertainty (e.g., right to refuse treatment, predicting dangerousness). As a consequence, critics contend that psychiatric citizens have been (and remain) subjected to "illness politics," a clinicolegal custom that mostly has led to their abandonment. The penalty for mental illness is manifested in such abandonment.

2. *Paternalism is mediated by mental health advocacy; a social practice designed to ensure, protect, and represent the rights of mental health consumers. However, this advocacy is governed by an ethic of psychological egoism, measured altruism, or both; philosophical perspectives that can never embody fully the interests of those for whom the practice was designed. At best, consumer rights are re-presented.*

Chapter 2 considered whether it was possible to promote the genuine interests of mental health citizens, recognizing the uneasy and strained historical relationship that legal and psychiatric decision brokers have endured, producing a flawed and disappointing system of care. For the mental health consumer, rights are assigned to and taken from them through the law. This is especially problematic, given that the advocate operates from a position of psychological egoism. As an ethical posture, psychological egoism mostly functions at an unconscious level informing and texturing how rights-claiming unfolds for the disordered citizen. Advocacy in mental health law is governed by clinicolegal interpretations of illness, dangerousness, competency, and the like. Given these realities, there is considerable room to question the philosophical basis upon which this advocacy is truly initiated. Thus, it follows that citizen justice and collective humanism remain largely diverted. The interests of mental health consumers are symbolically re-presented. Indeed, they are identified, spoken, codified, and legitimized through the re-presentation of others.

3. *The re-presentation of mental health consumer interests, and the limits that attach to them, are linked to identity politics; a political theory that balances competing and conflicting liberty rights by first reducing psychiatric difference to sameness.*

Among other things, chapter 3 assessed how competing and conflicting interests are balanced in psycholegal decision making. There are many articulated interests that underscore legal and psychiatric practices. Some of them include impartiality, objectivity, neutrality, order, the unitary subject, scientific certainty, quantification, rules, and accuracy. As spoken values, they operate at the level of conscious awareness and are applied to all people, presumably in an equitable and fair way. However, the problem with this logic is that people are not homogenous. Imposing order on variation reduces difference to sameness. This is the presence of identity politics; a clinicolegal standard that interprets and assigns meaning to the speech, thought, and behavior of psychiatric citizens from a shared, though noninclusive, perspective. The category of mental illness as difference is therefore devalued, and psycholegal decisions unfold accordingly.

4. *Regulating, containing, and/or correcting difference under the guise of paternalism, the re-presentation of consumer rights, and identity politics means that mental illness is "policed." The policing of psychiatric illness is a consequence of the social control thesis. In short, psychiatric citizens are disciplined not for what they do but for what they represent (i.e., difference).*

Chapter 4 presented and extended the social control thesis. Clinicolegal science, as a regime of truth, exercises its power to define and shape identities. This power, both technical and inventive, monitors, regulates, and corrects the behaviors and thoughts of mental health citizens. Thus, clinicolegal science represents power over others, fostering a disciplinary society where difference is normalized and depathologized. The psychiatric subject, exposed to discoveries in medicine and advances in law, is made functionally well, consistent with the modern episteme. However, the modern episteme, articulated at the level of consciousness, affirms the value of paternalism and the philosophy of identity politics. These important markers, in large part, constitute the "real dimension" of the penalty for mental illness. In addition, however, when coupled with psychological egoism the social control thesis, in substantial part, establishes the "symbolic dimension" of the penalty for psychiatric illness. Indeed, the plane of the real and the symbolic interactively operates through the speaking-subject. This axis reveals how the unconscious mind of law and psychiatry endorses values and meanings consistent with clinicolegal science, including the policing of difference.

5. *Legal and psychiatric decision brokers produce, sustain, and legitimize the social control thesis. In addition, however, mental health citizens reify, knowingly or not, the policing of difference. This reification occurs because they define and are defined by transcarceration. Transcarceration entails the routing of psychiatric subjects to and from the mental health and justice systems of which such citizens are a part and from which their identities emerge.*

Chapter 5 addressed the complicitous role of mental health consumers who both shape and are shaped by the discourse of transcarceration. Transcarceration is the "real" effect of the social control thesis. Indeed, for users of psychiatric services, the language and logic of civil and criminal confinement pervades their lives. Given that language, located in the Symbolic Order, activates conventional and prevailing speech and thought, the coherent narrative spoken and lived by psychiatric citizens, unconsciously represses and reduces their being. This notwithstanding, the discourse of transcarceration is spoken. As such, it always and already incompletely encodes the citizen's identity, while actively sustaining the process that is the penalty for mental illness.

6. *Transcarceration is the effect of the social control thesis, institutionally enacted through the psychiatric courtroom. Thus, the behavior of the mental health court, and the ideological values pertaining to it, reveal why mental illness is policed. On closer*

inspection, legal and psychiatric language structures thought in ways that are not neutral, in ways that convey hidden assumptions, in ways that embody circumscribed knowledge about psychiatric citizens. This is the phenomenon of desire-in-discourse.

Chapter 6 examined the discursive construction of law and psychiatry and how this construction gives rise to confinement determinations. The speaking-subject (e.g., the forensic mental health decision broker), embraces a particular language (i.e., clinicolegal discourse) saturated with unspoken desire. When articulated, this desire embodies only those values representing the psychiatric courtroom. As such, knowledge about illness, health, dangerousness, competence, confinement, execution, and so on is circumscribed and limited to the interpretations of forensic "experts." Thus, the disordered citizen appearing before a medicolegal tribunal or court is understood through a specialized grammar. The coordinates of this grammar are esteemed and validated by enactors of this discourse. Any attempt to communicate through alternative speech codes is objected to and dismissed or cleansed and relanguaged. In effect, all replacement grammars must be consistent with the coordinates of meaning advancing the desiring voice of psychiatric justice. The true, spoken identity and being of the psychiatric citizen is "linguistically" silenced. Accordingly, in the context of desire-in-discourse, disciplinary practices originate and are manifested in dominant speech ideologies with their corresponding effects.

7. *At the conscious level of speech production, desire-in-discourse represents a coherent narrative. This narrative or meaning is based on various binary oppositions contained within mental health civil and criminal law (e.g., well vs. ill; competent vs. incompetent), where what is spoken and made present (i.e., wellness, competence) conceals an absence awaiting recognition (the paradoxes of mental health law). Accordingly, ideology, with its marginalizing effects, is perpetuated in law and psychiatry.*

Chapter 7 investigated the problem with speech production in the psychiatric courtroom through a concrete example. At issue was how the U.S. Supreme Court constructed and articulated its position on the matter of incompetent death row prisoners who exercise their treatment refusal rights, in the face of imminent execution. Judges, too, function as speaking-subjects. In other words, what they talk and write about conveys unspoken desire. Within the plane of meaning and being the discourse on capital punishment for the mentally ill is built on a narratively coherent, although ideologically concealed, construction of reality. Absent from that which is spoken are the paradoxes of mental illness. For example, forced medication over objection is not "treatment." Indeed, deconstructively speaking, the one who treats, instead of giving, receives; and the one treated, instead of receiving, gives. Moreover, semiotically speaking, such middle ground solutions as negotiated treatment or contemplated treatment are dismissed because the logic of paternalism in mental health law does not include, nor does it value, such options. Thus, the penalty one endures for psychiatric disorder (i.e., the policing of difference) is mobilized in the unconscious mind of law and psychiatry.

8. *At the unconscious level of speech production, desire-in-discourse, constituting the text of civil and criminal mental health law, is situated in the Symbolic Order. This is the repository of prevailing language and culture. The "lack" that defines psychiatric citizens through clinicolegal metaphorical-metonymical expressions, fails to convey the fullness of their identity, humanity, and being. This is the presence of punishment, first and foremost assuming a discursive linguistic form.*

Earlier in chapter 8, I explored those unconscious and prethematic forces giving rise to clinicolegal speech. The Symbolic Order represents conventional language and thought. Accordingly, unconsciously selected words forming a speech chain (i.e., paradigm-syntagm) anchor, although incompletely and falsely, the inherent lack-in-being that, nonetheless, defines and names the psychiatric subject in law. Previously, this dynamic was described through the example of death row executions for the mentally ill. However, situated within the unconscious are those metaphorical-metonymical expressions that, when spoken as narrative constructions, always and already repress and reduce the humanity of the subject. Thus, as desire is mobilized in the prethematic mind of law and psychiatry, so, too, can we locate the presence of symbolic violence. Indeed, being is sacrificed at the alter of meaning. Harms of reduction and repression abound. Punishment, assuming a discursive linguistic form, prevails.

CONCLUSIONS

If decisions reached by law and psychiatry are, knowingly or not, always and already linguistically structured to punish the mentally ill, what then can be said about the legitimacy of *any* civil and criminal mental health law practice? This matter is of no small consequence. Indeed, the suggestion here is that symbolic violence, enacted deep within the unconscious mind of psycholegal thought, language, and culture, fundamentally marginalizes the identity and humanity of psychiatric citizens. This marginalization occurs *before* the trial, administrative hearing, or decision-making process unfolds, activated through such overt and/or spoken values as paternalism, identity politics, and transcarceration. Thus, the question under consideration is: What impact does such psychic harm have on clinicolegal decision making?

Generally speaking, there are three identifiable perspectives on this point (Arrigo, 1993c, pp. 12–23). The first position holds that the degree of individual violence or personal injury is so minor that citizen justice is not compromised. Thus, mental health law practices should remain unchanged as they fail to irreparably, seriously, or otherwise adversely harm the rights of the psychiatrically ill. This is the medical model or status quo perspective. The second position maintains that the degree of individual violence or personal injury is variable and, depending on circumstances, may compromise citizen justice. Thus, decisions made at the crossroads of law and psychiatry require careful and prudent review and, where necessary, specific adjustments to the mental health law system. This is the mainstream legal model or balanced perspective. The third position states that violence enacted through speech produces unintended social effects. These effects stem from a flawed process. Given that the process is suspect, citizen justice is always compromised. Thus, all mental health law practices should be thoroughly reevaluated: the harm enacted is real; the punishment inflicted is deep. This is the critical model or abolitionist perspective.

In the pages that remain, each of these outlooks is briefly reviewed. I am particularly interested in how mental illness is interpreted, given the respective outlooks. The focus on mental illness is extremely important. Indeed, one's interpretation or assessment of it signals a particular regard for law, psychiatry, and clinicolegal intervention (Williams & Arrigo, 2001a). Relatedly, I consider the justice policy implications that flow from these positions. Ultimately, I consider whether there are demonstrably clear and compelling grounds to abrogate the practice of civil and criminal incarceration for persons identified as psychiatrically disordered. If so, this determination invites speculation on the future of civil and criminal mental health law and policy.

The Medical Model Perspective

Supporters of this position assert that there is no harm. In other words, the use of clinicolegal language does not, in and of itself, produce violence or otherwise punish the mental health consumer, sufficient to warrant any change in the practice of psycholegal decision making. The status quo orientation draws attention to the "real" life experiences that the psychiatrically disordered confront, absent sustained confinement (e.g., homelessness, revolving-door care, deteriorating health, isolation, death) (Torrey, 1997). In this context, mental illness, as a state of being, exists categorically (Zusman, 1982). In the extreme, persons can be dangerous to themselves, others, or both and, therefore, must be treated, mindful of one's fundamental liberty guarantees (Appelbaum & Gutheil, 1991).

The justice policy implications linked to the medical model orientation are also worth noting. In short, the status quo perspective asserts that medical treatment and clinical intervention outweigh one's right to rot (e.g., Appelbaum & Gutheil, 1980; Arrigo, 1993c, pp. 13–18). The real issue is quality care, particularly for those persons who are obviously ill (Treffert, 1985). In this context, it would be criminal, for example, to not administer drug therapy or to not insist on confinement, given the presence of severe and persistent mental disease (Treffert, 1982; Zusman, 1982). Therefore, (medical) policy necessitates that the treatment needs of the patient be first and foremost protected (Appelbaum & Gutheil, 1991). To do otherwise would simply be unacceptable and unjust.

The Mainstream Legal Perspective

Advocates of this position contend that harm is possible. In other words, the use of clinicolegal language may, in particular instances, produce violence or otherwise erode the rights of psychiatric citizens. The most obvious illustration of this phenomenon is hate speech (Walker, 1994). Injury enacted through language would entail a showing of how such communication produced social harm (e.g., riots, looting, physical altercations) (Weinstein, 1999), or damaged the standing or reputation of a particular individual or constituency group (Sarat & Kearns, 1992). If sufficient proof is tendered, the practice of clinicolegal decision making would then be amended.

The balanced perspective attempts to weigh competing liberty interests. These interests focus on the rights of psychiatric citizens versus the demands of society. The mainstream legal position accepts the existence of mental illness (e.g., Wexler, 1981), believing that there are occasions when the confinement (civil or criminal) of psychiatric consumers is warranted (Gutheil, Appelbaum, & Wexler, 1983). Indeed, this perspective maintains that "incapacitation may not be punishment at all, since the purpose is not to inflict pain but to hold an individual until there is no risk of further harm or violence" (Arrigo, 1993c, p. 12). Thus, similar to the medical model framework, mainstream legalists contend that mental disorders exist absolutely; however, questions persist about whether, and under what specific conditions, clinical treatment supersedes liberty rights (e.g., Morse, 1982b). As a matter of justice policy, then, unless and until one can show how clinicolegal language is harmful, the balanced perspective weighs the other (competing and conflicting) interests at stake when controversial decisions are made at the crossroads of law and psychiatry.

The Critical Perspective

Proponents of this position maintain that the harm perpetrated through language is real (e.g., MacKinnon, 1993). That is to say, the spoken word can injure; it can exclude (Matsuda, Lawrence, & Delgado, 1993). The effect of this exclusion is the privileging of dominant ideologies and the marginalization of minority voices (Arrigo, Milovanovic, & Schehr, 2000, pp. 184–188; Matsuda, 1996). In the context of clinicolegal decision making, then, the grammar of law and psychiatry "names" identities, relationships, social interaction, and all forms of acceptable speech, thought, and behavior (Arrigo, 1996b). According to the abolitionist model, it is through the activity of defining the subject in law (i.e., the person as "patient," as "diseased," as "sick," as "incompetent," as "diminished") that violence, knowingly or not, is enacted. These descriptors convey unconscious values and implicit meanings that reduce and repress the humanity of psychiatric citizens.

In relation to mental illness, abolitionists seriously question the unconscious intent operating within and throughout this label (e.g., Williams & Arrigo, 2001a). In short, critics argue that the designation of psychiatric disorder creates a binary logic (i.e., an "us" versus "them"), dismissing the more fluid character of being human (Williams & Arrigo, 2001; Arrigo, 1996b). In other words, the phenomenon that is termed *mental illness* does not exist independent of an array of social, political, economic, and historical factors that are spoken. Once uttered as such, the discourse assumes a reality that becomes more "real" than the individual to whom the label is assigned. Thus, words or expressions embody not just implicit meanings but felt identities where psychological states, social conditions, and interpersonal dynamics once described as such, become a stand-in for the person or group to whom these descriptors are applied. In this way, the violence enacted by psycholegal decision-making "is inscribed in struggles to put violence in discourse and to control its discursive representations" (Sarat, 1993, pp. 24–25).

When the above critical observations are linked to how the unconscious mind of law and psychiatry is structured, consistent with the analysis entertained throughout this book, we understand that punishment *is* enacted through discourse. As a matter of justice policy, then, advocates of the critical perspective call for the elimination of all forms of civil and criminal confinement (e.g., MacLean & Pepinsky, 1991). Indeed, if the process embodies harm, victimization, exclusion, and so forth, activated deep within the inner network of psycholegal thought, then all the outcomes it yields and all the decisions it renders are, at the very least, suspect. In the extreme, they are irreparably flawed.

The abolitionist suggestion in the realm of clinicolegal decision-making should not be taken lightly. Aside from civil incarceration and criminal confinement, all other forensic practices (e.g., predictions of dangerousness, the ethics of advocacy, executions of the mentally ill) would also require significant and wholesale reformulation. Admittedly, there are serious consequences for adopting such a policy perspective. Indeed, the position recommended here calls for a dramatic reassessment of the theoretical premises and epistemological assumptions underscoring all legal and psychiatric decision-making (Williams & Arrigo, 2001a).

To date, important works along these lines, while sparse, are appearing. Challenges to the legitimacy of psycholegal practices (Fox, 1991, 1999; Melton,

1992; Haney, 1993) and calls for the development of a psychological jurisprudence (Fox, 1993; Arrigo, 2001c) seem to be the most promising. In brief, these efforts draw attention to where and how social change and citizen justice can be thoughtfully envisioned and systematically implemented. I submit that the future of humane and empowering decision-making situated at law and psychiatry's divide depends on these and similar liberatory efforts. We owe this much to the field of mental health law. We owe this much to the community of practitioners who make difficult decisions about the often complicated and troubling life experiences of psychiatric consumers. Indeed, in the final analysis, we owe this much to those who are, from the depths of the unconscious to the site of the psychiatric courtroom, needlessly and wrongfully punished.

Notes

PREFACE

1. See http://www.newreformation.org/elephant.htm (last visited April 31, 2001).

2. See e.g., Michael L. Perlin, "Morality and Pretextuality, Psychiatry and Law: Of 'Ordinary Common Sense,' Heuristic Reasoning, and Cognitive Dissonance," 19 *Bull. Am. Acad. Psychiatry and L.*, 131 (1991); Michael L. Perlin, "Psychodynamics and the Insanity Defense: 'Ordinary Common Sense' and Heuristic Reasoning," 69 *Neb. L. Rev.*, 3 (1990) (Perlin, "Psychodynamics").

3. See generally, Perlin, "Psychodynamics," supra note 2.

4. Manuscript, at xix.

5. I discuss this in, inter alia, Michael L. Perlin, "The Borderline Which Separated You From Me": The Insanity Defense, the Authoritarian Spirit, the Fear of Faking, and the Culture of Punishment, 82 *Iowa L. Rev*, 1375 (1997); Michael L. Perlin, *The Jurisprudence of the Insanity Defense* (1994) (Perlin, *Jurisprudence*), and Michael L. Perlin, *The Hidden Prejudice: Mental Disability on Trial* (2000) (Perlin, *The Hidden Prejudice*).

6. See generally, Michael L. Perlin, *Mental Disability Law: Civil and Criminal* (1989), and (2d ed., 1998, 1999, & 2000); Michael L. Perlin, *Mental Disability Law: Cases and Materials* (1999).

7. See e.g., Michael L. Perlin, "Mental Patient Advocacy by a Public Advocate," 54 *Psychiatric Q.* 169 (1982); Michael L. Perlin & Robert L. Sadoff, "Ethical Issues in the Representation of Individuals in the Commitment Process," 45 *Law and Contemp. Probs.*, 161 (Summer 1982); Michael L. Perlin, "Fatal Assumption: A Critical Evaluation of the Role of Counsel in Mental Disability Cases," 16 *Law and Hum. Behav.*, 39 (1992).

8. Manuscript, at 39 (emphasis added).

9. Ibid.

10. Ibid. at 53.

11. See e.g., Keri K. Gould & Michael L. Perlin, "'Johnny's in the Basement/Mixing Up His Medicine': Therapeutic Jurisprudence and Clinical Teaching," 24 *Seattle U. L. Rev.*, 339 (2000).

12. See e.g., Michael L. Perlin et al., "Therapeutic Jurisprudence: Understanding the Sanist and Pretextual Bases of Mental Disability Law," 20 *N. Eng. J. Crim. and Civ. Confinement*, 369 (1994); Michael L. Perlin, "Therapeutic Jurisprudence and the Civil Rights of Institutionalized Mentally Disabled Persons: Hopeless Oxymoron or Path to Redemption?" 1 *Psychology, Pub. Pol'y and L.*, 80 (1995); Michael L. Perlin, "'For the Misdemeanor Outlaw': The Impact of the ADA on the Institutionalization of Criminal Defendants with Mental Disabilities," 52 *Alabama L. Rev.*, 193 (2000); Michael L. Perlin, "'Their Promises of Paradise': Institutional Segregation, Community Treatment, the ADA, and *Olmstead v. L.C.*," 37 *Hous. L. Rev.* 999 (2000).

13. See generally, Perlin, *The Hidden Prejudice*, supra, note 5; Michael L. Perlin, "'Half-Wracked Prejudice Leaped Forth': Sanism, Pretextuality, and Why and How Mental Disability Law Developed as It Did," 10 *J. Contemp. Leg. Iss.*, 3 (1999).

14. See e.g., Perlin, *The Hidden Prejudice*, supra, note 5, at 36–47; Perlin, *Jurisprudence*, supra, note 5, at 383–387; Michael L. Perlin, On "Sanism," 46 *SMU L. Rev.*, 373 (1992).

CHAPTER 1.
CIVIL COMMITMENT AND PATERNALISM

1. This problem is exacerbated when considering the civil confinement of postconvicted sex offenders. For example, in 1994 Kansas enacted the Sexually Violent Predator Act, permitting the involuntary hospitalization of persons who, due to "mental abnormality" or a "personal disorder," were likely to participate in "predatory acts of sexual violence" (Kan. Stat. Ann. Sect. 52–29a01 et seq.). This statute was put to the test in the case of *Kansas v. Hendricks* (1997). Hendricks was a known child molester who was scheduled for release from prison shortly following the passage into law of the Act. The United States Supreme Court concluded that the statute comported with due process requirements, thereby making it possible for individuals, following release from prison, to be placed in a psychiatric hospital under a civil confinement order. The case of *Hendricks* is an example of paternalism, under the guise of public safety and potential dangerousness, that has far-reaching implications for the legitimacy of civil commitment in general and the rights of individuals in particular (e.g., Perlin, 1999, pp. 235–248). Indeed, it remains to be seen whether a person involuntarily hospitalized under *Hendricks* is truly mentally ill (i.e., an identified mental abnormality is not the same as a diagnosed psychiatric illness). Thus, the

civil confinement of predatory sexual offenders raises new constitutional and treatment challenges for law and psychiatry (for an overview of these matters see Winick & LaFond, 1998 [passim]).

CHAPTER 2. MEDICOLEGAL ADVOCACY FOR THE MENTALLY ILL

1. For example, Fox (1999) contends that, with an emphasis on justice, the law-psychology field could pose several relevant questions regarding the human condition and human social behavior, previously ignored or dismissed by the discipline. As he ponders it:

> How does the law ensure the maintenance of societal inequality and power imbalances? When does law provide the appearance of justice without the reality? Does the lack of consensus about how to define justice mean we cannot attack injustice? To what extent does reliance on law deflect attention from other solutions to societal problems? (Fox, 1999, p. 10)

2. Critics of mainstream psycholegal scholarship assert that, despite contributions from critical legal studies, feminist jurisprudence, postmodern inquiry, and the like, scant attention has been given to "law's potential downside even as [forensic researchers] examined discretionary factors in legal decision making and proposed relatively minor institutional reforms" (Fox, 1999, p. 10). Other disheartened commentators suggest that the law-psychology field remains constituted by practitioners who "still have blinders on when they look at the law and the legal system" (Melton, 1991, p. 1). These are blinders that signal "an abandoning of a sense of mission—the mission of legal change" (Haney, 1993, pp. 378–379).

3. Contributions from the therapeutic jurisprudence literature notwithstanding (e.g., Wexler & Winick, 1996; Winick, 1997a; Perlin, 1995; Arrigo & Tasca, 1999), some argue that these efforts largely assess how the state can function as a powerful instrument of control, coercion, and regulation in which psychology merely operates as the handmaiden of legal decision making (e.g., Finkel, 1995; Fox, 1997).

4. There is something approximating a tradition of this sort within mental health law circles dating back, at least, to the antipsychiatry movement of the 1960s. Indeed, on the American front, Szasz's (1963, 1987) investigations of insanity and jurisprudence (see also Ennis, 1972), Morse's (1978, 1982, 1988) analysis of "crazy behavior," morals, science, and liberty, Isaac and Armat's (1990) review of law and psychiatry's abandonment of the mentally ill, and Arrigo's (1993c, 1996b) critique of civil and criminal confinement law for the psychiatrically disordered are all exemplars of this perspective.

5. In his review of how the journal, *Law and Human Behavior*, has addressed this and similar critical questions, Ogloff (1999) notes that in order for legal psychology to advance knowledge, [researchers] must develop an understanding of "why" some phenomena in law exist. Thus, it is not enough to know *what* types of pretrial publicity affect jurors, for example, but *why* they react the way they do and *how* the media affects their decision making. . . . [O]nce we understand the cause of phenomena, we can begin to learn how the law can be revised, when necessary, to better reflect the reality [and ethics] of human behavior" (p. 4; see also, Ogloff, 2000).

6. Ethics in the law-psychology domain attempts to fit critical cases into abstract principles (e.g., the duty to warn versus client confidentiality, mandated conditions for reporting child sexual abuse, the ethics of advocacy by psychologists) (Wrightsman, 1997, pp. 40–47; Bersoff, 1995). The dilemma, of course, is that many of the nuances, complexities, and differences among the cases constituting real, unpredictable life are concealed and reduced to how such subtleties satisfy an artificial, and often homogenous, notion of personal and civic conduct.

7. In the extreme (and in some cases notwithstanding the best of advocacy intentions), the psychiatrically disordered become prisoners of confinement (Ennis, 1972; Arrigo, 1999b; Levy & Rubenstein, 1996). This means that they are repeatedly routed to and from the civil and criminal systems of institutional control (i.e., transcarcerated) with little opportunity to break free from this disciplinary cycle.

8. Consider, for example, the manner in which the administrative hearing unfolds in which a determination is made about prospects for sustained institutional confinement for a psychiatrically disordered petitioner. Resistance to the established code of comportment or opposition to the "ethic" of clinicolegal communication (i.e., appropriate speech, thought, and behavior), can thwart any expectation of release from civil or criminal custody (Arrigo, 1994).

9. I am cognizant of the violence research conducted through the MacArthur treatment studies. To date, these investigations indicate that persons with severe and untreated mental illness are more dangerous than members of the general population, especially when the individual suffers from a co-occurring substance abuse disorder, command hallucinations, or both (e.g., Steadman, 1996; see also Bardwell and Arrigo, 2002 for a detailed review of the MacArthur Treatment Competency Study). This research notwithstanding, the principal argument entertained in this chapter is the customary condition in which advocacy and rights-claiming efforts unfold for that constituency of persons identified as mentally ill. Indeed, aside from the few exceptions identified above, the mentally ill have not been proven to be any more violent than their non-men-

tally ill counterparts. Thus, the question of advocacy remains paramount to advancing the interests of (psychiatric) justice.

10. The use of the term *advocate* includes mental disability lawyers, psychiatric social workers and nurses, activist psychologists, and concerned family members of the disordered citizen. Each of these advocates assumes, depending on the individual case and the particular situation, the role of representing the perspective of the mental health systems user.

11. In critical criminological circles this process amounts to hegemony and reality construction (Milovanovic, 1994, pp. 149–150). The legitimacy of the clinicolegal system (and all of its ideological dimensions), becomes reified; that is, the medicolegal apparatus functions as the dominant arbiter of justice for the psychiatrically disordered through the unknowing consent of those who are governed by the very (confinement) system of which they are a part (Arrigo, 1993c, pp. 135–140; 1996b, pp. 129–174).

12. There is a sense in which this advocacy approximates a Marxian (1967) brand of false consciousness or what Cohen (1989) describes as "fabrications of justice" (p. 33). In short, "people accept the status quo out of lack of awareness that viable alternatives exist and out of ignorance as to how their rulers are violating their professed interest or out of ignorance of how they themselves are being harmed by what they think are their interests" (Parenti, 1996, pp. 210–211). False consciousness returns us to the hegemonic and reified legitimacy of the clinicolegal system alluded to earlier. For law-psychology applications of this phenomenon see, Fox (1999, pp. 11–15); Jost (1995, pp. 399–417); Haney (1991, pp. 184–187).

13. In mental health law circles, this decision making is often referred to as "substituted judgment." Questions concerning the efficacy of such practices center around whether it is *ever* possible to make choices that the psychiatrically disordered person would him- or herself make if the individual were competent to make them. For a brief, though accessible, review of this concept in the civil confinement context, see Arrigo (1992a, pp. 10–12). For a critical criminological assessment of this phenomenon in the criminal confinement context, see Arrigo and Williams (1999b, pp. 43–45).

14. Consider, for example, Warren's (1982) classic ethnographic study of civil commitment for the mentally ill in the fictitiously named "Metropolitan Court" in California. During the administrative hearing where a determination was made to extend or not involuntary confinement beyond the initial 72-hour observational period, attorneys, representing the interests of the institutionalized, routinely forfeited their role as zealous client advocates and adopted a psychiatrically informed commonsense and consensual definition of mental illness. Further, as she concluded, "attorneys viewe[d] their clients as crazy and therefore refraine[d] from standing firmly in the way of involuntary incarceration" (Warren, 1982, p. 140; see also Holstein, 1993).

CHAPTER 3.
THE RIGHT TO COMMUNITY-BASED TREATMENT

1. The term *mentally disabled* includes individuals with a diagnosed mental illness as well as those persons who are developmentally disabled. This chapter is concerned with those individuals whose disability is chronic or acute, requiring that the state do something about them (e.g., Costello & Preis, 1987; Perlin, 1999).

2. Interestingly, it appears as if there may be something of a notable shift, acknowledging the right to community-based treatment for the mentally disabled. In commenting on the right of institutionalized persons with mental disabilities to community services under the Americans with Disabilities Act, the Court in *Olmstead* concluded that:

> Unjustified isolation . . . is properly regarded as discrimination based on disability. . . . In evaluating the State's fundamental [responsibility] . . . [it] must consider . . . not only the cost of providing community-based care . . . but also the range of services the State provides others with mental disabilities, and the State's obligation to mete out those services equitably. (*Olmstead v. L.C.*, 1999, p. 2185)

This decision notwithstanding, the Court has yet to acknowledge an *unconditional* right to community-situated care and treatment for institutionalized psychiatric citizens. Assessing this matter constitutionally, sociologically, and philosophically is the subject of this chapter.

3. As previously described, the first group of cases focuses on the *Youngberg* court's rejection of the "least intrusive means" doctrine arguing that it forecloses *any* constitutionally based right to treatment services in the community. Conversely, the second group of cases finds that a constitutional right to community-based treatment is actually supported by *Youngberg* but maintains that minimally adequate treatment, supported by professional judgment, *is* community-based services (Costello & Preis, 1987, p. 1545).

4. In *Society for Good Will to Retarded Children*, the court maintained that the absence of treatment designated to improve a mentally retarded person's condition who is confined to a state institution is deprived of no constitutional protection. The state fails to grant a "*benefit of optimal treatment*" not mandated by the Constitution (p. 1250) (emphasis added).

5. Interpreting *Youngberg*, the court in *Society for Good Will to Retarded Children* submitted that the issue was not whether a "least restrictive environment" in general or a community placement in particular was a "superior" choice. At issue was whether keeping severely mentally retarded persons at the state institution "*[was] a rational decision based on professional judgment*" (p. 1249) (emphasis added). Although some experts testified at trial that some residents

would be "safer, happier and more productive" in smaller residences (pp. 1248–1249), the professional mental health consensus did not reflect that continued institutional confinement was appropriate. Therefore the court concluded that plaintiffs' institutional placement was not unreasonable.

6. Indeed, in *Lelsz*, the court arguable expanded the *Youngberg* holding from a presumption of validity to a presumption of correctness. The *Lelsz* language in effect argued that a state administrator's decision to institutionalize is not merely presumptively *valid* but presumptively *correct* (p. 1250).

7. In *Olson*, the federal district court plainly outlined the constitutional bases for community-situated treatment. Under the direction of the court, state officials were ordered to devise and implement a strategy to reduce the population size of mentally retarded facilities. The district court required state officials to include in their plan placing mentally retarded persons into adequate and appropriate community-based facilities, as well as ensuring the delivery of requisite support services (pp. 494–495). The district court stated that *Youngberg*'s holding rejected the "least intrusive means" standard, and therefore acknowledged a right to community-based treatment where the judgment of the medical profession agreed that said treatment was *necessary* to enable mentally retarded individuals to exercise their liberty interests guaranteed under the 14th Amendment. *Association of Retarded Children v. Olson*, 1982, pp. 488, 494).

8. Unlike the situations in *Clark* and *Thomas S.* where the question concerned the appropriate placement of individuals in the community, in *Lelsz* defendants' experts testified that community-situated services were "minimally adequate." However, it was clear that community placement was not the *only* remedy for *every* mentally disabled individual in the affected group (pp. 1250–1251).

9. The issue of complete consensus presents a problematic standard for the courts when addressing the appropriateness of institutional confinement and minimally adequate treatment (*Pennhurst State School & Hospital v. Halderman* (1984). Although experts agreed that institutional confinement was unreasonable and that developmentally disabled persons would be better served in the community, the parent-intervener challenged the professional consensus, especially with regard to severely disabled individuals. For more on the parents' claim see, Rhode (1983, pp. 1259–1260).

10. Significant inroads challenging the dominant view on the nature of mental illness (disease model) and on the nature of those persons so afflicted (patients that are ill) emerged in the 1960s (e.g., Lang, 1960, 1967; Szasz, 1963, 1974). Interestingly, while this antipsychiatry movement within the mental health community remained a peripheral orientation, it gained academic respectability within the discipline of sociology (e.g., Warren, 1982; Isaac & Armat, 1990; Holstein, 1993). These sociologists were interested in the socially constructed "label" (mental illness as deviance) that particular social groups

(clinicolegal profession) applied to people. Not only do these social groups make the rules that determine what constitutes deviance but they label these persons as outsiders (Becker, 1963) when their behavior violates the socially constructed rules (APA, 1994).

11. The APA's *Diagnostic and Statistical Manual of Mental Disorders-Revised* (1994), symbolizes an attitude toward the mentally disabled. Persons are understood as the sum of their symptoms, the sum of their deficiencies. This perspective is limited in that is does not address human possibility and competency that also constitute the fullness of the mentally disabled person's existence. Nonetheless, the medical community's barometer of psychiatric illness is regarded as *the* measure (e.g., Scull, 1984; Holstein, 1993; Arrigo, 1996b; Levy & Rubenstein, 1996; Perlin, 2000).

12. A more recent and compelling survey of the empirical data regarding the efficacy of psychotherapy and drug therapy for involuntarily confined mental patients as the *treatment of choice* concludes that: "[t]he best available evidence shows only that, at a very general level, providing both of these therapies to mentally ill individuals is better than doing nothing at all" (Durham & LaFond, 1988, p. 356). Moreover, the data does not establish that these treatment modalities for the nondangerous and involuntarily institutionalized mentally ill are effective (Durham & LaFond, 1988; LaFond & Durham, 1992).

13. The philosophical basis of this distinction was first popularized by Maurice Merleau-Ponty. Human beings are conscious of an intended reality that announces itself for all to see where meaning or truth resides between the intended observation and the object observed. This truth is intersubjectively real, provided the intentionality and the object observed are similarly, and with concern, considered by others. For those who do not engage reality in this way (like the mentally disabled) their consciousness is said to be other than the human order or virtually human (Merleau-Ponty, 1983).

14. The issue of substituted judgment was initially considered in "the right to refuse treatment" cases where the particular question for debate was terminally disabled person's "right to die" (e.g., *In re* Quinlan, 1976; *Garger v. New Jersey*, 1976; *Superintendent of Belchertown State School v. Saikewicz*, 1977; *In re* Storar, 1981). The substituted judgment doctrine was later applied to mentally ill persons not terminally ill but actively psychotic and dangerous (*In re* Richard Roe III, 1982).

15. Traditional psychiatry has been rigorously challenged for the past 50 years (e.g., Szasz, 1963; Levy & Rubenstein, 1996; Perlin, 2000). A growing body of feminist-inspired literature has challenged the paradigm of moral reasoning as defined as the discourse of justice and rights (e.g., MacKinnon, 1987; Smart, 1989; Gilligan, 1990; Fraser, 1997). Bringing these two perspectives together is an essential task if a critical theory of justice regarding the right to community-based treatment for the institutionalized mentally

disabled is to be unequivocally recognized. In part, this issue will be addressed in the last section of this chapter.

16. As Torrey (1997) observes, commenting on the devastation reaped at the hands of deinstitutionalization:

> For a substantial minority . . . deinstitutionalization has been a psychiatric Titanic. Their lives are virtually devoid of 'dignity' or 'integrity of body, mind, and spirit. 'Self-determination' often means merely that the person has a choice of soup kitchens. The 'least restrictive setting' frequently turns out to be a cardboard box, a jail cell, or a terror-filled existence plagued by both real and imaginary enemies. (p.112)

17. Arriving at statistically reliable and agreed on figures for "homelessness" in the United States is virtually impossible. This is because a representative portion of this populations prefers anonymity and seclusion making actual calculations no more than mere estimations. Estimates tend to range from 300,000 persons, according to the U.S. Department of Housing and Urban Development, to 3,000,000 persons, as reported by the Community for Creative Non-violence (e.g., Morrissey & Gounis, 1987; Caton, 1990).

18. In addition to the homelessness phenomenon, some psychiatrically disabled persons wind up in welfare hotels, poorly maintained personal care and boarding homes, local lock-up and detention centers, and, in the extreme, prison (Brakel, 1995; Arrigo, 1994a). For a more direct and cogent examination of how the criminal justice system (specifically the police) are routinely involved in "criminalizing" the lives of the mentally disabled see Teplin (1986); Patch & Arrigo (1998).

19. Aside from growing support modifying the civil commitment statutes of several states where petitioning for involuntary hospitalization for the psychiatrically disabled would be expanded, additional efforts focus on forced community treatment such as involuntary outpatient commitment. Specifically regarding the mentally ill, the American Psychiatric Association (APA) has led the campaign to modify existing state civil commitment statutes so that states would possess more power to treat *coercively* individuals with a mental health diagnosis in need of treatment (e.g., Stromberg & Stone, 1983; Schmidt, 1985). For more on forced treatment outside the community see Schwartz & Costanzo (1987).

20. These groups largely believe that the entire burden of deinstitutionalization should not fall on family members. As such, modifying existing state statutes to expand involuntary civil commitment would, in effect, reduce the harsh financial and emotional trauma families would otherwise bear (La Fond & Durham, 1992). This analysis raises an important question; namely, whose interests are really being served here? Indeed, to the extent that family members and

other caretakers support expanded civil commitment laws for their loved ones, this sentiment seriously erodes prospects for citizen justice (i.e., unencumbered choice-making) for the mentally disabled as a rights-claiming constituency (Arrigo, 1996b; Williams & Arrigo, 2000a).

21. The reference to liberty includes both its preservation and the exercise of it. This would entail the creation of a holistic system of comprehensive intervention approaches and models of care that would result in a continuum of seamless services. This system would necessarily provide the psychiatrically disabled with the right opportunity to actualize their potential to the fullest extent that their disability would permit *without* resorting to institutional confinement (*Mental Health Association v. Deukmejian*, 1986; Levy & Rubenstein, 1996).

22. The argument for this right could be made by examining state constitutions as well. For a more detailed treatment of this issue regarding the mentally ill under the doctrine of "independent and adequate state grounds," see Meisel (1982). I note that there are several problems with this state constitutional approach: (1) there is very little case law to assist with constitutional analysis which means that states will rely on Federal Constitutional interpretations; (2) statutorily based rights are subject to legislative modification which, in effect, results in a failure of continuity in community care; and (3) state courts may be unwilling to order state officials to implement constitutionally protected, state-based interests of individual plaintiffs (*Klostermann v. Cuomo*, 1984, p. 593).

23. Confinement without treatment violates the Eighth Amendment's cruel and unusual punishment proscription (e.g., *Robinson v. California*, 1962). In this case, the Supreme Court argued that while it is permissible to treat involuntarily committed drug addicts and mentally disabled persons, this treatment is *essential* in order to maintain one's liberty interests against cruel and unusual punishment. In the absence of such treatment for involuntarily committed individuals, this confinement amounts to punishment proscribed by the Eighth Amendment.

24. These concerns would include: (1) an "exchange" theory, which takes away the liberty interests of a mentally disabled person via indefinite institutional confinement. Such confinement affords the person less constitutionally protected liberty interests than a criminal defendant and necessitates compensation for such deprivation. This quid pro quo compensation is the benefit of treatment (see *O'Connor v. Donaldson*, 1975); (2) a protection from harm theory that implies that for state action to benefit presumably a mentally disabled person (specifically institutional confinement) it must not make the individual worse off than if the psychiatrically disabled person had not received such a benefit. This is an affirmative requirement to treat but not to improve the disabled person's condition (e.g., *Youngberg v. Romeo*, 1982, pp. 327–329; *Society for Goodwill to Retarded Children v. Cuomo*, 1990); (3) the least restrictive alterna-

tive theory which asserts that the state can take no more drastic and intrusive action into the lives of the involuntarily civilly committed than is necessary for the state to accomplish reasonably the purpose for its intrusion. In order for the state to succeed expeditiously and least invasively in its purpose, treatment must be prescribed to involuntarily committed, psychiatrically disabled persons (Spece, 1979, pp. 1052–1059; and (4) a right to treatment theory, which maintains that a mentally disabled person committed involuntarily to a state psychiatric facility is entitled to exhaustive procedural safeguards necessary to ensure the preservation of the individual's liberty interests. These protections would include notice, a hearing, individualized institutional programming, and periodic case reviews (Rubin, 1982).

25. For example, in *Baxstrom v. Herold* (1966), the Supreme Court maintained that the liberty interests of a confined mentally ill person would prevail when the evidence of the person's dangerousness was questionable. In the case of *Humphrey v. Cady*, 1972, civil commitment of a mentally ill individual capable of living safely outside the institution amounted to a "massive curtailment of liberty" (p. 509).

26. In this case, the Supreme Court dealt with the liberty interests of a mildly retarded deaf-mute declared incompetent to stand trial as a criminal defendant. The Court held that indefinite confinement authorized by a state statute violated the individual's due process rights. The Court reasoned that there was no reasonable relationship between the commitment and the purpose for which the commitment was ordered. Moreover, the commitment's duration could be no longer than was necessary for the state to accomplish its stated objective (*Jackson v. Indiana*, 1972, p. 738). Similar issues were raised in *O'Connor v. Donaldson* (1975). In this instance, the liberty interests of a mentally ill person who did not receive treatment during the nearly 15 years of his civil confinement were considered. The Supreme Court held that the state cannot constitutionally confine nondangerous, autonomous, psychiatric patients without providing some treatment (p. 576).

27. The constitutional right to community-situated treatment is not the same as the "least intrusive means" doctrine articulated at the beginning of this chapter. The essential difference is that the constitutional right to such treatment is not balanced against the state's 10th Amendment *parens patriae* role or its police power to prevent harm. Instead, the argument hinges on the acknowledgment that the only way to satisfy the court's implicit assumption regarding effective treatment, and maintain the holding in *Youngberg* regarding minimally adequate treatment required to preserve the 14th Amendment liberty interests, is to recognize that community-situated treatment accomplished these objectives.

28. The *parens patriae* power of the state encompasses two broad rights: the right to involuntarily confine someone for purposes of custodial care (e.g., food,

clothing, shelter, essential medical care), and the right to involuntarily confine someone for purposes of treatment (e.g., Peters et al., 1987; Reisner & Slobogin, 1997). For more on treatment with a therapeutic purpose see, *Robinson v. California* (1962) and *O'Connor v. Donaldson* (1975).

29. The relationship between custodial care of prison convicts and mental patients has been linked to a moral imprisonment. In both instances, to win release or even to ease one's life in the jail/asylum, a person must accept their place and situation as one of "self-alienation and moral servitude" (e.g., Goffman, 1967, p. 74). More recently, other commentators have suggested that if institutionalization is responsible for the pervasive sense of apathy among chronic mental patients, then both prisoners and the profoundly mentally disabled would resemble each other after five to ten years of confinement (Roth & Kroll, 1986; Isaac & Armat, 1990; Levy & Rubenstein, 1996; Williams & Arrigo, 2001).

30. The power of law with its unique method, including boundary definition, defining relevance, case analysis; and its unique language emphasizing objectivity, reasonableness, and impartiality, extends into most aspects of social life, always remaining legal and retaining for itself the mantel of legal power (Smart, 1989; Arrigo, 1995c; Fraser, 1997). Law's claim to truth is manifested in its lofty vision of itself: more than exercising power in concrete effects (judgments) is its ability to disqualify other nonlegal experiences or knowledges, or to regulate them to second-class statuses (MacKinnon, 1987). Therefore, unpacking or decoding what particular brand of legal justice is esteemed has significant implications for what particular laws (rights) will be recognized as the truth.

31. Psycholinguistic analysis of the law demonstrates a number of underlying themes, especially a need for order, unity, sameness, logic, reasonableness, impartiality, and formal equality. These notions represent standards valued by those who construct the law. The history of American jurisprudence convincingly demonstrates that these standards reflect the interest of white, middle-class males, predominately of European descent. Therefore, the socially constructed reality they have intended effectively discounts and subjugates all other realities to a lower prestige level. Not least among these oppressed groups would be the mentally disabled. For a prosaic account of how women's voices have been oppressed by the phallocentric language system see generally, Irigaray (1985). For feminist applications to law see, Cornell (1993) and Butler (1993, 1999). For a thorough overview of the concept of social construction of reality, see Berger &. Luckmann. (1966). For applications to the mentally ill, see Scheff (2000), for applications to law and the psychiatrically disordered, see Holstein (1993).

32. The holding in *Youngberg v. Romeo* (1982) is an excellent example of the Court's desire to maintain a sense of order and control (e.g., their version of truth and power) by applying the same moral reasoning lower courts relied on when assessing the case, or by utilizing related cases to create a sense of consistency and sameness.

33. In addition to impartiality's denial of difference is its inability to exist in an ideal state. Impartial reasoning can neither reduce difference to unity, nor maintain its claim to totality, because there is *always* something against which, or out of which, universal reality is asserted. This remaining perspective is a part of reality and, since reason seeks to comprehend *all* of reality, it must consider all perspectives with their unique and particular circumstances. However, impartial reason, as objective truth, depends on detachment and rests on universals. It must distance itself from particulars (feelings, special circumstances, personal inclinations, etc.) and exclude them from law's pronouncement of truth. Hence, law cannot apprehend the whole and cannot be unified (Nagel, 1986).

34. As I have argued in this chapter, the prevailing social reality in law an psychiatry regarding the mentally disabled includes disease-ridden, deviant-minded, and dangerous-prone images. Myth, symbol, and metaphor possess the capacity to alter prevailing social reality because they "possess the capacity to shatter and increase our sense of reality by shattering and increasing our language" (Ricoeur, 1973, p. 97). Enabling mentally ill and retarded people to describe their own worldviews and their own life stories is essential to disrupting the prevailing imagery surrounding this group of citizens. The legacy of institutional confinement constituted by law and science, with all of its claim to normalcy and order, denies these citizens this possibility.

35. Dispensing with such universally accepted symbols is an invitation not to substitute them with alternative symbols, as much as to acknowledge their inadequacy in representing the experiences of those whom they presume to serve. The difficulty in reconstituting images that more authentically represent the interests of the mentally ill and retarded is that any methodological reconstitution is a unity that effectively possesses the capacity to oppress those who do not subscribe to the particular paradigm (Irigaray, 1985a, pp. 68–85; Guattari, 1984; Baudrillard, 1988). The essential task is to decode multiple forms of meaning and to acknowledge and validate the particularity of experiences that signify the plurality of meaning situations hold for individual psychiatrically disabled citizens. In this regard, truth, knowledge, and power exist with no fixed determinations and no "essential" reality. Multiple forms of imagined and languaged expression are not situated in universal categories of reason or forms of rationality. Rather, they are communicative symbols signifying multiple realities (Cooper, 1967, 1978; Deleuze & Guattari, 1972; Baudrillard, 1983).

CHAPTER 4.
POLICING AND DISCIPLINING MENTAL ILLNESS

1. The link between Foucault's functional analysis of social control with nonlinear dynamics may appear somewhat contrived. After all, as I explain in

subsequent sections, Foucault presents a thesis in which resistance to regimes of power (i.e., law and psychiatry), is near impossible. However, resistance, flux, adaptability, and change are cornerstones of chaos theory. Thus, the linkage described is ostensibly an artificial or forced fit. Although I rely on Foucault's earlier writings to identify the ingredients of the social control phenomenon, his later works (Foucault, 1980, 1990) emphasize forms of micrological resistance. I allude to these works throughout the chapter and they represent an important backdrop from which to delineate a post-Foucauldian analysis informed by chaos theory principles.

2. Certainly there are multiple, competing forces parlaying for various and unrelated reasons to have their definitions of the civil commitment situation considered as essential. These other vested groups may have little specific interest in disciplining difference. Examples include social control through medicalization (Conrad and Schneider, 1992), state regulation (Jessop, 1990), and hegemonic power groups defining deviance (mental illness) consistent with the demands of those presently in power (Gramsci, 1971). The point, however, is that the likeliest explanation for the policing of public hygiene, given the conceptual and practical dilemmas of defining mental illness and dangerousness, is that psychiatric difference is normalized, depathologized, and homogenized consistent with Foucault's social control thesis.

3. I recognize that radical psychiatry, street advocates for the homeless mentally ill, and civil libertarians would challenge the extent to which "society" legitimately promotes the disciplining of psychiatric difference. But these criticisms only advance the efficacy of the argument; namely, that in the face of constituency resistance, clinicolegal science remains the avatar of justice and the source of knowledge/power concerning the behavior (and thus existence) of the mentally ill.

CHAPTER 5.
TRANSCARCERATION AND MENTALLY ILL "OFFENDERS"

1. As I subsequently describe in the section chronicling the three case studies, I interacted with literally hundreds of persons suffering from a myriad of social, psychological, and economic difficulties. The cases selected for purposes of this inquiry are representative of the type of client populations with which I worked. Thus, the results from my analysis are generalizable only to the specific subgrouping of MIOs identified in this ethnography. Clearly, then, the findings should not be linked to the experiences of all psychiatrically disordered offenders.

2. The information collected during the 1984–1991 time period included initial client contact data, personal interviews, case reports, psychosocial histo-

ries, content and processes progress notes, and criminal confinement and psychiatric hospitalization records. Documentation for the latter two required client/patient releases of information. Much of the field reporting described here was direct, personal, and recorded verbatim. During the eight year period in which client information was documented, I interviewed more than 350 individuals. The case studies described in this study are representative of three types of mentally ill offenders: (1) persons who are defined as chemically addicted and experience difficulty with receiving ongoing mental health services (the case of Edith); (2) persons who are defined as mentally ill and cycle in and out of psychiatric treatment centers (the case of Jim); and (3) persons who are defined as mentally ill and criminally responsible, repeatedly and alternately institutionalized and incarcerated (the case of Larry).

3. Admittedly, one could argue that the effect of transcarceration (short-term hospital care and sustained criminal confinement) was salubrious for Edith, James, and Larry. For example, Edith desired emotional relief through psychiatric intervention, communicating her investment in civil commitment. James seemed well and was discharged, following psychiatric treatment. Larry was medically stabilized while confined. However, the violence enacted through the language of transcarceration considerably denied these individuals the opportunity to describe their identities beyond or outside of confinement discourse. Thus, the language of transcarceration, embodied in how the three case study subjects defined their existences and in how the structural and organizational forces impacting their lives interpreted them, produced profoundly disturbing social consequences.

CHAPTER 7.
EXECUTING THE MENTALLY ILL

1. The legal history of this debate can be traced to the matter of *Nobles v. Georgia* (1897). Interestingly, the Court concluded that no competency for execution hearing was constitutionally required when the death row prisoner was mentally incompetent. In the wake of *Nobles* (1897), courts and legislatures routinely found that there was no legal basis to execute an incompetent death row prisoner. As I will demonstrate, however, this standard was substantially amended in subsequent case law by the United States Supreme Court.

2. The three most compelling cases exploring the legal boundaries of this issue include: *Ford v. Wainwright* (1986); *Washington v. Harper* (1990); and *Perry v. Louisiana* (1990). The related case of *Riggins v. Nevada* (1992) while worth noting, is not specifically germane to this chapter's investigation. *Riggins* (1992) involved medication refusal during the pretrial and trial stage and *not* while the individual was incarcerated. Indeed, the expressed purpose of *Riggins* (1992) was

to explore the conditions under which a psychiatrically ill person resisting antipsychotic medication could be rendered "competent to stand trial." Clearly, then, *Riggins* (1992) is not a death row inmate case or one addressing the rights of incompetent prisoners.

3. The notion that all language is method represents an important theme contained in the structural and poststructural sociology of knowledge process. The structural approach (here aligned with my subsequent structural legal semiotic analysis) focuses on the "underlying rules which organize phenomena into a social system" (Best & Kellner, 1991, p. 18). The poststructural approach (here aligned with my subsequent legal deconstructionist investigation) claims that root assumptions, foundational truths, linear cause-effect relations, and the neutrality of the scientific method are not ascertainable because language structures thought in way which are never neutral. Deconstructionism points to the "hierarchy of values which attempt not only to guarantee truth [falsely], but also work to exclude and devalue allegedly inferior terms or positions [values]" (Best & Kellner, 1991, p. 21; see also MacDonell, 1986; Rorty, 1979). For a practical assessment of deconstructionism with relevant sociolegal implications, see Fuchs & Ward, 1994. For more direct applications to the sociology of law, see Milovanovic, 1994. For more on the development of what discourse analysis is and how it furthers critical inquiry into the nature of social phenomena, see Foucault, 1972, 1973; Kristeva, 1980, 1986; Lacan, 1977; Barthes, 1988; Derrida, 1976; Greimas, 1990.

4. As Johnson (1998) describes it: "[death] row is the most total of institutions, the penitentiary most demanding of penitence, the prison most debilitating and disabling in its confinement. On death row the allegorical pound of flesh is just the beginning. Here the whole person is consumed. The spirit is captured and gradually worn down, then the body is disposed of" (pp. 70–71). This troubling reality is intensified when the medicolegal tension of drug treatment or its refusal is considered for incompetent prisoners awaiting execution (Heilbrun et al., 1992)

5. In related matters, the U.S. Supreme Court had previously and summarily found unconstitutional interventions amounting to medical punishment. I note, however, that in the *Ford* (1986) decision the Court did *not* address the related matter of whether a state could *coercively treat* (and thus restore to competency) a mentally disordered prisoner awaiting execution for purposes of capital punishment.

6. I note that the U.S. Supreme Court has previously held that the state does possess a legitimate penal interest in capital punishment sufficient to withstand Eight Amendment scrutiny. However, the Court in *Ford* (1986) found that the administration of medical treatment, within a correctional context for an incompetent death row inmate, was an intrusive intervention that could not overcome the Eighth Amendment challenge.

7. I recognize that the U.S. Supreme Court originally granted certiorari in *Perry v. Louisiana* (1990) to assess the "treatment to execute" matter prior to its determination in *Harper* (1990). However, the Court chose to remand *Perry* (1990) to the State Supreme Court of Louisiana for further consideration which, temporarily, left unresolved the matter presented to it in *Perry* (1990). By presenting legal background on *Harper* (1990) before an analysis of *Perry* (1990), I draw attention to the progression of constitutional and legal thought in the area of treatment refusal rights for prisoners, competency determinations, and death row executions. In addition, I demonstrate the apparent legal uncertainty inherent in the Court's assessment of these weighty issues.

8. Walter Harper had been imprisoned in the state of Washington following a 1976 conviction for robbery. He received psychiatric treatment for six years, including the involuntary consumption of psychotropic medication. In 1982, while incarcerated, Harper began refusing to take the antipsychotic drugs prescribed to him and, consequently, his condition deteriorated to the degree that he engaged in violent conduct. Under Washington's Department of Corrections and the Special Offender Center (SOC), it was determined that Harper suffered from a mental disorder, was gravely disabled, and posed a likelihood of serious harm to himself and others in the prison. Given these findings, Harper was forced to consume antipsychotic medication. He filed a suit alleging that the SOC failed to provide him with a judicial hearing before involuntarily medicating him in violation of his 14th Amendment due process protections and his 8th Amendment rights against cruel and unusual punishment.

9. At the trial stage, the court argued that forcible medication was necessary and reasonable because the state interest in carrying out the verdict imposed by the jury overrode any interest that Mr. Perry had in avoiding unwanted medication. Perry appealed arguing that he had a right to refuse treatment in the form of antipsychotic medication. The U.S. Supreme Court remanded the case to the state for reconsideration, given the intervening matter of *Harper v. Washington* (1990). The Supreme Court of Louisiana addressed the concern posed in *Perry* (1992) in the matter of *State v. Perry* (1992).

10. It is also worth noting that there are several clinical and ethical implications involved in restoring to competency a prisoner on death row, even when, ostensibly, it is in the offender's best medical interest. The effect is that while the individual would be restored and made psychologically "well," he or she would then be executed following the administered psychiatric treatment.

11. Semiotics is the study of "signs" and "sign systems." A sign is any written or verbal expression. It can be a word, phrase, gesture, extraverbal cue, silence, noise, and so on provided it conveys some meaning beyond what is written, spoken, or observed. Thus, a sign signifies something beyond itself; that is, beyond what is written, spoken, or observed. When signs are clustered together within a particular domain of inquiry (e.g., sports, war, computer science), we

may speak of a system of signs or a (coordinated) sign language system. Law, and more particularly law and psychiatry, functions as a sign system because medicolegal discourse utilizes specialized expressions, words, or phrases that convey unique meaning within its own system of communication.

12. This emphasis on wholeness is in opposition to the atomistic view of the world in which things exist only in relation to other things, and these relationships exist only as part of a whole. Philosophically, then, structuralism is the very antithesis of the existentialist-humanist notion of a world in which each subject or individual is understood as an individual rather than merely a part of the whole.

13. Coincidentally, it was in this regard that the structuralists celebrated the disappearance of the subject. "The subject was dismissed, or radically decentered, as merely an effect of language, culture, or the unconscious, and denied causal or creative efficacy" (Best & Kellner, 1991, p. 19)

14. There are differing perspectives on the meaning of signs. For purposes of this chapter, given the more structural orientation described here, I rely on the Greimasian approach (through the linguistics of Saussure) as appropriated by Bernard Jackson. Accordingly, a sign is constituted by a *signifier* and a *signified*. The signifier is the acoustic-visual image (i.e., the naming of a thought). The signified is the content we assign, through spoken or written language, to the signifier. For example, words or phrases such as "diminished capacity," "informed consent," "execution," "right to refuse treatment," "mental illness," "guilty but mentally ill," "dangerous," "reasonableness," and the like are signifiers. We fill in their meaning, give them value, through other words or phrases that express these ideas. Language is a system of signs that expresses ideas or signifieds through differing signifiers that produce meaning.

15. As Balkin (1987) accurately points out in his presentation of Derridean legal deconstruction, "[as everyone thinks], we mean more that we say, we also say more than we mean. Our words seem to perform tricks that we had not intended, establish connections that we had not considered, lead to conclusions that were not present in our minds when we spoke or wrote" (p. 778).

16. Clearly, the radicality of deconstruction I propose is not a complete destabilization of meaning ad infinitum. More specifically, I am not rejecting the modernist notions of progress, emancipation, reason, and the subject in a wholesale fashion. This would be a revolutionary project in law and, more particularly, medicolegal discourse beyond the scope of the present chapter. What I am contesting, however, is the legitimacy and institutional authority that follows from ossified meaning, privileged as the *dominant* interpretation rendering alternatives readings and, consequently, different expressions in law and legal thought nonjusticiable.

17. Indeed, as Balkin (1987) concludes: "Deconstruction by its very nature is an analytic tool and not a synthetic one. It can displace a hierarchy momen-

tarily, it can shed light on otherwise hidden dependencies of concepts, but it cannot propose new hierarchies of thought or substitute new foundations. These are by definition logocentric projects, which deconstruction defines itself against" (p. 786).

18. Milovanovic (1994b) describes the Derridean notion of trace in relation to legal deconstruction as follows: "In deconstructive strategies, one must start with the idea that any term (presence) always implies a hidden one (absence); both are essential to any meaning of each. The *trace* is that part that exists in each and maintains the relation. In many ways, it is the 'glue.' For those practicing deconstruction, the challenge is to identify the absent term which maintains the term that is felt as present" (pp. 101–102).

19. Perhaps the most widely discussed and debated example of "ungrounding" comes from Derrida's investigation of speech and writing. Drawing attention to the work of Rousseau, Lévi-Strauss, and Saussure, Derrida notes that there is a nonaccidental preference for speech over writing in their respective philosophies. The former term is privileged as presence, while the corresponding latter term is delegitimized as absence. Derrida demonstrates that, notwithstanding all the limitations of writing, "speech is a type of 'writing' that suffers from all the inadequacies attributed to writing" (Balkin, 1987, p. 757). Thus, the logocentricism (i.e., primacy) of speech is undone by deconstructing the terms in the binary opposition.

20. The most glaring of limitations is that just as we cannot say with absolute certainty what mental illness really is, we cannot say with absolute certainty what good mental health is either. Indeed, as the examples suggest, on some occasions it is even better to be more "crazy" than not. This notion of how arguments undo themselves gives rise to Derrida's logic of the supplement (Derrida, 1976, p. 144; Balkin, 1987, pp. 758–759). There are two meanings for the term *supplement*. The first of these refers to adding something to an already sufficient thing. For example, a professor gives a complete lecture to a class but places on reserve in the university's library the previously prepared notes for the lecture. The notes represent the lecture. The second meaning of the term *supplement* is to fill something in with what it lacks in order to make it self-sufficient. The lecture needs the notes in order to be complete for the students. The logic of the supplement demonstrates how the second term in a hierarchical position (e.g., being mentally ill, insanity) can only supplement the first term (e.g., being mentally healthy, sanity) in the sense of being an addition to something complete when the first term in the binary opposition can be supplemented "by having a lack that could be fulfilled" (Balkin, 1987, p. 759). What is missing in the binary value of mental health? Mental health is not an objective state made present to society; rather, it is but *one* condition of being, representing (and masquerading around as) *the* objective state of existence. Mental health appears to possess Derridean presence; however, similar to mental illness,

it is a sham. Both are modes of being. Both are mediations of authentic existence not absolute ways of comportment. The latter is delayed through the representation of mental health, mental illness, and its sundry variations.

21. The terms are not chosen randomly. They logically arise from the operation of contraries and contradictions, signifying the binary oppositions. Thus, the terms or values themselves are not only an expression of the semiotic square but an accurate representation of how nonlegal discourse informs and translates the events of a given case into legal discourse.

22. This point cannot be overemphasized. What it demonstrates is how the events of a case unconsciously get codified by jurists into legal language. This transformation is the result of placing nonlegal language on the semiotic square along with legal discourse where the former grammar makes possible the translation of the latter grammar.

23. My exploration specifically requires that I unpack the underlying structure of meaning formed through unconscious semiotic production. Although certainly useful in their own right, the semantical value of *variable treatment* contained between the binary oppositions "receiving treatment" and "not receiving treatment," as well as the semantical value of *variable refusal* located between the binary tension "receiving treatment" and "not receiving treatment" will not be systematically investigated. The semiotic terms "treatment assent" and "not receiving treatment" are, however, germane to other binary oppositions and, accordingly, will be examined elsewhere in this structural legal semiotic analysis.

24. Long-term institutionalization in a mental health unit of a prison, pending the results of a competency determination to exercise one's right to refuse treatment, is precisely the result envisioned by this possibility. Indeed, this was the type of placement in which Walter Harper was housed. Recall, that he was detained in a Special Offender Center under the Washington State Department of Corrections.

25. I do not, however, address the least noteworthy relationships. For example, the oppositional terms "competent" and "not competent" yield the meaning *variably competent*. The oppositional values "competent" and "incompetent" produce the semantic meaning *variably incompetent*. What these relationships suggest is that the Court esteems more totalizing understandings for the sign of competency. In other words, precisely because the U.S. Supreme Court does not recognize shades of competency or degrees of incompetency in its decision making capacity, it can only interpret and validate behavior that falls into this "either or" context (Arrigo, 1996b, pp. 177–180). The result is that an assortment of differences (within the competency and incompetency constructs) remain concealed, glossed over, and repressed as outside the juridical sphere. Thus, the possibility for promoting and codifying alternative readings of the law, and of psychiatric justice, are denied. I note further that the Court's

inability to recognize how competency and incompetency occur on different continua, parallels the previous semiotic assessment on the relationship between the binary oppositions "treatment assent" and "not receiving treatment."

26. The logic of legal deference implies an acceptance of psychiatry's understanding of mental illness (*Youngberg v. Romeo*, 1982). Psychiatry generally endorses a disease model; that is, people with diagnoses are identified as "ill" and not "well" (Arrigo, 1992b, pp. 10–11). This logic is consistent with the medical imperative in which sickness is presumed, regardless of intervening anomalies (Szasz, 1987, pp. 45–103; Scheff, 2000). Moreover, psychiatry argues that treatment, in the form of antipsychotic medication, can produce efficacious results. In response to these clinical observations, the court system, legal tribunals, or both assign a *presumption of validity* to these diagnostic statements. In *Youngberg v. Romeo* (1982) Justice Powell concluded that there is no reason to believe that the wisdom of judges and juries is any more accurate in such matters than the wisdom of mental health experts (pp. 322–323). Regrettably, however, "[t]he best available evidence shows . . . that, at a very general level, providing [drug] therap[y] to mentally ill individuals is better than doing nothing at all" (Durham & LaFond, 1988, p. 356).

27. This phenomenon is known as "revolving door" institutionalization. The nature of involuntary civil commitment laws are such that one can only be confined as long as the person poses a threat of danger to oneself, others, or both. Once those symptoms giving rise to psychiatric hospitalization dissipate, mental health law requires that the person be released from confinement. Although release typically includes a discharge plan with out-patient therapy and medication, if the plan is not followed it can lead to the reappearance of those very symptoms that precipitated involuntary hospitalization. This process repeats itself such that the cycle of care is revolving.

28. Emerson (1983) indicates that the problem with the gift is that it: (1) holds itself out as a threat to one's independence; (2) leads to a real or implied contractual debt; and (3) produces unwanted feelings of inferiority in the receiver and dependence in the giver.

29. I recognize that there are those mentally confined or treated persons who welcome the gift of treatment or, retrospectively, come to appreciate it. In some mental health circles, this has been coined "thank you" therapy (e.g., Stone, 1975). However, there are also those who do not welcome the gift of treatment (e.g., Beck & Golowka, 1988, p. 565; Kane et al., 1983, pp. 374–377; Schwartz et al., 1988, pp. 1049–1054).

30. Power is also implied when the treat involves reciprocity. Once you bestow your gift, I can never completely repay you. Even if I return to you many more gifts, your initial act of generosity creates a chasm of reciprocation that can never be filled. Even though it may remain unspoken or repressed, this is because we both know that it was you who treated me first (Arrigo & Williams, 2000a).

31. I note tha the literature is replete with clinical studies questioning the efficacy of the "cure" of drug treatment (e.g., Gardos & Cole, 1976, pp. 34–36). In the case of some patients, the Court has even considered "dug-free holidays" as a way to assess medication necessity (*Rogers v. Okin*, 1980, p. 656; *Rennie v. Klein*, 1978, p. 1146).

32. For example, in some instances, the death row prisoner is characterized as not making a competent, knowledgeable, voluntary choice to exercise treatment refusal (Winick, 1997a, pp. 347–365).

33. This is exactly the constitutional and policy debate, implicit or not, in mental health law circles when the right to refuse treatment doctrine is invoked. For example, when medication refusal was invoked in *Harper* (1990), the *limits* of exercising this right were expressly ascertained. The Court reasoned that the prisoner's protection against bodily intrusiveness could not be sustained when the forced treatment was in his best medical interest and when it protected others from a risk of danger he posed while unmedicated (*Washington v. Harper*, 1990, pp. 227, 248, n. 18).

34. One general standard balances the value of the individual's freedom to choose, albeit potentially incorrectly, against society's interest in ensuring that such a choice is not harmful to others, albeit largely paternalistic. "The justification presumably is that the injury caused by denying such [mentally ill patients] autonomy would be exceeded by the harm produced by honoring the choices of incompetent people" (Winick, 1997a, p. 348).

35. Commenting on the ideological nature of the law, Balkin (1987) states that "[l]egal doctrines both reflect and regulate social life. The choice of protected rights and of enforcement techniques reflect views, whether obvious or obscure, about social relations. Law tells a story about what people are and should be" (pp. 761–762).

CHAPTER 8.
LAW, PSYCHIATRY, AND PUNISHMENT

1. For Lacan (1977), the combinatory effects of these Three Orders are depicted in his famous *Schema L* and his *Graphs of Desire*. Both represent Lacan's quadripartite subject (pp. 193–194, 303–316). In the quadrilateral subject we have a more robust delineation of the speaking-being mobilizing the psychic apparatus when confronted with its own lack. For a brief, though accessible, overview of the Three Orders see, Caudill (1997, pp. 8–9, 102–103).

2. In Lacanian (1977) psychoanalytic semiotics, a signifier represents the subject for another signifier, which represents the subject for another signifier, and so on (an infinite regress) (p. 74). For Lacan (1985), the search for completeness, consistency, and precision, were illusory because they dismissed

the integral role of the person through whom signifiers were embodied with meaning and desire (pp. 143–147).

3. Foucault's work on disciplinary institutions (e.g., 1965, 1972, 1976, 1977) and Habermas's critique of steering mechanisms (e.g., 1975, 1984, 1987) offer some direction for explicating a theory in which desire is territorialized and vanquished (Deleuze and Guattari, 1987). In brief, these investigations point out how certain technological breakthroughs or scientific discoveries promote new models of communicating meaning (e.g., advances in forensic sciences inform our response to crime and its control). Thus, certain discourses are privileged as knowledge and truth. These discourses, as mechanisms of control and domination, exercise power by esteeming only those assertions, advancing that desire in language reflecting the new technologies or the new scientific discoveries. All attempts to esteem alternative models of expression, despite subjecting prevailing knowledge/truth principles to a legitimation crisis, are neutralized by way of sociolinguistic hegemony and reification (Arrigo, 1997e). For various feminist critiques of these notions see Kristeva (1980, 1984) and Irigaray, (1985a, 1990). For applications to feminist jurisprudence see Cornell (1990, 1993), Smart (1989), and Young (1996).

References

Abraham, F., Abraham, R., & Shaw, C. (1990). *A visual introduction to dynamical systems theory for psychology*. Santa Cruz, CA: Aerial.

Abu-Jamal, M. (1995). *Live from death row*. Reading, MA: Addison-Wesley & Sons.

Adorno, T. W. (1973). *Negative dialectics* (E. B. Ashton, Trans). New York: Seabury Press.

Alexander, F. G., & Selesnick, S. T. (1966). *The history of psychiatry: An evaluation of psychiatric thought and practice form prehistoric times to the present*. New York: Harper & Row.

Alexander, R. (1992). Determining appropriate criteria in the evaluation of correctional mental health treatment for inmates. *Journal of Offender Rehabilitation, 18* (1–2), 119–134.

Althusser, L. (1971). *Lenin and philosophy and other essays* (B. Brewster, Trans.). London: New Left Books.

Altman, A. (1990). *Critical legal studies: A liberal critique*. Princeton, NJ: Princeton University Press.

American Psychiatric Association (1987). *Diagnostic and statistical manual of mental disorders* (3rd Rev. ed.). Washington, DC: Author.

American Psychiatric Association (1994). *Diagnostic and statistical manual of mental disorders* (4th ed.). Washington, DC: Author.

Appelbaum, P. S. (1984). Standards for civil commitment: A critical review of empirical research. *International Journal of Law & Psychiatry, 7* (2), 133–144.

Appelbaum, P. S. (1986). Competency to be executed: another conundrum for mental health professionals. *Hospital and Community Psychiatry, 37* (7), 682–684.

Appelbaum, P. S., & Grisso, T. (1995). The MacArthur treatment competence study, I: Mental illness and competency to consent to treatment. *Law & Human Behavior, 19* (2), 105–126.

Appelbaum, P. S., & Gutheil, T. G. (1980). The Boston state hospital case: "Involuntary mind control, the constitution and the right to rot." *American Journal of Psychiatry, 137* (6), 720–723.

Appelbaum, P. S., & Gutheil, T. G. (1981). The right to refuse treatment: The real issue is quality of care. *Bulletin of the American Academy of Psychiatry and the Law*, 9 (3), 199–202.

Appelbaum, P. S., & Gutheil, T. G. (1991). *Clinical handbook of psychiatry and the law* (2nd ed.). Baltimore: Williams &Wilkins.

Appelbaum, P. S., Lidz, C. W., & Meisel, A. (1987). *Informed consent: Legal theory and clinical practice.* New York: Oxford University Press.

Appelbaum, P. S., & Roth, L. (1982). Competency to consent to research. *Archives of General Psychiatry, 39* (8), 951–958.

Arce, A. A., & Vaegare, J. (1984). Identifying the Mentally Ill Among the Homeless. In H. R. Lamb (Ed.), *The homeless mentally ill: A task force report of the American Psychiatric Association* (pp. 75–89). Washington, DC: The Association.

Aristotle (1956). *Nicomachean ethics.* Cambridge, MA: Harvard University Press.

Arnaud, A. J. (1973) *Essai d'analyse structurale du code civil francais* [Essay on the structural analysis of the French civil code]. Paris: Librairie generale de droit et de jurisprudence.

Arrigo, B. A. (1992a). Deconstructing jurisprudence: An experiential feminist critique. *Journal of Human Justice, 4* (1), 13–30.

Arrigo, B. A. (1992b). The logic of identity and the politics of justice: Establishing a right to community-based treatment for the institutionalized mentally disabled. *New England Journal on Criminal and Civil Confinement, 18* (1), 1–31.

Arrigo, B. A. (1993a). Civil commitment, semiotics, and discourse on difference: A historical critique of the sign of paternalism. In R. Kevelson (Ed.), *Flux, complexity and illusion in law* (pp. 13–30). New York: Peter Lang.

Arrigo, B. A. (1993b). An experientially-informed feminist jurisprudence: Rape and the move toward praxis. *Humanity and Society, 17*, 28–47.

Arrigo, B. A. (1993c). *Madness, language, and the law.* New York: Harrow and Heston.

Arrigo, B. A. (1993d). Paternalism, civil commitment, and illness politics: Assessing the current debate and outlining a future direction. *Journal of Law and Health, 17* (2), 131–168.

Arrigo, B. A. (1994a). Rooms for the misbegotten: On social design and social deviance. *Journal of Sociology and Social Welfare, 21* (4), 95–113.

Arrigo, B. A. (1994b). Legal discourse and the disordered criminal defendant: Contributions from psychoanalytic semiotics and chaos theory. *Legal Studies Forum*, 8 (1), 93–112.

Arrigo, B. A. (1995a). Deconstructing classroom instruction: Contributions of the postmodern sciences for crimino-legal education. *Social Pathology, 1* (2): 115–148.

Arrigo, B. A. (1995b). The peripheral core of law and criminology: On postmodern social theory and conceptual integration. *Justice Quarterly, 12,* (3), 121–126.

Arrigo, B. A. (1995c). Rethinking the language of law, justice, and community: Postmodern feminist jurisprudence. In D.S. Caudill and S.J. Gold (Eds.), *Radical philosophy of law: Contemporary challenges to mainstream legal theory and practice* (pp. 88–107). Atlantic Heights, NJ: Humanities Press.

Arrigo, B. A. (1995d). Subjectively in law, medicine and science: A semiotic perspective on punishment. In C. Sistare (Ed.), *Punishment: Social control and coercion* (pp. 69–92). New York: Peter Lang.

Arrigo, B. A. (1996a). The behavior of law and psychiatry: Rethinking knowledge construction and the guilty but mentally ill verdict. *Criminal Justice and Behavior, 23* (4), 572–592.

Arrigo, B. A. (1996b). *The contours of psychiatric justice: A postmodern critique of mental illness, criminal insanity, and the law.* New York: Garland.

Arrigo, B. A. (1996c). Desire in the psychiatric courtroom: On Lacan and the dialects of linguistic oppression. *Current Perspectives in Social Theory, 16,* 159–187.

Arrigo, B. A. (1996d). Toward a theory of punishment in the psychiatric courtroom: On language, law, and Lacan. *Journal of Crime and Justice, 19* (1), 15–32.

Arrigo, B. A. (1997a). The constitution of constitutive theory in law and criminology: Revisiting the past and forging the future. *Theoretical Criminology, 1* (3), 392–396.

Arrigo, B. A. (1997b). Dimensions of social justice in an SRO: Contributions from chaos theory, policy, and practice. In D. Milovanovic (Ed.), *Chaos, criminology, and social justice* (pp. 179–194). Westport, CT: Praeger.

Arrigo, B. A. (1997c). Recommunalizing drug offenders: The 'drug peace' agenda. *Journal of Offender Rehabilitation, 23* (3/4), 53–73.

Arrigo, B. A. (1997d). Insanity defense reform and the sign of abolition: Re-visiting Montana's experience. *International Journal for the Semiotics of Law, 10* (29), 191–211.

Arrigo, B. A. (1997e). Transcarceration: Notes on a psychoanalytically-informed theory of social practice in the criminal justice and mental health systems. *Crime, Law and Social Change, 27* (1), 31–48.

Arrigo, B. A. (1998). Marxist criminology and Lacanian psychoanalysis: Outline for a general constitutive theory of crime. In J. I. Ross (Ed.), *Cutting the edge: Current perspectives in radical and critical criminology* (pp. 40–62). New York: Praeger.

Arrigo, B. A. (1999a). Martial metaphors and medical justice: Implications for law, crime, and deviance. *Journal of Political and Military Sociology, 27,* 307–322.

Arrigo, B. A. (2000a). *Introduction to forensic psychology: Issues and controversies in crime and justice.* San Diego, CA: Academic Press.

Arrigo, B. A. (2001a). Back to the future: The place of justice in forensic psychological research and practice. *Journal of Forensic Psychology Practice, 1* (1), 1–7.

Arrigo, B. A. (2001b). Transcarceration: A constitutive ethnography of mentally ill offenders. *The Prison Journal, 81* (2), 162–186.

Arrigo, B. A. (2001c). The critical perspective in psychological jurisprudence: Theoretical advances and epistemological assumptions. *International Journal of Law and Psychiatry.*

Arrigo, B. A., Milovanovic, D., & Schehr, R. (2000). The French connection: Implications for law, crime, and social justice. *Humanity & Society, 24* (2), 162–203.

Arrigo, B. A., & Schehr R. (1998). Restoring justice for juveniles: Toward a critical analysis of victim offender mediation. *Justice Quarterly, 15* (4), 629–666.

Arrigo, B. A., & Tasca, J. (1999). Right to refuse treatment, competency to be executed, and therapeutic jurisprudence: Toward a systematic analysis. *Law and Psychology Review, 24,* 1–47.

Arrigo, B. A., & Williams, C. R (1999a). Chaos theory and the social control thesis: A post-Foucauldian analysis of mental illness and involuntary civil commitment. *Social Justice, 26* (1), 177–207.

Arrigo, B. A, & Williams, C. R. (1999b). Law, ideology and critical inquiry: The case of treatment refusal for incompetent prisoners awaiting execution. *New England Journal On Criminal and Civil Confinement, 25* (2), 367–412.

Arrigo, B. A., & Williams, C. R. (2000a). The impossibility of democratic justice and the 'gift' of the majority: On Derrida, deconstruction, and the search for equality. *Journal of Contemporary Criminal Justice, 16* (3), 321–343.

Arrigo, B. A., & Williams, C. R. (2000b). Reading prisons: A metaphoric-organizational approach. *Sociology of Crime, Law, and Deviance, 2,* 191–231.

Bacal, H. A., & Newman, K. M. (1990). *Theories of object relations: Bridges to self psychology.* New York: Columbia University Press.

Bachrach, L. L. (1983). *Deinstitutionalization.* San Francisco: Jossey-Bass.

Balkin, J. M. (1987). Deconstructive practice and legal theory. *Yale Law Journal,* 96 (4), 743–786.

Barak, G. (1993). Media, crime, and justice: A case for constitutive criminology. *Humanity and Society, 17* (3), 272–296.

Barak, G., & Henry, S. (1999). An integrated-constitutive theory of crime, law, and social justice. In B. A. Arrigo (Ed.), *Social justice/criminal justice: The maturation of critical theory in law, crime, and deviance* (pp. 152–175). Belmont, CA: West/Wadsworth.

Bardach, E. (1972). *The skill factor in politics: Repealing the mental commitment laws in California*. Berkeley: University of CA Press.

Bardwell, M. C. & Arrigo, B. A. (2002). Competency to stand trial: A law, psychology, and policy assessment. *Journal of Psychiatry and Law*, 30 (2).

Barthes, R. (1964). *Essais critiques* [Critical essays]. Paris: Editions du Seuil.

Barthes, R. (1977). *Elements of semiology* (A. Lavers & C. Smith, Trans.). New York: Hill and Wang.

Barthes, R. (1988). *The semiotic challenge* (1st ed.) (R. Howard, Trans.). New York: Hill and Wang.

Barton, S. (1994). Chaos, self-organization, and psychology. *American Psychologist*, *49*, 5–14.

Bataille, G. (1988). *The accursed share: An essay on general economy: Vol. 1. Consumption* (R. Hurley, Trans.). New York: Zone Books.

Baudrillard, J. (1983). *Simulacra and Simulations* (P. Foss, P. Patton, & Philip Beitchman, Trans.). Ann Arbor, MI: University of Michigan Press.

Baudrillard, J. (1988). Symbolic exchange and death. M. Poster (Ed.), *Selective Writings*. Stanford, CA: Stanford University Press.

Bazelon, D. L. (1975). Institutionalization, deinstitutionalization and the adversary process. *Columbia Law Review*, *75*, 897–912.

Beck, J. C., & Golowka, E. A. (1988). A study of enforced treatment in relation to Stone's "Thank You" Theory. *Behavioral Sciences and the Law*, 6 (4), 559–566.

Becker, H. S. (1963). *Outsiders: Studies in the sociology of deviance*. London: Free Press of Glencoe.

Bedau, H. (1984). *Death is different: Studies in morality, law, and politics*. Boston: Northeastern University Press.

Bedau, H. (1987). *The case against the death penalty*. New York: American Civil Liberties Union.

Belcher, J. R. (1988). Defining the service needs of homeless mentally ill persons. *Hospital and Community Psychiatry*, 39 (11), 1203–1205.

Bender, J. M. (1984). After abolition: The present state of the insanity defense in Montana. *Montana Law Review*, *45*, 133–150.

Bentham, J. (1879/1961). *Introduction to the principles of morals and legislation*. New York: Hafner.

Bentham, J. (1962). The rationale of punishment. In J. Bowring (Ed.), *The works of Jeremy Bentham* (Vol. 1). New York: Russell and Russell.

Benveniste, E. (1971). *Problems in general linguistics*. Coral Gables, Florida: University of Miami Press.

Berger, P. L., & Luckmann, T. (1966). *The social construction of reality: A treatise on the sociology of knowledge*. Garden City, NY: Doubleday.

Berman, A. (1988). *From the new criticism to deconstructionism: The reception of structuralism and post-structuralism*. Urbana, IL: University of Illinois Press.

Bersoff, D. N. (1995). *Ethical conflicts in psychology*. Washington, DC: American Psychological Association.

Best, S., & Kellner, D. (Eds.). (1991). *Postmodern theory: Critical interrogations*. New York: Guilford Press.

Blackstone, W. (1783). *Commentaries*. London: W. Straham.

Blanck, G., & Blanck, R. (1974). *Ego psychology: Theory and practice*. New York: Columbia University Press.

Bleicher, B. K. (1967). Compulsory community care for the mentally ill. *Cleveland Law Review, 16*, 93–115.

Blumer, H. (1969). *Symbolic interactionism: Perspective and method*. Englewood Cliffs, NJ: Prentice-Hall.

Bonnie, R. (1993). The competence of criminal defendants: Beyond Dusky and Drope. *University of Miami Law Review, 47*, 539–566.

Borch-Jacobsen, M. (1991). *The absolute master*. Stanford, CA: Stanford University Press.

Bourdieu, P. (1977). *Outline of a theory of practice*. Cambridge, MA: Cambridge University Press.

Bourdieu, P. (1984). *Distinction: A social critique of the judgement of taste*. Cambridge, MA: Harvard University Press.

Bourdieu, P. (1987). The force of law: Toward a sociology of the juridical field. *The Hastings Law Journal, 38*, 814–853.

Bourdieu, P., & Wacquant, L. J. D. (1992). *An invitation to reflexive sociology*. Chicago: University of Chicago Press.

Bowie, M. (1991). *Lacan*. Cambridge, MA: Harvard University Press.

Boyce, J. N., & Jackson, D. S. (1982). Is the system guilty? *Time* (July 5, 1982), p. 26.

Bracher, M. (1988). Lacan's theory in the four discourses. *Prose Studies, 11*, 32–49.

Bracher, M. (1993). *Lacan, discourse, and social change: A psychoanalytic cultural criticism*. Ithaca, NY: Cornell University Press.

Braddock, D. (1981). Deinstitutionalization of the retarded: Trends in public policy. *Hospital & Community Psychiatry, 32*, 607–610.

Brakel, S. J. (1985). *The mentally disabled and the law*. Buffalo, NY: William S. Hein & Company.

Briggs, J., & Peat, F. D. (1989). *Turbulent Mirror*. New York: Harper and Row.

Brooks, A. D. (Ed.). (1974). *Law, psychiatry, and the mental health system*. Boston: Little, Brown.

Brooks, A. D. (1980). The constitutional right to refuse antipsychotic medications. *Bulletin of the American Academy of Psychiatry and Law*, 8, 179–221.

Brooks, A. D. (1987). The right to refuse antipsychotic medications: Law and policy. *Rutgers Law Review*, *39*, 339–376.

Brown, L., & Gilligan, C. (1993). *Meeting at the Crossroads*. Cambridge, MA: Harvard University Press.

Bursten, B. (1986). Post-hospital mandatory outpatient treatment. *American Journal of Psychiatry*, *143* (10), 1255–1258.

Butler, J. (1993). *Bodies that matter*. New York: Routledge.

Butler, J. (1999). *Subjects of desire*. New York: Columbia University Press.

Bütz, M. (1992). Chaos: An omen of transcendence in the psychotherapeutic process. *Psychological Reports*, *71*, 827–843.

Bütz, M. (1997). *Chaos and complexity: Implications for psychological theory and practice*. Bristol, PA: Taylor and Francis.

Bütz, M. (1992). The fractal nature of the development of the self. *Psychological Reports*, *71*, 1043–63.

Callahan, L., Mayer, C., & Steadman, H. J. (1987). Insanity defense reform in the United States—post Hinckley. *Mental and Physical Disability Law Reporter*, *11*, 54–59.

Cameron, J. D. (1988). Balancing the interests: The move towards less restrictive commitment of New York's mentally ill. *New England Journal on Criminal And Civil Confinement*, *14*, 91–106.

Caputo, J. (Ed.). (1997). *Deconstruction in a nutshell: A conversation with Jacques Derrida*. New York: Fordham University Press.

Castel, R., Castel, F., & Lovell, A. (1982). *The psychiatric society*. New York: Columbia University Press.

Caton, C. L. M. (1990). *Homelessness in America* (New York: Oxford University Press).

Caton, C. L. M., & Gralnick, A. (1987). A review of issues surrounding length of psychiatric hospitalization. *Hospital and Community Psychiatry*, 38 (8), 858–863.

Caudill, D. S. (1997). *Lacan and the subject of law: Toward a psychoanalytical critical legal theory*. Atlantic Highlands, NJ: Humanities Press.

Chodoff, P. (1976). The case for involuntary hospitalization of the mentally ill. *American Journal of Psychiatry*, *133* (5), 496–501.

Chambers, D. L. (1972). Alternatives to civil commitment of the mentally ill: Practical guides and constitutional imperatives. *Michigan Law Review*, *70*, 1107–1200.

Cleary, E. W. (1972). *McCormick's handbook of law and evidence* (2nd ed.). St. Paul, MN: West Publishing Company.

Cocozza, J., & Steadman, H. J. (1976). The failure of psychiatric predictions of dangerousness: Clear and convincing evidence. *Rutgers Law Review*, *29*, 1084–1101.

Cohen, F. (1992). Inmates with mental disorders: A guide to law and practice. *Mental and Physical Disability Law Reporter, 16* (4), 462–470.

Cohen, R. L. (1989). Fabrications of justice. *Social Justice Research, 3*, 31–46.

Cohen, S. (1979). The punitive city: Notes on the dispersal of social control. *Contemporary Crises, 3*, 339–363.

Cohen, S. (1985). *Visions of social control.* Oxford: Polity Press.

Comment. (1974). Developments in the law—civil commitment of the mentally ill. *Harvard Law Review, 87*, 1190–1346.

Comment. (1983). Guidelines for legislation on the psychiatric hospitalization of adults. *American Journal of Psychiatry, 140*, 672–679.

Conley, D. T. (1986). A Szasian approach to the right to refuse treatment: My view from the trenches. In D. Rapoport. & J. Parry (Eds.), *The right to refuse antipsychotic medication.* Washington, DC: American Bar Association.

Conrad, J., & Schneider W. (1992). *Deviance and medicalization: From badness to sickness.* Philadelphia: Temple University Press.

Coombe, R. J. (1989). Room for maneuver: Toward a theory of practice in critical legal studies. *Law and Social Inquiry, 14*, 69–121.

Cooper, D. G. (1967). *Psychiatry and anti-psychiatry.* New York: Tavistock Publications.

Cooper, D. G. (1978). *The Language of Madness.* London: Allen Lane.

Cornell, D. (1991). *Beyond accommodation: Ethical feminism, deconstruction and the law.* New York: Routledge.

Cornell, D. (1992). The philosophy of the limit: System theory and feminist legal reform. In D. Cornell, M. Rosenfeld, & G. Carlson (Eds.), *Deconstruction and the possibility of justice* (pp. 68–91). New York: Routledge.

Cornell, D. (1993). *Transformations: Recollective imagination and sexual difference.* New York: Routledge.

Costello, J. C., & Preis, J. J. (1987). Beyond least restrictive alternative: A constitutional right to treatment for mentally disabled persons in the community. *Loyola Law Review, 20*, 1527–1557.

Culler, J. D. (1981). *The pursuit of signs: Semiotics, literature, deconstruction.* Ithaca, NY: Cornell University Press.

Culler, J. D. (1982). *On deconstruction: Theory and criticism after structuralism.* Ithaca, NY: Cornell University Press.

Cumming, E., & Cumming, J. (1957). *Closed ranks: An experiment in mental health education.* Cambridge, MA: Harvard University Press.

Dain, N. (1964). *Concepts of insanity in the United States, 1789–1865.* New Brunswick, NJ: Rutgers University Press.

Darwall, S. L. (1983). *Impartial reason.* Ithaca, NY: Cornell University Press.

Davies, P. (1989). *The new physics.* New York: Cambridge University Press.

DeGeorge, R. T., & DeGeorge, F. M. (Eds.). (1972). *The structuralists from Marx to Lévi-Strauss* (1st ed.). Garden City, NY: Anchor Books.

Deleuze, G., & Guattari, F. (1977). *Anti-Oedipus: Capitalism and schizophrenia.* (R. Hurley, M. Seem, & P. R. Lane, Trans.). New York: Viking Press.

Deleuze, G., & Guattari, F. (1986). *Kafka: Toward a Minor Literature.* Minneapolis, MN: University of Minnesota Press.

Deleuze, G., & Guattari, F. (1987). *A thousand plateaus.* Minneapolis, MN: University of Minnesota Press.

Derrida, J. (1973). *Speech and phenomena and other essays on Husserl's theory of signs* (D. B. Allison, Trans.). Evanston: Northwestern University Press.

Derrida, J. (1976). *Of grammatology* (G. Chakravorty Spivak, Trans.). (1st American ed.). Baltimore: Johns Hopkins University Press.

Derrida, J. (1978). *Writing and difference* (A. Bass, Trans.). Chicago: University of Chicago Press.

Derrida, J. (1981). *Positions* (A. Bass, Trans.). Chicago: University of Chicago Press.

Derrida, J. (1982). *Margins of philosophy* (A. Bass, Trans.). Chicago: University of Chicago Press.

Deutsch, A. (1948). *The shame of the states.* New York: Harcourt, Brace.

Deutsch, A. (1949). *The mentally ill in America: A history of their care and treatment from colonial times* (2nd ed.). New York: Columbia University Press.

Dews, P. (1987). *The logics of disintegration: Post-structural thought and the claims of critical theory.* New York: Verso.

Diamond, B. (1974). The psychiatric prediction of dangerousness. *University of Pennsylvania Law Review, 123,* 439–452.

Dicks, S. (1990). *Death row: Interviews with inmates, their families, and opponents of capital punishment.* Jefferson, NC: McFarland.

Dorwart, R. A. (1988). A ten-year follow-up study on the effects of deinstitutionalization. *Hospital and Community Psychiatry, 39* (3), 287–291.

Doudera, A. E., & Swazey, J. P. (Eds.). (1982). *Refusing treatment in mental health institutions-values in conflict.* Ann Arbor, MI: AUPHA Press.

Durham, M. L., & LaFond, J. Q. (1985). The empirical consequences and policy implications of broadening the statutory criteria for civil commitment. *Yale Law & Policy Review,* 3, 395–446.

Durham, M. L., & LaFond, J. Q. (1988). A search for the missing premise of involuntary therapeutic commitment: Effective treatment of the mentally ill. *Rutgers Law Review, 40,* 305–368.

Durham, M. L., & Pierce, G. L. (1982). Beyond deinstitutionalization: A commitment law in evolution. *Hospital and Community Psychiatry, 33,* 216–219.

Dworkin, G. (1979). Paternalism. In P. Laslett and J. Fishkin (Eds.), *Philosophy, politics, & society* (pp. 78–96). New Haven: Yale University Press.

Eco, U. (1979). *A theory of semiotics.* Bloomington, IN: Indiana University Press.

Einstadter, W. J., & Henry, S. (1995). *Criminological theory: An analysis of its underlying assumptions.* Fort Worth, TX: Harcourt Brace.

Eisenstein, J., & Jacob, H. (1971). *Felony justice*. Boston: Little, Brown.
Emerson, R. W. (1983). *Essays & Lectures* (J. Porte, Ed.). New York: Viking Press.
Ennis, B. J. (1972). *Prisoners of psychiatry: Mental patients, psychiatrist, and the law*. New York: Harcourt Brace Jovanovich.
Ennis, B. J., & Litwack T. R. (1974). Psychiatry and the presumption of expertise: Flipping the coins in the courtroom. *California Law Review, 62*, 693–752.
Ennis, B. J., & Siegel L. (1974). *The rights of mental patients: The basic ACLU guide to a mental patient's rights*. New York: Richard T. Baron.
Ewing, P. (1987). Diagnosing and treating "insanity" on death row: Legal and ethical perspectives. *Behavioral Sciences and the Law*, 5 (2), 175–185.
Eysenck, H. J. (1952). The effects of psychotherapy: An evaluation. *Journal of Consulting Psychology, 16*, 309–318.
Feeley, M. (1979). *The process is the punishment*. New York: Russell Sage Foundation.
Finkel, N. J. (1995). *Commonsense justice: Jurors' notions of the law*. Cambridge, MA: Harvard University Press.
Fitzpatrick, P. (1984). Law and societies. *Osgoode Hall Law Journal, 22*, 115–138.
Foucault, M. (1965). *Madness and civilization: A history of insanity in the age of reason* (R. Howard, Trans.). New York: Pantheon Books.
Foucault, M. (1972). *The archeology of knowledge* (1st American ed.) (A. M. Sheridan Smith, Trans.). New York: Pantheon Books.
Foucault, M. (1973). *Birth of a clinic: An archeology of medical perception*. New York: Pantheon Books.
Foucault, M. (1973). *The order of things*. New York: Vintage Books.
Foucault, M. (1975). *I, Pierre Riviére, having slaughtered my mother, my sister, and my brother . . . A case of parricide in the 19th Century*. New York: Pantheon Books.
Foucault, M. (1976). *Mental illness and psychology* (1st ed.) (A. Sheridan, Trans.). New York: Harper & Row.
Foucault, M. (1977). *Discipline and punish: The birth of a prison*. New York: Pantheon Books.
Foucault, M. (1980). *Power/knowledge: Selected interviews and other writings, 1972–1977*. New York: Pantheon Books.
Foucault, M. (1990). *Michel Foucault: Interviews and other writings 1977–1984* (L. Kritzman, Ed.). New York: Routledge.
Fox, D. R. (1991). Social science's limited role in resolving psycholegal social problems. *Journal of Offender Rehabilitation, 17*, 117–124.
Fox, D. R. (1993). Psychological jurisprudence and radical social change. *American Psychologist, 48*, 234–241.
Fox, D. R. (1997). Psychology and law: Justice diverted. In D. R. Fox & I. Prilleltensky (Eds.), *Critical psychology: An introduction* (pp. 217–232). London: Sage.

Fox, D. R. (1999). Psycholegal scholarship's contribution to false consciousness about injustice. *Law and Human Behavior, 23*, 9–30.

Fraser, N. (1997). *Justice interruptus: Critical reflections on the "postsocialist" condition*. New York: Routledge.

Freidson, E. (1970). *Professional dominance: The social structure of medical care* (1st ed.). New York: Atherton Press.

Freire, P. (1972). *Pedagogy of the oppressed*. New York: Herder and Her.

Freud, S. (1914). *The psychopathology of everyday life*. New York: Macmillian.

Freud, S. (1916). *Wit and its relation to the unconscious*. New York: Brentano's.

Freud, S. (1927). *The ego and id* (J. Riviere, Trans.). London: L. & Virginia Woolf at the Hogarth Press, and the Institute of Psycho-analysis.

Freud, S. (1949). Three essays on the theory of sexuality. In J. Strachey (Ed.), *The standard edition*. London: The Hogarth Press.

Freud, S. (1954). *The origins of psychoanalysis: Letters to Wilhelm Fliess, drafts, and notes: 1897–1902* (M. Bonaparte, A. Freud, & E. Kris, Eds.). (E. Mosbacher & J. Strachey, Trans.). New York: Basic.

Freud, S. (1965). *The interpretation of dreams*. New York: Avon Books.

Friedman, M. (1989). The impracticality of impartiality. *Journal of Philosophy, 86*, 645–656.

Fromm, E. (1947). *Escape from freedom*. New York: Holt, Rinehart, and Winston.

Fuchs, S., & Ward, S. (1994). What is deconstruction, and where and when does it take place: Making facts in science building cases in law. *American Sociological Review, 59*, 481–505.

Fuller, L. (1964). *The morality of law*. New York: Yale University Press.

Gardos, G., & Cole, J. O. (1976). Maintenance antipsychotic therapy: Is the cure worse than the disease. *American Journal of Psychiatry, 133* (1), 32–36.

Garland, D. (1990). *Punishment and modern society: A study in social theory*. Chicago: The University of Chicago Press.

Geller, J. L. (1989). *The Massachusetts experience with funded deinstitutionalization: A decade of promises, products and problems under the Brewster v. Dukakis consent decree*. Boston: University of Massachusetts Medical School & Massachusetts Department of Mental Health.

Gergen, K. (1991). *The saturated self*. New York: Basic Books.

Gergen, K. (1999). *An invitation to social construction*. London: Sage.

Giddens, A. (1984). *The constitution of society: Outline of a theory of structuration*. Oxford, United Kingdom: Polity Press.

Giddens, A. (1990). *Consequences of modernity*. Stanford, CA: Stanford University Press.

Gilligan, C. (1982). *In a different voice*. Cambridge, MA: Harvard University Press.

Gilligan, C., Lyons, N. P., & Hanmer, T. J. (Eds.). (1990). *Making connections*. Cambridge, MA: Harvard University Press.

Goerner, S. (1994). *Chaos and the evolving ecological universe*. Langhorne, PA: Gordon and Breach Science Publishers.

Goffman, E. (1961). *Asylums: Essays of the social situation of mental patients and other inmates*. Garden City, NY: Anchor Books.

Goffman, E. (1967). *Interaction ritual: Essays in face to face behavior*. Chicago: Aldine.

Goldman, H. H., Adams, N. H., & Taube, C. A. (1983a). The alchemy of mental health policy: Homelessness and the fourth cycle of reform. *American Journal of Public Health, 34*, 129–134.

Goldman, H. H., Adams, N. H., & Taube, C. A. (1983b). Deinstitutionalization: The data demythologized. *Hospital & Community Psychiatry, 34* (2), 129–134.

Goldman H. H., & Morrissey, J. P. (1985). The alchemy of mental health policy: Homelessness and the fourth cycle of reform. *American Journal of Public Health, 75*, 727–731.

Goodrich, P. (1987). *Legal discourse*. New York: St. Martin's Press.

Goodrich, P. (1990). *Languages of law: From logics of memory to nomadic masks*. London: Weidenfeld and Nicholson.

Gormley, M. J. (1984). Substantial judgment: A modern application. *New England Journal of Criminal and Civil Confinement, 10*, 353–382.

Gould, K. K., & Perlin, M. L. (2000). "Johnny's in the basement mixing up his medicine": Therapeutic jurisprudence and clinical teaching. *Seattle University Law Review, 24* (2), 339–372.

Gramsci, A. (1971). *Prison notebooks*. New York: International Publications.

Greimas, A. (1987). *On meaning: Selected writings* (P. J. Perron & F. H. Collins, Trans.). Minneapolis, MN: University of Minnesota Press.

Greimas, A. (1990). *The social sciences: a semiotic view* (P. Fabbi & F. H. Collins, Trans.). Minneapolis, MN: University of Minnesota Press.

Grisso, T. (1986). *Evaluating competencies: Forensic assessments and instruments*. New York: Plenum Press.

Greene, L. R., & De La Cruz, A. (1981). Psychiatric day treatment as an alternative to and transition from full-time hospitalization. *Community Mental Health Journal, 17* (3), 191–202.

Grob, G. N. (1973). *Mental institutions in America: Social policy to 1875*. New York: Free Press.

Grob, G. N. (1983a). Historical origins of deinstitutionalization. In L. L. Bachrach (Ed.), *Deinstitutionalization* (pp. 30–74). San Francisco: Jossey-Bass.

Grob, G. N. (1983b). *Mental illness and American society, 1875–1940*. Princeton, NJ: Princeton University Press.

Grob, G. N. (1994). *The mad among us: A history of the care of America's mentally ill*. New York: Free Press.

Grosz, E. A. (1990). *Jacques Lacan: A feminist introduction*. New York: Routledge.

Guattari, F. (1984). *Molecular revolution: Psychiatry and politics* (3rd ed.). (R. Sheed, Trans). New York: Penguin.

Gutheil, T. G. (1980). Legal guardianship in drug refusal: An illusory solution. *American Journal of Psychology, 137* (3), 347–352.

Gutheil, T. G. (1985). Rogers v. Commissioner: Denouncement of an important right-to-refuse treatment case. *American Journal of Psychiatry, 142* (2), 213–216.

Gutheil, T. G., & Appelbaum, P. S. (1983). *Substituted judgment: Best interest in disguise, the Hastings Center Report*. Garrison, NY: The Hastings Center.

Gutheil, T. G., Appelbaum, P. S., & Wexler, D. B. (1983). The inappropriateness of least restrictive alternative analysis for involuntary interventions with the mentally ill. *Journal of Psychiatry and Law, 11*, 7–17.

Habermas, J. (1975). *Legitimation crises*. Boston: Beacon Press.

Habermas, J. (1984). *The theory of communicative action: Vol. 1. Reason and the rationalization of society*. Boston: Beacon Press.

Habermas, J. (1987). *The theory of communicative action: Vol. 2. Life world and system: A critique of functionalist reason*. Boston: Beacon Press.

Haddad, L. K. (1974–1975). Predicting the Supreme Court's response to the criticism of the psychiatric predictions of dangerousness in civil commitment proceedings. *University of Pennsylvania Law Review, 123*, 439–488.

Halleck, S. L. (1975). *Coping with the legal onslaught*. San Francisco: Jossey-Bass.

Haney, C. (1991). The 14th Amendment and symbolic legality: Let them eat due process. *Law and Human Behavior, 14*, 183–204.

Haney, C. (1993). Psychology and legal change: The impact of a decade. *Law and Human Behavior, 17*, 371–398.

Hart, M. A. (1974). Civil commitment of the mentally ill in California: The Lanterman-Petris-Short Act. *Loyola of Los Angeles Law Review, 7*, 93–136.

Hawkes, T. (1977). *Structuralism and semiotics*. Barkeley, CA: University of California Press.

Hayles, N. K. (1990). *Chaos bound: Orderly disorder in contemporary literature and science*. Ithaca, NY: Cornell University Press.

Heidegger, M. (1958). *The question of being* (W. Kluback & J. T. Wilde, Trans.). New Haven, CT: College & University Press.

Heilbrun, K., Radelet, M., & Dvoskin, J. (1992). The debate on treating individuals incompetent for execution. *American Journal of Psychiatry, 149* (5), 596–605.

Heinbecker, P. (1986). Two year's experience under Utah's *mens rea* insanity law. *Bulletin of the American Academy of Psychiatry and Law, 14* (2), 185–191.

Henry, S., & Lanier, M. M. (1998). The prism of crime: Arguments for an integrated definition of crime. *Justice Quarterly*, *15* (4), 609–629.

Henry, S., & Lanier, M. M. (2001). *Defining crime*. Boston, MA: Allyn & Bacon.

Henry, S., & Milovanovic, D. (1991). Constitutive criminology: The maturation of critical theory. *Criminology*, *29* (2), 293–315.

Henry, S., & Milovanovic, D. (1996). *Constitutive criminology: Beyond postmodernism*. London: Sage.

Henry, S., & Milovanovic, D. (1999). *Constitutive theory at work: Agency and resistance in the constitution of crime and punishment*. Albany, NY: SUNY Press.

Herman, D. H. J. (1973). Preventive detention, a scientific view of man, and state power. *University of Illinois Law Review, 1973*, *73*, 673–699.

Hermann, D. (1990). Autonomy, self-determination, the right of involuntary committed persons to refuse treatment, and the use of substituted judgement in medication decisions involving incompetent persons. *International Journal of Law and Psychiatry*, *13* (4), 361–385.

Herr, S. S. (1979). *The new clients: Legal services for mentally retarded persons*. Washington, DC: National Legal Services Corp.

Herr, S. S. (1983). *Legal rights and mental health care*. Lexington, MA: Lexington Books.

Hiday, V. A., & Goodman, R. R. (1982). The least restrictive alternative to involuntary hospitalization, outpatient commitment: Its use and effectiveness. *Journal of Psychiatry and Law*, *10* (1), 81–86.

Hiday, V. A., & Scheid-Cook, T. (1987). The North Carolina experience with outpatient commitment: A critical reappraisal. *International Journal of Law and Psychiatry*, *10*, 215–241.

Hinds, J. T. (1990). Involuntary outpatient commitment for the chronically mentally ill. *Nebraska Law Review*, *69*, 346–412.

Hobbes, T. (1651/1950). *Leviathan*. New York: Dutton.

Hoch, C., & Slayton, R. A. (1989). *New homeless and old: Community and the skid row hotel*. Philadelphia: Temple University Press.

Hoffman, B. (1977). Living with your rights off. *Psychiatric Annals*, *7*, 84–89.

Holdsworth, W. S. (1922/1966). *A history of English law*. A. L. Goohart and G. Hanbury (eds.). London: Methuen and Company, Ltd., Sweet & Maxwell, Ltd.

Holstein, J. A. (1993). *Court-ordered insanity: Interpretive practice and involuntary commitment*. New York: Aldine de Gruyter.

Hombs, M. E., & Snyder, M. (1982). *Homelessness in America: A forced march to nowhere* (2nd ed.). Washington, DC: Community for Creative Non-Violence.

Howe, A. (1994). *Punish and critique: Towards a feminist analysis of penalty*. London: Routledge.

Hughes, S. D. (1984). Civil commitment: guardianship, substantial judgment, and right to refuse psychiatric treatment. *Gonzaga Law Review, 20*, 479–509.

Hunt, A. (1986). The theory of critical legal studies. *Oxford Journal of Legal Studies*, 6, 1–45.

Hunt, A. (1987). The critique of law: What is "critical" about critical theory? *Journal of Law and Society, 14*, 5–19.

Hunt, A. (1993). *Exploration in law and society: A constitutive theory of law*. New York: Routledge.

Irigaray, L. (1985a). *Speculum of the other woman* (G. C. Gill, Trans.). Ithaca, NY: Cornell University Press.

Irigaray, L. (1985b). *This sex which is not one* (C. Porter, Trans.). Ithaca, NY: Cornell University Press.

Irigaray, L. (1990). *The ethics of sexual difference* (C. Burke, Trans.). Oxford, United Kingdom: Blackwell.

Irwin, J., & Austin, J. (1997). *It's about time*. Belmont, CA: Wadsworth.

Isaac, R. J., & Armat, V. C. (1990). *Madness in the streets: How psychiatry and the law abandoned the mentally ill*. New York: Free Press.

Jackson, B. S. (1985). *Semiotics and legal theory*. Boston: Routledge & Kegan Paul.

Jackson, B. S. (1991). *Law fact and narrative coherence*. Merseyside, United Kingdom: Deborah Charles.

Jackson, B. S. (1995). *Making sense in law*. Liverpool, United Kingdom: Deborah Charles.

Jakobson, R. Two aspects of language and two types of aphasic disorder. In *Fundamental of language*, R. Jakobson and M. Halle (Eds.), (pp. 69–96). Paris: Mouton.

Jessop, B. (1990). *State theory: Putting the capitalist state in its place*. Cambridge: Polity Press.

Johnson, R. (1998). *Death work: A study of the modern execution process* (2nd ed.). Belmont, CA: Wadsworth.

Jones, K. (1972). *A history of the mental health services*. London: Routledge & Kegan Paul.

Jost, J. T. (1995). Negative illusions: Conceptual clarification and psychological evidence concerning false consciousness. *Political Psychology*, 16, 394–427.

Julien, P. (1994). *Jacques Lacan's return to Freud: The real, the symbolic, and the imaginary* (D. Simiu, Trans.). New York: NYU Press.

Kagehiro, D. K., & Laufer, W. S. (1992). Preface. In D. K. Kagehiro & W. S. Laufer (Eds.), *Handbook of forensic psychology* (pp. xi–xiii). New York: Springer-Verlag.

Kahle, S., & Sales, B. (1980). Due process of law and the attitudes of professionals toward involuntary civil commitment. In P. Lipsitt and B. Sales (Eds.), *New Directions in Psychological Research*, 6, 201–223.

Kairys, D. (Ed.). (1982). *The politics of law* (1st ed.). New York: Pantheon Books.

Kane, J. M., Quitkin, F., Rifkin, A., Wagner, J., Rosenberger, G., & Borenstein, M. (1983). Attitudinal changes of involuntarily committed patients following treatment. *Archives of General Psychiatry*, 40 (2), 374–377.

Kant, I. (1785/1959. *Foundations of the metaphysics of morals* (L. W. Beck, Trans.). Indianapolis, IN: Bobbs-Merrill.

Kauffman, S. (1991). Antichaos and adaptation. *Scientific American*, 265 (2), 78–84.

Kaufmann, W. A. (Ed.). (1956). *Existentialism from Dostoevsky to Sartre*. New York: Meridian Books.

Keilitz, I. (1985). Least restrictive treatment of involuntary patients: Translating concepts into practice. *St Louis University Law Journal*, 29, 691–745.

Keilitz, I. (1987). Researching and reforming the insanity defense. *Rutgers Law Review*, 39, 289–322.

Kevelson, R. (1987). *Charles S. Peirce's method of methods*. Philadelphia: J. Benjamins.

Kevelson, R. (1988). *The law as a system of signs*. New York: Plenum Press

Kevelson, R. (1990). *Peirce, paradox, praxis: The image, the conflict, and the law*. New York: Mouton de Gruyter.

Kiesler, C. A. (1982a). Mental hospitals and alternative care: Noninstitutionalization as potential public policy for mental patients. *American Psychology*, 37 (12), 1323–1339.

Kiesler, C. A. (1982b). Public and professional myths about mental hospitalization: An empirical reassessment of policy-related beliefs. *American Psychologist*, 37 (12), 1323–1339.

Kittrie, N. N. (1972). *The right to be different: Enforced therapy*. Baltimore: Johns Hopkins University Press.

Klein, D. F. (1980). *Diagnosis and drug treatment of psychiatric disorders: Adults and children* (2nd ed.). Baltimore: Williams and Wilkins.

Klein, D. F., & Davis, J. M. (1969). *The diagnosis and drug treatment of psychiatric disorders*. Baltimore: Williams and Wilkins.

Klein, J. I. (1986). A legal advocate's perspective on the right to refuse treatment. In D. Rapoport & J. Parry (Eds.), *The right to refuse antipsychotic medication* (pp. 80–86). Washington, DC: American Bar Association.

Knorr-Cetina, K. (1981). Introduction: The Micro-sociological challenge of macro-sociology: Towards a reconstruction of social theory and methodology. In K. Knorr-Cetina & A. V. Cicourel (Ed.), *Advances in social theory and methodology: Toward an integration of micro- and micro-sociologies* (pp. 1–47). Boston: Routledge and Kegan Paul.

Kohut, H. (1971). *The analysis of the self*. New York: International Universities Press.

Kristeva, J. (1977). *Polylogue*. Paris: Seuil.

Kristeva, J. (1979, Autumn). *Il n'y a pas de maitre a langage. Nouvelle Revue de Psychanalyse*, 20, 119–149.

Kristeva, J. (1980). *Desire in language: A semiotic approach to literature and art* (L. Roudiez, Ed.). (T. Gora, A. Jardine, & L. S. Roudiez, Trans.). New York: Columbia University Press.

Kristeva, J. (1986). *Revolution in poetic language*. New York: Columbia University Press.

Kutner, L. (1962–1963). The illusions of due process in commitment proceedings. *Northwestern University Law Review*, 57, 383–409.

Lacan, J. (1975). *Encore*. Paris, France: Edition du Seuil.

Lacan, J. (1977). *Ecrits: A selection* (A. Sheridan, Trans.). New York: Norton.

Lacan, J. (1981). *The four fundamental concepts of psycho-analysis*. New York: Norton.

Lacan, J. (1985). *Feminine sexuality*. New York: Norton.

Lacan, J. (1988). *The seminars of Jacques Lacan: Book II. The ego in Freud's theory and the technique of psychoanalysis 1954–1955*. Cambridge, MA: Cambridge University Press.

Lacan, J. (1991). *L'envers de la Psychanalyse*. Paris: Editions du Seuil.

Laclau, E. (1989). Preface. In S. Zieck (Ed.), *The sublime object of ideology* (pp. ix–xv). New York: Verso.

Laclau, E., & Mouffe, C. (1985). *Hegemony and socialist strategy*. New York: Verso.

LaFond, J. Q. (1981). An examination of the purposes of involuntary civil commitment. *Buffalo Law Review*, 30, 499–535.

LaFond, J. Q., & Durham, M. L. (1992a). *Back to the asylum: The future of mental health law and policy in the United States*. New York: Oxford University Press.

LaFond, J. Q., & Durham, M. L. (1992b). *The future of mental health policy in the United States*. New York: Oxford University Press.

Laing, R. D. (1967). *The politics of experience*. New York: Pantheon Books.

Laing, R. D. (1969). *Divided self: An existential study in sanity and madness*. Baltimore: Penguin Books.

Lamb, H. R. (1979). The new asylums in the community. *Archives of General Psychiatry*, 36 (2), 129–134.

Lamb, H. R. (1982). The mentally ill in an urban county jail. *Archives of General Psychiatry*, 39 (1), 17–22.

Lamb, H. R. (1984a). Deinstitutionalization and the homeless mentally ill. *Hospital and Community Psychiatry*, 35 (9), 899–907.

Lamb, H. R. (Ed.). (1984b). *The homeless mentally ill: A task force report of the American Psychiatric Association*. Washington, DC: The Association.

Lamb, H. R. (1989). Involuntary treatment for the homeless mentally ill. *Notre Dame Journal of Law, Ethics, and Public Policy*, 4, 269–280.

Lamb, H. R., & Goertzel, V. (1977). The long-term patient in the era of community treatment. *Archives of General Psychiatry, 34* (6), 679–682.

Lamb, H. R., & Mills, M. J. (1984). Deinstitutionalization and the homeless mentally ill. *Hospital and Community Psychiatry, 35*, 899–907.

Lamb, H. R., & Mills, M. J. (1988). Needed changes in law and procedure for the chronically mentally ill. *Hospital and Community Psychiatry, 37*, 475–480.

Lamb, H. R., & Weinberger, L. E. (1998). Persons with severe mental illness in jails and prisons: A review. *Psychiatric Services, 49* (4), 483–492.

Landau, I. (1993). Early and later deconstruction in the writings of Jacques Derrida. *Cardozo Law Review, 14*, 1895–1909.

Lanier, M. M., & Henry, S. (1998). *Essential criminology*. Boulder, CO: Westview/Harper Collins.

Lecercle, J. (1985). *Philosophy through the looking glass: Language, nonsense, desire*. London: Hutchinson.

Lee, J. S. (1990). *Jacques Lacan*. Amherst, MA: University of Massachusetts.

Lerman, P. (1982). *Deinstitutionaliztion and the welfare state*. New Brunswick, NJ: Rutgers University Press.

Lévi-Strauss, C. (1962). *The savage mind*. Chicago: University of Chicago Press.

Lévi-Strauss, C. (1963). *Structural anthropology* (C. Jacobson & B. Grundfest Schoept, Trans.). New York: Basic Books.

Levy, R., & Rubenstein, L. (1996). *The rights of people with mental disabilities*. Carbondale, IL: Southern Illinois University Press.

Liebman, F., & Leibman, N. (1991). Developing trends in prisoners' rights to mental health treatment. *American Journal of Forensic Psychology*, 9 (1), 19–28.

Lipetz, M. (1983). *Routine justice: Processing cases in women's court*. New Brunswick, NJ: Transaction Books.

Lipton, A. A., & Simon, F. S. (1985). Psychiatric diagnosis in a state hospital: Manhattan State revisited. *Hospital and Community Psychiatry*, 36, 368–373.

Livermore, A., Malmquist, R., & Meehl, S. (1968). On the justifications for civil commitment. *University of Pennsylvania Law Review, 75*, 84–112.

Locke, J. (1968). *The works of John Locke* (Vols. 1–10). Aalen: Scientia Verlag.

Lyotard, J. F. (1984). *The postmodern condition: A report on knowledge*. Minneapolis, MN: University of Minnesota Press.

MacCabe, C. (1979). *James Joyce and the revolution of the world*. London: MacMillan.

MacDonell, D. (1986). *Theories of discourse*. New York: B. Blackwell.

MacGraw, B. D., Farthing-Capowich, D., & Keilitz, I. (1985). The guilty but mentally ill plea and verdict: Current state of the knowledge. *Villanova Law Review, 169*, 205–221.

MacKinnon, C. A. (1987). *Feminism unmodified: Discourses on life and law*. Cambridge, MA: Harvard University Press.

MacKinnon, C. A. (1989). *Towards a feminist theory of the state*. Cambridge, MA: Harvard University Press.

MacKinnon, C. (1993). *Only words*. Cambridge: Harvard University Press.

MacLean, B., & Pepinsky, H (1991). *We who would take no prisoners: Selections from the fifth international conference on penal abolition*. Vancouver: The Collective Press.

Machiavelli, N. (1640/1985). *The prince* (H. C. Mansfield, Trans.). Chicago: University of Chicago Press.

Manning, P. (1979). Metaphors in the field: Varieties of organizational discourse. *Administrative Science Quarterly, 24*, 660–671.

Manning, P. (1988). *Symbolic communication: Signifying calls and the police response*. Cambridge, MA: Harvard University Press.

Marcel, G. (1950/1951). *The mystery of being* (R. Hague, Trans.). Chicago: Regnery.

Marx, K. (1967). *Capital*. (F. Engels, Ed.). New York: International Publishers.

Marx, K. (1984). *The eighteenth Brumaire of Louis Bonaparte*. Toronto, Canada: Norman Bethune Institute.

Matsuda, M. (1996). *Where is your body? And other essays on race, gender, and the law*. Boston, MA: Beacon Press.

Matsuda, M., Lawrence, C., & Delgado, R. (Ed.). (1993). *Words that wound: Critical race theory, assaultive speech, and the First Amendment*. Boulder, CO: Westview.

Mauss, M. (1990). *The gift: The form of reason for exchange in archaic societies*. (W. D. Halls, Trans.). New York: W. W. Norton.

May, R. (1983). *The discovery of being*. New York: W. W. Norton.

Mayer, C. (1987). *Insanity defense reforms: Pre-and post-Hinckley*. Paper presented at the annual meeting of the Law and Society Association, Washington, DC.

McCleary, R. (1992). *Dangerous men: The sociology of parole*. New York: Harrow and Heston.

McCormick, C. (1972). *Laws of evidence*. (2nd ed.). St Paul, MN: West.

McGarry, A. L. (1976). The holy legal war against state-hospital psychiatry. *New England Journal of Medicine, 294* (6), 318–320.

McGraw, B.D., Farthing-Capowich, D., & Keilitz, I. (1985). The "guilty but mentally ill" plea and verdict: Current state of the knowledge. *Villanova Law Review, 30*, 117–191.

McKnight, J. L. (1987). Regenerating community. *Social Policy*, 3, 54–58.

Meisel, A. (1979). The exceptions to the informed consent doctrine: Striking a balance between competing values in medical decisionmaking. *Wisconsin Law Review*, 413–462.

Meisel, A. (1982). The rights of the mentally ill under state constitutions. *Law & Contemporary Problems, 45*, 7–46.

Meisel, A., & Roth, L. (1983). Toward an informed discussion of informed consent: A review of and critique of empirical studies. *Arizona Law Review, 25*, 265–289.

Melton, G. B. (1988). The significance of law in the everyday lives of children and families. *Georgia Law Review, 22*, 851–895.

Melton, G. B. (1990). Realism in psychology and humanism in law: Psycholegal studies at Nebraska. *Nebraska Law Review*, 69, 251–277.

Melton, G. B. (1991, Summer). President's column. *American Psychology-Law Society News*, 1–3.

Melton, G. B. (1992). The law is a good thing (psychology is, too): Human rights in psychological jurisprudence. *Law and Human Behavior, 16*, 381–398.

Melton, G. B., Petrila, J., Poythress, N., & Slobogin, C. (1987). *Psychological evaluations for the courts: A handbook for mental health professionals and lawyers*. New York: Guilford Press.

Meltzoff, J., & Kornreich, M. (1970). *Research in psychotherapy*. New York: Atherton Press.

Melville, S. (1987). Psychoanalysis and the place of *jouissance*. *Critical Inquiry, 13*, 349–370.

Merleau-Ponty, M. (1983). *The structure of behavior*. (A. L. Fisher, Trans.). Pittsburgh, PA: Duquesne University Press.

Metz, C. (1983). *The imaginary signifier*. Bloomington, IN: Indiana University Press.

Metzner, J. (1998). An introduction to correctional psychiatry: Part III. *Journal of the American Academy of Psychiatry and the Law, 26* (1), 107–115.

Mill, J. S. (1863/1951). *Utilitarianism*. New York: Dutton.

Miller, J. (1982). The least restrictive alternative: Hidden meanings and agenda. *Community Health Law*, 8, 46–51.

Miller, R. D. (1985). Commitment to outpatient treatment: A national survey. *Hospital and Community Psychiatry*, 36, (3), 265–267.

Miller, R. D. (1988). Evaluation and competency to be executed: A national survey and analysis. *Journal of Psychiatry and Law, 16*, 67–92.

Miller, R. D., & Fiddleman, P. B. (1984). Outpatient commitment: Treatment in the least restrictive environment. *Hospital & Community Psychiatry, 35* (2), 147–151.

Mills, M. J., & Cummins, B. D. (1982). Deinstitutionalization reconsidered. *Journal of Law & Psychiatry, 5* (3/4), 271–284.

Milovanovic, D. (1986). Juridico-linguistic communicative markets: towards a semiotic analysis. *Contemporary Crises, 10*, 281–304.

Milovanovic, D. (1988). Jailhouse lawyers and jailhouse lawyering. *International Journal of the Sociology of Law, 16*, 455–475.

Milovanovic, D. (1992a). *Postmodern law and disorder: Psychoanalytic semiotics, chaos and juridic exegesis*. Liverpool, United Kingdom: Deborah Charles.

Milovanovic, D. (1992b). Rethinking subjectivity in law and ideology: A semiotic perspective. *Journal of Human Justice, 4* (1), 31–53.

Milovanovic, D. (1993). Lacan, chaos and practical discourse in law. In R. Kevelson (Ed.), *Flux, complexity, illusion in law* (pp. 311–337). New York: P. Lang.

Milovanovic, D. (1994a). The decentered subject in law: Contributions of topology, psychoanalytic semiotics and chaology. *Studies in Psychoanalytic Theory, 3*, 93–127.

Milovanovic, D. (1994b). *A primer in the sociology of law*. New York: Harrow and Heston.

Milovanovic, D. (1995). Postmodern law and subjectivity: Lacan and the linguistic turn. In D. Caudill & S. Gold (Eds.), *Radical philosophy of law: Contemporary challenges to mainstream legal theory and practice* (pp. 38–53). Atlantic Heights, NJ: Humanities Press.

Milovanovic, D. (1996). "Rebellious lawyering": Lacan, chaos, and the development of alternative juridico-semiotic forms. *Legal Studies Forum, 20* (3), 295–321.

Milovanovic, D. (Ed.) (1997a). *Chaos, criminology and social justice: The new orderly (dis)order*. Westport, CT: Praeger.

Milovanovic, D. (1997b). *Postmodern criminology*. New York: Garland.

Milovanovic, D., and Henry, S. (1991). Constitutive Penology. *Social Justice, 18*, 204–224.

Moi, T. (1985). *Sexual/textual politics: Feminist literary theory*. London: Methuen.

Monahan, J. (1981a). The Clinical Prediction of Violent Behavior. *National Institute of Mental Health* (DHHS Publication No. ADM 81–921). Washington, DC: U.S. Government Printing Office.

Monahan, J. (1981b). *U.S. Department of Health and Human Services: The clinical prediction of violent behavior*. Washington, DC: U.S. Government Printing Office.

Monahan, J. (1996). Violence prediction: The past 20 years and the next 20 years. *Criminal Justice and Behavior, 23* (1), 107–120.

Monahan, J., & Wexler, D. (1978). Definite maybe: Proof and probability in civil commitment. *Law and Human Behavior, 2*, 37–42.

Montesquieu, C. (1748/1989). *The spirit of laws*. New York: Cambridge University Press.

Morgan, G. (1983). More on metaphor: Why we cannot control tropes in administrative science. *Administrative Science Quarterly, 28*, 601–607.

Morris, G. H. (1986). The supreme court examines civil commitment issues: A retrospective and prospective assessment. *Tulane Law Review, 60*, 927–953.

Morris, N. (1982). *Madness and the Criminal Law.* Chicago: University of Chicago Press.

Morrissey, J. P., & Goldman, H. H. (1984). Cycles of reform in the care of the chronically mentally ill. *Hospital and Community Psychiatry, 35* (8), 785–793.

Morrissey, J. P., & Goldman, H. H. (1986). Care and Treatment of the Mentally Ill in the United States: Historical Developments and Reforms. *Annals of the American Academy of Political and Social Sciences, 484*, 12–27.

Morrissey, J. P., & Gounis, K. (1987). *Homelessness in America: Emerging issues in the construction of a social problem, location and stigmas: Emerging themes in the study of mental health and mental illness.* New York: Praeger.

Morse, S. J. (1978). Crazy behavior, morals, and science: An analysis of mental health law. *California Law Review, 51*, 527–654.

Morse, S. J. (1982a). A preference for liberty: The case against involuntary commitment of the mentally disordered. *California Law Review, 70*, 54–106.

Morse, S. J. (1982b). *The court of the last resort: Mental illness and the law.* Chicago: University of Chicago Press.

Morse, S. J. (1988). Treating crazy people less specially. *West Virginia Law Review, 90*, 353–382.

Mulvey, E. P., Geller, J. L., & Roth, L. H. (1987). The promise and peril of involuntary outpatient commitment. *American Psychologist, 42* (6), 571–584.

Murray, E. L. (1986). *Imaginative thinking and human existence.* Pittsburgh, PA: Duquesne University Press.

Murray, E. L. (Ed.). (1987). *Imagination and phenomenological psychology.* Pittsburgh, PA: Duquesne University Press.

Musto, D. R. (1975). What ever happened to "community mental health"? *Public Interest, 39*, 53–79.

Myers, J. E. B. (1983–1984). Involuntary civil commitment of the mentally ill: A system in need of change. *Villanova Law Review, 29*, 367–433.

Nagel, T. (1986). *The view from nowhere.* New York: Oxford University Press.

Nardulli, P. (1978). *The courtroom elite.* Cambridge, MA: Ballinger.

Nietzsche, F. W. (1966). *Beyond good and evil: Prelude to a philosophy of the future.* New York: Random House.

Nietzsche, F. W. (1995). *Thus spoke Zarathustra: A book for all and none.* (W. Kaufmann, Trans.). New York: Modern Library.

Nietzsche, F. W. (1996). *Human, all too human.* (M. Farber & S. Lehmann, Trans.). Lincoln, NE: University of Nebraska Press.

Ogden, C. K., & Richards, I. A. (1926). *The meaning of meaning: A study of the influence of language upon thought and of the science of symbolism.* Richards, NY: Harcourt, Brace.

Ogloff, J. R. P. (1992). *Law and psychology: The broadening of the discipline.* Durham, NC: Carolina Academic Press.

Ogloff, J. R. P. (1999). Law and Human Behavior: Reflecting back and looking forward. *Law and Human Behavior, 23* (1), 1–7.

Ogloff, J. R. P. (2000). Two steps forward and one step backward: The law and psychology movement(s) in the 20th century. *Law and Human Behavior, 24* (4), 457–483.

Ogloff, J. R. P., Roesch, R., & Hart, S. (1994). Mental health services in jails and prisons: Legal, clinical, and policy issues. *Law and Psychology Review, 18*, 109–136.

Omer, H., & Strenger, C. (1992). The pluralist revolution: From one true meaning to an infinity of constructed ones. *Psychotherapy, 29* (2), 253–261.

Paczak, S. (1989). Pennsylvania standard for involuntary civil commitment of the mentally ill: Clear and present danger? *Duquesne University Law Review, 27*, 325–353.

Parenti, M. (1996). *Dirty tricks: Reflection on politics, media, ideology, conspiracy, ethnic life, and class power*. New York: City Light.

Parloff, M. B. (1978). *Assessment of psychological treatment of mental health disorders: Current status and prospects*. Rockville, MD: National Institute of Mental Health.

Parry, A., & Doan, R. (1994). *Story re-visions: Narrative therapy in the postmodern world*. New York: Guildford Press.

Parry-Jones, W. L. (1972). *The trade in lunacy: A study of private madhouses in England in the eighteenth and nineteenth centuries*. London: Routledge.

Patch, P. C., & Arrigo B. A. (1998). Police officer attitudes and use of discretion in situations involving the mentally ill: The need to narrow the focus. *International Journal of Law and Psychiatry, 22* (1), 23–55.

Pecheux, M. (1982). *Language, semantics, and ideology*. New York: St. Martin's Press.

Peirce, C. S. (1956). *The philosophy of Peirce: Selected writings*. (J. Bulcher, Ed.). London: Routledge & Kegan Paul.

Peirce, C. S. (1965). *The collected papers of Charles Sanders Peirce*. (C. Hartshorne & P. Weiss, Ed.). Cambridge, MA: Harvard University Press.

Pepinsky, H. (1991). *The geometry of violence*. Bloomington, IN: Indiana University Press.

Pepper, B., & Ryglewicz, H. (1982). Testimony for the neglected: The mentally ill in the post-deinstitutionalization age. *American Journal of Orthopsychiatry, 52* (3), 388–392.

Perlin, M. L. (1982). Mental patient advocacy by a public advocate. *Psychiatric Quarterly, 54*, 169–178.

Perlin, M. L. (1989, 1998, 1999, 2000). *Mental disability law: Civil and criminal*. Charlottesville, VA: Michie Co.

Perlin, M. L. (1990). Psychodynamics and the insanity defense: "Ordinary common sense" and heuristic reasoning. *Nebraska Law Review, 69*, 109–139.

Perlin, M. L. (1991). Morality and pretextuality, psychiatry and law: Of "ordinary commonsense," heuristic reasoning, and cognitive dissonance. *Bulletin of the American Academy of Psychiatry and Law, 19,* 131–150.

Perlin, M. L. (1992a). On sanism. *Southern Methodist University Law Review, 46,* 373–491.

Perlin, M. L. (1992b). Fatal assumption- A critical evaluation of the role of counsel in mental disability cases. *Law and Human Behavior, 16,* 39–59.

Perlin, M. L. (1994a). *The jurisprudence of the insanity defense.* Durham, NC: Carolina Academic Press.

Perlin, M. L. (1994b). Therapeutic jurisprudence: Understanding the sanist and pretextual bases of mental disability law. *New England Journal on Criminal and Civil Confinement, 20,* 369–383.

Perlin, M. L. (1995). Therapeutic jurisprudence and the civil rights of institutionalized mentally disabled persons: Hopeless oxymoron or path to redemption? *Psychology, Public Policy, and the Law, 1,* 85–95.

Perlin, M. L. (1997). "The borderline which separated you from me": The insanity defense, the authoritarian spirit , the fear of faking, and the culture of punishment. *Iowa Law Review, 82,* 1375–1414.

Perlin, M. L. (1999a). *Mental disability law: Cases and materials.* Durham, NC: Carolina Academic Press.

Perlin, M. L. (1999b). "Half-wracked prejudice leaped forth": Sanism, pretextuality, and why and how mental disability law developed as it did. *Journal of Contemporary Legal Issues, 10,* 3–36.

Perlin, M. L. (2000a). *The hidden prejudice: Mental disability on trial.* Washington, DC: American Psychological Association.

Perlin, M. L. (2000b). Their promises of paradise: Institutional segregation, community treatment, the ADA, and Olmstead v. L. C. *Houston Law Review, 37,* 999–1054.

Perlin, M. L., Gould, K. K., & Dorfman, D. D. (1995). Therapeutic jurisprudence and the civil rights of institutionalized mentally disabled persons: Hopeless oxymoron or path to redemption? *Psychology, Public Policy, and Law, 1,* 80–119

Perlin, M. L., & Sadoff, R. L. (1982). Ethical issues in the representation of individuals in the commitment process. *Law and Contemporary Problems, 45,* 161–192.

Peters, R. (1987). The effects of statutory change on the civil commitment of the mentally ill. *Law & Human Behavior, 11,* 73–99.

Petrella, R. C., Benedek, E. P., Banks, S. C., & Packer, I. K. (1985). Examining the application of the guilty but mentally ill verdict in Michigan. *Hospital and Community Psychiatry,* 36 (3), 254–259.

Pfohl, S. (1978). *Predicting dangerousness: The social construction of psychiatric reality.* Lexington, MA: Lexington Books.

Pfohl, S. (1984). Predicting dangerousness: A social deconstruction. In L Teplin (Ed.), *Mental health and criminal justice* (pp. 201–226). Beverly Hills, CA: Sage.

Plato (1957). *The republic of Plato*. (A. D. Lindsay, Trans.). New York: E. P. Dutton.

Pollock-Byrne, J. M. (1989). *Ethics in crime and justice: Dilemmas and decisions*. Belmont, NY: Wadsworth.

Pool, R. (1989). "Is it healthy to be chaotic?" *Science*, *243*, 604–607.

Pope, H. G., Jr., & Lipinski, J. F., Jr. (1978). Diagnosis in schizophrenia and manic-depressive illness. *Archives of General Psychiatry*, *35*, 811–828.

Porter, E., & Gleick, J. (1990). *Nature's chaos*. New York: Viking.

Poythress, N. G. (1978). Psychiatric expertise in civil commitment: Training attorneys to cope with expert testimony. *Law and Human Behavior*, *2*, 1–23.

Prigogine, I., & Stengers, I. (1984). *Order out of chaos*. New York: Bantam Books.

Rachman, S. J. (1973). The effects of psychological treatment. In H.J. Eysenck (Eds.), *Handbook of Abnormal Psychology* (pp. 805–819). San Diego, CA: R. R. Knapp.

Ragland-Sullivan, E. (1986). *Jacques Lacan and the philosophy of psychoanalysis*. Chicago: University of Illinois Press.

Rapson, R. (1980). The right of the mentally ill to receive treatment in the community. *Columbia Journal of Law and Social Problems*, *16* (193), 236–239.

Reisner, R., & Slobogin, C. (1990). *Law and the mental health system: Civil and criminal aspects*. St. Paul, MN: West Publishing.

Reisner, R., & Slobogin, C. (1997). *Law and the mental health system: Criminal and civil aspects* (2nd ed.). St. Paul, MN: West.

Rhode, D. L. (1983). Class conflicts in class actions. *Stanford Law Review*, *34*, 1183–1262.

Rhoden, N. K. (1980). The right to refuse psychotropic drugs. *Harvard Civil Rights and Civil Liberties Law Review*, *15*, 363–413.

Rhoden, N. K. (1982). The limits of liberty: Deinstitutionalization, homelessness and libertarian theory. *Emory Law Journal*, *31*, 375–440.

Ricoeur, P. (1973). Creativity of language. *Philosophy Today*, *17*, 97–101.

Ricoeur, P. (1975). *The rule of metaphor*. (R. Czerny, K. McLaughlin, & J. Costello, Trans.). Paris: Sevil.

Robitscher, J. B. (1975). Implementing the rights of the mentally disabled: Judicial, legislative and psychiatric action (quoting H. Solomon). In F. Ayd (Ed.), *Medical, moral, and legal issues in mental health care* (pp. 142–178). Baltimore: Williams & Wilkins.

Roesch, R. (1995). Creating change in the legal system: Contributions from community psychology. *Law and Human Behavior*, *19*, 325–343.

Rorty, R. (1978). Philosophy as a kind of writing: An essay on Derrida. *New Literary History, 10*, 141–153.

Rorty, R. (1979). *Philosophy in the mirror of nature*. Princeton, NJ: Princeton University Press.

Rosenau, P. M. (1992). *Postmodernism and the social sciences: Insights, inroads, and intrusions*. Princeton, NJ: Princeton University Press.

Rosenthal (1993, April 7). Who will turn violent? Hospitals have to guess. *New York Times*, p. C1.

Rossi-Landi, F. (1977). *Linguistics and economics*. The Netherlands: Mouton.

Roth, L. H. (1977). Tests of competency to consent to treatment. *American Journal of Psychiatry, 134* (3), 279–284.

Roth, L. H. (1979). A commitment law for patients, doctors, and lawyers. *American Journal of Psychiatry, 136* (9), 1121–1127.

Roth, L. H. (1986). The right to refuse treatment: Law and medicine at the interface. *Emory Law Journal, 35*, 139–161.

Roth, L. H., & Appelbaum, P. S. (1982). What we do and do not know about treatment refusals in mental institutions. In A. E. Doudera, & J. P. Swazey (Eds.), *Refusing treatment in mental health institutions-values in conflict* (pp. 179–196). Ann Arbor, MI: AUPHA Press.

Roth, M., & Kroll, J. (1986). *The reality of mental illness*. New York: Cambridge University Press.

Rothman, D. (1971). *The discovery of the asylum: Social order and disorder in the new republic* (1st ed.). Boston: Little, Brown.

Rothman, D. (1980). *Conscience and convenience: The asylum and its alternatives in progressive America* (1st ed.). Boston: Little, Brown.

Rousseau, J. (1762/1764/1950). *The social contract and discourses*. New York: Hutton.

Rubenstein, L. S. (1983). The American Psychiatric Association's proposals on civil commitment. *Clearinghouse Review, 17*, 558–562.

Rubin. E. L. (1982). Generalizing the trial model of procedural due process: A new basis for the right to treatment. *Harvard C.R.-C.L. Law Review, 17*, 61–132.

Saks, M. J. (1986). The law does not live by eyewitness testimony alone. *Law and Human Behavior, 10* (3), 279–280.

Salecl, R. (1988). Homage to the great one. *Prose Studies, 11*, 84–93.

Salyer, L. (1991). The constitutive nature of law in American history. *Legal Studies Forum, 15*, 1, 61–64.

Sarat, A. (1993). Speaking of death. *Law and Society Review, 27*, 19–58.

Sarat, A., & Kearns, T. (1992). *Law's violence*. Ann Arbor, MI: Michigan University Press.

Sartre, J. P. (1956). *Being and nothingness* (H. E. Barnes, Trans.). New York: Washington Square Press.

Sarup, M. (1989). *Post-structuralism and post-modernism*. Athens, GA: University of Georgia Press.

Sarup, M. (1993). *Post-structuralism and post-modernism* (2nd ed.). Athens, GA: University of Georgia Press.

Saussure, F. de. (1966). *Course in general linguistics* (C. Bally & A. Sechehaye, Ed.). New York: McGraw-Hill.

Sayler, L. (1991). The constitutive nature of law in American history. *Legal Studies Forum, 15* (1), 61–64.

Scheff, T. (1969). *Being mentally ill: A sociological theory*. New York: Aldine de Gruyter.

Scheff, T. (1984). *Being mentally ill: A sociological theory* (2nd ed.). New York: Aldine de Gruyter.

Scheff, T. (2000). *Being mentally ill: a sociological theory* (3rd ed.). New York: Aldine de Gruyter.

Schehr, R. (1996). *New social movement theory*. New York: Praeger.

Schmidt, W. C. (1985). Critique of the American Psychiatric Association's guidelines for the state legislation on civil commitment of the mentally ill. *New England Journal On Criminal and Civil Confinement, 11*, 1–43.

Schoonover S. C., & Bassuk, E. L. (1983). Deinstitutionalization and the private general hospital: Inpatient unit implications for clinical care. *Hospital & Community Psychiatry, 34* (2), 135–139.

Schopenhauer, A. (1851/1970). *Essays and aphorisms* (R. J. Hollingdale, Trans.). New York: Penguin.

Schrift, A. D. (Ed.). (1997). *The logic of the gift: Toward an ethic of generosity*. New York: Routledge.

Schwartz, H. I., & Roth, L. (1989). Informed consent and competency in psychiatric practice. *Journal of Psychiatry and the Law, 8*, 409–427.

Schwartz, H. I., Vingiano, W., & Bezirganian-Perez, C. (1988). Autonomy and the right to refuse treatment: Patients' attitudes after involuntary medication. *Hospital and Community Psychiatry, 39* (10), 1049–1054.

Schwartz, M., & Freidrichs, D. (1994). Postmodern thought and criminological discontent: New metaphors for understanding violence. *Criminology, 32* (2), 221–246.

Schwartz, S. J., & Costanzo, C. E. (1987). Compelling treatment in the community: Distorted doctrines and violated values. *Loyola Los Angeles Law Review, 20*, 1329–1429.

Scull, A. T. (1979). *Museums of madness: The social organization of insanity in nineteenth-century England*. London: Allen Lane.

Scull, A. T. (1981). *Madhouses mad-doctors and madmen: The social history of psychiatry in the Victorian Era*. Philadelphia: University of Pennsylvania Press.

Scull, A. T. (1984). *Decarceration: Community Treatment and the Deviant-A Radical View* (2nd ed.). New Brunswick, NJ: Rutgers University Press.

Scull, A. T. (1989). *Social order/mental disorder: Anglo-American psychiatry in historical perspective*. Berkeley, CA: University of California Press.

Sebeok, T. A. (Ed.). (1986). *Encyclopedic dictionary of semiotics*. New York: Mouton de Gruyter.

Sedgwik, P. (1982). *Psychopolitics*. New York: Harper & Row.

Sellers, S. (Ed.). (1991). *Feminist criticism, theory and practice*. New York: Routledge.

Series, C. (1992). Fractals, reflections and distortions. In N. Hall (Ed.), *Exploring chaos* (pp. 138–146). New York: W. W. Norton.

Serres, M. (1982). *Hermes: Literature, science, philosophy*. Baltimore: Johns Hopkins University Press.

Shah, S. A. (1974). Some interactions of law and mental health in the handling of social deviance. *Catholic University Law Review, 23*, 4, 674–719.

Shah, S. A. (1977). Dangerousness: Some definitional, conceptual and public policy issues. Perspectives In Law and Psychology (Vol. 1). *The criminal justice system* (pp. 91–119). New York: Plenum Press.

Shah, S. A. (1981). Legal and mental health system interactions: Major developments and research needs. *International Journal of Law and Psychiatry, 4* (3), 219–270.

Shell, R. W. (1979–1980). Psychiatric testimony: Science of fortune-telling?. *Barrister, 7*, 6–8; 55.

Showalter, E. (1985). *The female malady: Women, madness, and English culture 1830–1980*. New York: Pantheon Books.

Shultz-Ross, R. A. (1993). Theoretical difficulties in the treatment of mentally ill prisoners. *Journal of Forensic Sciences, 38* (2), 426–431.

Silverman, K. (1983). *The subject of semiotics*. New York: Oxford University Press.

Silverman, K. (1988). *The acoustic mirror: The female voice in psychoanalysis and cinema*. Bloomington, IN: Indiana University Press.

Simon, R., & Aaronson, D. (1988). *The insanity defense: A critical assessment of law and policy in the post-Hinkley era*. New York: Praeger.

Simpson, D. (1984). Involuntary civil commitment: The dangerousness standard and its problems. *University of North Carolina Law Review*, 63, 241–256.

Singer, R. G. (1985). The aftermath of an insanity acquittal: The Supreme Court's recent decision in Jones v. United States. *Annals of the American Academy of Political and Social Science, 1*, 114–124.

Slovenko, R. (1977). Criminal justice procedures in civil commitment. *Hospital and Community Psychiatry, 28* (11), 817–826.

Small, M. A. (1993). Legal psychology and therapeutic jurisprudence. *Saint Louis University Law Journal, 37*, 675–700.

Small, M. A. (1997 August). *Content analysis of Law and Human Behavior articles*. Paper presented at the 105th Annual Meeting of the American Psychological Association, Chicago, IL.

Smart, C. (1989). *Feminism and the power of the law*. New York: Routledge.

Smart, C. (1990). Feminist approaches to criminology or postmodern woman meets atavistic man. In L. Gelsthorpe & A. Morris (Eds.), *Feminist perspectives in criminology* (pp. 70–84). Philadelphia: Open University Press.

Smart, C. (1992). The women of legal discourse. *Social and Legal Studies: An International Journal, 1*, 29–44.

Smith, G. A., & Hall, J. A. (1982). Evaluating Michigan's guilty but mentally ill verdict: An empirical study. *Journal of Law Reform, 16*, 75–112.

Smith, F. M. L. (1980). *The benefits of psychotherapy*. Baltimore: Johns Hopkins University Press.

Smith, P. (1988). *Discerning the subject*. Minneapolis, MN: University of Minnesota Press.

Spece, R. G., Jr. (1979). Justifying invigorated scrutiny and the least restrictive alternative as a superior forum of intermediate review: Civil commitment and the right to treatment as a case study. *Arizona Law Review, 21*, 1049–1094.

Spence, K. (1956). *Behavior theory and conditioning*. New Haven, CT: Yale University Press.

Spitzer, R. L., & Fleiss, J. L. (1974). A reanalysis of the reliability of psychiatric diagnosis. *British Journal of Psychiatry, 25*, 341–347.

Steadman, H. J., McGreevy, M., Morrisey, J., Callahan, L., Clark, T., Robbins, P., & Cirincione, C. (1993). *Before and after Hinckley: Evaluating insanity defense reform*. New York: Guilford Press.

Steadman, H. J., McCarty, D., & Morrissey, J. (1989). *The mentally ill in jail: Planning for essential services*. New York: Guilford Press.

Stein, L. I., & Test, M. A. (1980). Alternative to mental hospital treatment: Conceptual model, treatment, and clinical evaluation. *Archives of General Psychiatry, 37* (4), 392–397.

Stone, A. (1975). *Mental health law: A system in transition*. Rockville, MD: U.S. Department of Health, Education, and Welfare, Public Health Service, Alcohol, Drug Abuse, and Mental Health Administration, National Institute of Mental Health, Center for Studies of Crime and Delinquency; Washington: for sale by the Superintendent of Documents, U.S. Government Printing Office.

Stonequist, E. V. (1934). *The marginal man*. New York: Charles Scribner's Sons.

Stromberg, C. D., & Stone, A. A. (1983). A model state law on civil commitment of the mentally ill. *Harvard Journal on Legislation, 20*, 275–396.

Sturrock, J. (Ed.). (1979). *Structuralism and since: From Lévi-Strauss to Derrida*. New York: Oxford University Press.

Sullivan, R. (1996). The birth of the prison: Discipline or punish? *Journal of Criminal Justice, 24* (5), 449–458.

Szasz, T. S. (1963). *Law, liberty and psychiatry: An inquiry into the social uses of mental health practices*. New York: Macmillan.

Szasz, T. S. (1970). *Ideology and insanity: Essay on the psychiatric dehumanization of man*. Garden City, NY: Anchor Books.

Szasz, T. S. (1970). *The manufacture of madness*. New York: Harper & Row.

Szasz, T. S. (1973). *The second sin*. Garden City, NY: Anchor Press.

Szasz, T. S. (1974). *The myth of mental illness: Foundations of a theory of personal conduct*. New York: Harper and Row.

Szasz, T. S. (1977). *Psychiatric slavery: When confinement and coercion masquerade as cure*. New York: Free Press.

Szasz, T. S. (1984). The therapeutic state: Psychiatry in the mirror of current events. Buffalo, NY: Prometheus Books.

Szasz, T. (1987). *Insanity: The idea and its consequences*. New York: Wiley & Sons.

Talbott, J. A. (1979). Deinstitutionalization: Avoiding the disasters of the past. *Hospital and Community Psychiatry, 30*, 621–624.

Talbott, J. A. (1980). Toward a public policy on the chronic mentally ill patient. *American Journal of Orthopsychiatry, 50* (1), 43–53.

Tanay, E. (1980). The right to refuse treatment and the abolition of involuntary hospitalization of the mentally ill. *Bulletin of the American Academy of Psychiatry & the Law*, 8, 1014.

Tapp, J. L., & Levine, F. J. (1977a). Epilogue in psychology and law. In J. L. Tapp & F. J. Levine (Eds.), *Law, justice and the individual in society* (pp. 363–368). New York: Holt, Rinehart.

Tapp, J. L., & Levine, F. J. (1977b). Psychological and legal issues. In J. L. Tapp & F. J. Levine (Eds.), *Law, justice and the individual in society* (pp. 3–9). New York: Holt, Rinehart.

Teplin, L. A. (1986). Keeping the peace: The parameters of police discretion in relation to the mentally disordered. In *Research Report Series of the National Institute of Justice*. Washington, DC: U.S. Department of Justice.

Thomas, J. (1988). *Prisoner litigation: The paradox of the jailhouse lawyer*. Totowa, NJ: Allen and Littlefield.

Tiefenbrun, S. (1986). Legal semiotics. *Cardozo Arts and Entertainment Law Review, 5*, 89–156.

Tifft, L. L. (1995). Social harm definitions of crime. *The Critical Criminologist, 7*, 9–13.

Toch, H. (1998). *Corrections: A humanistic perspective*. New York: Harrow and Heston.

Torrey, E. F. (1997). *Out of the shadows: Confronting America's mental illness crisis*. New York: John Wiley & Sons.

Treffert, D. A. (1982). Legal "rites" criminalizing the mentally ill. *Hillside Journal of Clinical Psychiatry, 3* (2): 123–137.

Treffert, D. A. (1985). The obviously ill patient in need of treatment: A fourth standard for civil commitment. *Hospital and Community Psychiatry, 36* (3), 259–269.

Treffert, D. A., & Krajeck, P. A. (1976). In search of a sane commitment statute. *Psychiatric Annals*, 6, 283–294.

Turnbull, H. R. (Ed.). (1981). *The least restrictive alternative: principles and practices*. Washington, DC: Task Force on Least Restriction, Legislative and Social Issues Committee, American Association on Mental Deficiency.

Tushnet, M. (1986). Critical legal studies: An introduction to its origins and underpinnings. *Journal of Legal Education, 36* (4), 505–517.

Tushnet, M. (1991). Critical legal studies: A political history. *Yale law journal, 100*, 1515–1537.

Unger, R. (1986). *The critical legal studies movement*. Cambridge, MA: Harvard University Press.

Vail, D. J. (1966). *Dehumanization and the institutional career*. Springfield, IL: C. C. Thomas.

Van Eenwyk, J. R. (1991). Archetypes: The strange attractors of the psyche. *Journal of Analytical Psychology, 36*, 1–25.

Volosinov, V. N. (1986). *Marxism and the philosophy of language*. (L. Matejka & I. R. Titunik, Trans.). Cambridge, MA: Harvard University Press.

Voltaire, F. (1759/1961). *Candide*. New York: Signet.

Voltaire, F. (1734/1980). *Letters on England*. New York: Penguin.

Uniform Probate Code Sections 5–309 (1990).

Walker, S. (1985). *Sense and nonsense about crime: A policy guide*. Monterey, CA: Brooks/Cole.

Walker, S. (1994). *Hate speech: The history of an American controversy*. Lincoln, Nebraska: University of Nebraska Press.

Wallace, D. H. (1987). Incompetency for execution: The supreme court challenges the ethical standards of the mental health profession. *Journal of Legal Medicine, 8*, 265–281.

Warren, C. A. B. (1982). *The court of last resort: Mental illness and the law*. Chicago: University of Chicago Press.

Washington Revue Code Annual. (1985). Sec, 71.05 et seq. St Paul: West.

Weber, M. (1958). Politics as a vocation. In H. Gerth & C. Mills (Trans., Eds.), *From Max Weber: Essays in sociology* (pp. 77–128). New York: Oxford University Press.

Wegner, T., & Tyler, B. (1993). *Fractal creations*. Corte Madera, CA: The Waite Group.

Weiner, B. A. (1985). Treatment rights. In S. J. Brakel, J. Perry, & B. A. Weiner (Eds.), *The mentally disabled and the law* (3rd ed.), (pp. 327–351). Chicago: American Bar Foundation.

Weiner, R. L. (1993). Introduction: Law and psychology-beyond mental health and legal procedure. *Saint Louis University Law Journal, 37*, 499–502.

Weinstein, J. (1999). *Hate speech, pornography, and the radical attack of free speech doctrine*. Boulder, CO: Westview.

Wettstein, R. W. (1984). The prediction of violent behavior and the duty to protect third parties. *Behavioral Sciences and the Law, 2*, 291–317.

Wettstein, R. W. (Ed.). (1998). *Treatment of offenders with mental disorders*. New York: Guilford Press.

Wexler, D. B. (1981). *Mental health law: Major issues*. New York: Plenum Press.

Wexler, D. B., & Winick, B. J. (1996). *Law in a therapeutic key: Developments in therapeutic jurisprudence*. Durham, NC: Carolina Academic Press.

Whitford, M. (1991). *Luce Irigaray: Philosophy in the feminine*. London: Routledge.

Whorf, B. (1967). *Language, thought, and reality*. (J. B. Caroll, Ed.). Cambridge, MA: The MIT Press.

Williams, C. (1998). The abrogation of subjectivity in the psychiatric courtroom: Toward a psychoanalytic semiotic analysis. *International Journal for the Semiotics of Law, 11* (32), 181–192.

Williams, C. (1999). Inside the outside and outside the inside: Negative fusion from the margins of humanity. *Humanity and Society, 23*, 70–91.

Williams, C. R., & Arrigo, B. A. (2000a). The philosophy of the gift and the psychology of advocacy: Critical reflections on forensic mental health intervention. *International Journal for the Semiotics of Law, 13* (2), 215–242.

Williams, C. R., & Arrigo, B. A. (2001a). *Law, psychology, and justice: Chaos theory and the new (dis)order*. Albany, NY: State University of New York Press.

Williams, C. R., & Arrigo, B. A. (2001b). Law, psychology, and the "new sciences": Rethinking mental illness and dangerousness. *International Journal of Offender Therapy and Comparative Criminology*, 46 (1).

Winick, B. J. (1977). Psychotropic medication and competency to stand trial. *American Bar Foundation Research Journal, 3*, 769–782.

Winick, B. (1979/1980). The right to refuse mental health treatment: A first amendment perspective. *Miami Law Review, 34*, 1–??.

Winick, B. (1981). Legal limits on correctional therapy and research. *University of Minnesota Law Review, 65*, 331–420.

Winick, B. (1986). The right to refuse psychotropic medication: Current state of law and beyond. In D. Rapoport, & J. Perry (Eds.), *The right to refuse antipsychotic medication* (pp. 7–31). Washington, DC: American Bar Association.

Winick, B. (1992). Competency to be executed: A therapeutic jurisprudence perspective. *Behavioral Science and the Law, 10*, 317–338.

Winick, B. J. (1993). New directions in the right to refuse mental health treatment: The implications of Riggins v. Nevada. *William and Mary Bill of Rights Journal, 2* (2), 205–238.

Winick, B. J. (1995a). Ambiguities in the meaning of mental illness. *Psychology, Law, and Public Policy, 1* (3), 534–611.

Winick, B. J. (1995b). The side effects of incompetency labeling and the implication for mental health law. *Psychology, Public Policy, and the Law, 1* (1), 6–42.

Winick, B. J. (1997a). *The right to refuse mental health treatment.* Washington, DC: American Psychological Association.

Winick, B. J. (1997b). *Therapeutic jurisprudence applied: Essays on mental health law.* Durham, NC: Carolina Academic Press.

Winick, B. J & LaFond, J. Q. (1998). Special Theme: *Sex Offenders: Scientific, Legal, and Policy Perspectives. Psychology, Public Policy, and Law, 4* (1/2), 1–572.

Wise, P. (1985). *Chaos in the courtroom.* New York: Praeger.

Wolff, K. H. (Ed.). (1950). *The sociology of Georg Simmel* (K. H. Wolff, Trans.). Glencoe, IL: Free Press.

Wolinsky, S. H. (1991). *Trances people live with: Healing approaches to quantum psychology.* Norfolk, CT: Bramble.

Wolinsky, S. H. (1993). *Quantum consciousness: The guide to experiencing quantum psychology.* Norfolk, CT: Bramble.

Wrightsman, L. S. (1997). *Psychology and the legal system.* Pacific Grove, CA: Brooks/Cole.

Young, A. (1996). *Imagining crime.* London: Sage.

Young, I. (1990). *Justice and the politics of difference.* Princeton, NJ: Princeton University Press.

Young, T. R. (1991a). Chaos theory and symbolic interaction. *Journal of Symbolic Interaction, 14,* 3–21.

Young, T. R. (1991b). Chaos and social change: metaphysics of the postmodern. *The Social Science Journal, 28* (3), 289–305.

Young, T. R. (1992). Chaos theory and human agency: Humanist sociology in a postmodern age. *Humanity and Society, 16* (4), 441–460.

Young, T. R. (1997a). Challenges: for a postmodern criminology. In D. Milovanovic (Ed.), *Chaos, criminology, and social justice: The new orderly (dis)order* (pp. 29–51). Westport, CT: Praeger.

Young, T. R. (1997b). The abc's of crime: Attractors, bifurcations, and chaotic dynamics. In D. Milovanovic (Ed.), *Chaos, criminology, and social justice: The new orderly (dis)order* (pp. 77–96). Westport, CT: Praeger.

Zilboorg, G. (1941). *A history of medical psychology.* New York: W. W. Norton.

Zlotkin, D. (1981). First do no harm: Least restrictive alternative analysis and the right of mental patients to refuse treatment. *West Virginia Law Review, 83,* 375–448.

Zola, I. K. (1972). Medicine as an institution of social control. *Sociological Review, 20,* 487–503.

Zusman, J. (1982). The need for intervention: The reasons for state control of the mentally disordered. In C. A. B. Warren (Ed.), *The court of last resort: Mental illness and the law* (pp. 110–136). Chicago: Chicago University Press.

CASES CITED

Addington v. Texas, 441 U.S. 418 (1979).
Aden v. Younger, 57 Cal. App. 3d 662 (Ct. App. Cal. 4th App. D. 1976).
Argersinger v. Hamlin, 407 U.S. 25 (1972).
Association of Retarded Citizens of North Dakota v. Olson, 561 F. Supp. 473 (D.N.D. 1982), *aff'd in part, modified and remanded on other grounds*, 713 F. 2d 1384 (8th Cir. 1983).
Barefoot v. Estelle, 103 S. Ct. 3383, 463 U.S. 880 (1983).
Baxstrom v. Herold, 383 U.S. 107 (1966).
Bee v. Greaves 744 F. 2d 1387 (10th Cir. 1984).
Boggs v. N.Y. City Health and Hosp. Corp., 132 A.D. 2d 340 (A.D. N.Y. 1987).
Childress v. Thomas S., 479 U.S. 869 (1986).
Clark v. Cohen, 794 F. 2d 79 (3rd Cir. Pa. 1986).
Cohen v. Clark, 794 U.S. 962 (1986).
Colyar v. Third Judicial Dist. Court, 469 F. Supp. 424 (D. Utah 1979).
Davis v. Hubbard, 506 F. Supp. 915 (N.D. Ohio 1980).
Dodd v. Hughes, 81 Nev. 43, 398 P. 2d 540 (Nev. 1965).
Donaldson v. O'Connor 493 F. 2d 507 (5th Cir. 1974), *vacated and remanded*, O'Connor v. Donaldson 422 U.S. 563 (1975).
Doremus v. Farrell, 407 F. Supp. 509 (D. Neb. 1975).
Dusky v. United States, 363 U.S. 402 (1960).
Estelle v. Gamble, 429 U.S. 97 (1976).
Fontain v. Ravenel, 58 U.S. 369 (1855).
Foucha v. Louisiana, 504 U.S. 71 (1992).
Ford v. Wainwright, 477 U.S. 399 (1986).
Gannett Co. v. De Pasquale, 443 U.S. 368 (1979).
Garger v. New Jersey, 429 U.S. 922 (1976).
Gideon v. Wainwright, 392 U.S. 1 (1963).
Gregg v. Georgia, 428 U.S. 153 (1976).
Griswold v. Connecticut, 381 U.S. 479 (1965).
Halderman v. Pennhurst State School & Hospital, 446 F. Supp. 1295 (E.D. Pa 1977), *aff'd in part and rev'd in part*, 612 F. 2d 84 (3rd Cir. 1979), *rev'd* 451 U.S. 1 (1981), *on remand*, 673 F. 2d 647 (3rd Cir. 1982), *rev'd* 465 U.S. 89 (1984).
Hammon v. Hill, 228 F. 999 (D. Pa. 1915).
Hawaii v. Standard Oil Co., 415 U.S. 251 (1972).
Hawks v. Lazaro, 202 S.E. 2d 109 (Sup. Ct. App. W. Va. 1974).
Humphrey v. Cady, 405 U.S. 504 (1972).
Hutton v. City of Camden, 39 N.J.L. 122 (N.J. 1876).
In re Barker, 2 Johns. Ch. 232 (N.Y. 1816).
In re Colyar, 660 P. 2d 738 (1983).

In re Gault, 387 U.S. 1 (1967).
In re Guardianship of Richard Roe III, 421 N.E. 2d 40 (Mass. 1981),
In re Oakes, 8 Law Rep. 123 (Mass. 1845).
In re Quinlan, 355 A. 2d 647 (N.J. 1976), *cert. denied sub. nom.*
In re Richard Roe III, 421 NE 2d 40 (Mass. 1982).
In re Storar, 420 N.E. 2d 64 (N.Y. 1981), *cert. denied*, Storar v. Storar 454 U.S. 858 (1981).
Jackson v. Indiana, 406 U.S. 715 (1972).
Johns. Ch. 232 (N.Y. Ch. 1816).
Johnson v. Silvers, 742 F. 2d 823 (4th Cir. Md. 1984).
Jones v. Gerhardstein, 400 N.W. 2d 12 (W.S. Ct. App. 1986).
Jones v. United States, 463 U.S. 354 (1983).
Kansas v. Hendricks, 117 S. Ct. 2072 (1997).
Kirk v. Thomas S. V. Brooks, 476 U.S. 1124 (1986).
Klostermann v. Cuomo, 463 N.E. 2d 588 (N.Y. 1984).
Lake v. Cameron, 382 U.S. 863 (1965).
Lake v. Cameron, 364 F. 2d 657 (D.C. Cir. 1966), *cert. denied.*
Law Rep. 122 (N.Y. Ch. 1816).
Lelsz v. Kavanagh, 807 F. 2d 1234 (5th Cir. 1987).
Lessard v. Schmidt, 349 F. Supp. 1078 (E.D. Wis. 1972), 414 U.S. 473 (1974), 379 F. Supp. 1376 (E.D. Wis. 1974), *vacated and remanded on other grounds*, 421 U.S. 957 (1975), 413 F. Supp. 1318 (E.D. Wis. 1976).
Lynch v. Baxley, 386 F. Supp. 378 (M.D. Ala. 1974).
Mackey v. Procunier, 477 F. 2d 877 (9th Cir. 1973).
Matter of Harry M. 468 N.Y.S. 2d. 359 (2nd Dept. 1983).
McIntosh v. Dill, 205 P. 917 (Okla. 1922), *cert denied*, 260 U.S. 721 (1922).
Mental Health Association v. Deukmejian, 233 Cal. Rptr. 130 (Ct. App. Cal. 1986).
Mills v. Rogers, 457 U.S. 291 (1982).
Mormon Church v. United States, 136 U.S. 1 (1890).
Nebraska Press Association v. Stuart, 427 U.S. 539 (1976).
Nelson v. Heyne, 491 F. 2d 352 (7th Cir. 1974), *cert. denied*, 417 U.S. 976 (1974).
Nobles v. Georgia, 168 U.S. 398 (1897).
O'Connor v. Donaldson, 422 U.S. 563 (1975).
Olmstead v. L.C., 119 St. Ct. 2176 (1999).
Parham v. J.R., 442 U.S. 584 (1979).
Pennhust State School & Hospital v. Halderman, 466 F. Supp. 1295 (E.D. Pa. 1977); *aff'd in part and rev'd in part*, 612 F. 2d 84 (3d Cir. 1979), *rev'd*, 451 U.S. 1 (1981), *on remand*, 673 F. 2d 647 (3d Cir. 1982), *rev'd*, 465 U.S. 89 (1984).
Perry v. Louisiana, 498 U.S. 38 (1990).
Phillips v. Thompson, 715 F. 2d 365 (7th Cir. 1983).

Poe v. Ullman, 367 U.S. 497 (1961).
Powell v. Alabama, 287 U.S. 45 (1932).
Press-Enterprise Co. v. Superior Court, 478 U.S. 1 (1986).
Price v. Sheppard, 239 N.W. 2d 905 (Minn. 1976).
Project Release v. Provost, 722 F. 2d 960 (2nd Cir. 1983).
Proffit v. Florida, 428 U.S. 242 (1976).
Project Release v. Prevost, 722 F. 2d 960 (2nd Cir. 1983).
R.A.J. v. Miller, 590 F. Supp. 1319 (N.D. Tex. 1984).
Rennie v. Klein, 458 U.S. 1119 (1982), 462 F. Supp. 1131 (D.N.J. 1978), 476 F. Supp. 1294 (D.N.J. 1979), 653 F. 2d 836 (3rd Cir. 1981).
Rennie v. Klein, 653 F. 2d 836 (3rd Cir. 1981).
Riggins v. Nevada, 504 U.S. 127 (1992).
Riggins v. State, 808 P. 2d 535 (Nev. 1991).
Rivers v. Katz, 495 N.E. 2d 337 (N.Y. 1986).
Robinson v. California, 370 U.S. 660 (1962).
Rodgers v. Commissioner of Depts. of Mental Health, 458 N.E. 2d 308 (Mass. 1983).
Roe v. Wade, 410 U.S. 113 (1973).
Rogers v. Okin, 634 F. 2d 650 (1st Cir. 1980), 738 F. 2d 1 (1st Cir. 1984).
Romeo v. Youngberg, 644 F. 2d 147 (3rd Cir. 1980).
Rone v. Firemen, 473 F. Supp. 92 (N.D. Ohio 1979).
Rouse v. Cameron, 373 F. 2d 451 (D.C. Cir. 1966).
Society of Good Will to Retarded Children v. Cuomo 737 F. 2d. 1239 (2d Cir. 1984).
Smith v. Goguen, 415 U.S. 566 (1974).
State v. Krol, 68 N.J. 236, 344 A. 2d 289 (N.J. 1975).
State v. Perry, 610 S. 2d 746 (La. 1992).
Stensvad v. Reivitz, 601 F. Supp. 128 (W.D. Wis. 1985).
Superintendent of Belchertown State School v. Saikewicz, 370 N.E. 2d 417 (Mass. 1977).
Thomas S. v. Morrow, 781 F. 2d 367 (4th Cir. 1986), *cert. denied*, 476 U.S. 1124 (1986), *cert. denied*, 479 U.S. 869 (1986), *and cert. denied*, 106 S. Ct. 1992 (1986).
Truman v. Thomas, 611 P. 2d 902 (Cal. 1980).
Von Luce v. Rankin, 588 S.W. 2d 445 (Ark. 1979).
Washington v. Harper, 494 U.S. 210 (1990).
Winters v. Miller, 404 U.S. 984 (1971), 446 F. 2d 65 (2d Cir. 1971).
Woe v. Cuomo, 729 F. 2d 96 (2nd Cir. 1984), *cert denied*, 469 U.S. 936 (1984).
Wyatt v. Aderholt, 503 F. 2d 1305 (5th Cir. Ala. 1974).
Wyatt v. Stickney, 344 F. Supp. 373 (M.D. Ala. 1972).
Youngberg v. Romeo, 457 U.S. 307 (1982).
Zinermon v. Burch, 494 U.S. 113 (1990).

Index

Made in the USA
Middletown, DE
21 December 2014